首斬り朝

SAMURAI 首斬り朝
EXECUTIONER

Punished is not the man himself,
but the evil that resides in him.

story
KAZUO KOIKE

art
GOSEKI KOJIMA

™

DARK HORSE MANGA™

translation
DANA LEWIS

lettering & retouch
DIGITAL CHAMELEON

publisher
MIKE RICHARDSON

editor
TIM ERVIN-GORE

assistant editor
PHILIP SIMON

book design
DARIN FABRICK

art director
LIA RIBACCHI

Published by Dark Horse Comics, Inc., in association
with MegaHouse and Koike Shoin Publishing Company.

Dark Horse Comics, Inc.
10956 SE Main Street, Milwaukie, OR 97222
www.darkhorse.com

First edition: July 2004
ISBN: 1-59307-207-4

1 3 5 7 9 10 8 6 4 2

Printed in Canada

To find a comics shop in your area, call the
Comic Shop Locator Service toll-free at 1-888-266-4226.

首斬り朝

WHEN THE DEMON KNIFE WEEPS

By **KAZUO KOIKE**
& **GOSEKI KOJIMA**

VOLUME

1

A NOTE TO READERS

Samurai Executioner is a carefully researched re-creation of Edo-Period Japan. To preserve the flavor of the work, we have chosen to retain many Edo-Period terms that have no direct equivalents in English. Japanese is written in a mix of Chinese ideograms and a syllabic writing system, resulting in numerous synonyms. In the glossary, you may encounter words with multiple meanings. These are words written with Chinese ideograms that are pronounced the same but carry different meanings. A Japanese reader seeing the different ideograms would know instantly which meaning it is, but these synonyms can cause confusion when Japanese is spelled out in our alphabet. *O-yurushi o* (please forgive us)!

SAMURAI EXECUTIONER

首斬り朝

TABLE OF CONTENTS

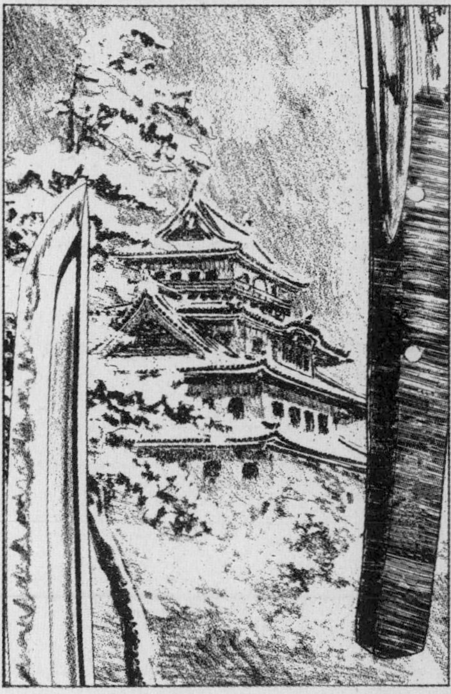

the first

When the Demon Knife Weeps

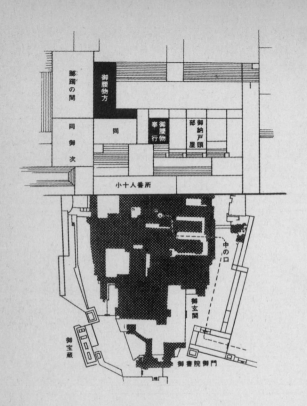

膜閣の間

御膝物方

同御次

同

御膝物奉行

御納戸頭部屋

小十人番所

中の口

御玄関

御宝蔵

御書院御門

THE *O-KOSHIMONO-BUGYŌ*. IN THE DAYS OF THE *SHOGUN*,
HE OVERSAW THE SWORDS GIFTED BY JAPAN'S RULER TO THE
DAIMYŌ FEUDAL LORDS, AND THE SWORDS THE *DAIMYŌ* PRESENTED
TO THEIR LORD AS SIGNS OF FEALTY. IT WAS A TRUSTED POSITION,
BRINGING FIVE-HUNDRED *KOKU* IN PAY, AND A STIPEND OF
THREE-HUNDRED BALES OF RICE.

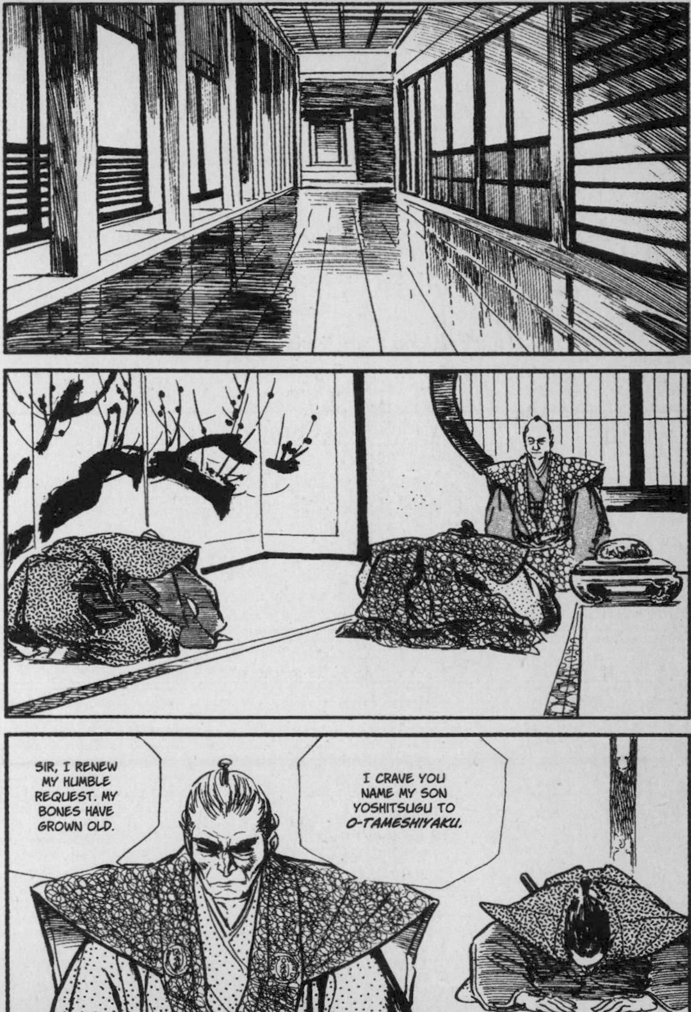
SIR, I RENEW MY HUMBLE REQUEST. MY BONES HAVE GROWN OLD.
I CRAVE YOU NAME MY SON YOSHITSUGU TO *O-TAMESHIYAKU.*

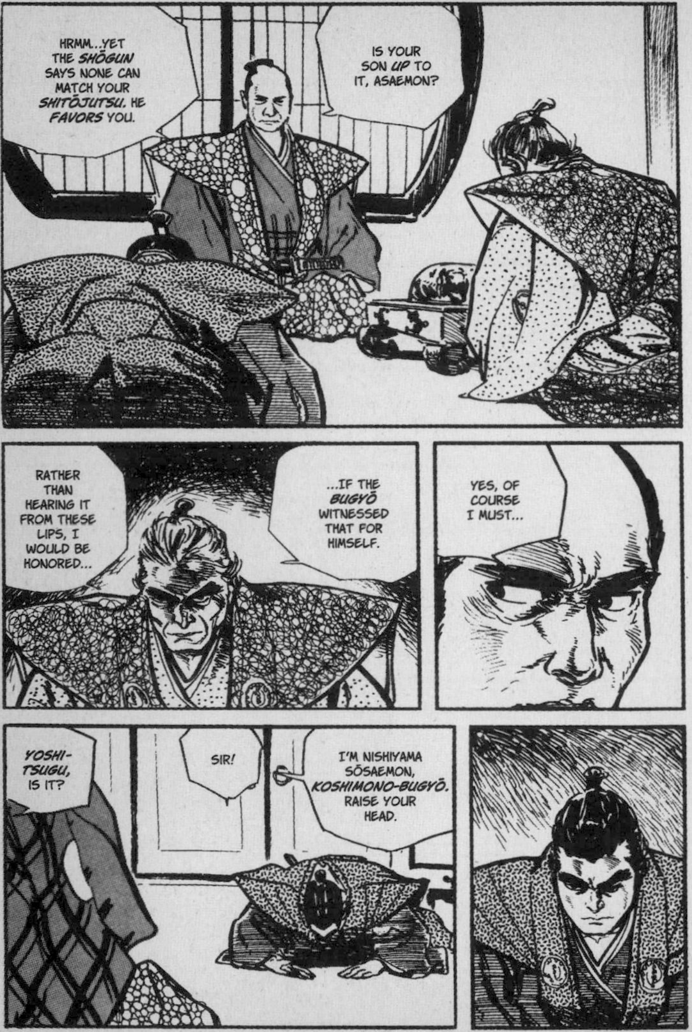
HRMM...YET THE SHŌGUN SAYS NONE CAN MATCH YOUR SHITŌJUTSU. HE FAVORS YOU.
IS YOUR SON UP TO IT, ASAEMON?
RATHER THAN HEARING IT FROM THESE LIPS, I WOULD BE HONORED...
...IF THE BUGYŌ WITNESSED THAT FOR HIMSELF.
YES, OF COURSE I MUST...
YOSHI-TSUGU, IS IT?
SIR!
I'M NISHIYAMA SŌSAEMON, KOSHIMONO-BUGYŌ. RAISE YOUR HEAD.

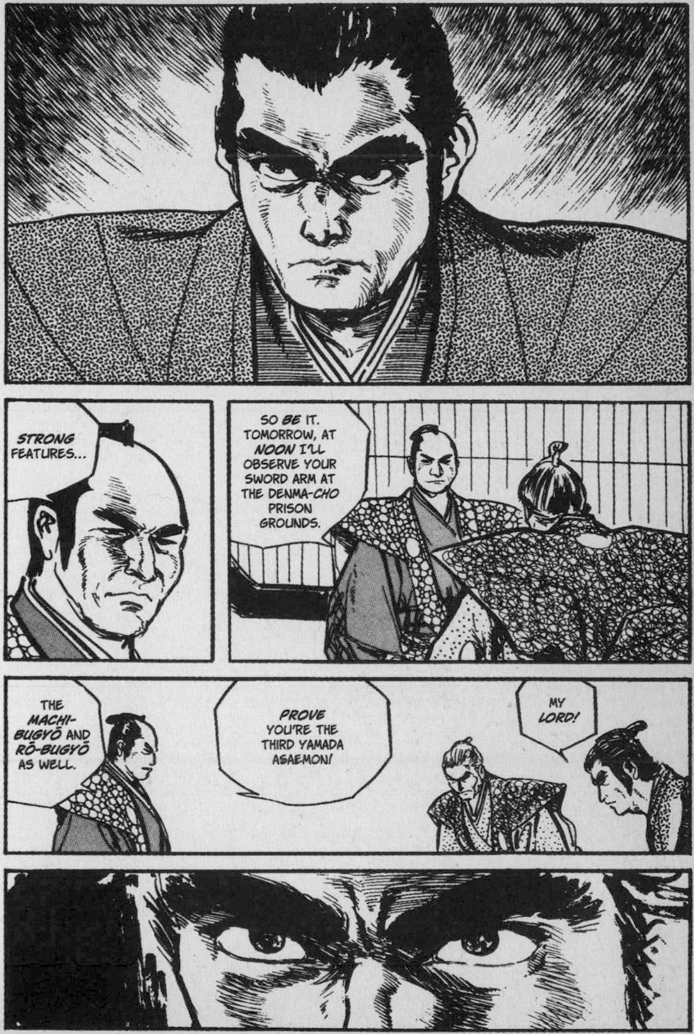

STRONG FEATURES...
SO BE IT. TOMORROW, AT NOON I'LL OBSERVE YOUR SWORD ARM AT THE DENMA-CHO PRISON GROUNDS.
THE MACHI-BUGYŌ AND RŌ-BUGYŌ AS WELL.
PROVE YOU'RE THE THIRD YAMADA ASAEMON!
MY LORD!

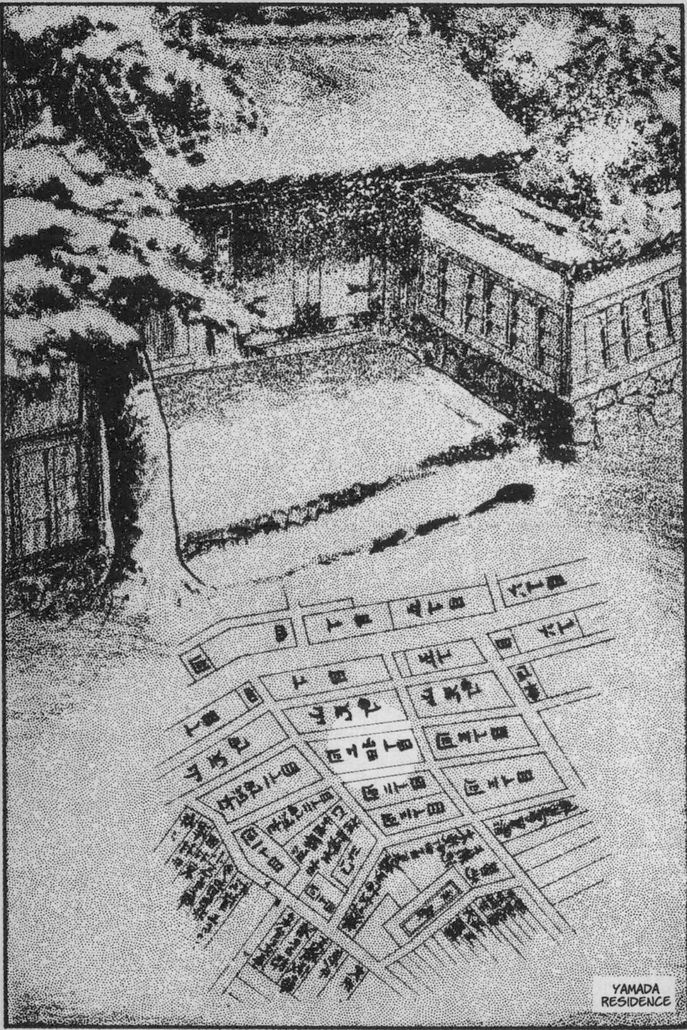
YAMADA RESIDENCE

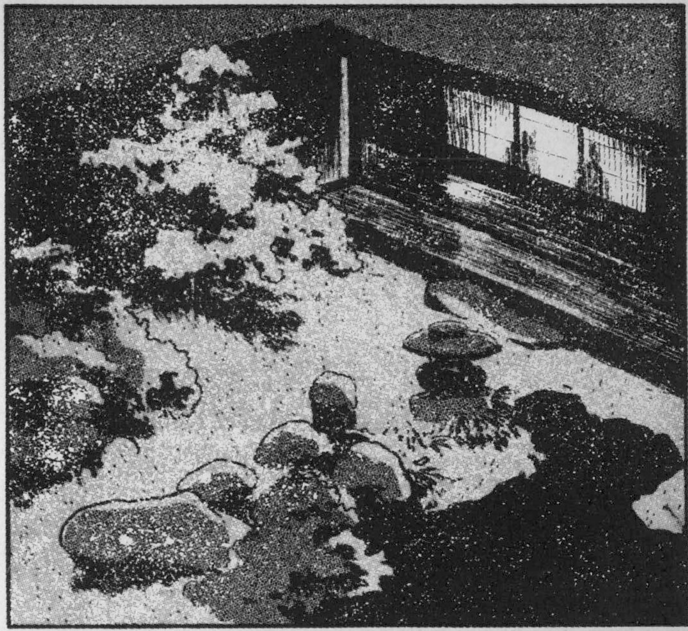

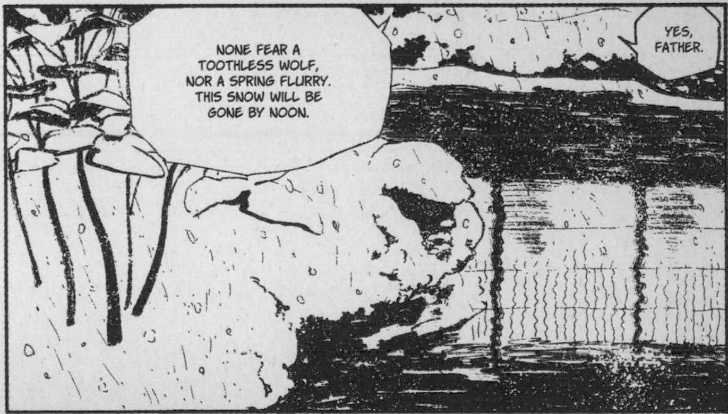
NONE FEAR A TOOTHLESS WOLF, NOR A SPRING FLURRY. THIS SNOW WILL BE GONE BY NOON.
YES, FATHER.

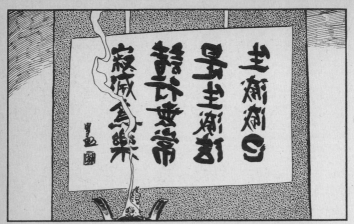

YOSHI-TSUGU!

SIR.

HOW OLD WERE YOU AT YOUR FIRST *TAMESHI?*

TEN, FATHER.

16

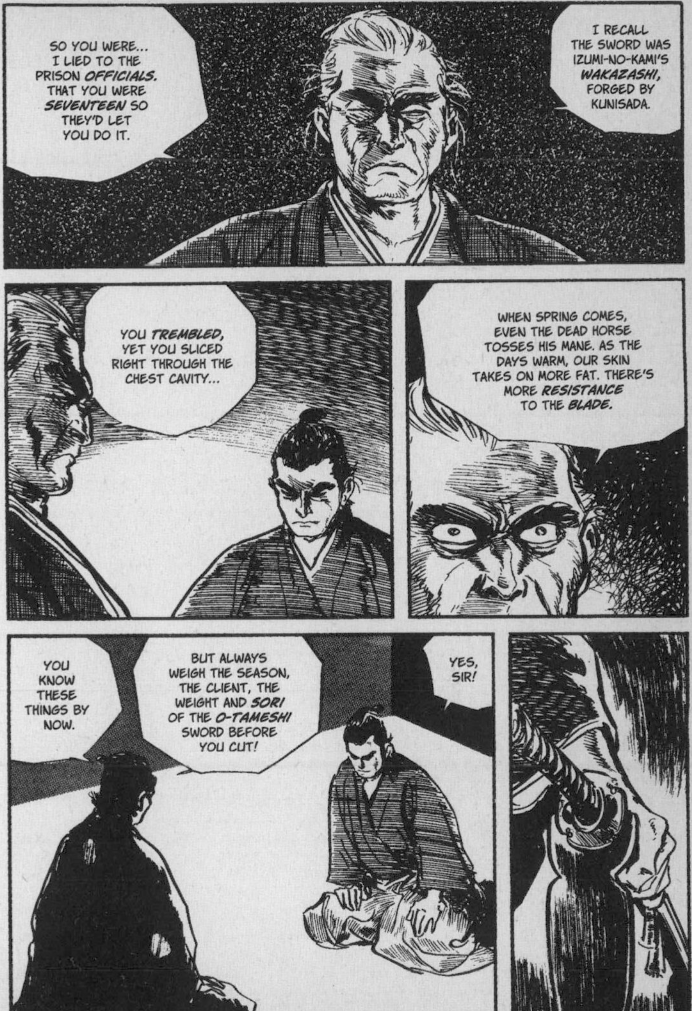
SO YOU WERE... I LIED TO THE PRISON OFFICIALS. THAT YOU WERE SEVENTEEN SO THEY'D LET YOU DO IT.
I RECALL THE SWORD WAS IZUMI-NO-KAMI'S WAKAZASHI, FORGED BY KUNISADA.
YOU TREMBLED, YET YOU SLICED RIGHT THROUGH THE CHEST CAVITY...
WHEN SPRING COMES, EVEN THE DEAD HORSE TOSSES HIS MANE. AS THE DAYS WARM, OUR SKIN TAKES ON MORE FAT. THERE'S MORE RESISTANCE TO THE BLADE.
YOU KNOW THESE THINGS BY NOW.
BUT ALWAYS WEIGH THE SEASON, THE CLIENT, THE WEIGHT AND SORI OF THE O-TAMESHI SWORD BEFORE YOU CUT!
YES, SIR!

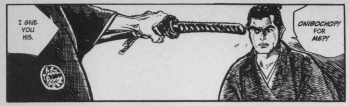

I GIVE YOU HIS.

ONIBOCHO?! FOR *ME*?!

OF COURSE! YOU'RE MY *HEIR*.

WHEN YOU USE THIS SWORD, YOUR HEART MAY AT TIMES GO OUT TO THOSE YOU CUT.

NO MATTER HOW YOU HARDEN YOUR HEART LIKE *STEEL*.

YET THAT *MAKES* YOU A O-TAME-SHIYAKU.

OUR HANDS BREATHE *SPIRIT* INTO THE *BLADE*. WE GIVE IT *LIFE*.

....

....

IN MY LIFETIME, TAMESHI ON TWO HUNDRED TORSOS. THREE HUNDRED DECAPITATIONS...

THE WAY OF THE WARRIOR? THE WAY OF SLAUGHTER? THE ANSWER LIES ON THE WAY TO HELL.

18

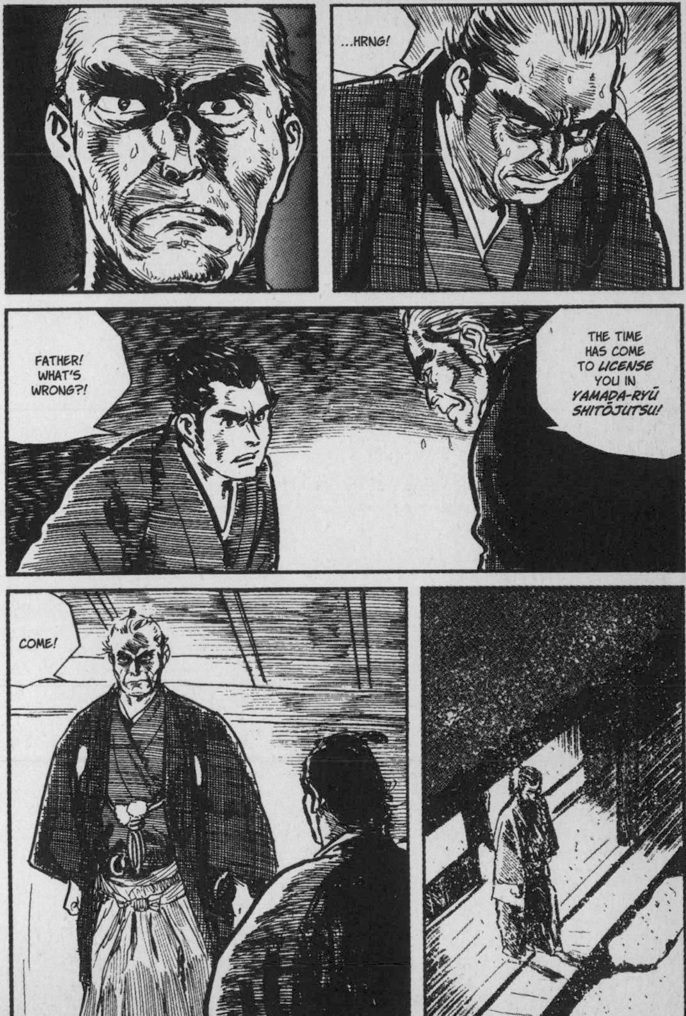
...HRNG!
FATHER! WHAT'S WRONG?!
THE TIME HAS COME TO *LICENSE* YOU IN *YAMADA-RYŪ SHITŌJUTSU!*
COME!

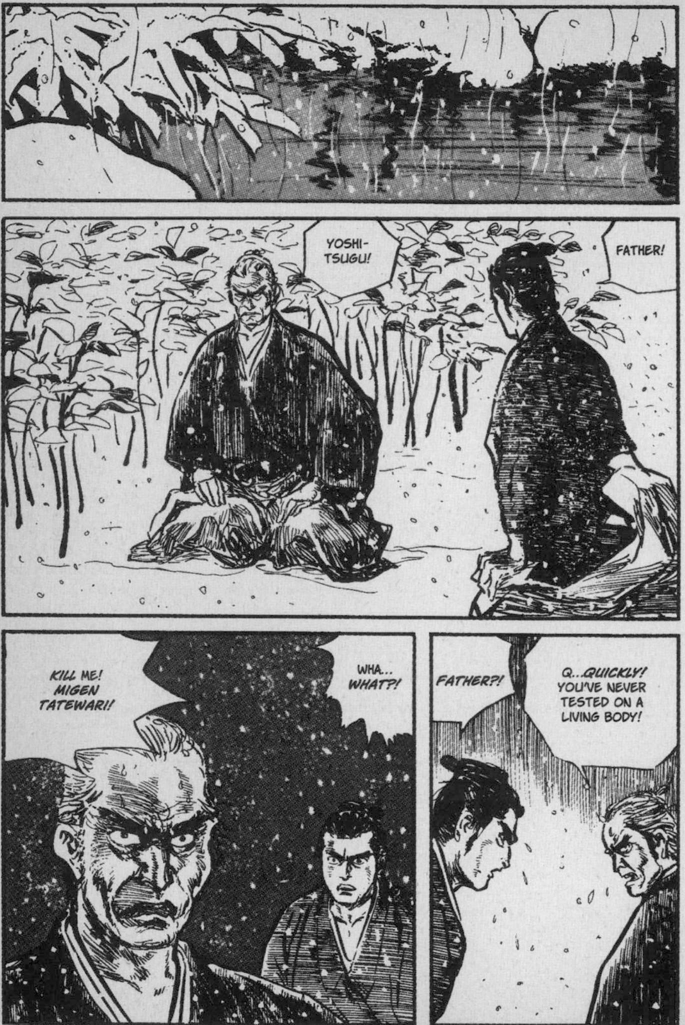
YOSHI-TSUGU!
FATHER!
KILL ME! MIGEN TATEWARI!
WHA... WHAT?!
FATHER?!
Q...QUICKLY! YOU'VE NEVER TESTED ON A LIVING BODY!

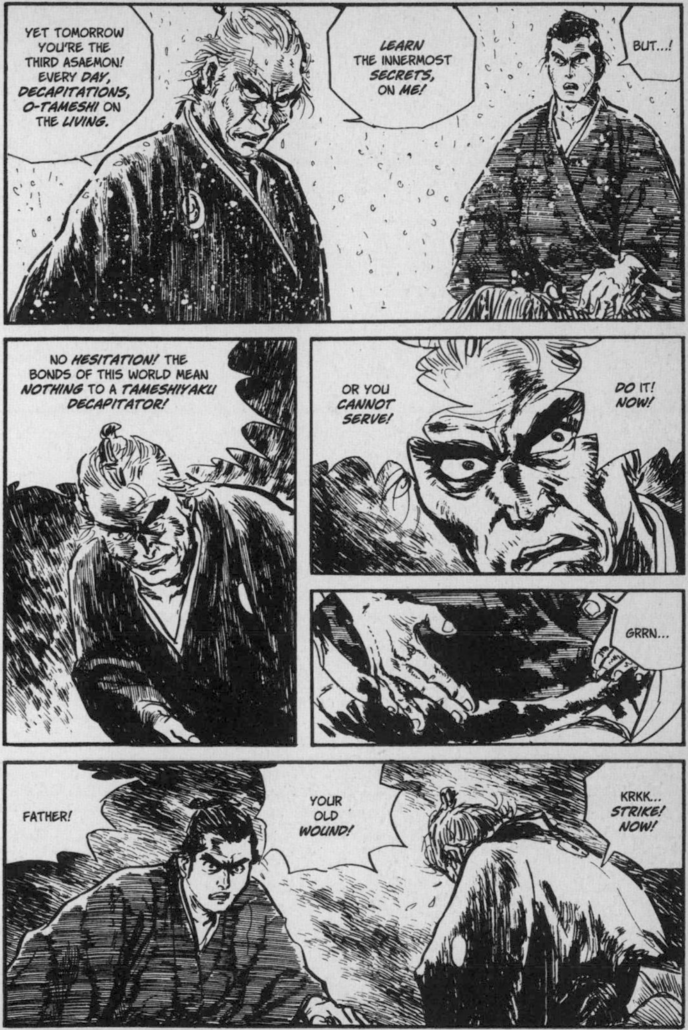
YET TOMORROW YOU'RE THE THIRD ASAEMON! EVERY *DAY*, *DECAPITATIONS*, *O-TAMESHI* ON THE *LIVING*.
LEARN THE INNERMOST *SECRETS*, ON *ME!*
BUT...!
NO *HESITATION!* THE BONDS OF THIS WORLD MEAN *NOTHING* TO A *TAMESHIYAKU DECAPITATOR!*
OR YOU *CANNOT SERVE!*
DO IT! NOW!
GRRN...
FATHER!
YOUR OLD *WOUND!*
KRKK... *STRIKE! NOW!*

I LICENSE YOU IN YAMADA-RYU!

THE SUTRAS OF THE GRIP!

FIRST FINGER, *SHOGYŌ MUJŌ!* SECOND FINGER, *ZESHŌ MEPPŌ!* THIRD, *SHŌMETSU MEKKI!* FOURTH, *JAKUMETSU IRAKU!*

SHOGYŌ MUJŌ!

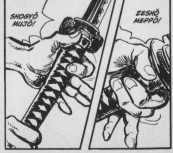

ZESHŌ MEPPŌ!

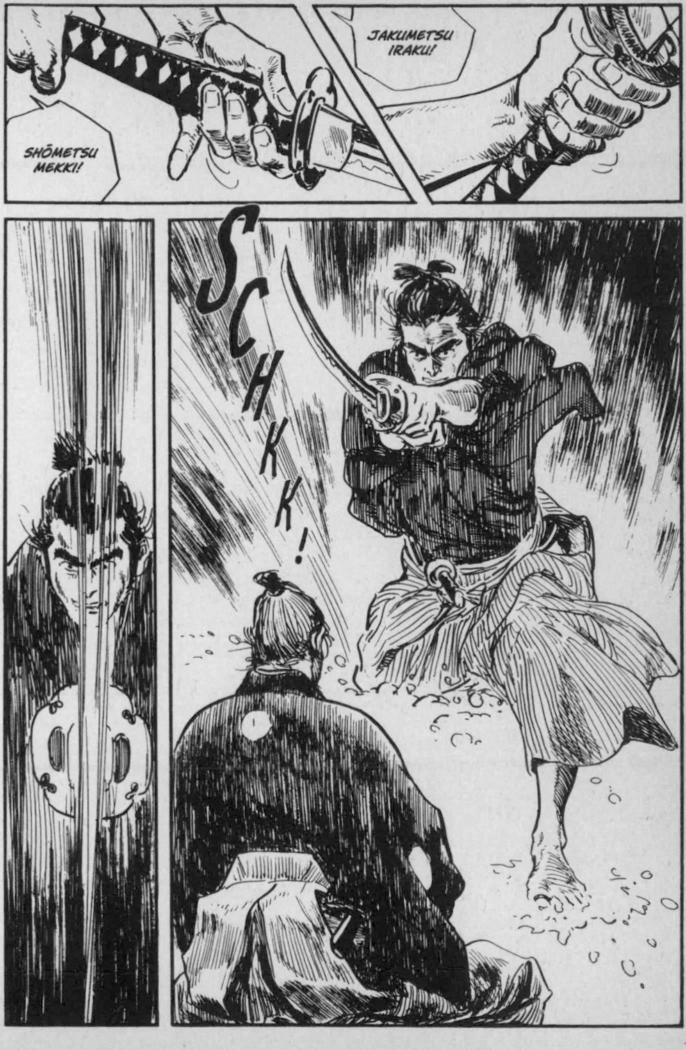
SHŌMETSU MEKKI!
JAKUMETSU IRAKU!
SCHKKK!

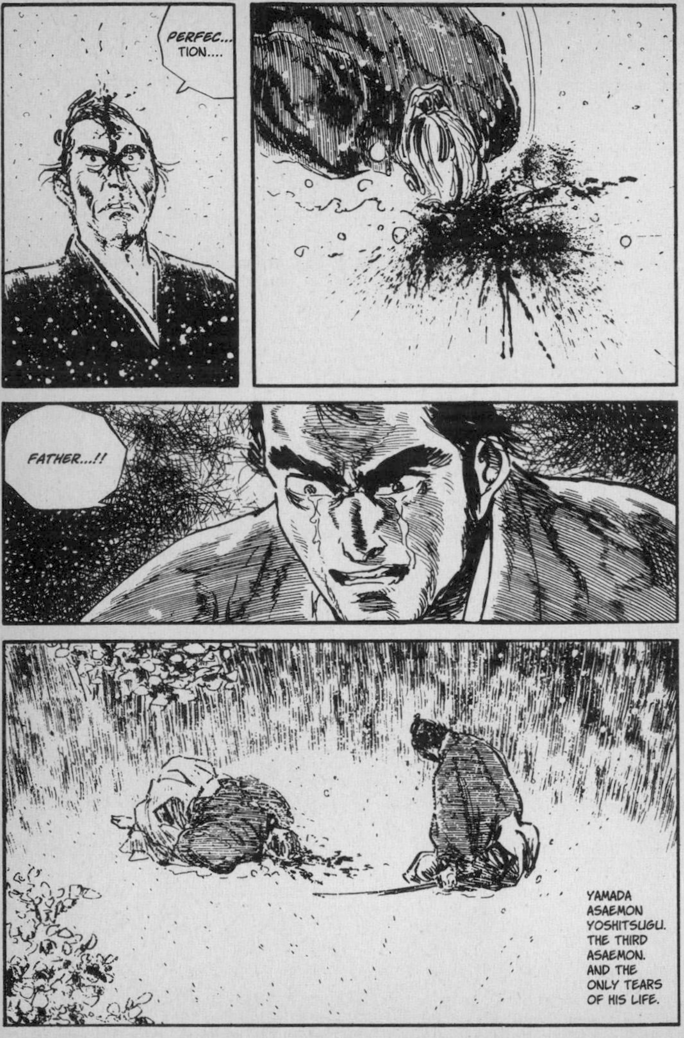
PERFEC... TION....
FATHER...!!
YAMADA ASAEMON YOSHITSUGU. THE THIRD ASAEMON. AND THE ONLY TEARS OF HIS LIFE.

the second

Yamada
Asaemon
the
Third

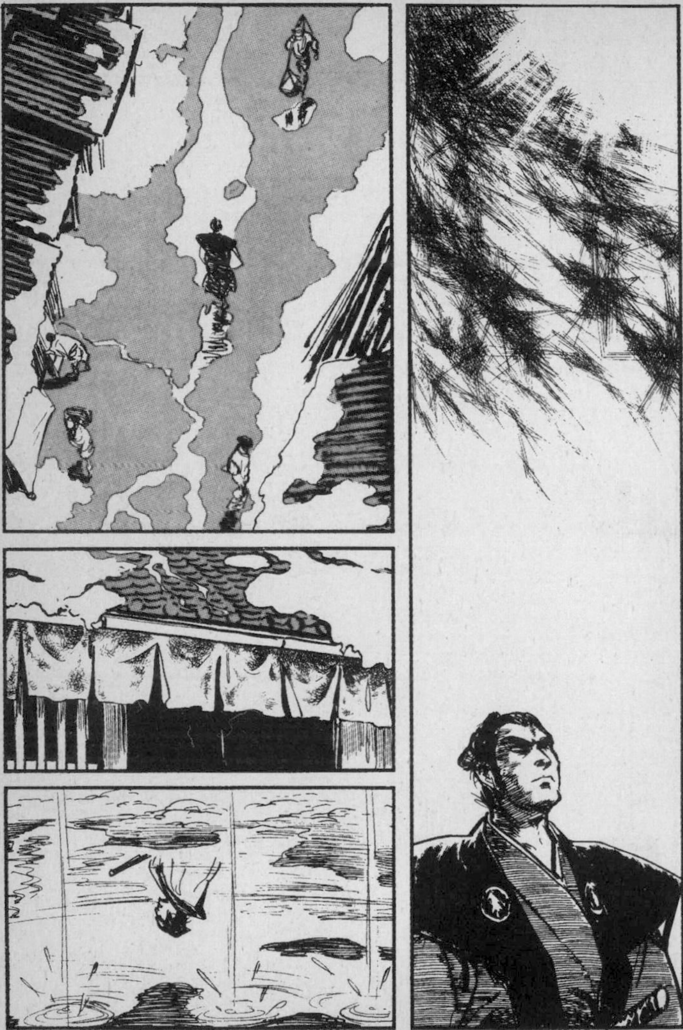

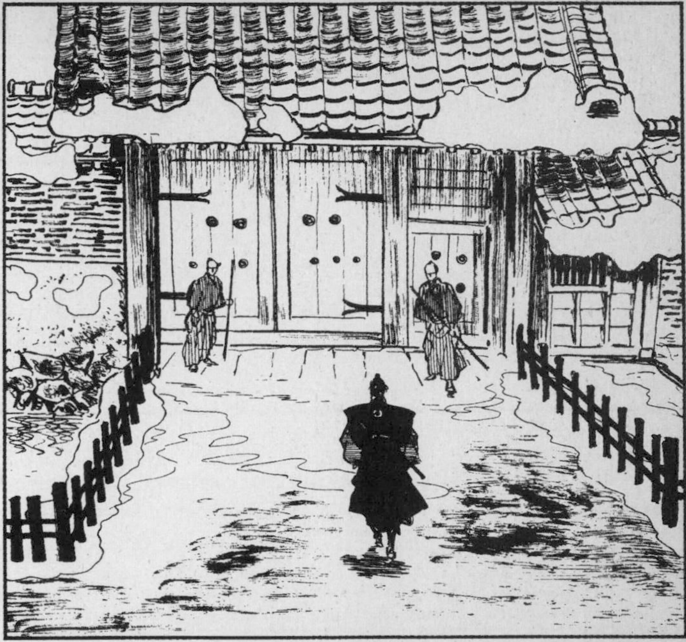

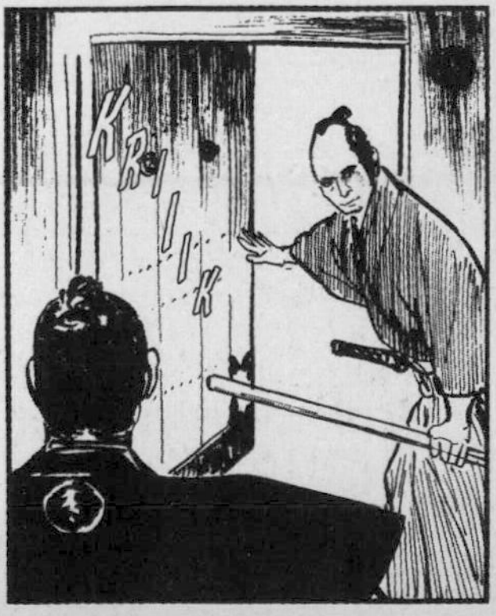
KRIIIK

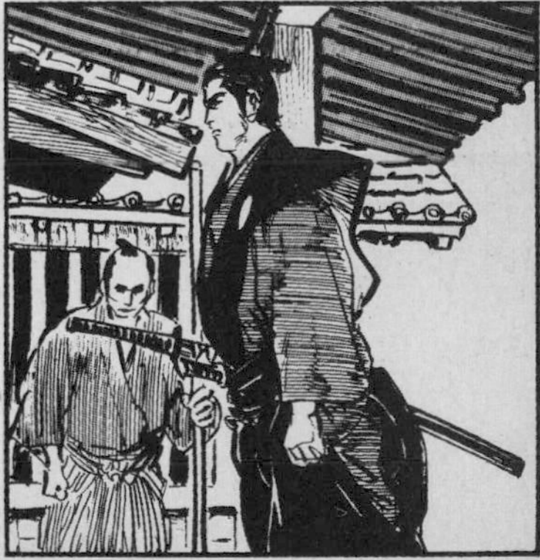

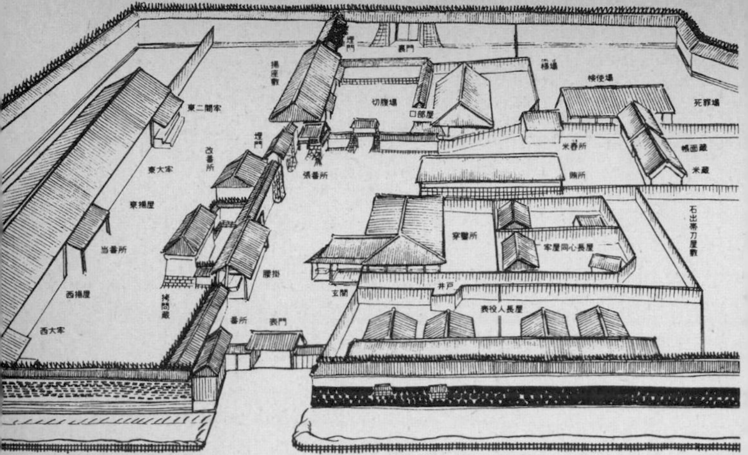
埋門
裏門
揚座敷
様場
検使場
死罪場
東二間牢
切腹場
口部屋
埋門
改番所
米舂所
帳面蔵
東大牢
張番所
賄所
米蔵
東揚屋
穿鑿所
石出帯刀屋敷
当番所
牢屋同心長屋
腰掛
井戸
西揚屋
拷問蔵
玄関
表役人長屋
西大牢
番所
表門

THE TENMACHO PRISON GROUNDS WERE LOCATED IN NIHONBASHI, AND COVERED MORE THAN SEVENTY-SEVEN *TSUBO*.

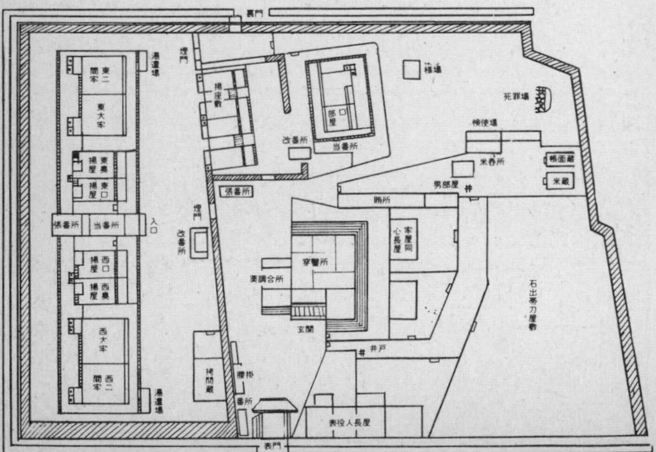
裏門
埋門
湯遣場
東二間牢
東大牢
揚座敷
口部屋
様場
死罪場
検使場
改番所
当番所
東奥揚屋
東口揚屋
米舂所
帳面蔵
男部屋
米蔵
張番所
賄所
張番所
当番所
入口
埋門
改番所
牢屋同心長屋
穿鑿所
西口揚屋
薬調合所
西奥揚屋
石出帯刀屋敷
西大牢
玄関
井戸
西二間牢
拷問蔵
腰掛
湯遣場
番所
表役人長屋
表門

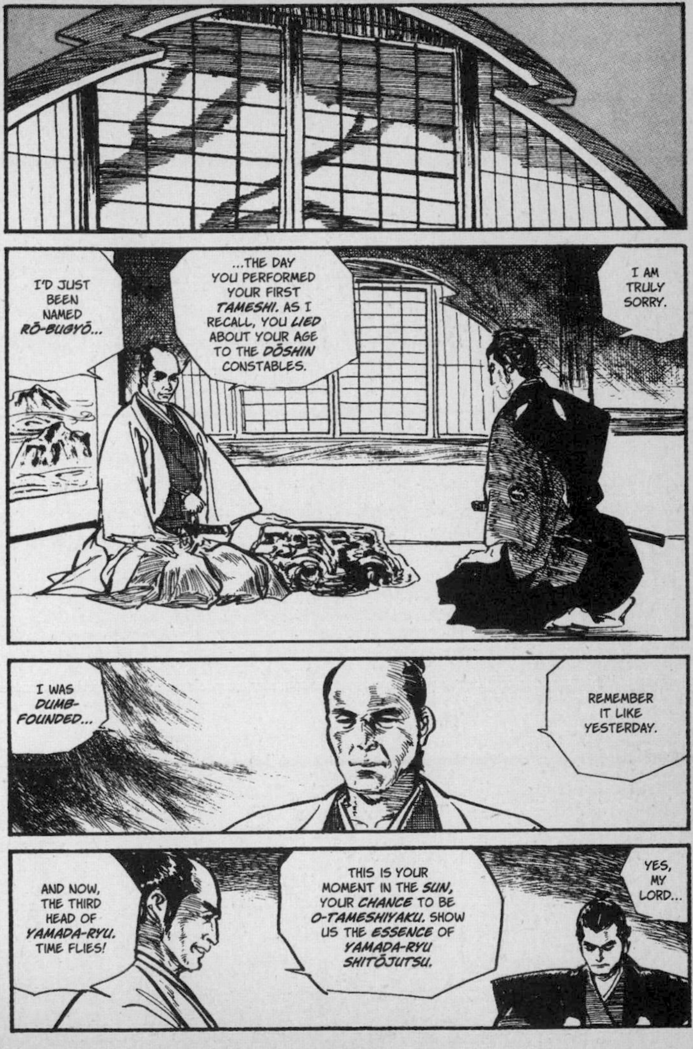
I'D JUST BEEN NAMED *RŌ-BUGYŌ*...
...THE DAY YOU PERFORMED YOUR FIRST *TAMESHI.* AS I RECALL, YOU *LIED* ABOUT YOUR AGE TO THE *DŌSHIN* CONSTABLES.
I AM TRULY SORRY.
I WAS *DUMB-FOUNDED*...
REMEMBER IT LIKE YESTERDAY.
AND NOW, THE THIRD HEAD OF *YAMADA-RYU.* TIME FLIES!
THIS IS YOUR MOMENT IN THE *SUN,* YOUR *CHANCE* TO BE *O-TAMESHIYAKU.* SHOW US THE *ESSENCE* OF *YAMADA-RYU SHITŌJUTSU.*
YES, MY LORD...

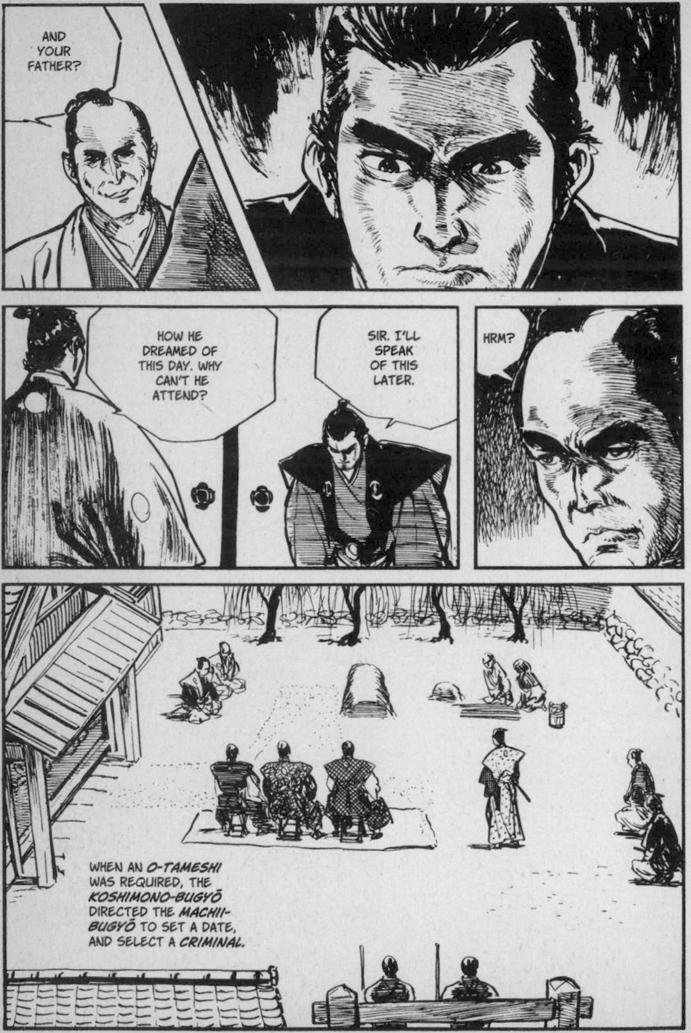
AND YOUR FATHER?
HOW HE DREAMED OF THIS DAY. WHY CAN'T HE ATTEND?
SIR. I'LL SPEAK OF THIS LATER.
HRM?
WHEN AN *O-TAMESHI* WAS REQUIRED, THE *KOSHIMONO-BUGYŌ* DIRECTED THE *MACHII-BUGYŌ* TO SET A DATE, AND SELECT A *CRIMINAL.*

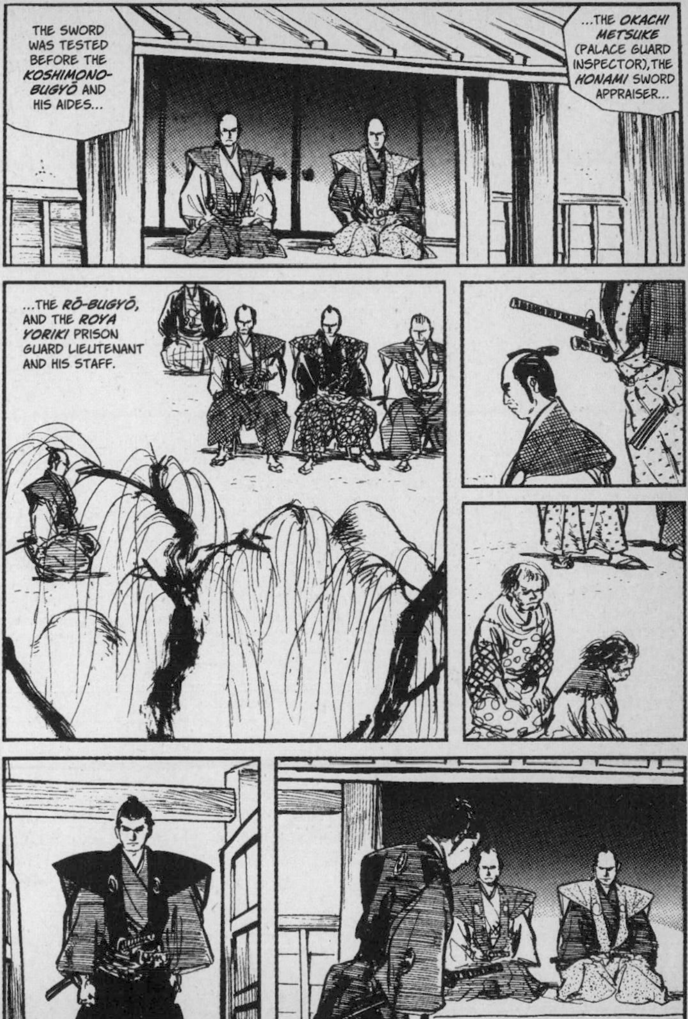
THE SWORD WAS TESTED BEFORE THE KOSHIMONO-BUGYŌ AND HIS AIDES...
...THE OKACHI METSUKE (PALACE GUARD INSPECTOR), THE HONAMI SWORD APPRAISER...
...THE RŌ-BUGYŌ, AND THE ROYA YORIKI PRISON GUARD LIEUTENANT AND HIS STAFF.

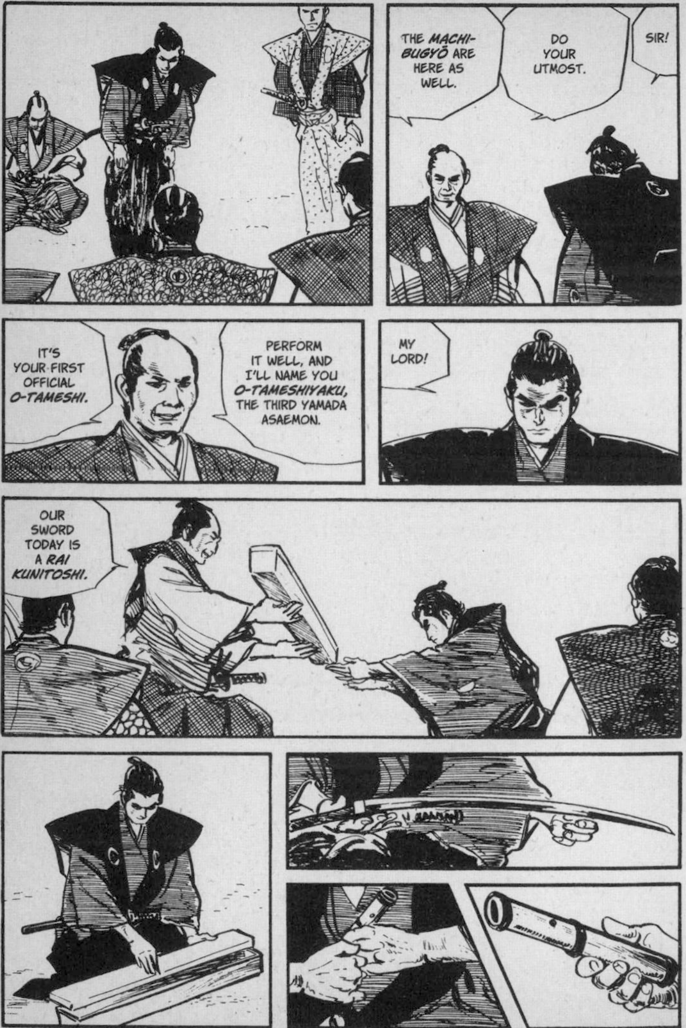
THE *MACHI-BUGYŌ* ARE HERE AS WELL.
DO YOUR UTMOST.
SIR!
IT'S YOUR FIRST OFFICIAL *O-TAMESHI.*
PERFORM IT WELL, AND I'LL NAME YOU *O-TAMESHIYAKU,* THE THIRD YAMADA ASAEMON.
MY LORD!
OUR SWORD TODAY IS A *RAI KUNITOSHI.*

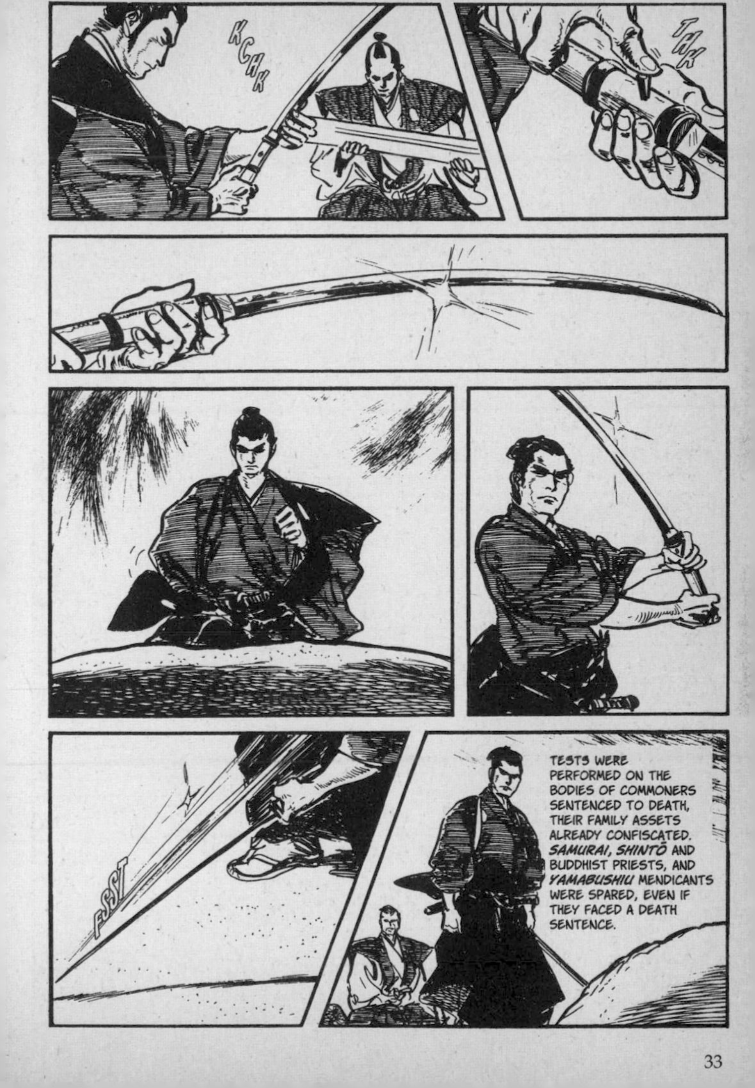
KCHK
THK
FSST
TESTS WERE PERFORMED ON THE BODIES OF COMMONERS SENTENCED TO DEATH, THEIR FAMILY ASSETS ALREADY CONFISCATED. *SAMURAI, SHINTŌ* AND BUDDHIST PRIESTS, AND *YAMABUSHIU* MENDICANTS WERE SPARED, EVEN IF THEY FACED A DEATH SENTENCE.

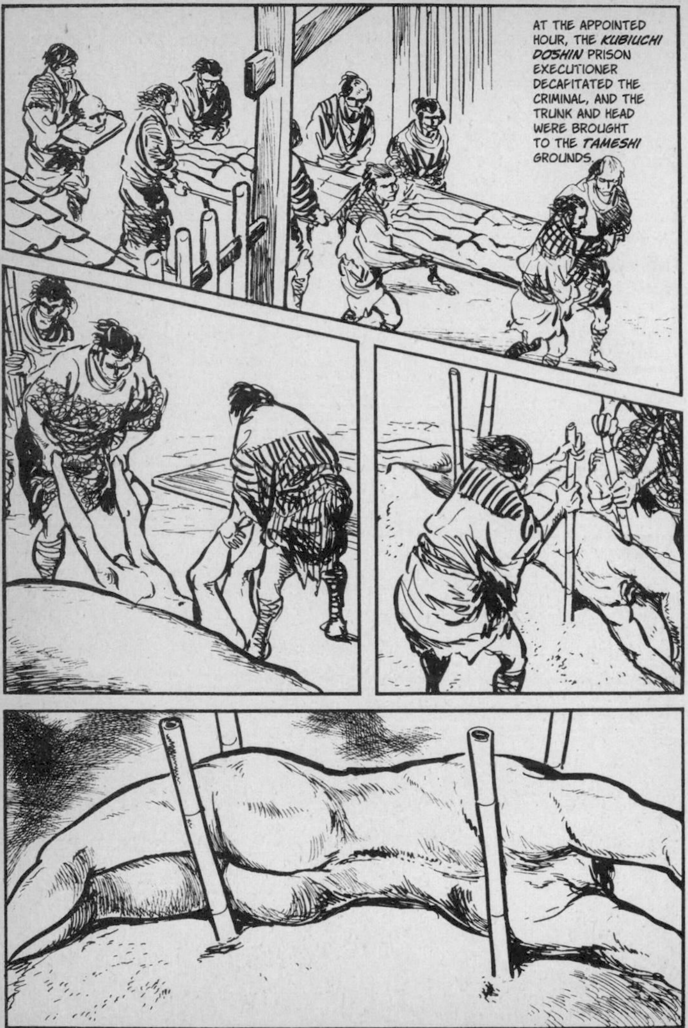
AT THE APPOINTED HOUR, THE *KUBIUCHI DOSHIN* PRISON EXECUTIONER DECAPITATED THE CRIMINAL, AND THE TRUNK AND HEAD WERE BROUGHT TO THE *TAMESHI* GROUNDS.

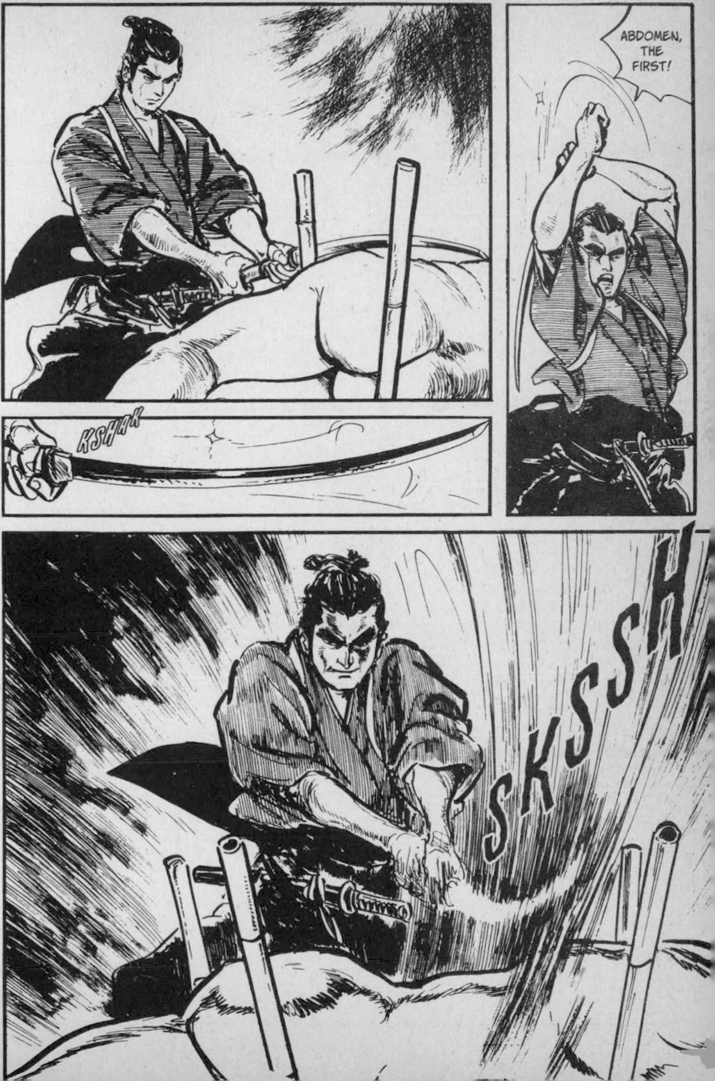
KSHAK
ABDOMEN, THE FIRST!
SKSSH

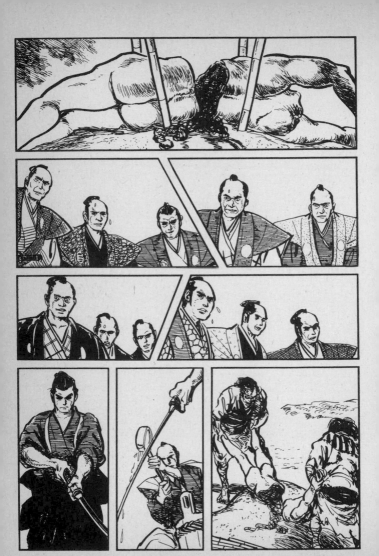

MIGEN
TATE-
WARI!!

SKRAK

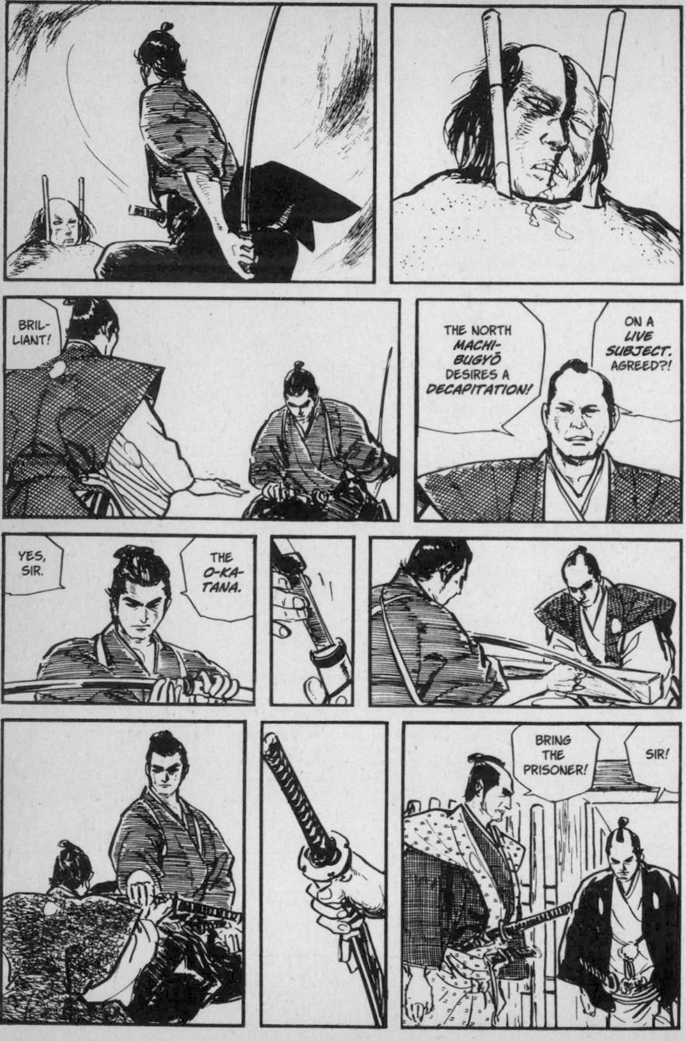
BRIL-
LIANT!
THE NORTH MACHI-BUGYŌ DESIRES A DECAPITATION!
ON A LIVE SUBJECT. AGREED?!
YES, SIR.
THE O-KA-TANA.
BRING THE PRISONER!
SIR!

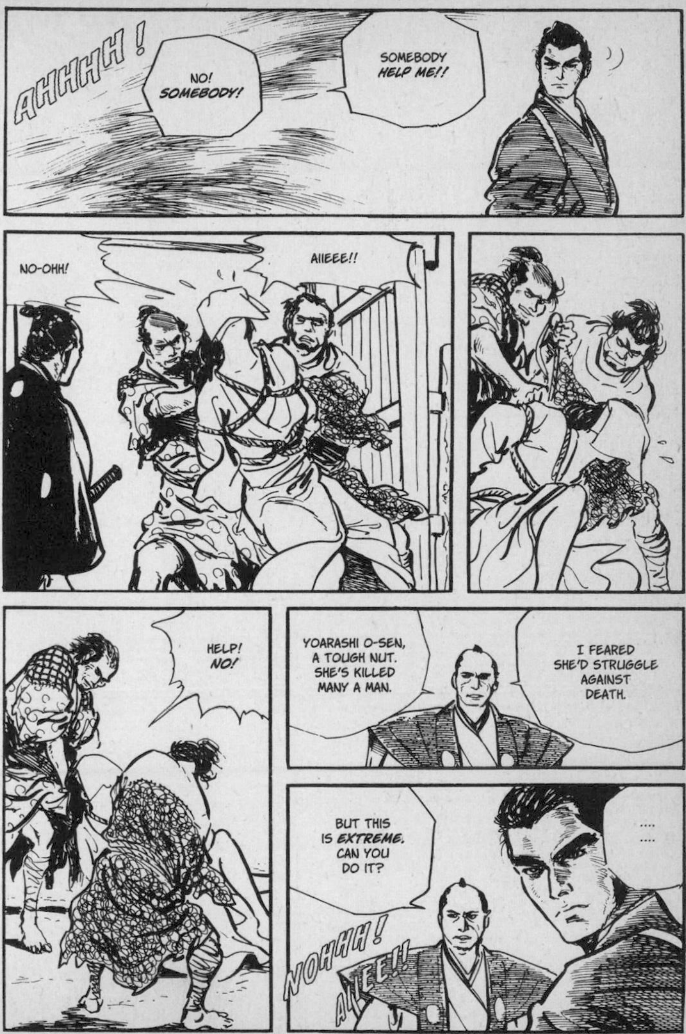
AHHHH!
NO! SOMEBODY!
SOMEBODY HELP ME!!
NO-OHH!
AIIEEE!!
HELP! NO!
YOARASHI O-SEN, A TOUGH NUT. SHE'S KILLED MANY A MAN.
I FEARED SHE'D STRUGGLE AGAINST DEATH.
BUT THIS IS EXTREME. CAN YOU DO IT?
....
....
NOHHH!
AIIEE!!

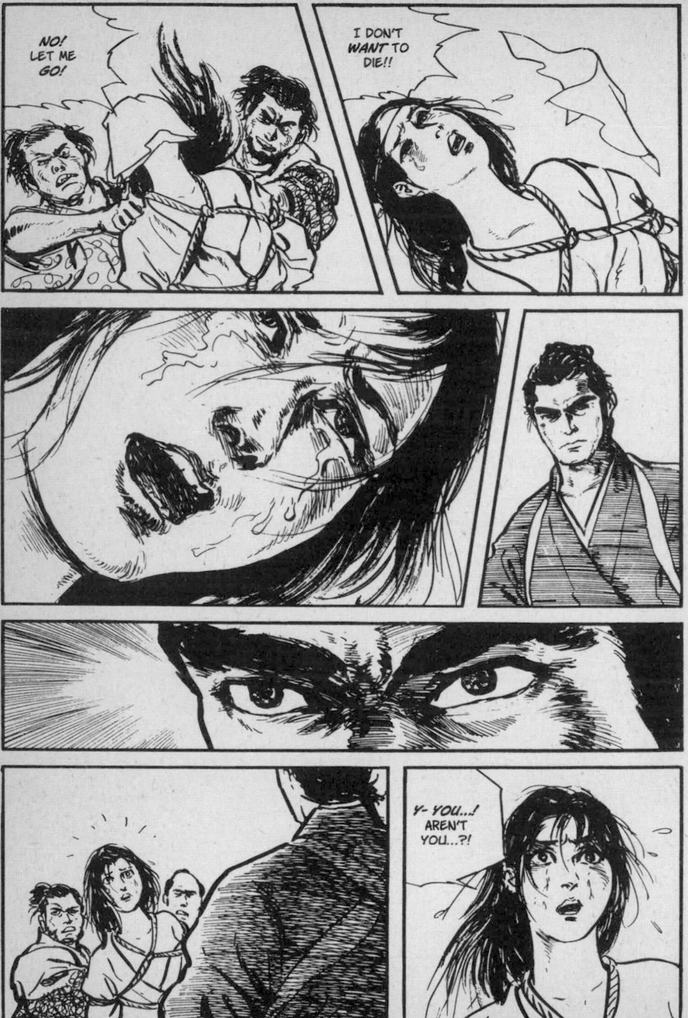
NO! LET ME GO!
I DON'T WANT TO DIE!!
Y- YOU...! AREN'T YOU...?!

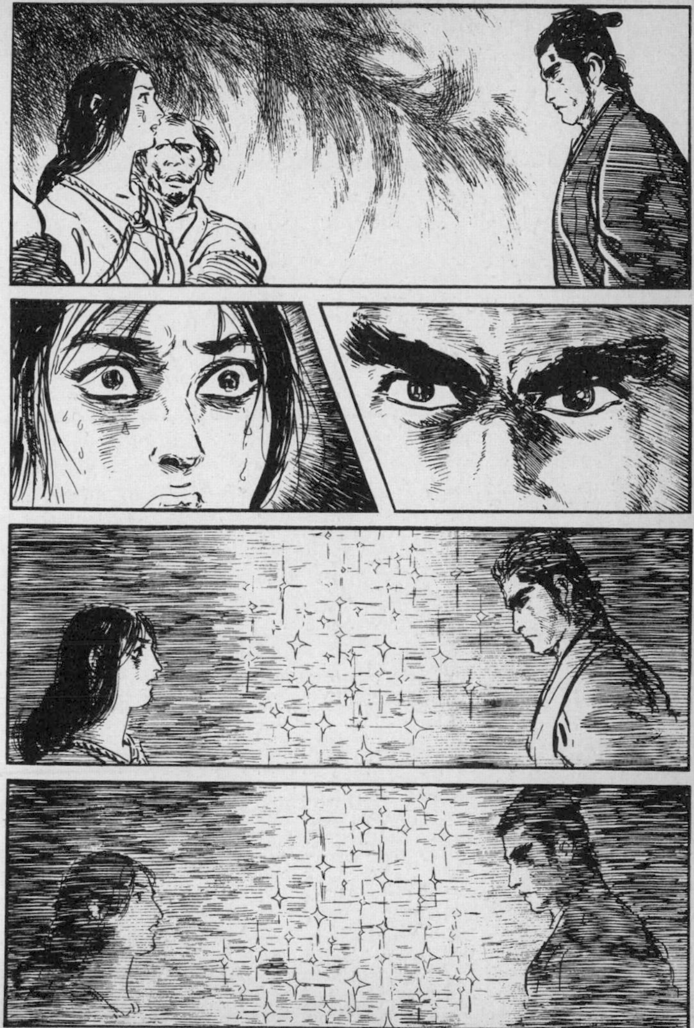

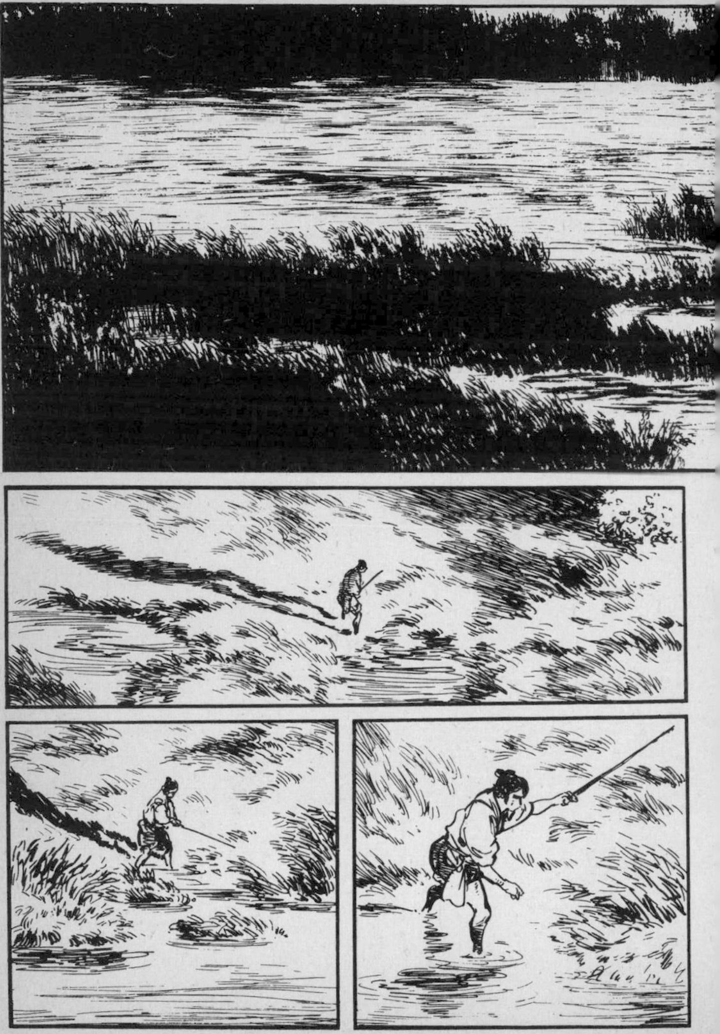

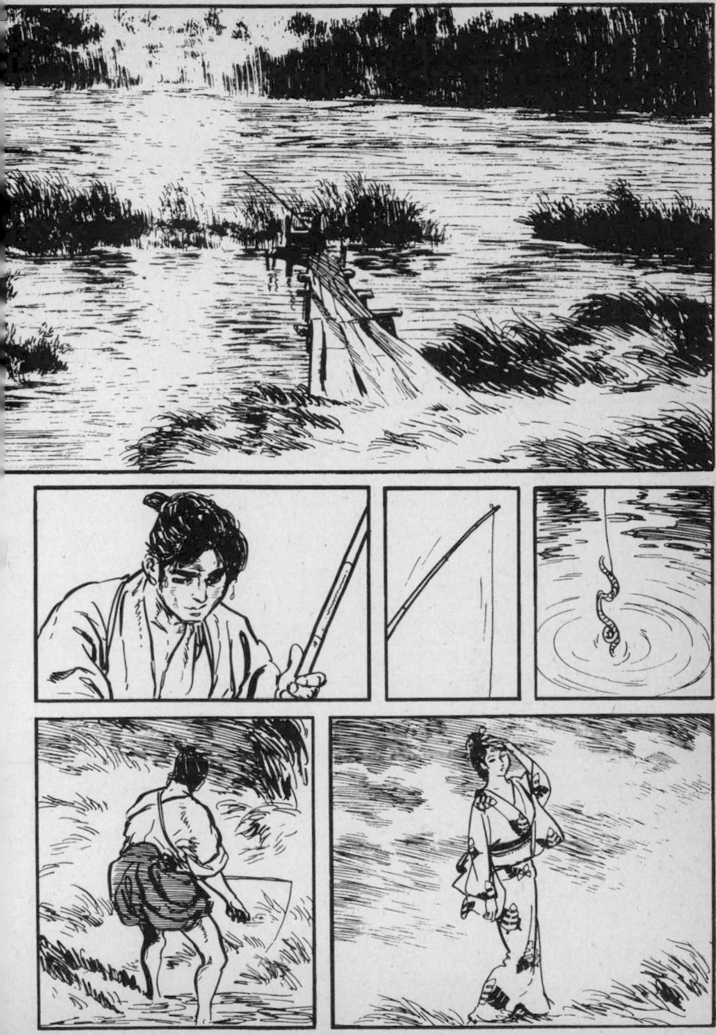

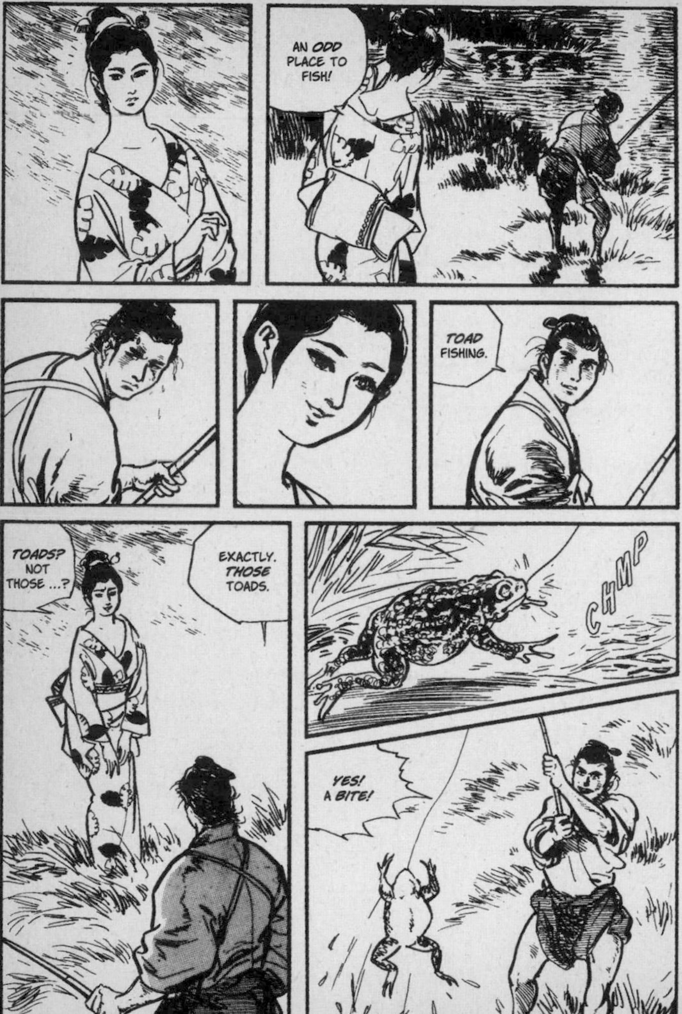
AN ODD PLACE TO FISH!
TOAD FISHING.
TOADS? NOT THOSE ...?
EXACTLY. THOSE TOADS.
CHMP
YES! A BITE!

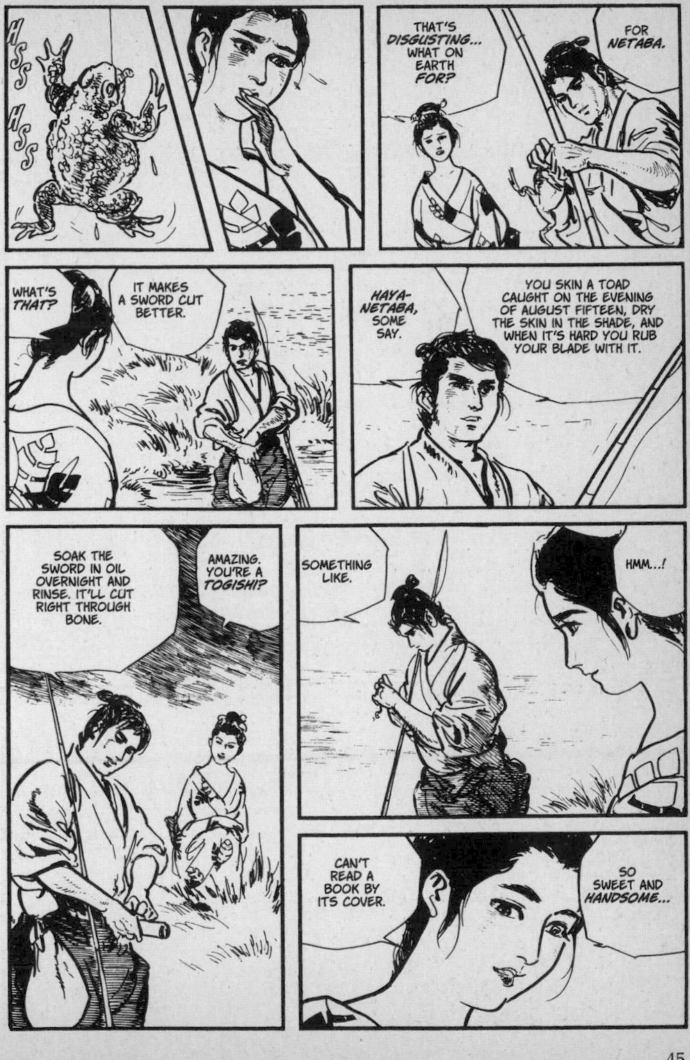
HSS HSS
THAT'S DISGUSTING... WHAT ON EARTH FOR?
FOR NETABA.
WHAT'S THAT?
IT MAKES A SWORD CUT BETTER.
HAYA-NETABA, SOME SAY.
YOU SKIN A TOAD CAUGHT ON THE EVENING OF AUGUST FIFTEEN, DRY THE SKIN IN THE SHADE, AND WHEN IT'S HARD YOU RUB YOUR BLADE WITH IT.
SOAK THE SWORD IN OIL OVERNIGHT AND RINSE. IT'LL CUT RIGHT THROUGH BONE.
AMAZING. YOU'RE A TOGISHI?
SOMETHING LIKE.
HMM...!
CAN'T READ A BOOK BY ITS COVER.
SO SWEET AND HANDSOME...

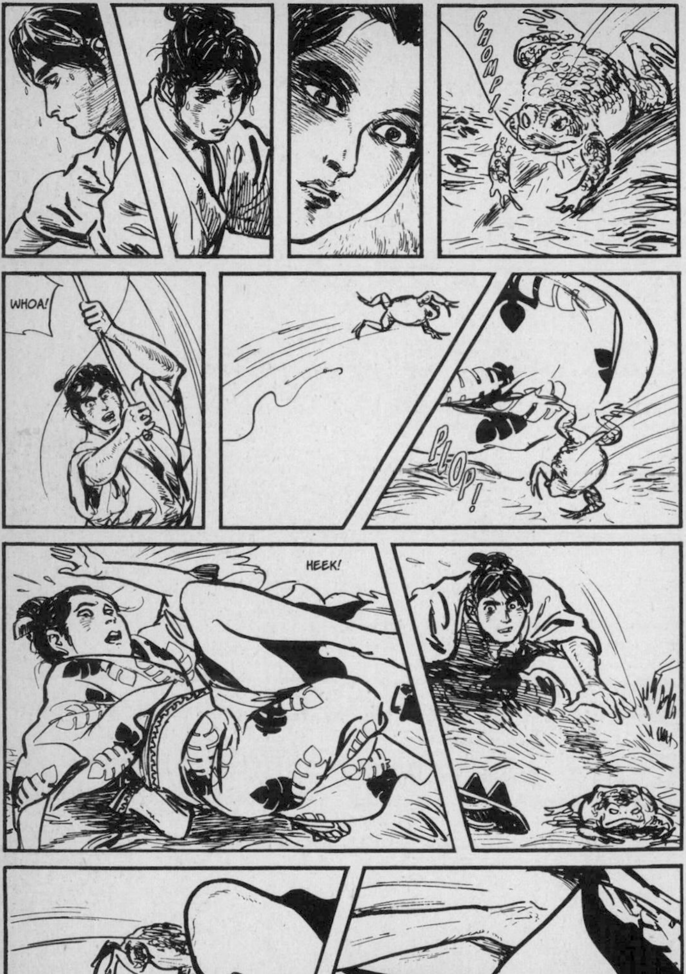
CHOMP!
WHOA!
PLOP!
HEEK!

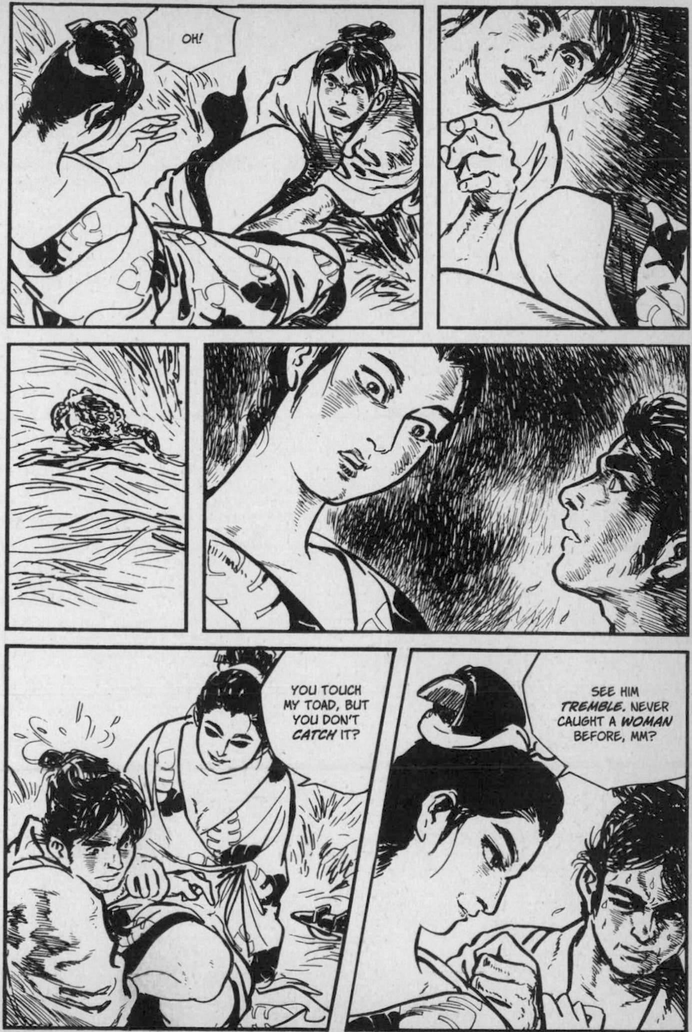
OH!
YOU TOUCH MY TOAD, BUT YOU DON'T *CATCH* IT?
SEE HIM *TREMBLE.* NEVER CAUGHT A *WOMAN* BEFORE, MM?

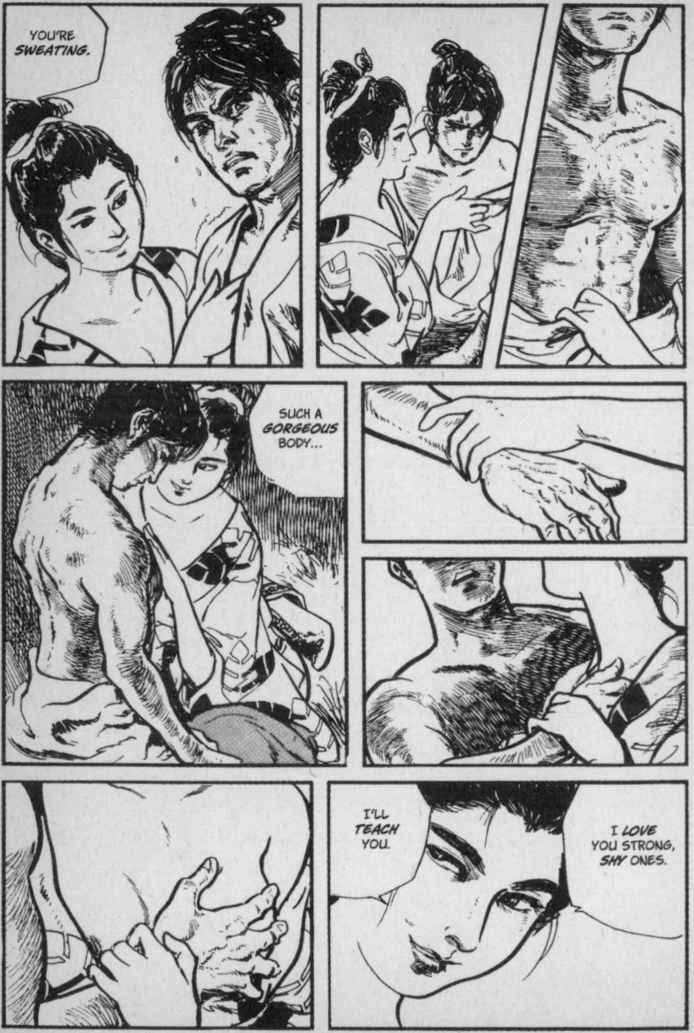
YOU'RE SWEATING.
SUCH A GORGEOUS BODY...
I'LL TEACH YOU.
I LOVE YOU STRONG, SHY ONES.

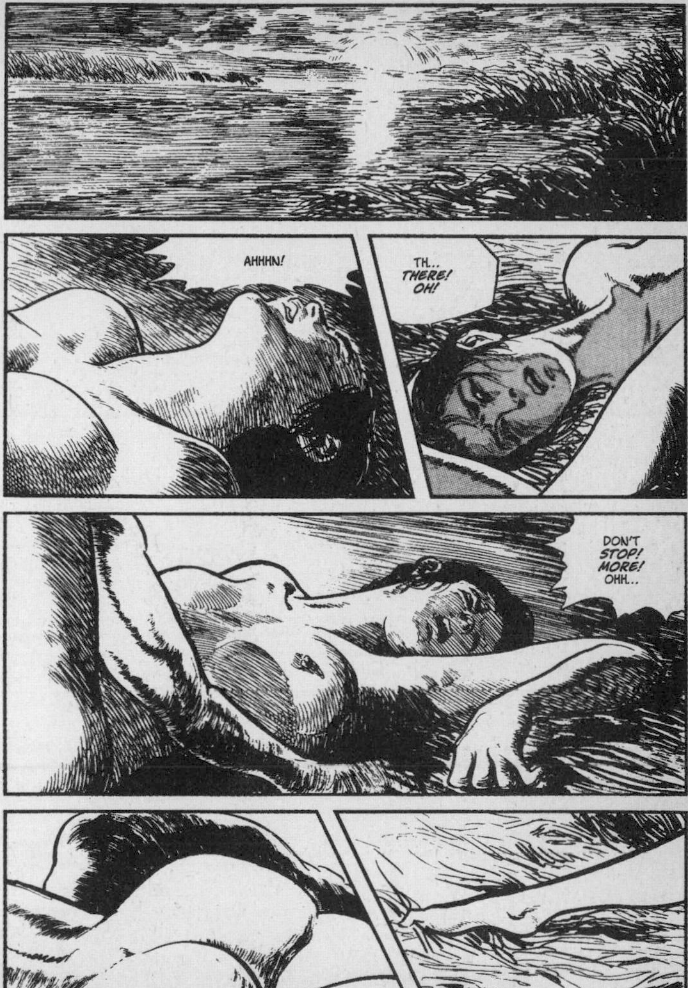
AHHHN!
TH... THERE! OH!
DON'T STOP! MORE! OHH...

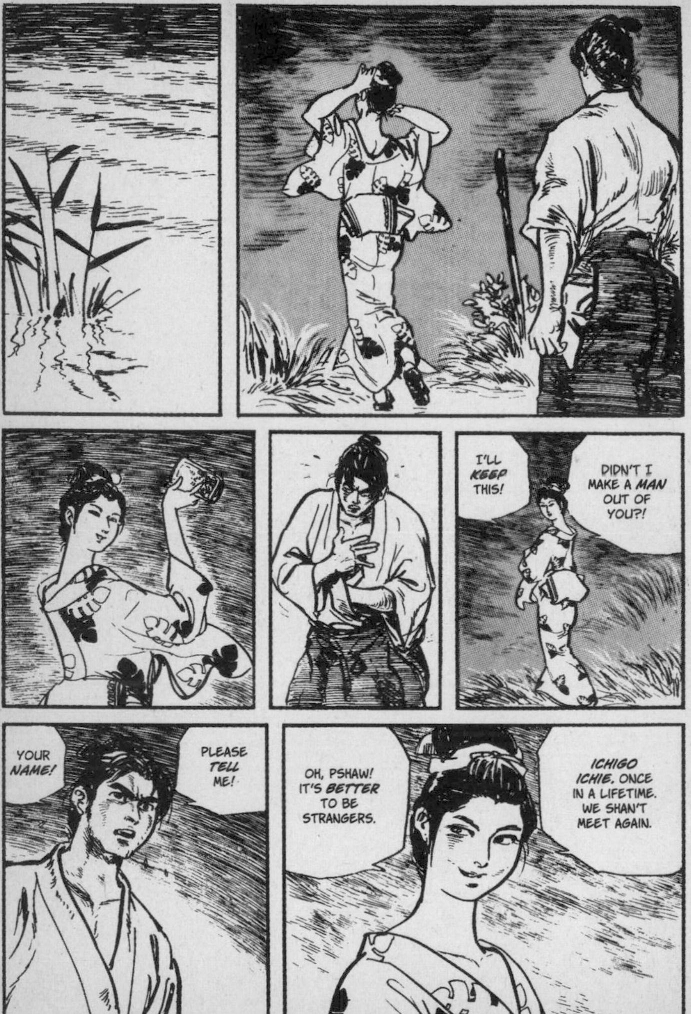
I'LL KEEP THIS!
DIDN'T I MAKE A MAN OUT OF YOU?!
YOUR NAME!
PLEASE TELL ME!
OH, PSHAW! IT'S BETTER TO BE STRANGERS.
ICHIGO ICHIE. ONCE IN A LIFETIME. WE SHAN'T MEET AGAIN.

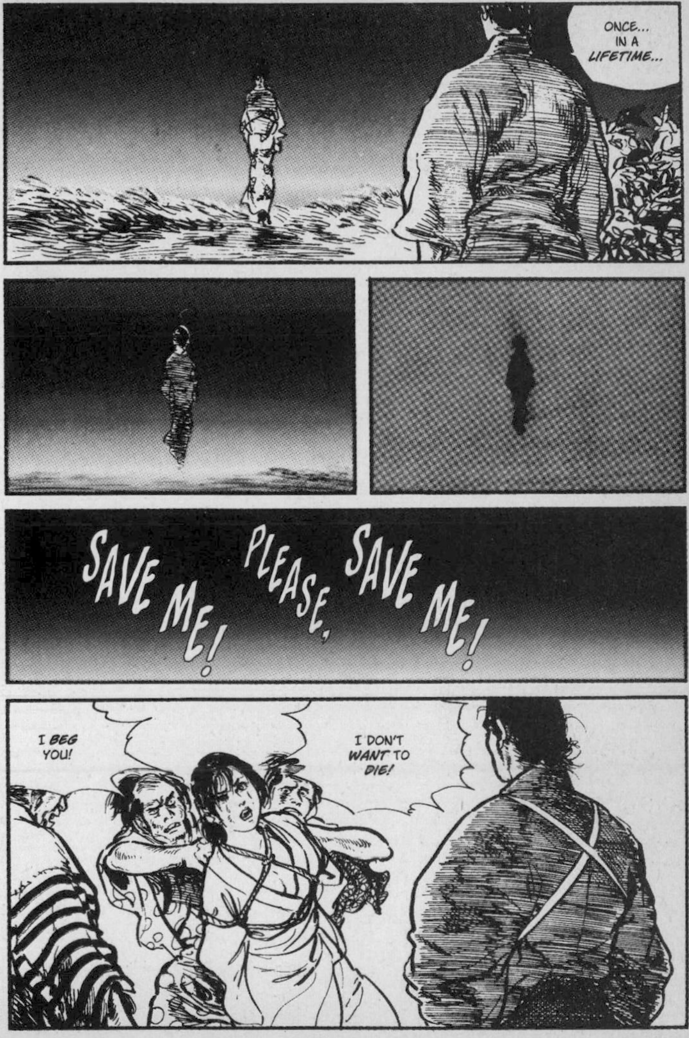
ONCE... IN A LIFETIME...
SAVE ME! PLEASE, SAVE ME!
I BEG YOU!
I DON'T WANT TO DIE!

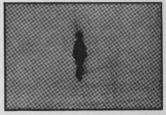

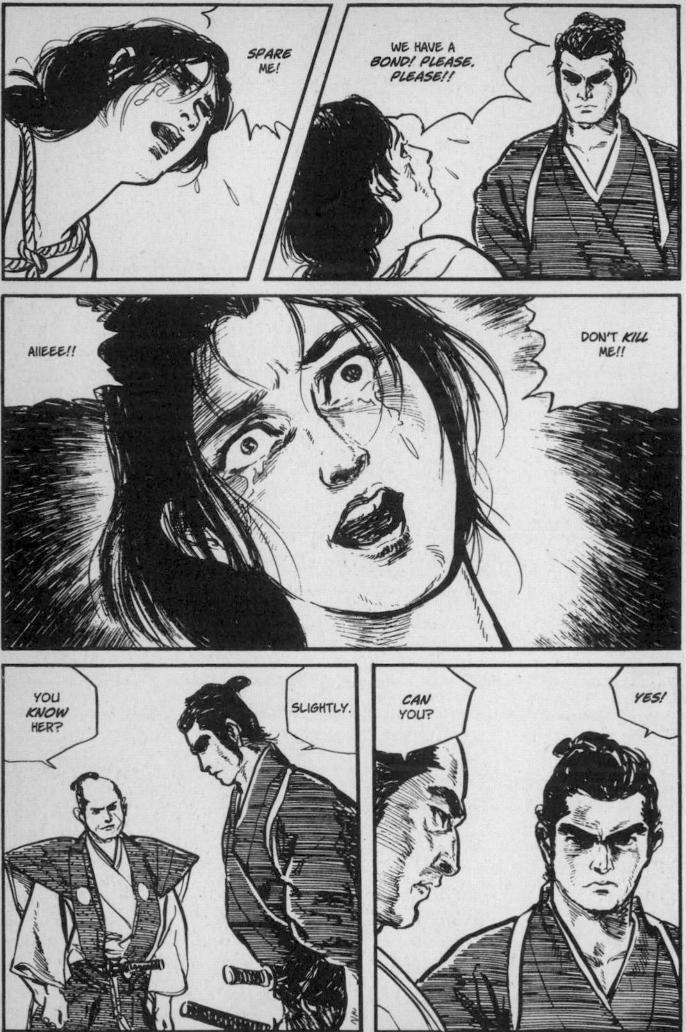
SPARE ME!
WE HAVE A BOND! PLEASE. PLEASE!!
AIIEEE!!
DON'T KILL ME!!
YOU KNOW HER?
SLIGHTLY.
CAN YOU?
YES!

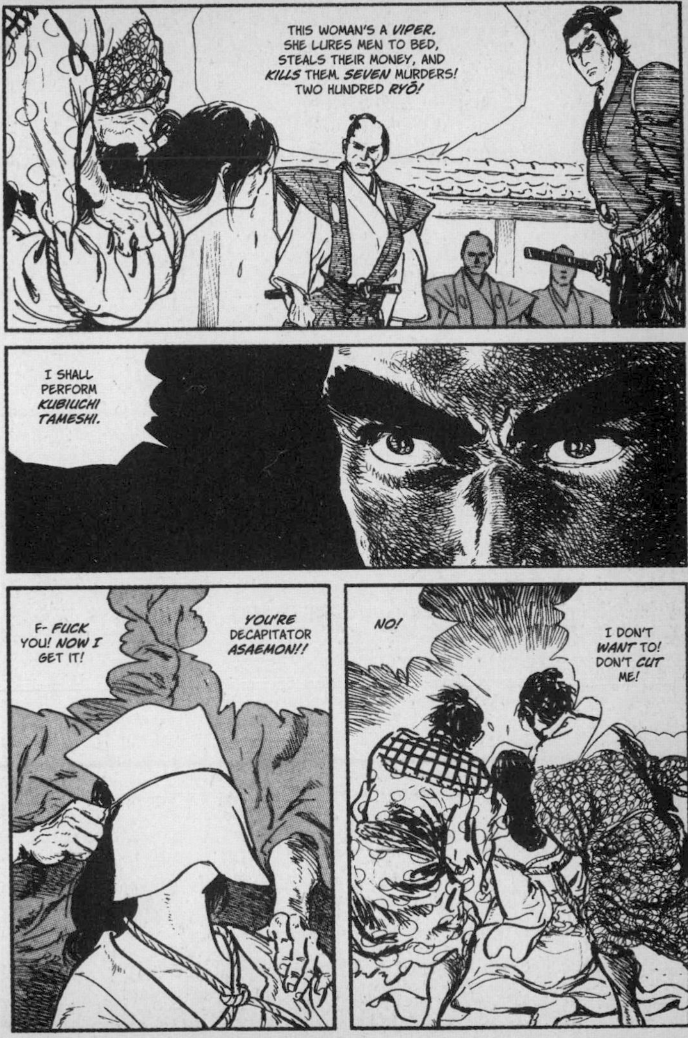
THIS WOMAN'S A VIPER. SHE LURES MEN TO BED, STEALS THEIR MONEY, AND KILLS THEM. SEVEN MURDERS! TWO HUNDRED RYŌ!
I SHALL PERFORM KUBIUCHI TAMESHI.
F- FUCK YOU! NOW I GET IT!
YOU'RE DECAPITATOR ASAEMON!!
NO!
I DON'T WANT TO! DON'T CUT ME!

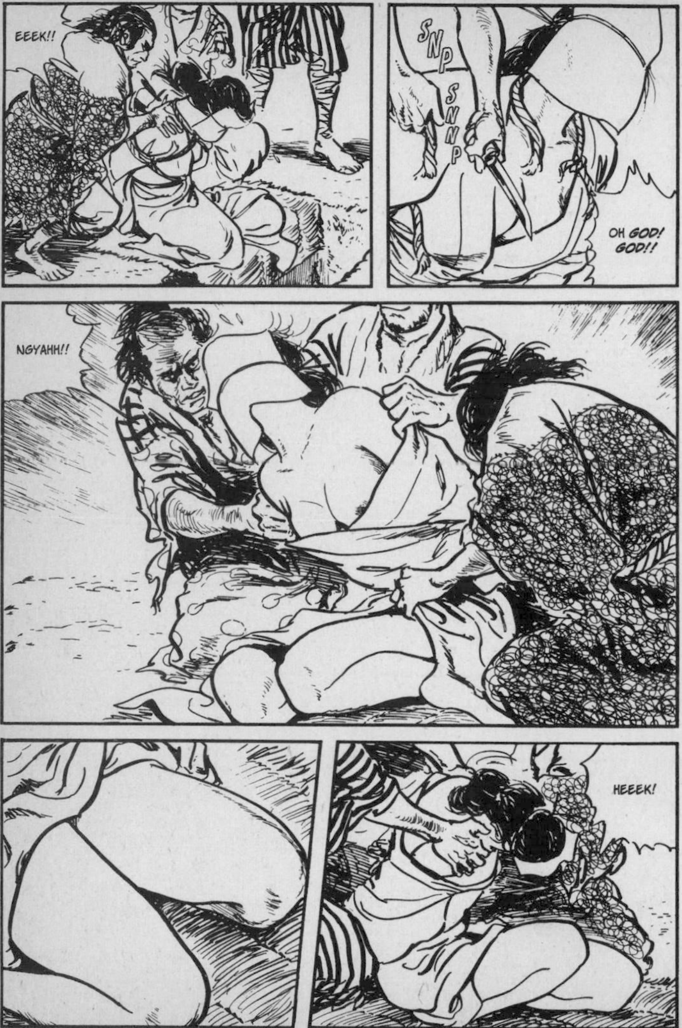
EEEK!!
SNP
SNNP
OH GOD! GOD!!
NGYAHH!!
HEEEK!

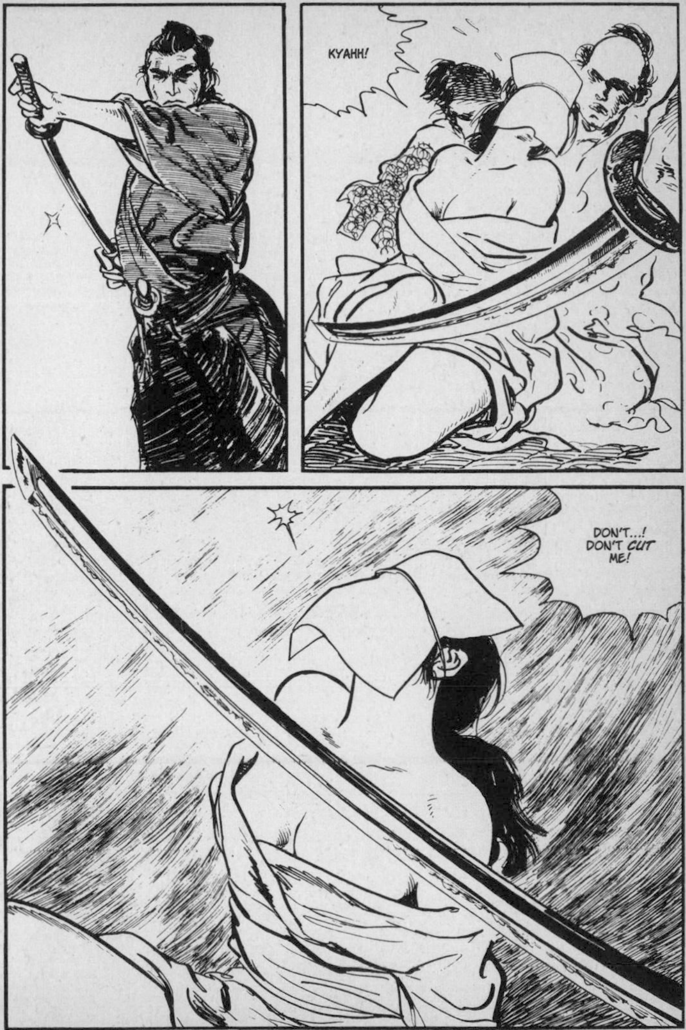
KYAHH!
DON'T...! DON'T CUT ME!

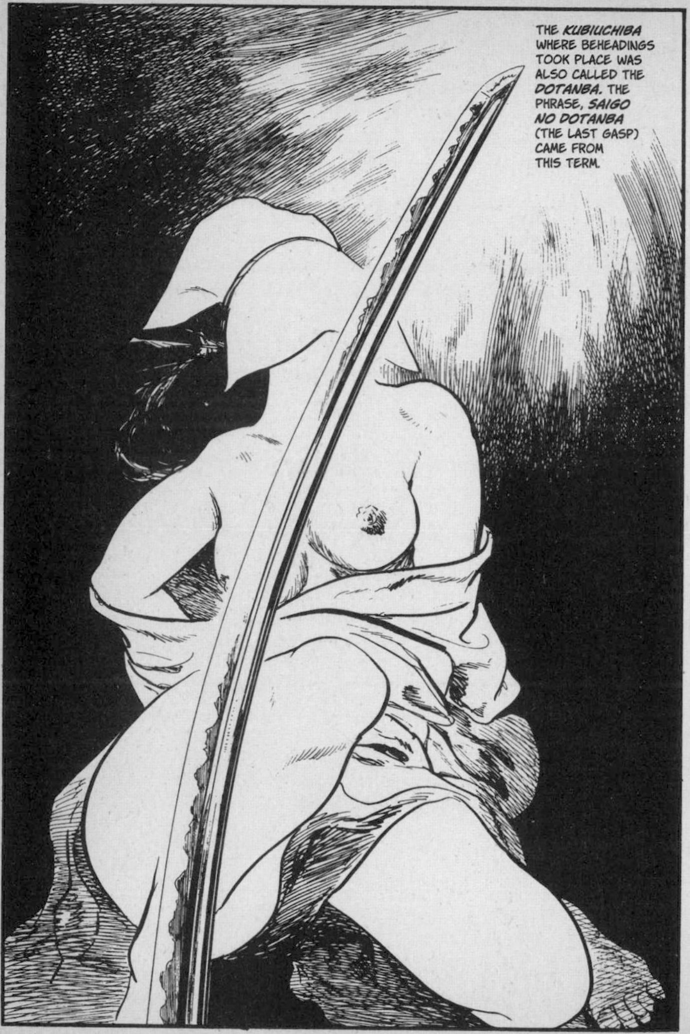
THE *KUBIUCHIBA* WHERE BEHEADINGS TOOK PLACE WAS ALSO CALLED THE *DOTANBA*. THE PHRASE, *SAIGO NO DOTANBA* (THE LAST GASP) CAME FROM THIS TERM.

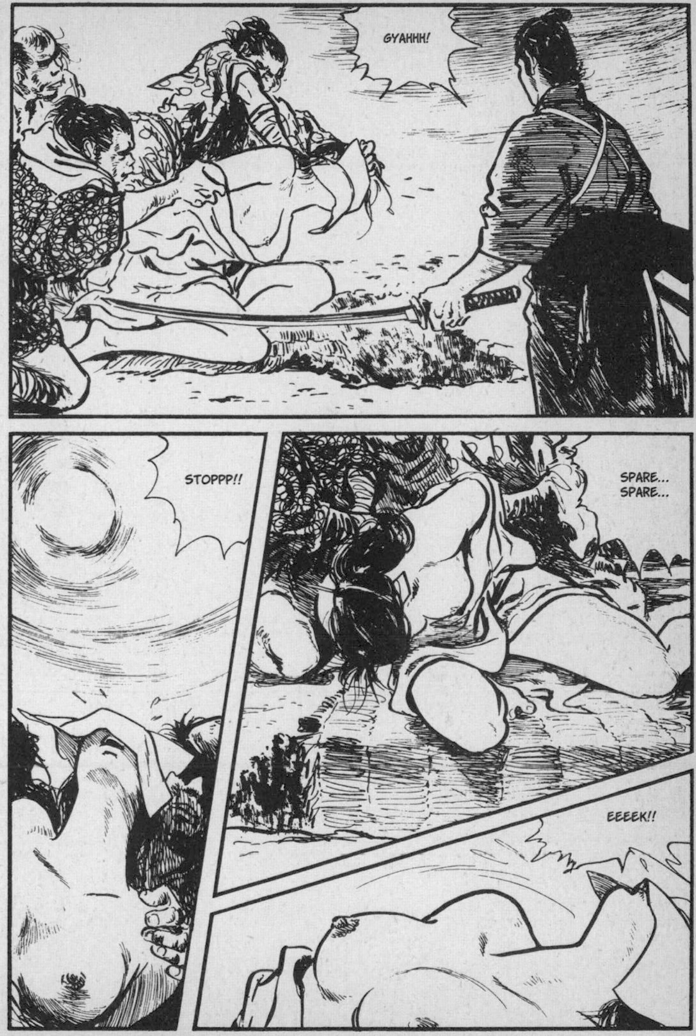
GYAHHH!
STOPPP!!
SPARE...
SPARE...
EEEEK!!

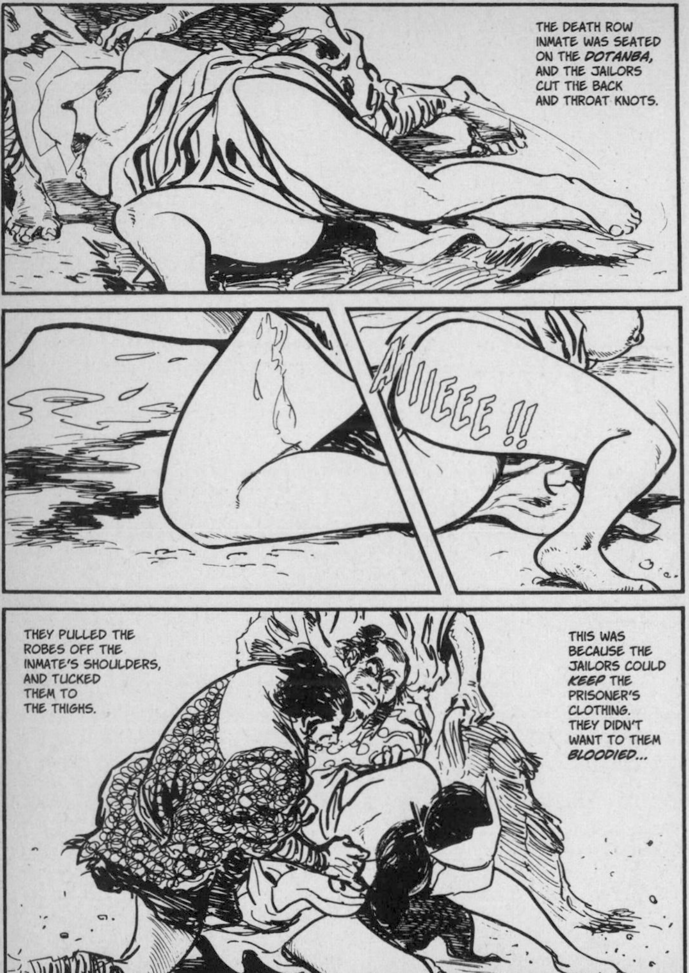
THE DEATH ROW INMATE WAS SEATED ON THE *DOTANBA,* AND THE JAILORS CUT THE BACK AND THROAT KNOTS.
AIIIEEE !!
THEY PULLED THE ROBES OFF THE INMATE'S SHOULDERS, AND TUCKED THEM TO THE THIGHS.
THIS WAS BECAUSE THE JAILORS COULD *KEEP* THE PRISONER'S CLOTHING. THEY DIDN'T WANT TO THEM *BLOODIED...*

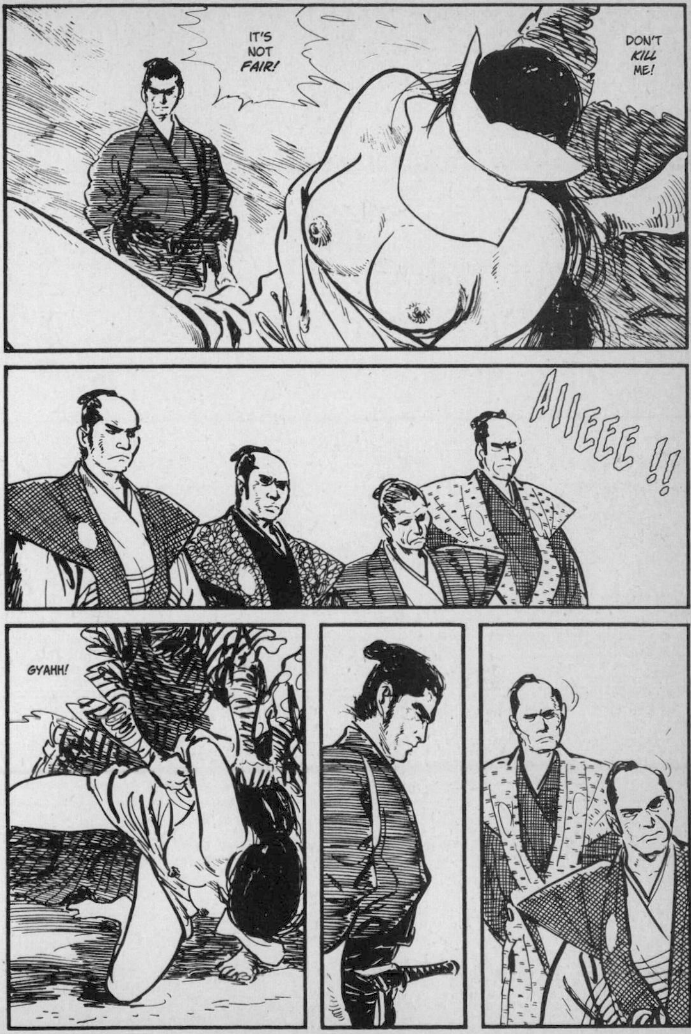
IT'S NOT FAIR!
DON'T KILL ME!
AIIEEE !!
GYAHH!

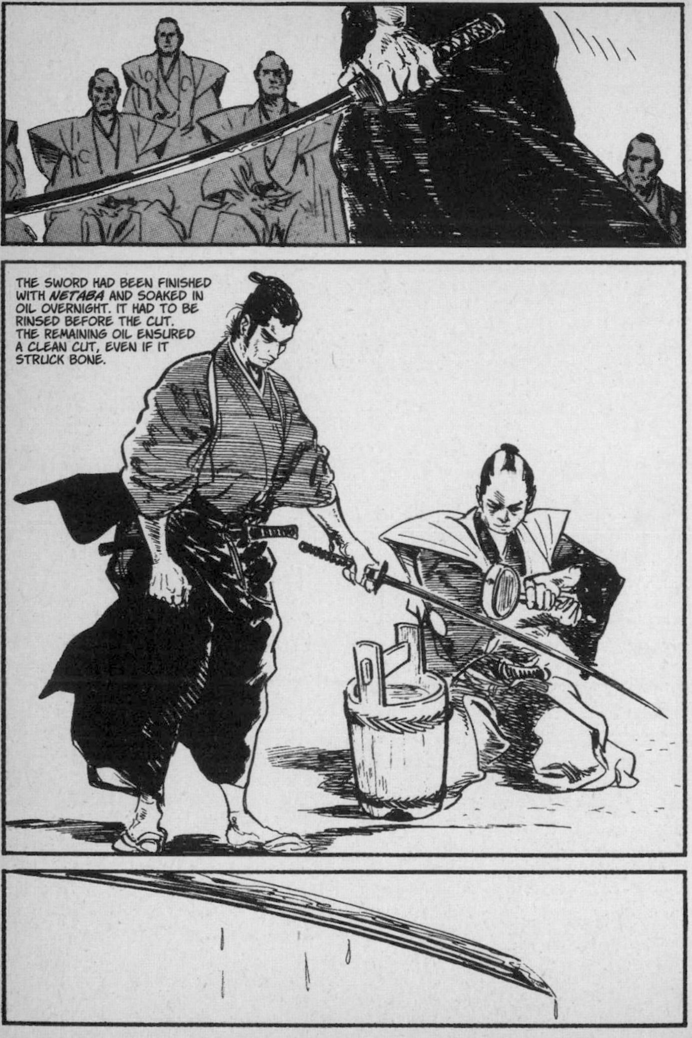
THE SWORD HAD BEEN FINISHED WITH *NETABA* AND SOAKED IN OIL OVERNIGHT. IT HAD TO BE RINSED BEFORE THE CUT. THE REMAINING OIL ENSURED A CLEAN CUT, EVEN IF IT STRUCK BONE.

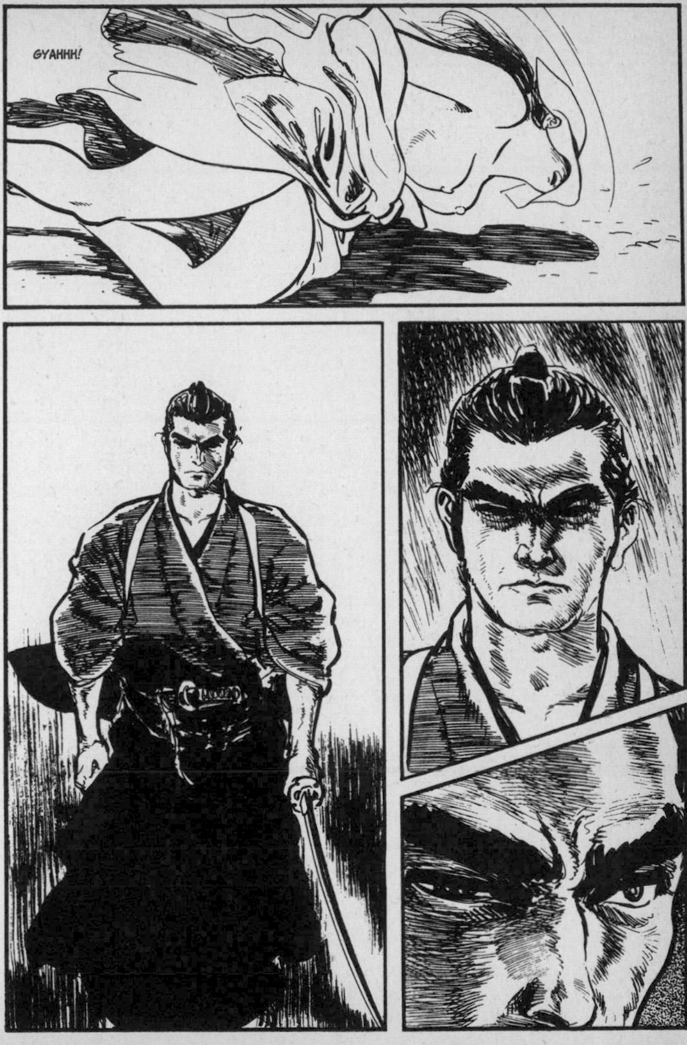
GYAHHH!

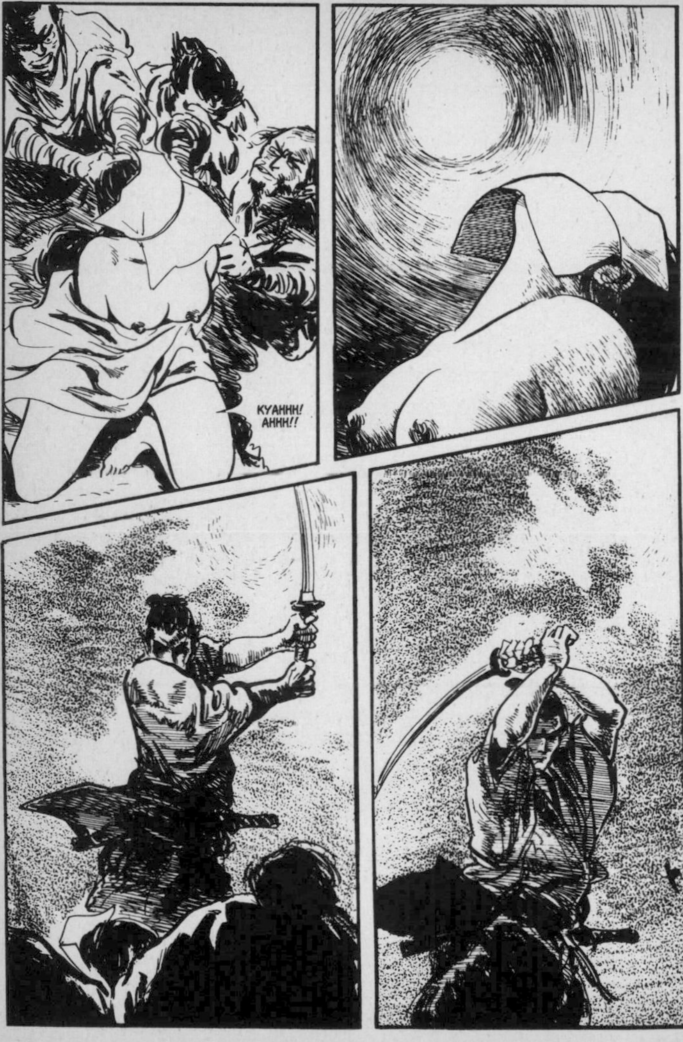
KYAHHH!
AHHH!!

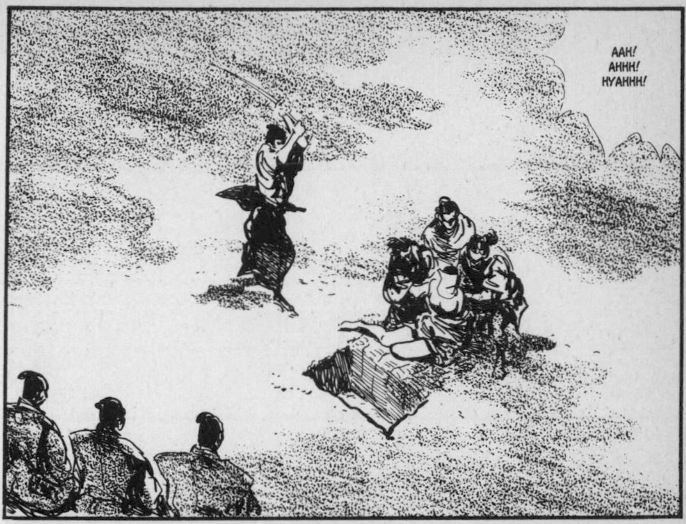
AAH!
AHHH!
HYAHHH!
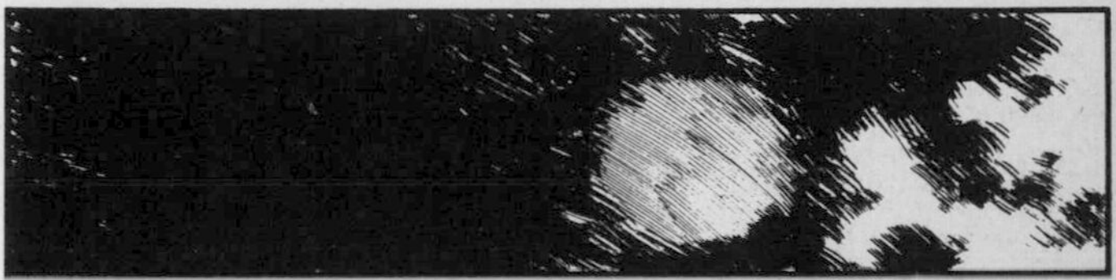
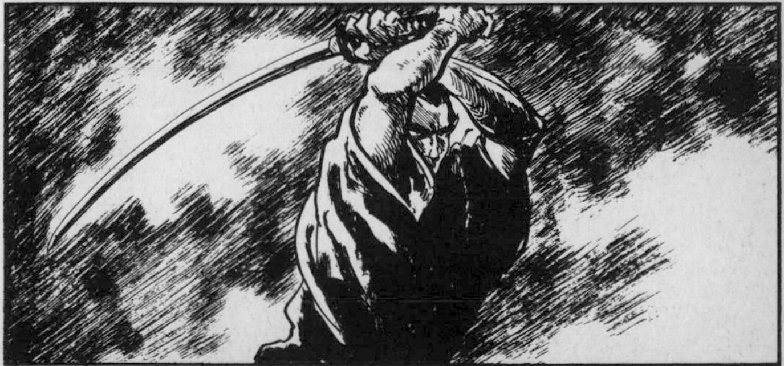

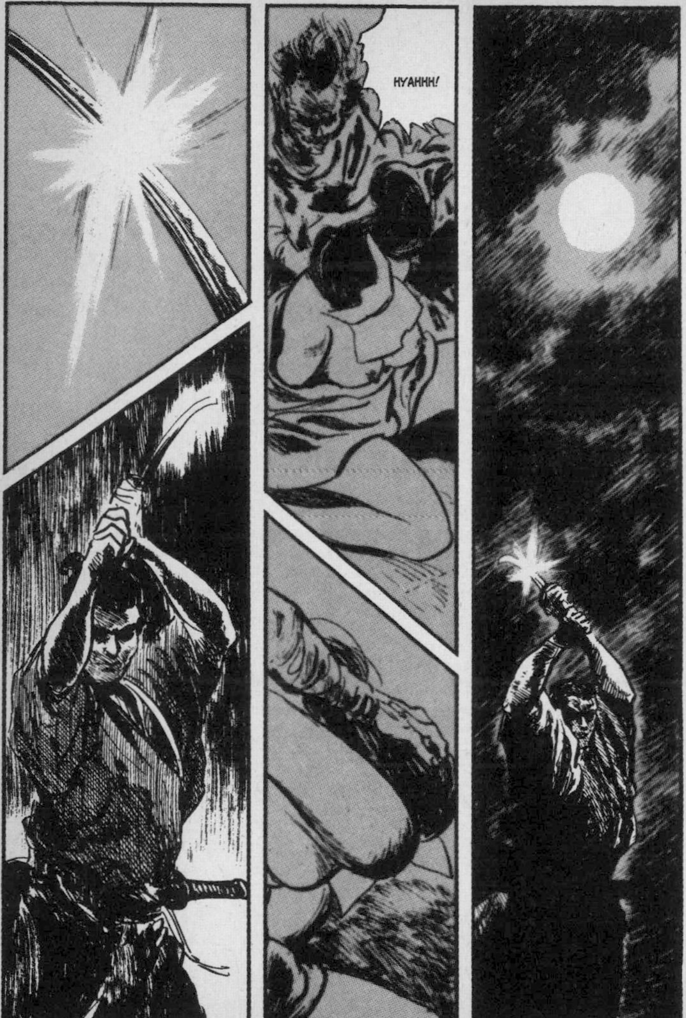
HYAHHH!

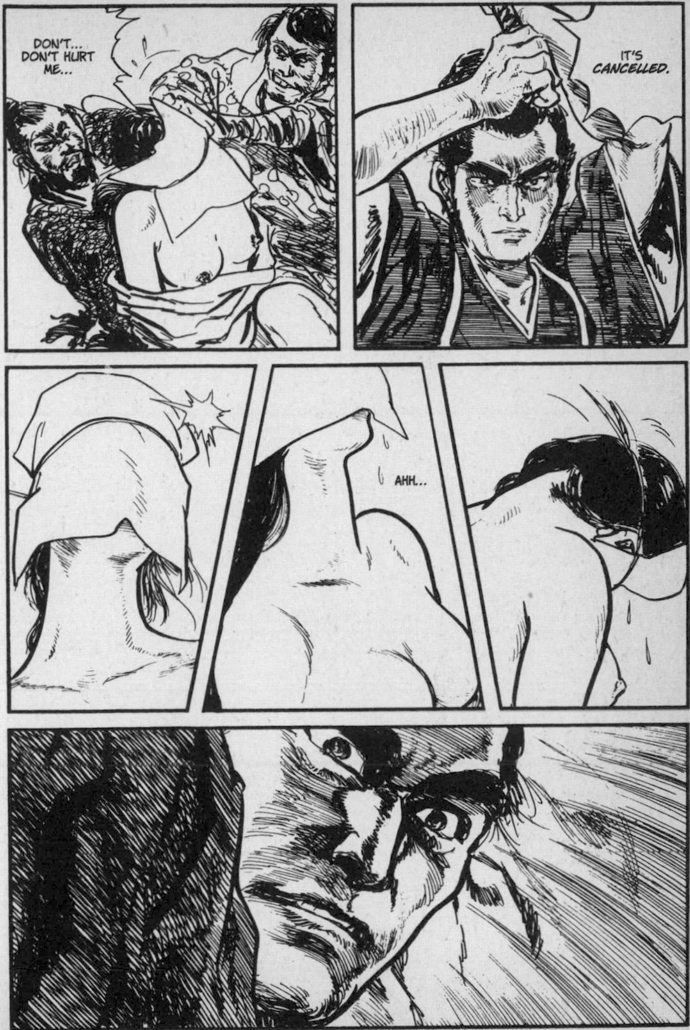
DON'T... DON'T HURT ME...
IT'S CANCELLED.
AHH...

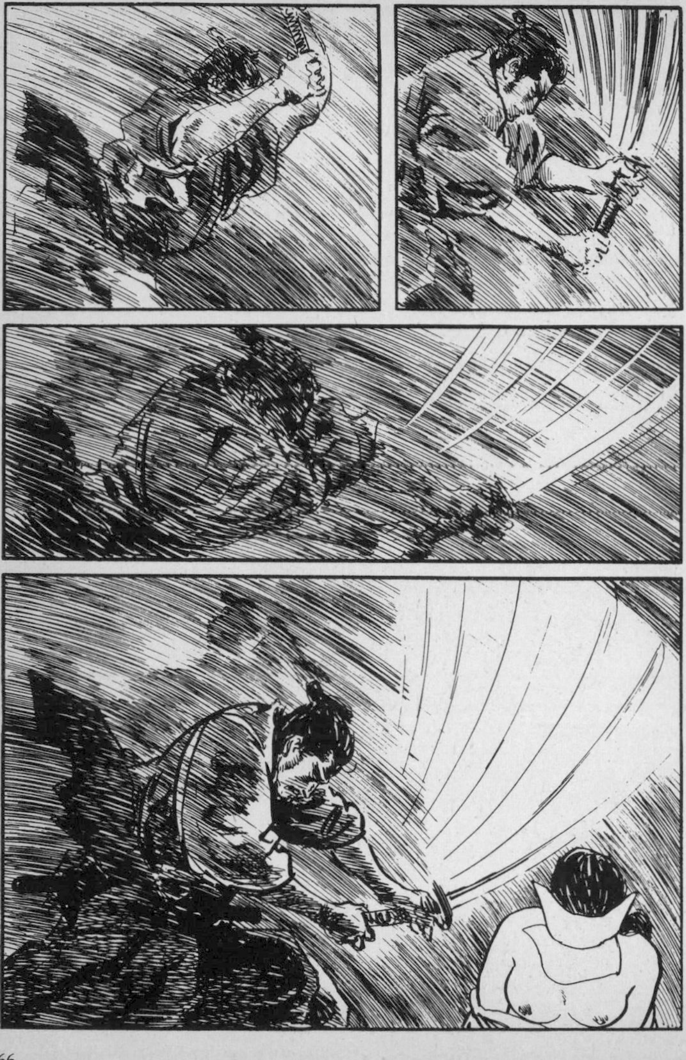

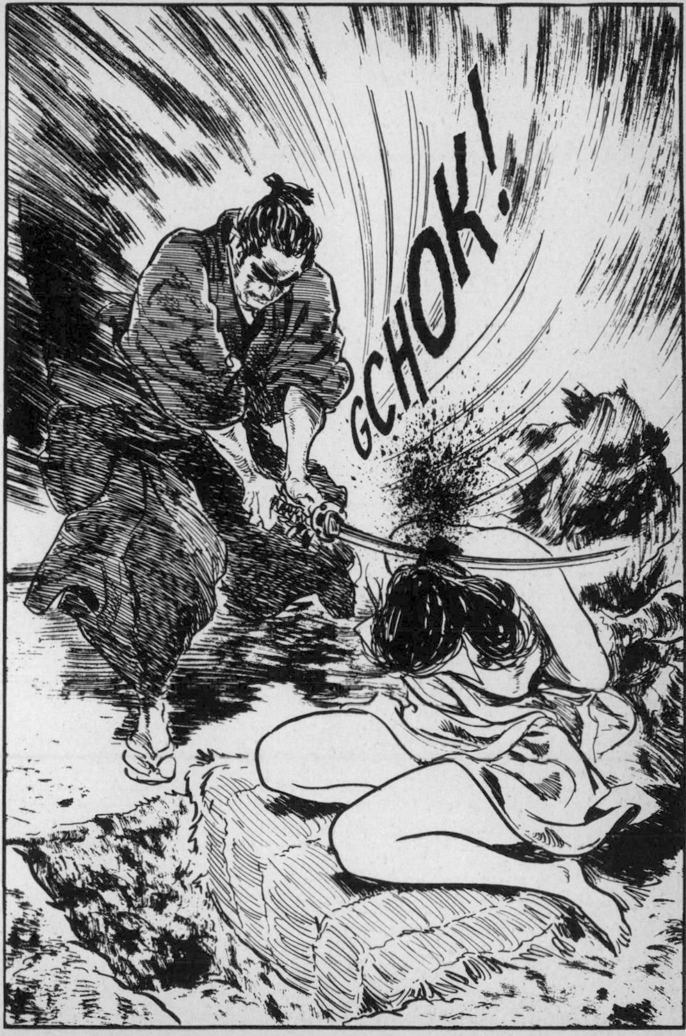
GCHOK!

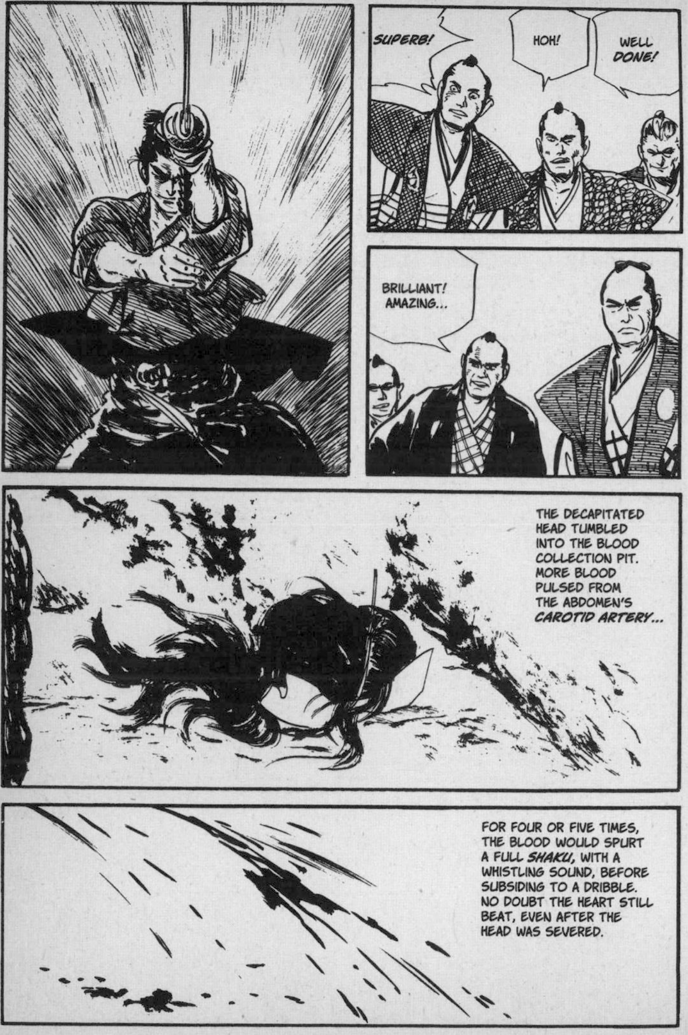
SUPERB!
HOH!
WELL DONE!
BRILLIANT! AMAZING...
THE DECAPITATED HEAD TUMBLED INTO THE BLOOD COLLECTION PIT. MORE BLOOD PULSED FROM THE ABDOMEN'S CAROTID ARTERY...
FOR FOUR OR FIVE TIMES, THE BLOOD WOULD SPURT A FULL SHAKU, WITH A WHISTLING SOUND, BEFORE SUBSIDING TO A DRIBBLE. NO DOUBT THE HEART STILL BEAT, EVEN AFTER THE HEAD WAS SEVERED.

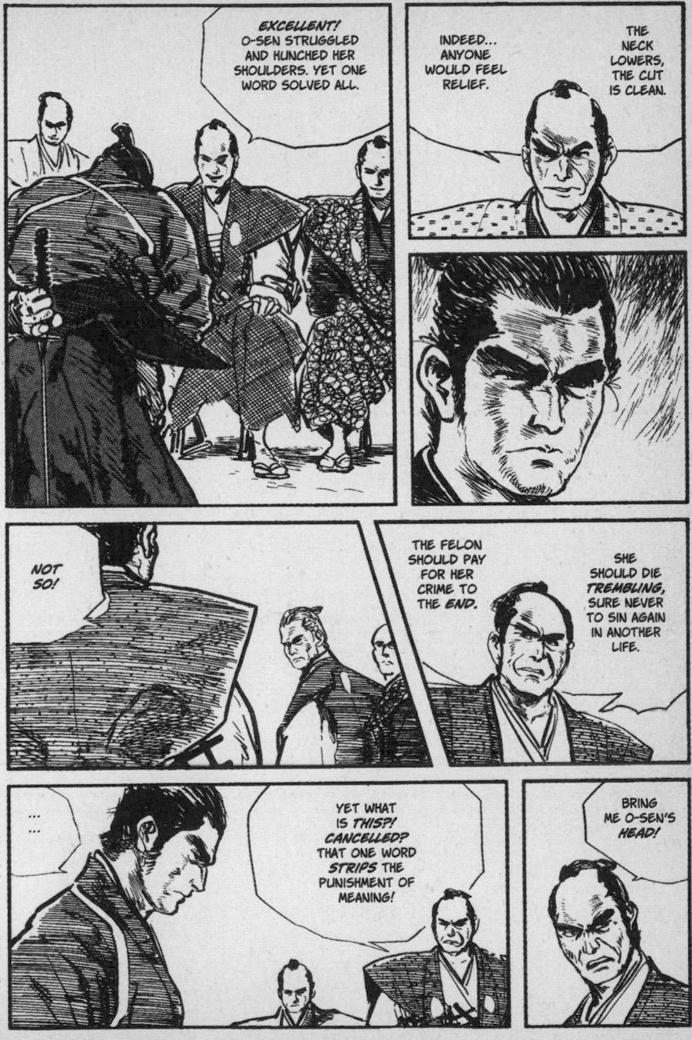

EXCELLENT! O-SEN STRUGGLED AND HUNCHED HER SHOULDERS. YET ONE WORD SOLVED ALL.
INDEED... ANYONE WOULD FEEL RELIEF.
THE NECK LOWERS, THE CUT IS CLEAN.
NOT SO!
THE FELON SHOULD PAY FOR HER CRIME TO THE END.
SHE SHOULD DIE TREMBLING, SURE NEVER TO SIN AGAIN IN ANOTHER LIFE.
...
...
YET WHAT IS THIS?! CANCELLED? THAT ONE WORD STRIPS THE PUNISHMENT OF MEANING!
BRING ME O-SEN'S HEAD!

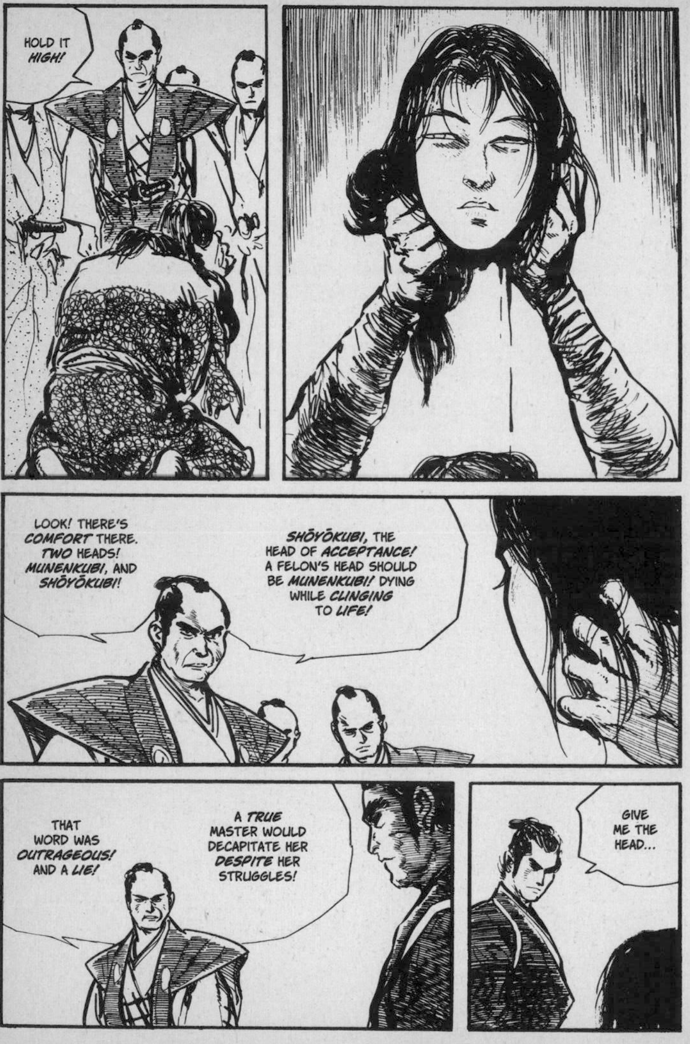
HOLD IT HIGH!
LOOK! THERE'S COMFORT THERE. TWO HEADS! MUNENKUBI, AND SHŌYŌKUBI!
SHŌYŌKUBI, THE HEAD OF ACCEPTANCE! A FELON'S HEAD SHOULD BE MUNENKUBI! DYING WHILE CLINGING TO LIFE!
THAT WORD WAS OUTRAGEOUS! AND A LIE!
A TRUE MASTER WOULD DECAPITATE HER DESPITE HER STRUGGLES!
GIVE ME THE HEAD...

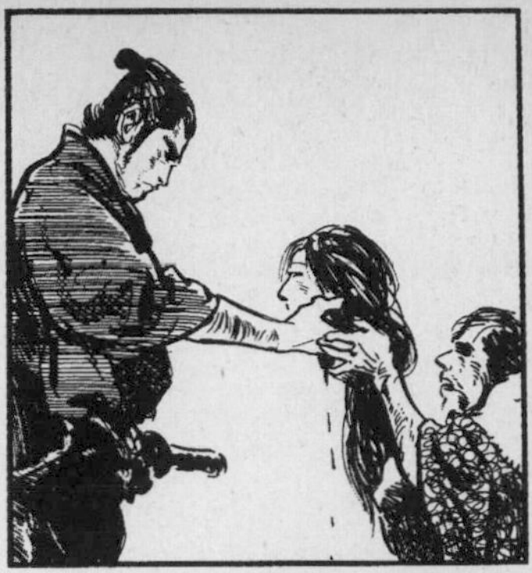
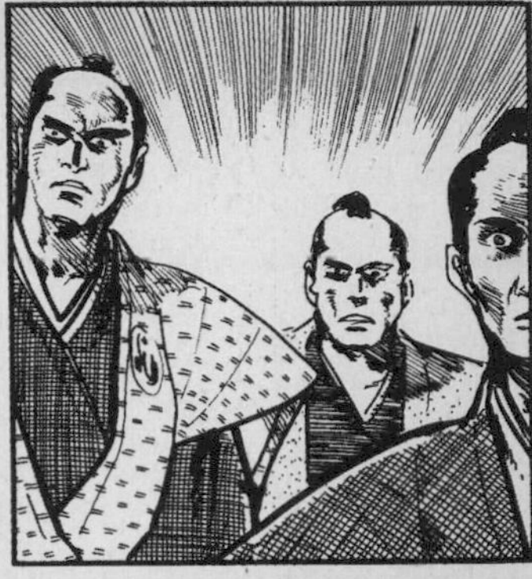
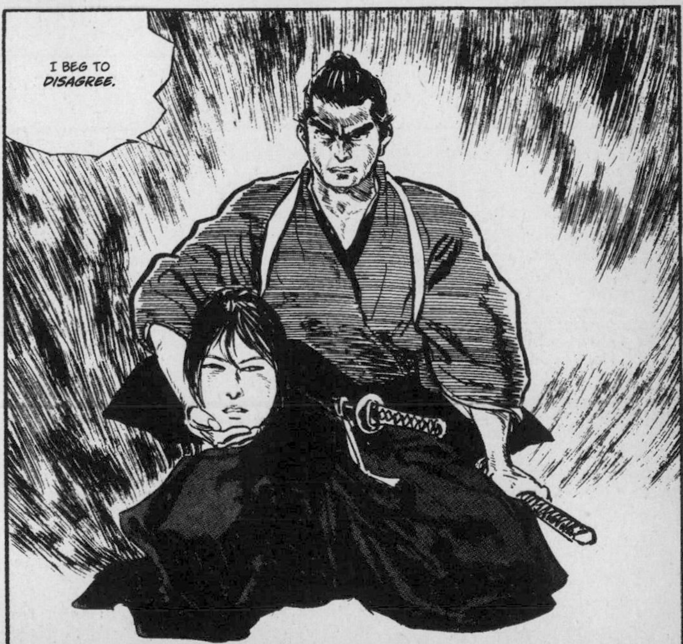
I BEG TO DISAGREE.

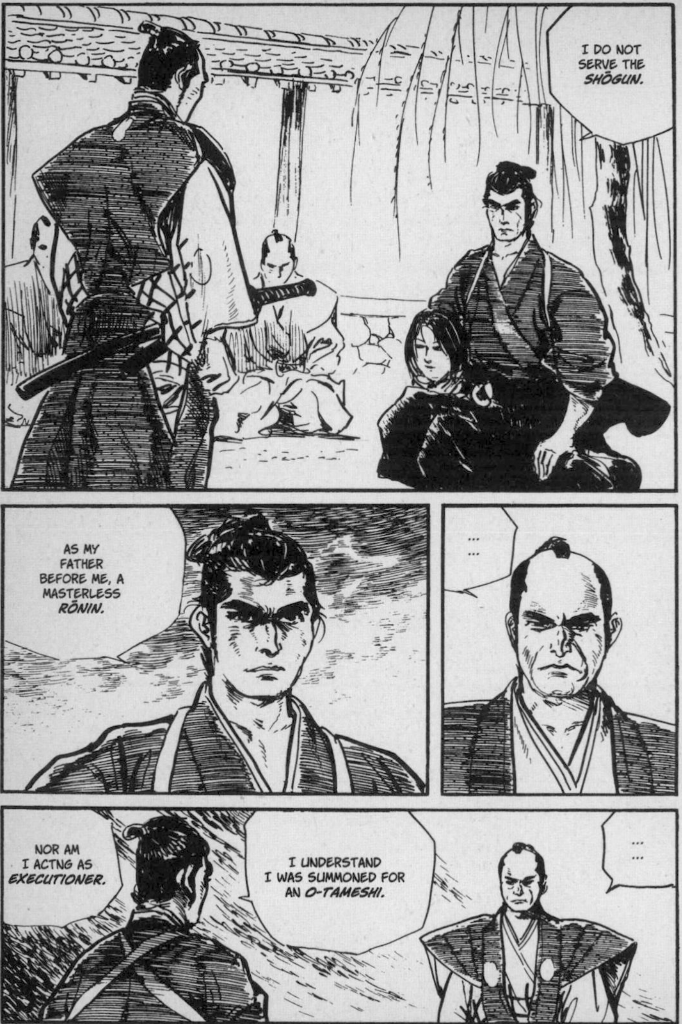
I DO NOT SERVE THE *SHŌGUN.*
AS MY FATHER BEFORE ME, A MASTERLESS *RŌNIN.*
...
...
NOR AM I ACTNG AS *EXECUTIONER.*
I UNDERSTAND I WAS SUMMONED FOR AN *O-TAMESHI.*
...
...

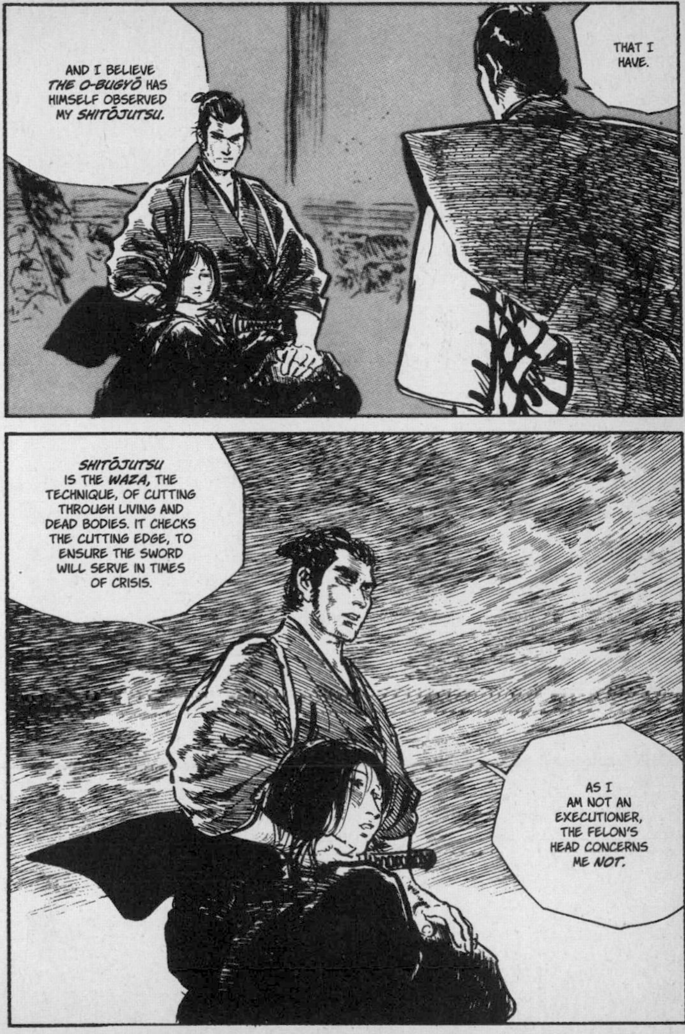
AND I BELIEVE THE O-BUGYŌ HAS HIMSELF OBSERVED MY SHITŌJUTSU.
THAT I HAVE.
SHITŌJUTSU IS THE WAZA, THE TECHNIQUE, OF CUTTING THROUGH LIVING AND DEAD BODIES. IT CHECKS THE CUTTING EDGE, TO ENSURE THE SWORD WILL SERVE IN TIMES OF CRISIS.
AS I AM NOT AN EXECUTIONER, THE FELON'S HEAD CONCERNS ME NOT.

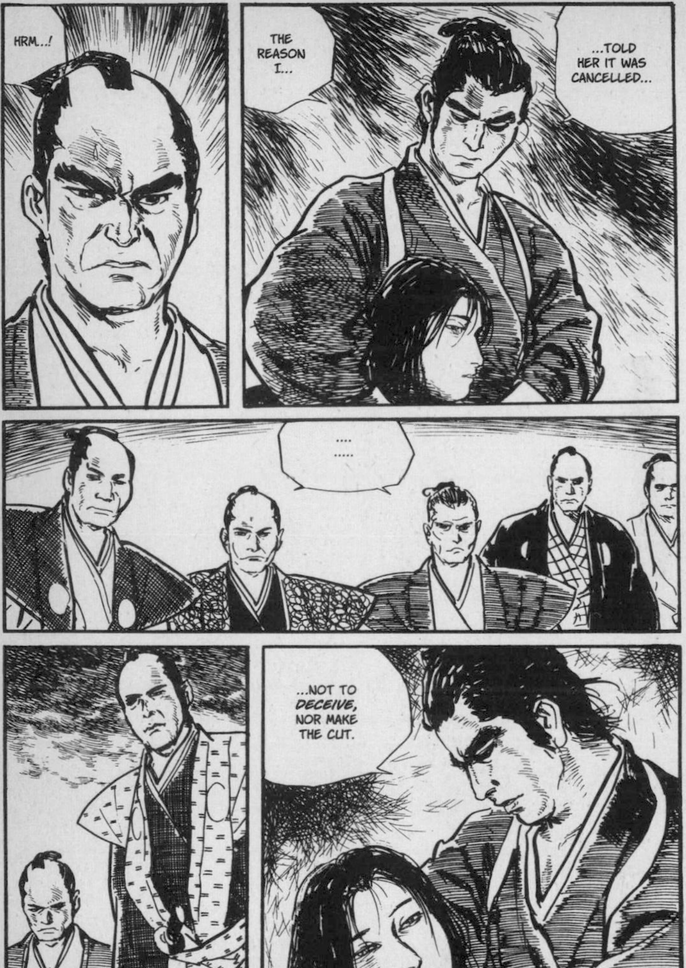
HRM...!
THE REASON I...
...TOLD HER IT WAS CANCELLED...
....
.....
...NOT TO DECEIVE, NOR MAKE THE CUT.

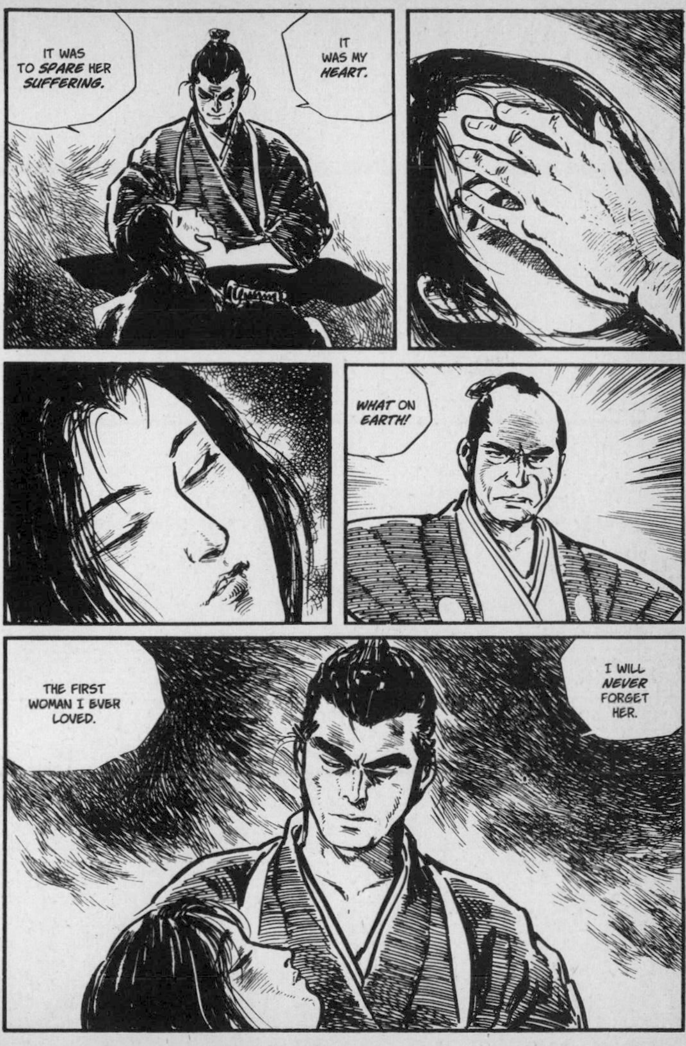
IT WAS TO SPARE HER SUFFERING.
IT WAS MY HEART.
WHAT ON EARTH!
THE FIRST WOMAN I EVER LOVED.
I WILL NEVER FORGET HER.

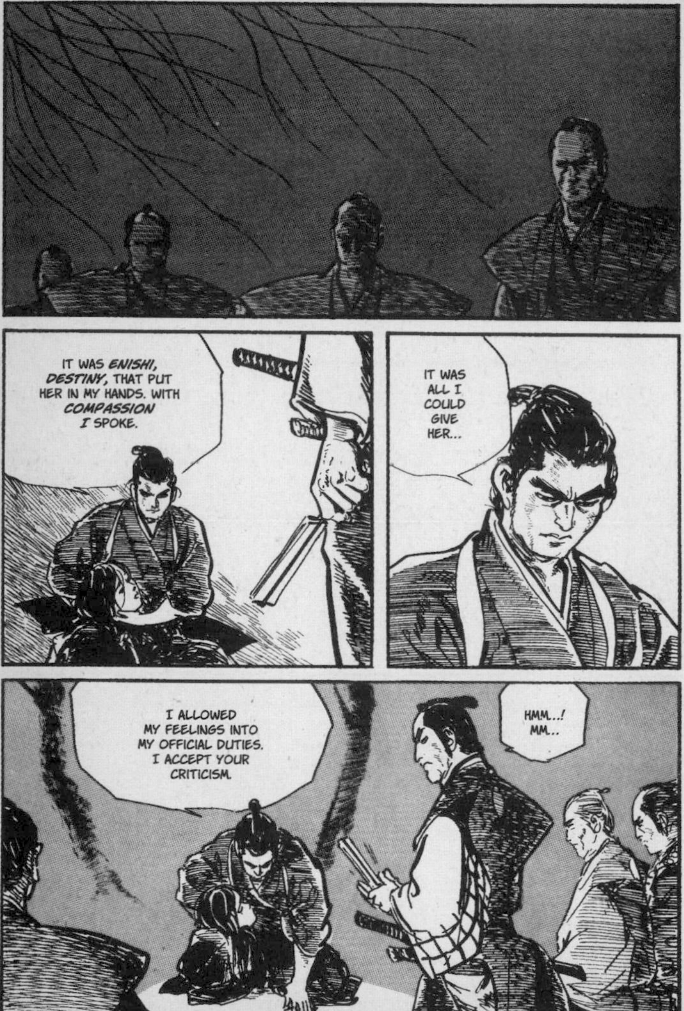
IT WAS *ENISHI, DESTINY,* THAT PUT HER IN MY HANDS. WITH *COMPASSION* *I* SPOKE.
IT WAS ALL I COULD GIVE HER...
I ALLOWED MY FEELINGS INTO MY OFFICIAL DUTIES. I ACCEPT YOUR CRITICISM.
HMM...! MM...

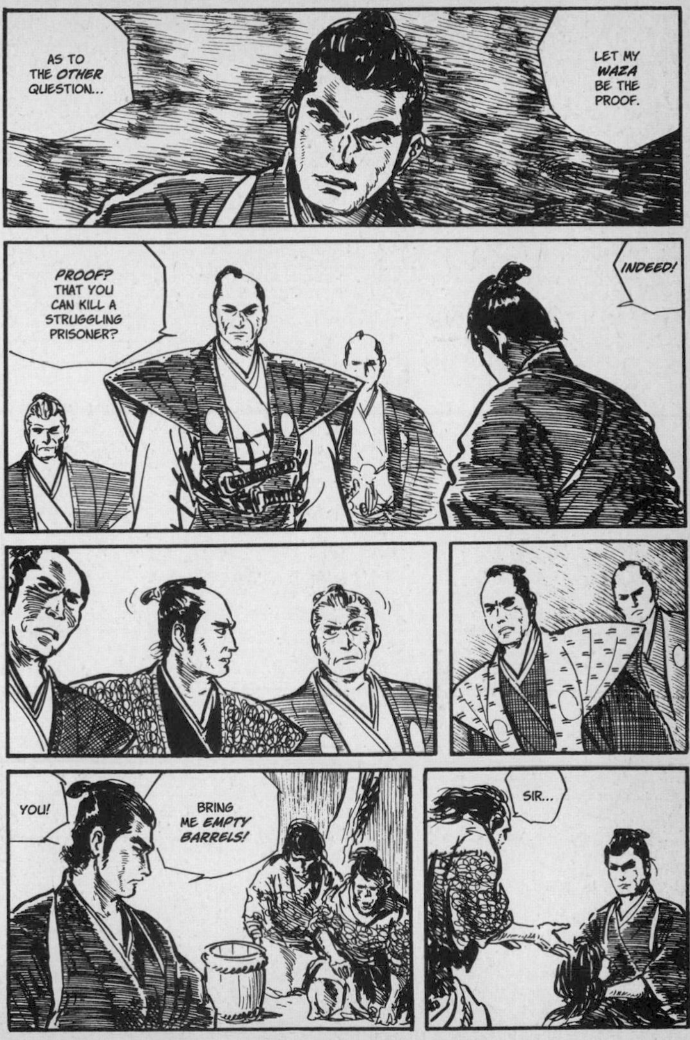
AS TO THE *OTHER* QUESTION...
LET MY *WAZA* BE THE PROOF.
PROOF? THAT YOU CAN KILL A STRUGGLING PRISONER?
INDEED!
YOU!
BRING ME *EMPTY BARRELS!*
SIR...

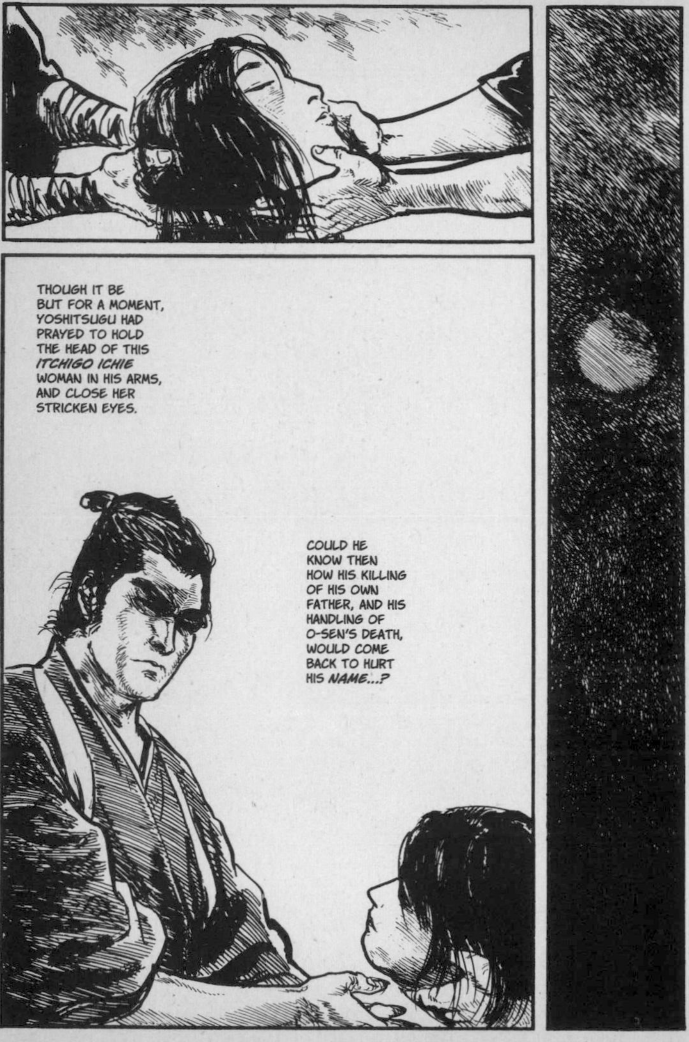
THOUGH IT BE BUT FOR A MOMENT, YOSHITSUGU HAD PRAYED TO HOLD THE HEAD OF THIS *ITCHIGO ICHIE* WOMAN IN HIS ARMS, AND CLOSE HER STRICKEN EYES.
COULD HE KNOW THEN HOW HIS KILLING OF HIS OWN FATHER, AND HIS HANDLING OF O-SEN'S DEATH, WOULD COME BACK TO HURT HIS *NAME...?*

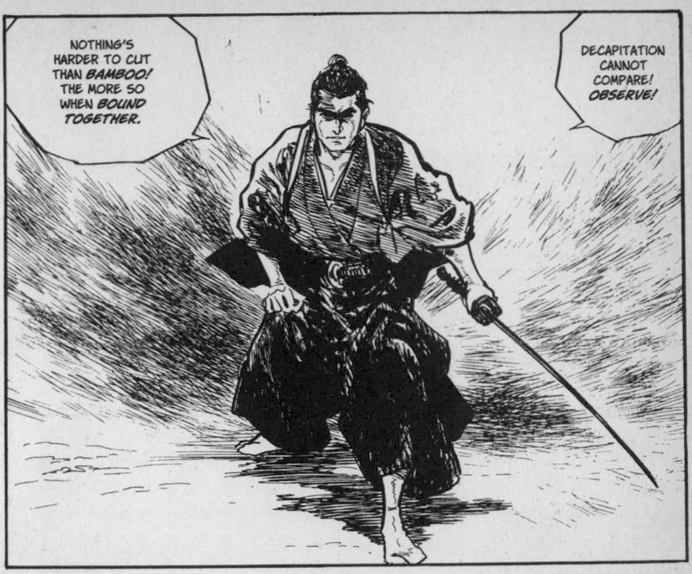
NOTHING'S HARDER TO CUT THAN BAMBOO! THE MORE SO WHEN BOUND TOGETHER.
DECAPITATION CANNOT COMPARE! OBSERVE!
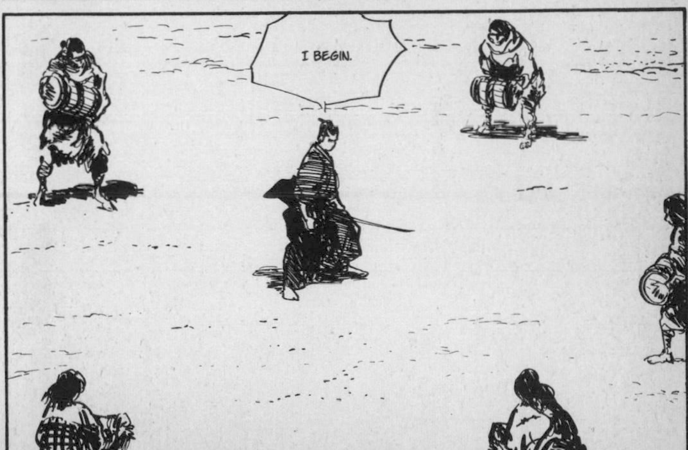
I BEGIN.

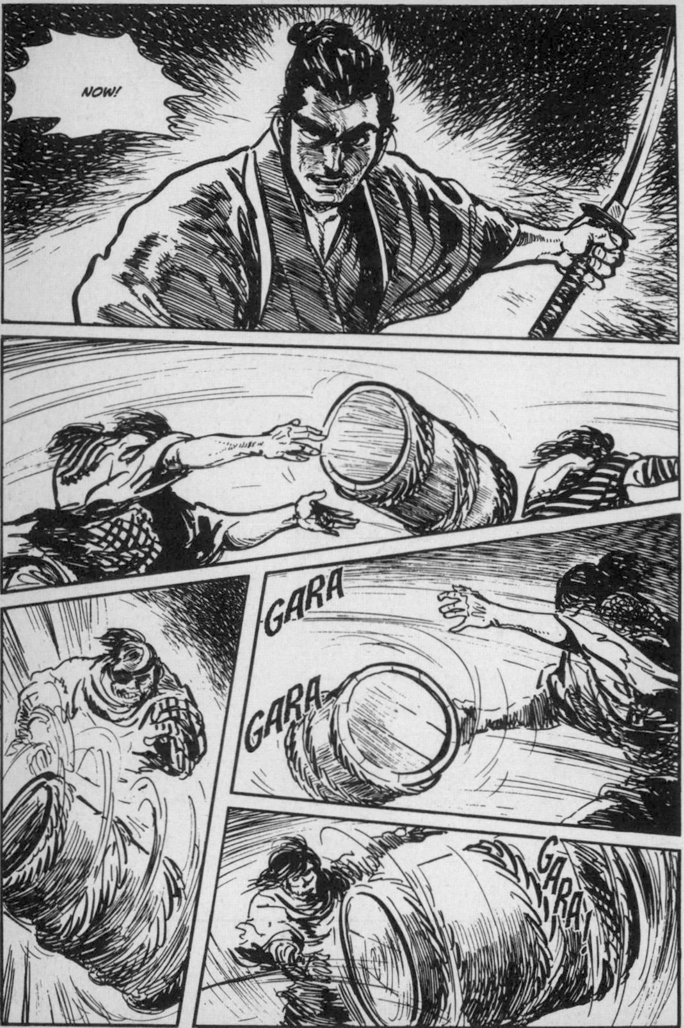
NOW!
GARA
GARA
GARA!

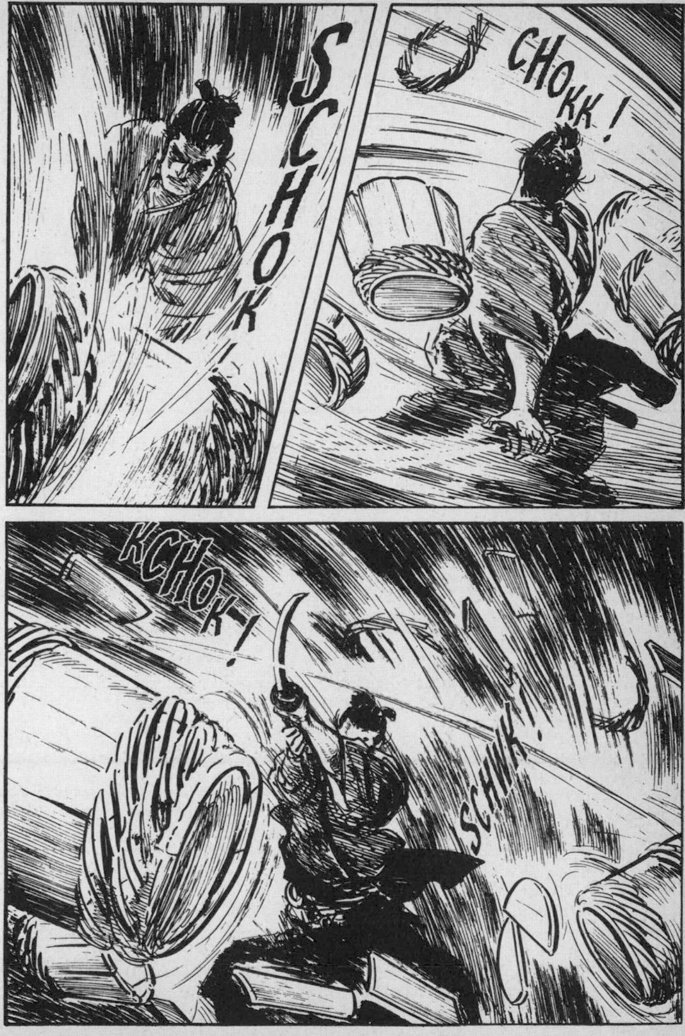
SCHOK!
CHOKK!
KCHOK!
SCHIK!

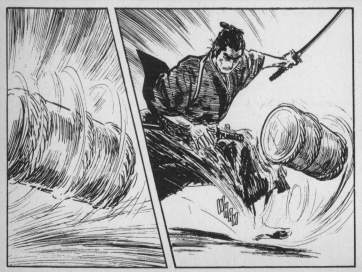

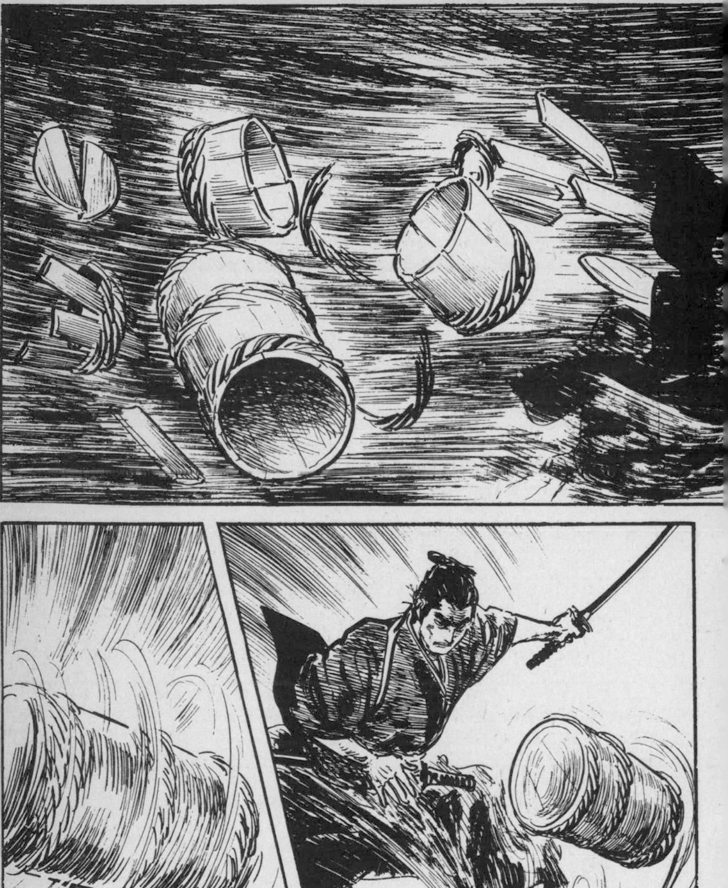
WHAM

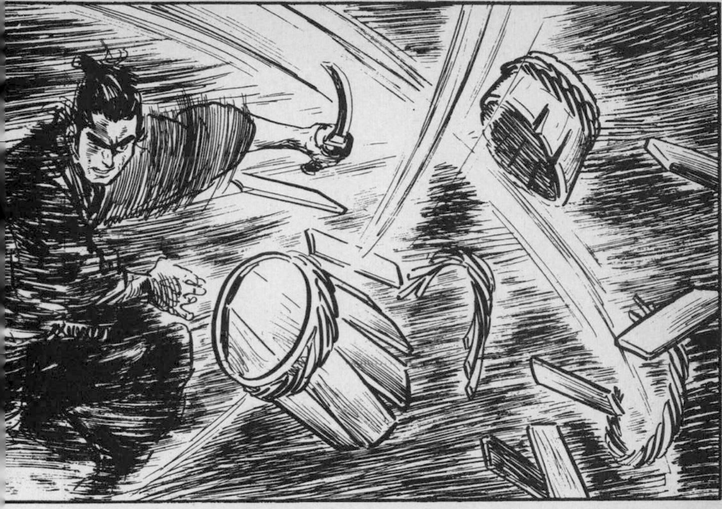

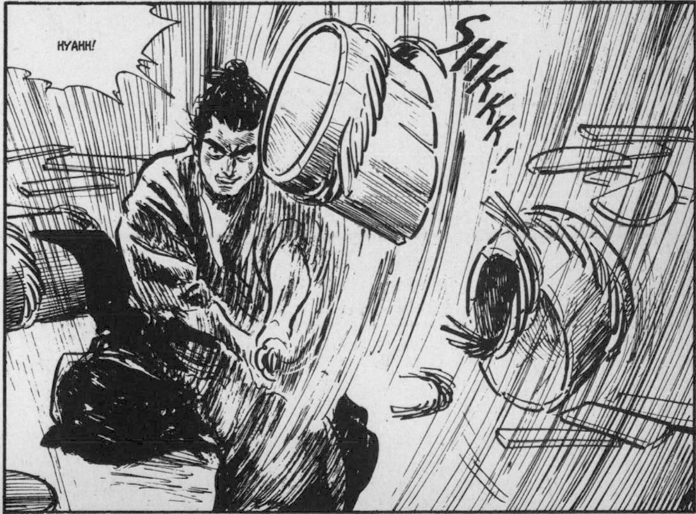
HYAHH!
SHKKK!

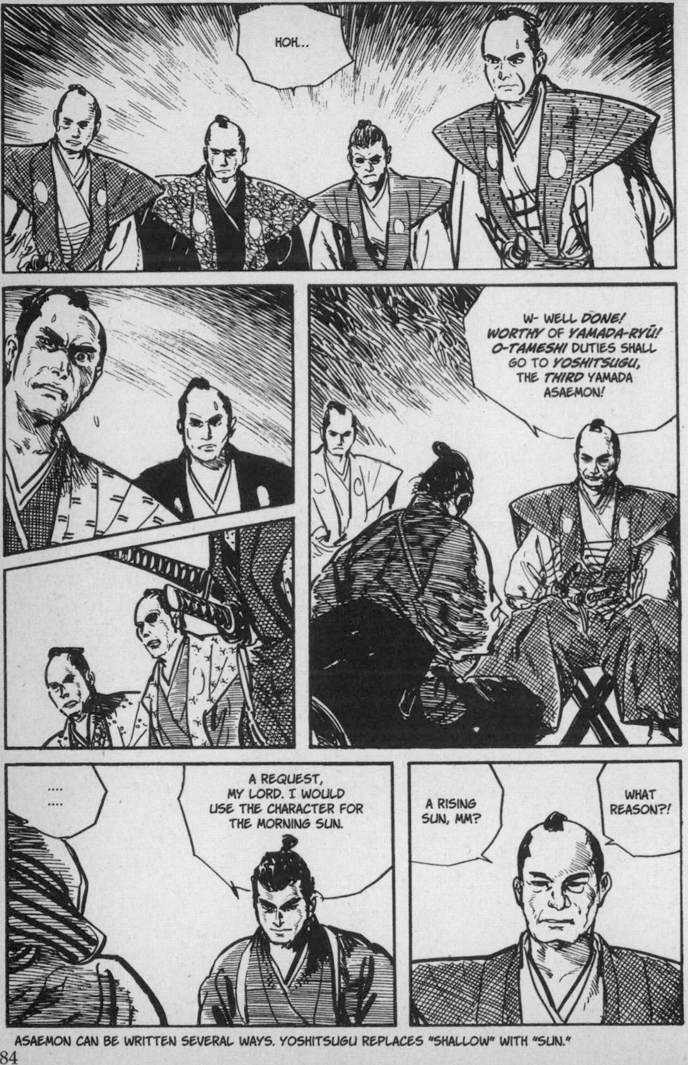
HOH...
W- WELL DONE! WORTHY OF YAMADA-RYŪ! O-TAMESHI DUTIES SHALL GO TO YOSHITSUGU, THE THIRD YAMADA ASAEMON!
....
....
A REQUEST, MY LORD. I WOULD USE THE CHARACTER FOR THE MORNING SUN.
A RISING SUN, MM?
WHAT REASON?!

ASAEMON CAN BE WRITTEN SEVERAL WAYS. YOSHITSUGU REPLACES "SHALLOW" WITH "SUN."

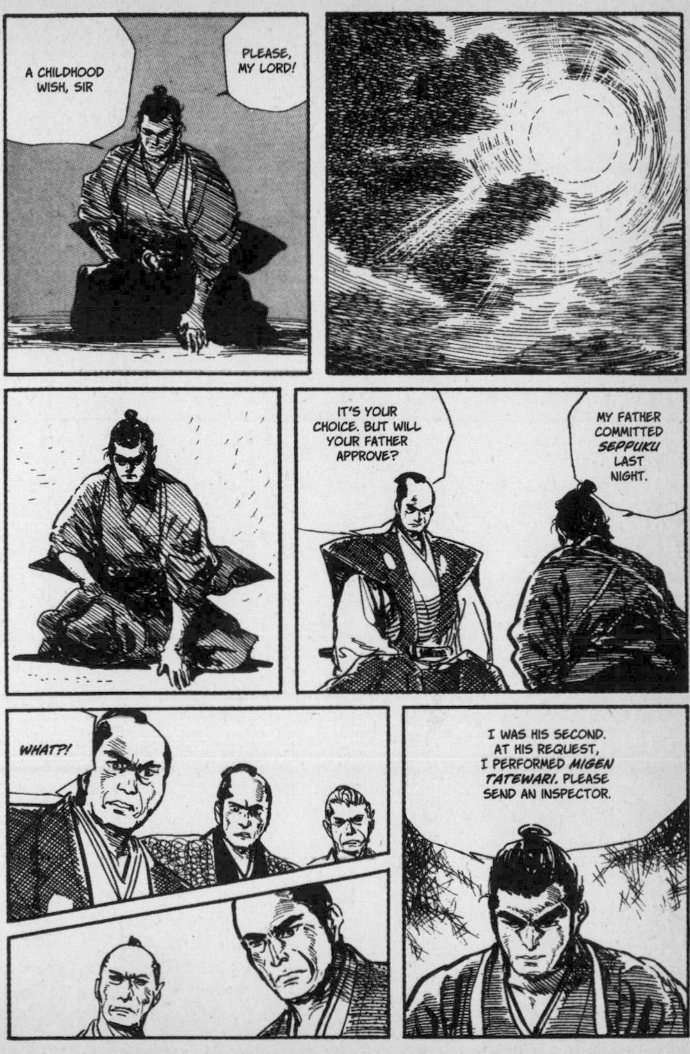
A CHILDHOOD WISH, SIR
PLEASE, MY LORD!
IT'S YOUR CHOICE. BUT WILL YOUR FATHER APPROVE?
MY FATHER COMMITTED *SEPPUKU* LAST NIGHT.
WHAT?!
I WAS HIS SECOND. AT HIS REQUEST, I PERFORMED *MIGEN TATEWARI.* PLEASE SEND AN INSPECTOR.

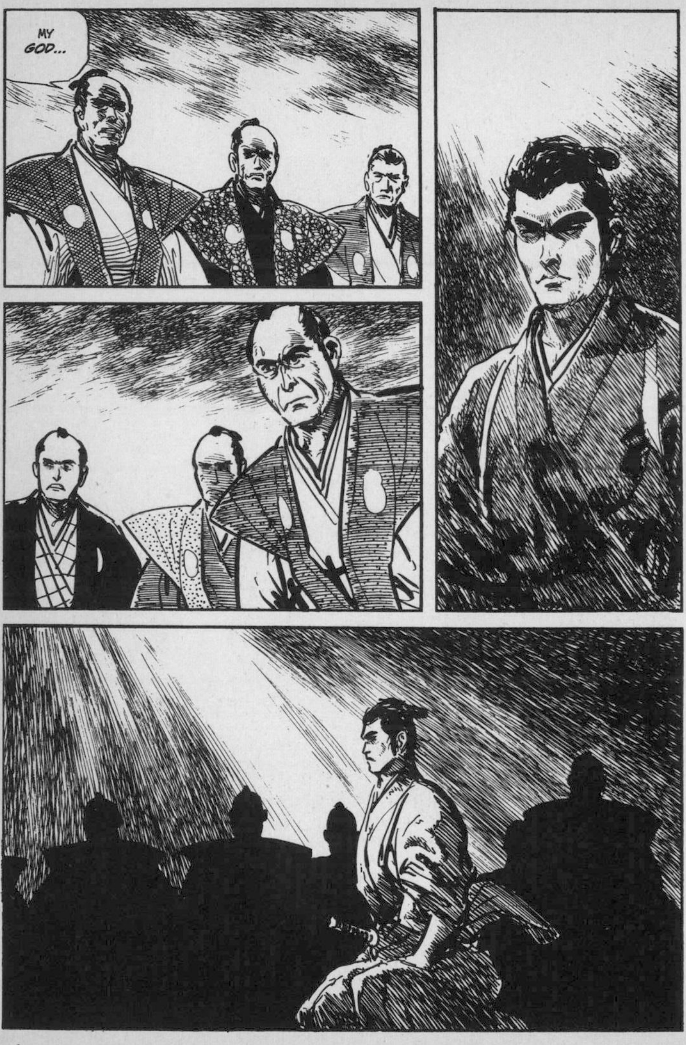
MY GOD...

the third

Monkey
Fire
Song

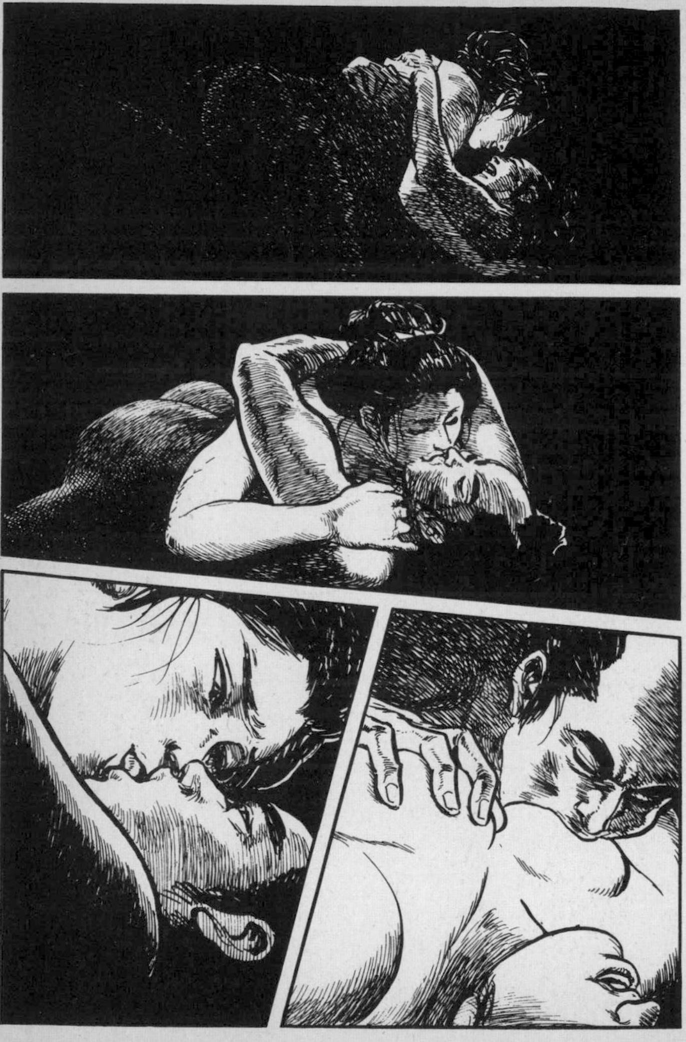

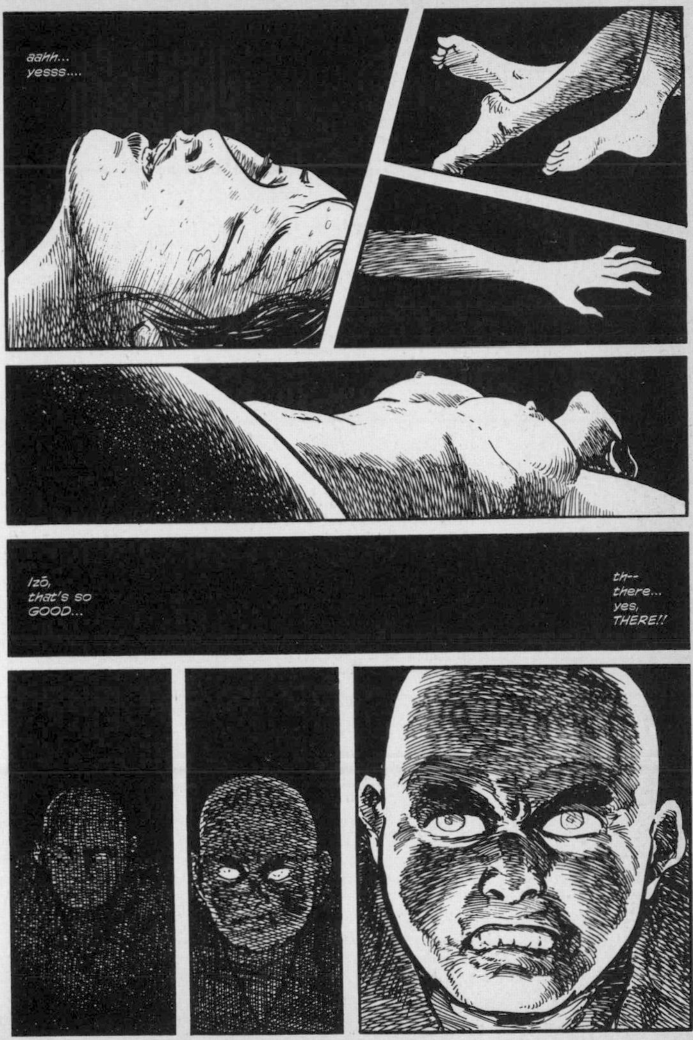
aahh... yesss....
Izō, that's so GOOD...
th-- there... yes, THERE!!

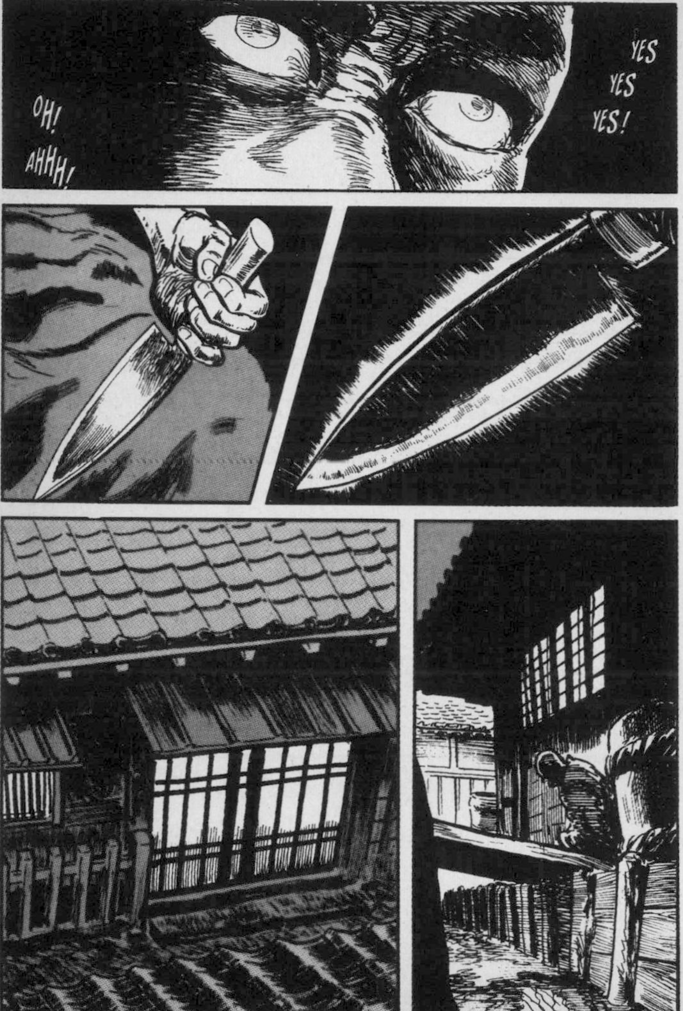
OH! AHHH!
YES YES YES!

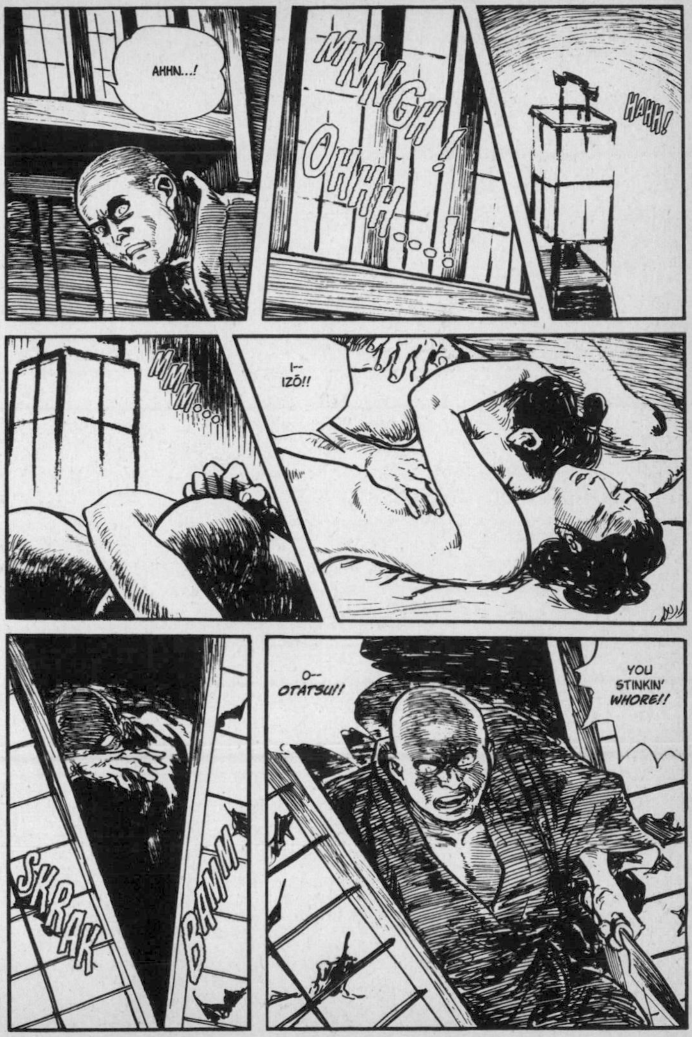
AHHN...!
MNNGH!
OHHH...!
HAHH!
MMM...
I-- IZŌ!!
SKRAK
BAMM
O-- OTATSU!!
YOU STINKIN' WHORE!!

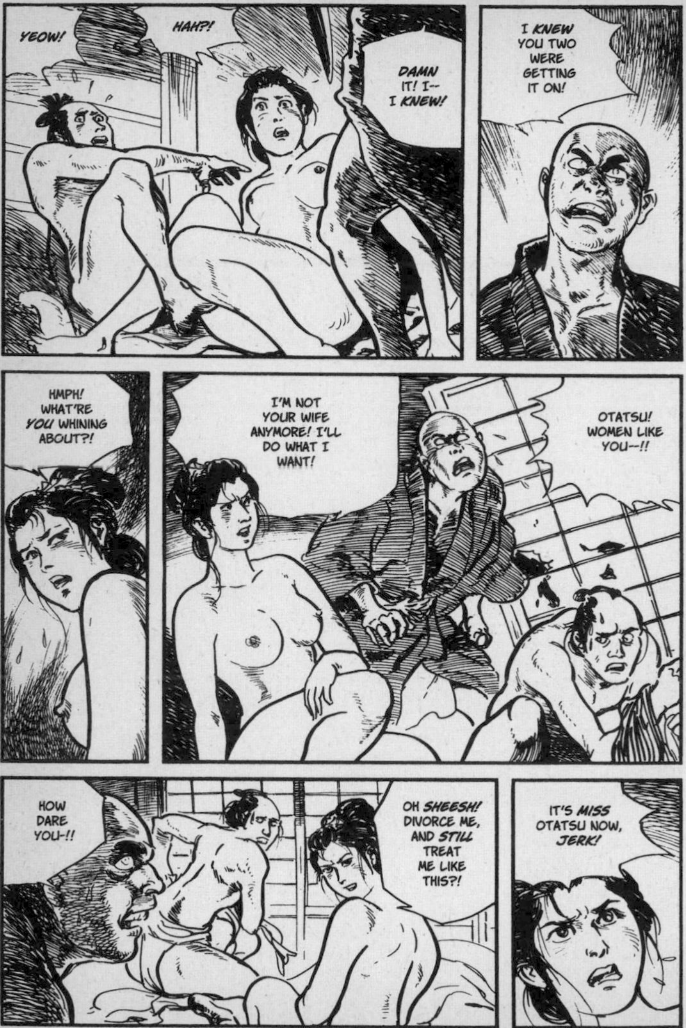
YEOW!
HAH?!
DAMN IT! I-- I KNEW!
I KNEW YOU TWO WERE GETTING IT ON!
HMPH! WHAT'RE YOU WHINING ABOUT?!
I'M NOT YOUR WIFE ANYMORE! I'LL DO WHAT I WANT!
OTATSU! WOMEN LIKE YOU--!!
HOW DARE YOU-!!
OH SHEESH! DIVORCE ME, AND STILL TREAT ME LIKE THIS?!
IT'S MISS OTATSU NOW, JERK!

I DIVORCED YOU TO *CATCH* YOU!

RED-HANDED!

AND SURE ENOUGH!

YOU-- *YOU!*

HEEK!

ACT LIKE A *MAN*, IZŌ! HE'S *BLIND*.

OTATSUUU!!

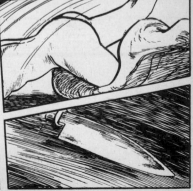

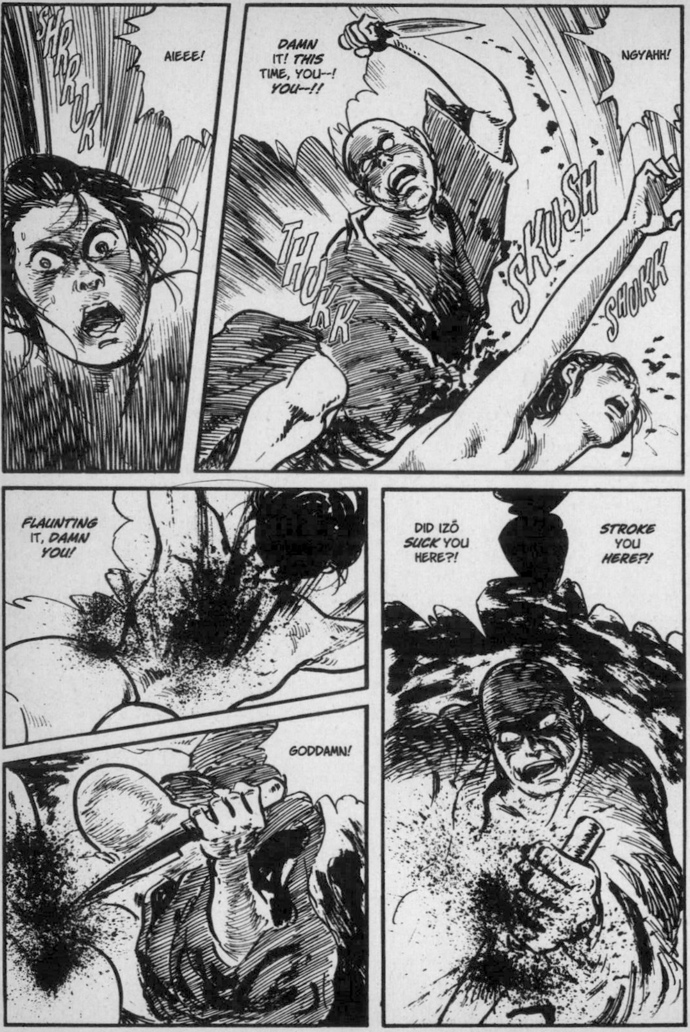
SHRRUK
AIEEE!
DAMN IT! THIS TIME, YOU--! YOU--!!
NGYAHH!
THUKK
SKUSH
SHUKK
FLAUNTING IT, DAMN YOU!
GODDAMN!
DID IZŌ SUCK YOU HERE?!
STROKE YOU HERE?!

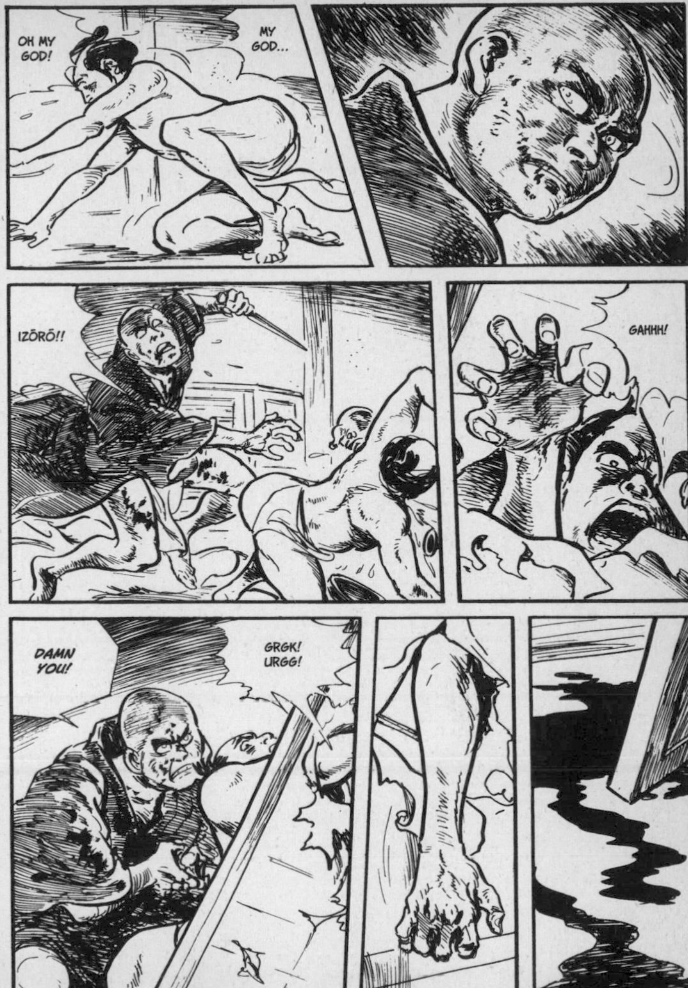
OH MY GOD!
MY GOD...
IZŌRŌ!!
GAHHH!
DAMN YOU!
GRGK! URGG!

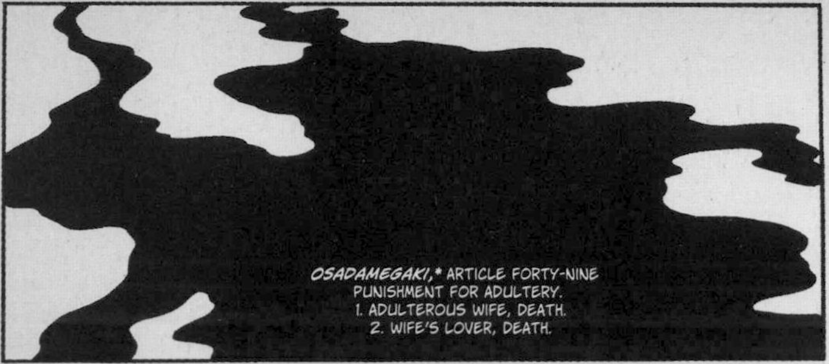
OSADAMEGAKI,* ARTICLE FORTY-NINE
PUNISHMENT FOR ADULTERY.
1. ADULTEROUS WIFE, DEATH.
2. WIFE'S LOVER, DEATH.

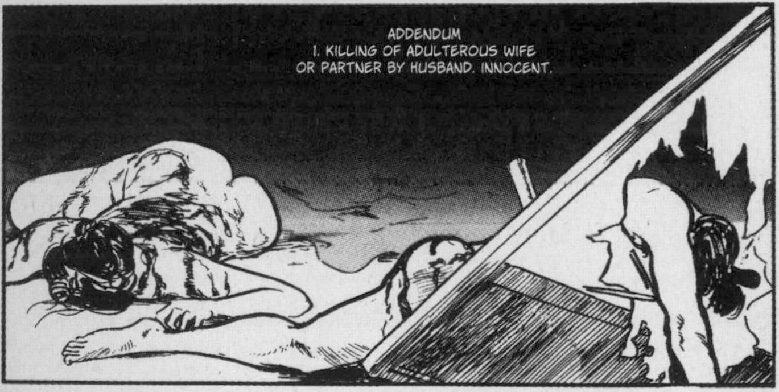
ADDENDUM
1. KILLING OF ADULTEROUS WIFE
OR PARTNER BY HUSBAND. INNOCENT.

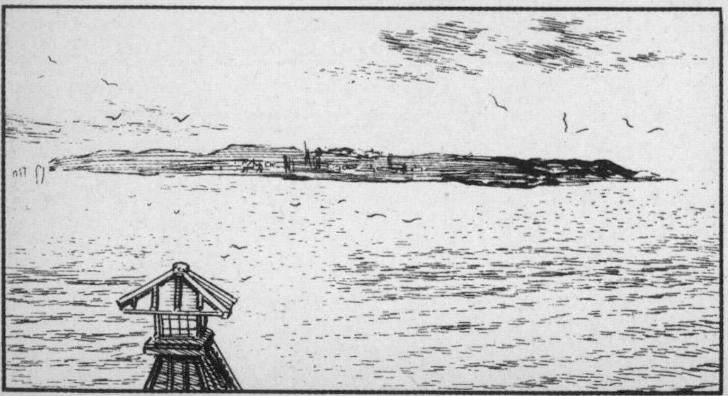

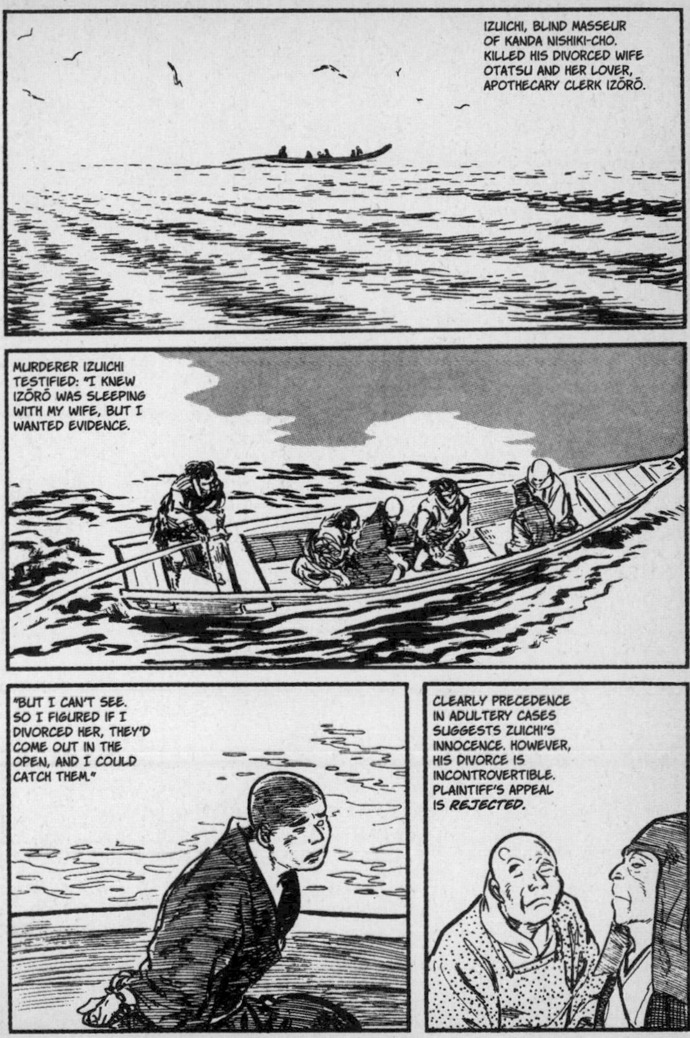
IZUICHI, BLIND MASSEUR OF KANDA NISHIKI-CHO. KILLED HIS DIVORCED WIFE OTATSU AND HER LOVER, APOTHECARY CLERK IZŌRŌ.
MURDERER IZUICHI TESTIFIED: "I KNEW IZŌRŌ WAS SLEEPING WITH MY WIFE, BUT I WANTED EVIDENCE.
"BUT I CAN'T SEE. SO I FIGURED IF I DIVORCED HER, THEY'D COME OUT IN THE OPEN, AND I COULD CATCH THEM."
CLEARLY PRECEDENCE IN ADULTERY CASES SUGGESTS ZUICHI'S INNOCENCE. HOWEVER, HIS DIVORCE IS INCONTROVERTIBLE. PLAINTIFF'S APPEAL IS *REJECTED.*

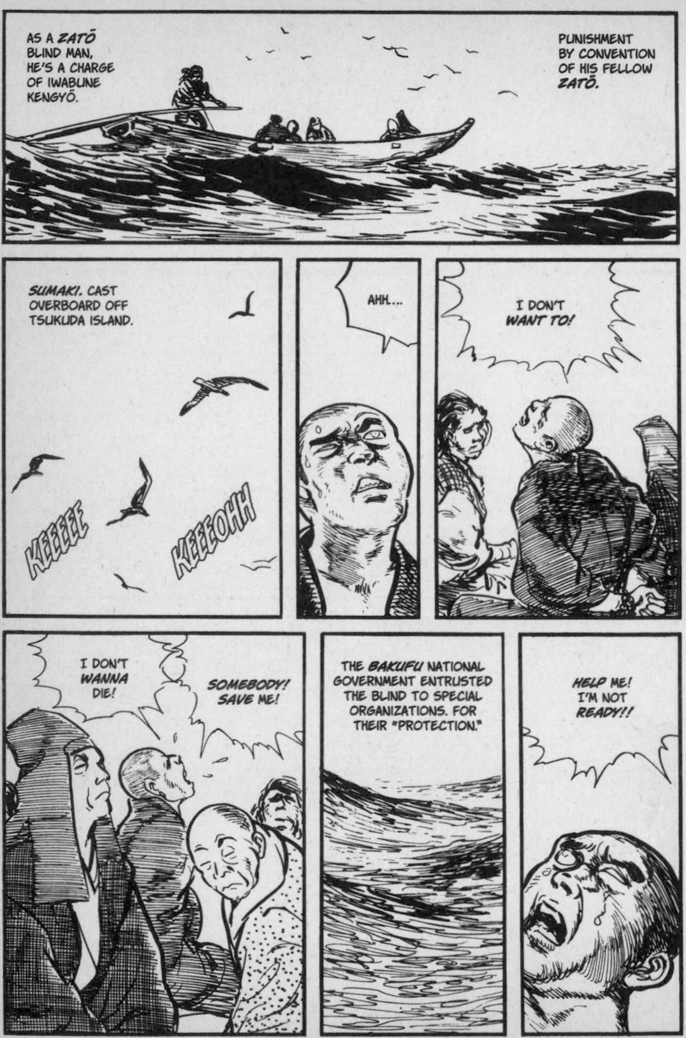
AS A ZATŌ BLIND MAN, HE'S A CHARGE OF IWABUNE KENGYŌ.
PUNISHMENT BY CONVENTION OF HIS FELLOW ZATŌ.
SUMAKI. CAST OVERBOARD OFF TSUKUDA ISLAND.
KEEEEE
KEEEOHH
AHH...
I DON'T WANT TO!
I DON'T WANNA DIE!
SOMEBODY! SAVE ME!
THE BAKUFU NATIONAL GOVERNMENT ENTRUSTED THE BLIND TO SPECIAL ORGANIZATIONS. FOR THEIR "PROTECTION."
HELP ME! I'M NOT READY!!

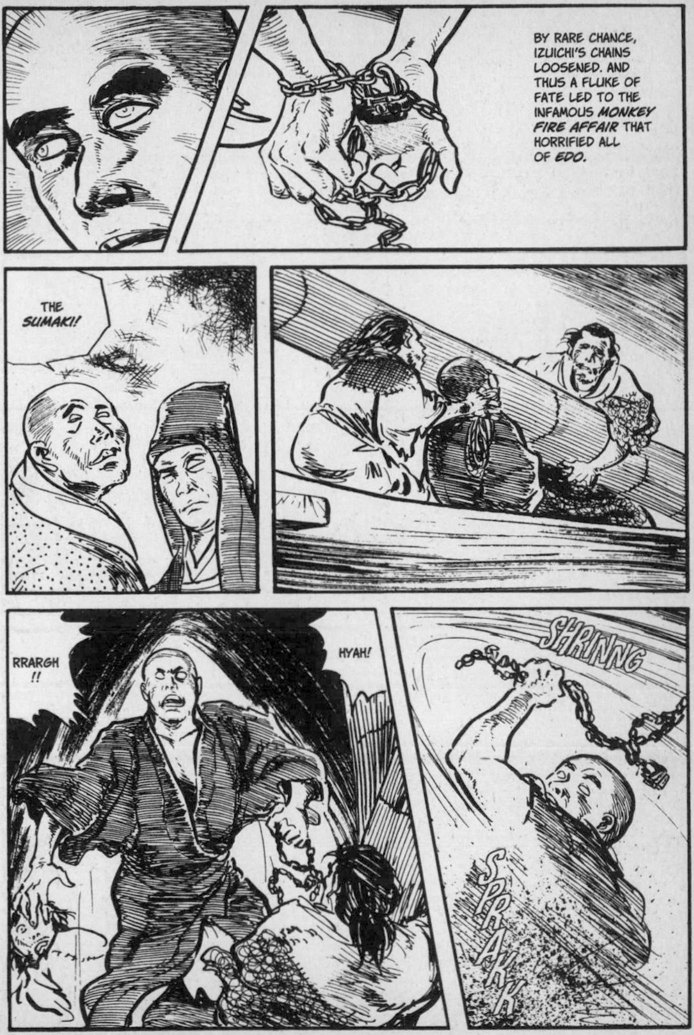
BY RARE CHANCE, IZUICHI'S CHAINS LOOSENED. AND THUS A FLUKE OF FATE LED TO THE INFAMOUS *MONKEY FIRE AFFAIR* THAT HORRIFIED ALL OF *EDO.*
THE *SUMAKI!*
RRARGH !!
HYAH!
SHRINNG
SPRAKK

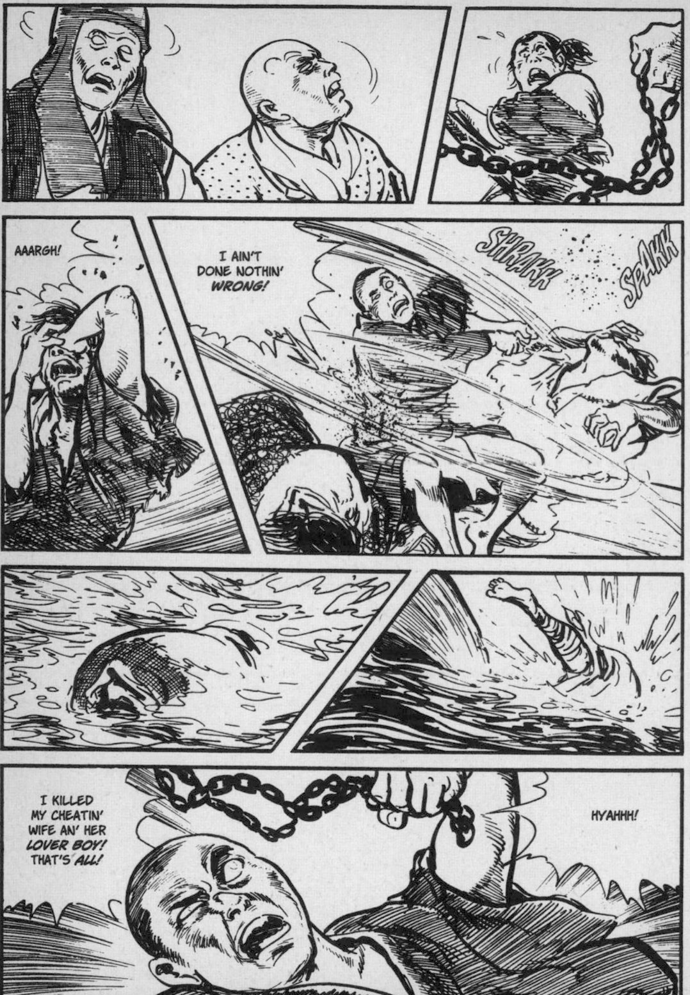
AAARGH!
I AIN'T DONE NOTHIN' WRONG!
SHRAKK
SPAKK
I KILLED MY CHEATIN' WIFE AN' HER LOVER BOY! THAT'S ALL!
HYAHHH!

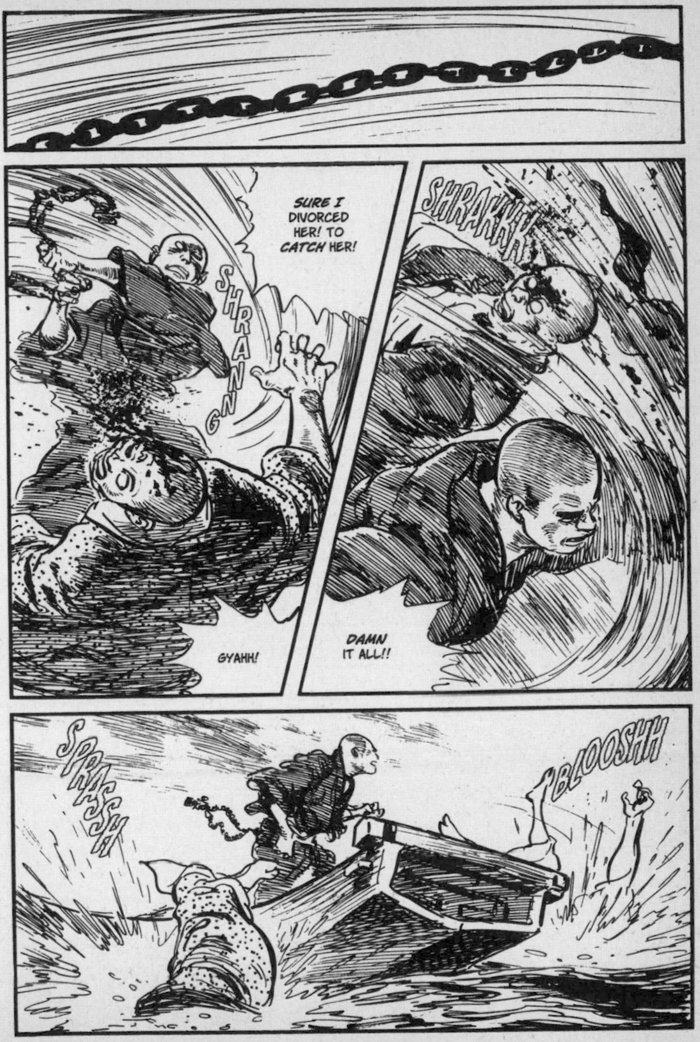
SURE I DIVORCED HER! TO CATCH HER!
SHRANNG
GYAHH!
SHRAKKK
DAMN IT ALL!!
SPRASSH
BLOOSHH

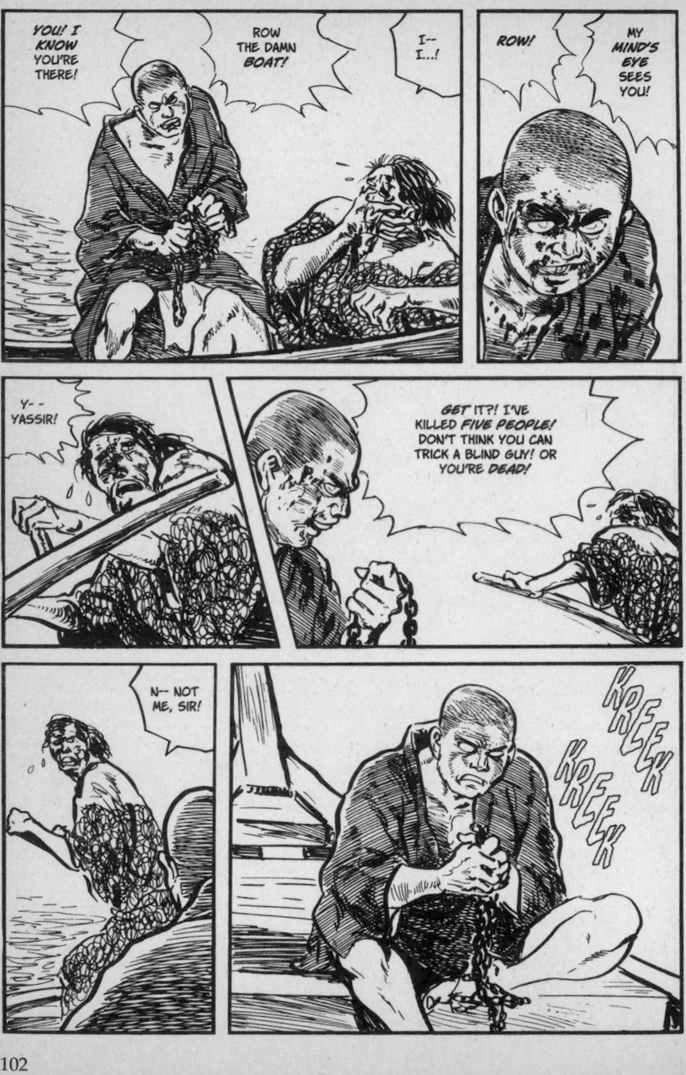

YOU! I KNOW YOU'RE THERE!
ROW THE DAMN BOAT!
I-- I...!
ROW!
MY MIND'S EYE SEES YOU!
Y-- YASSIR!
GET IT?! I'VE KILLED FIVE PEOPLE! DON'T THINK YOU CAN TRICK A BLIND GUY! OR YOU'RE DEAD!
N-- NOT ME, SIR!
KREEK
KREEK

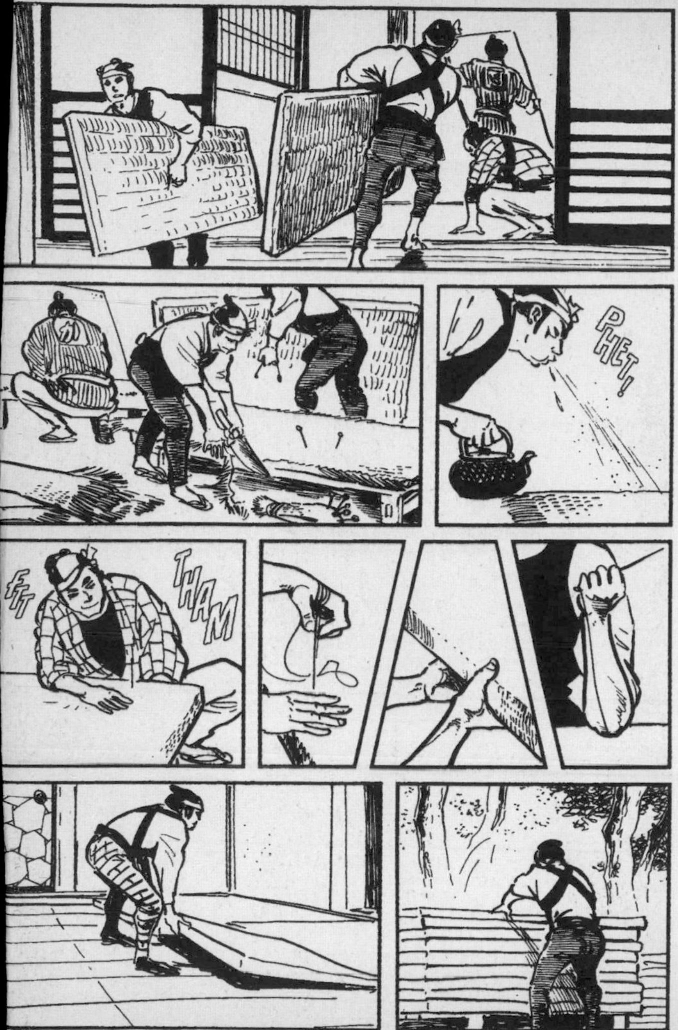
PHET!
FTT
THAM

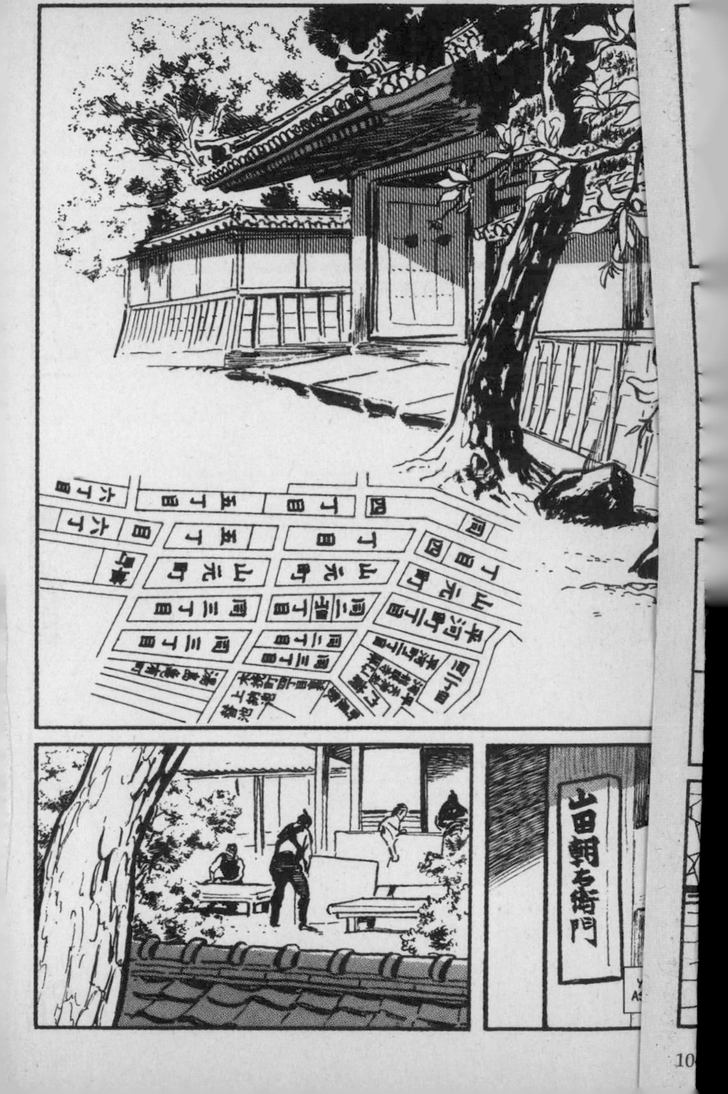
山田朝右衛門

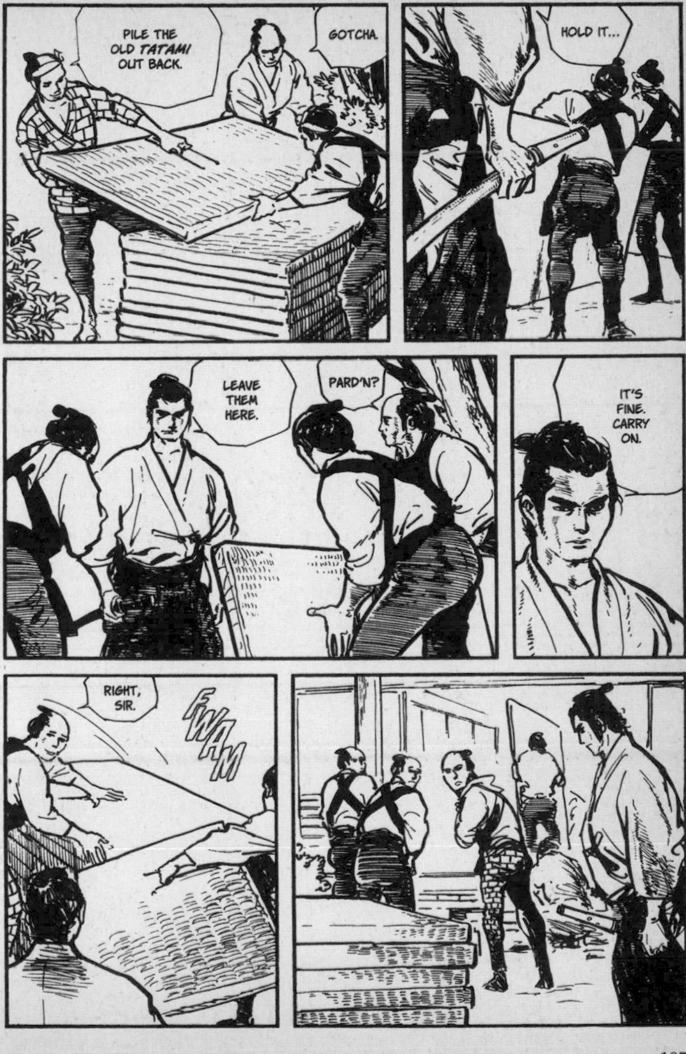
PILE THE OLD *TATAMI* OUT BACK.
GOTCHA.
HOLD IT...
LEAVE THEM HERE.
PARD'N?
IT'S FINE. CARRY ON.
RIGHT, SIR.
FWAM

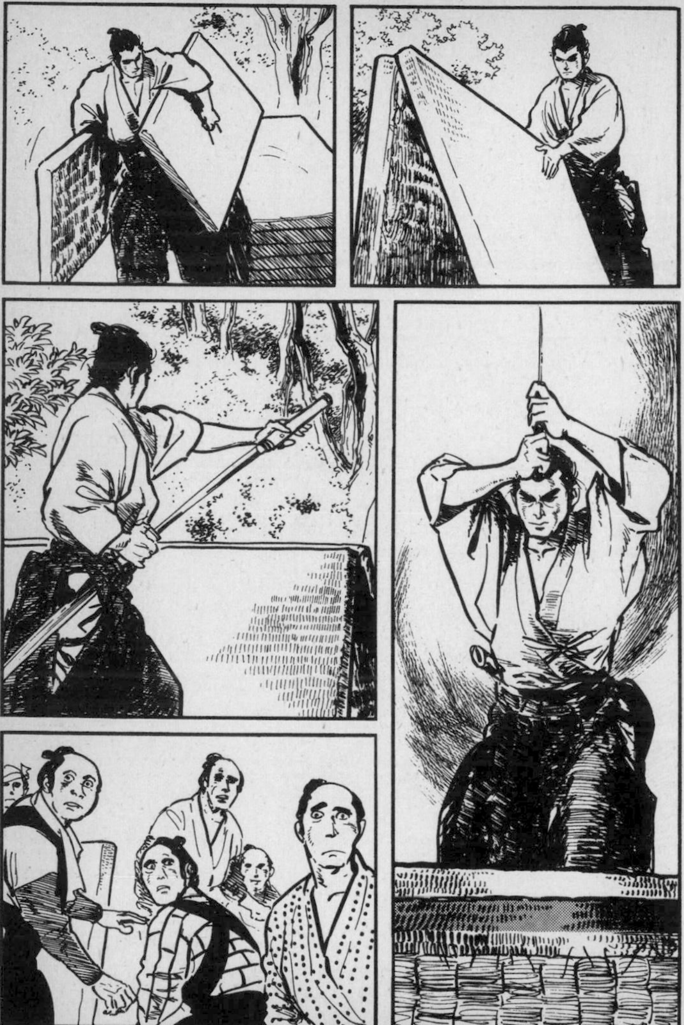

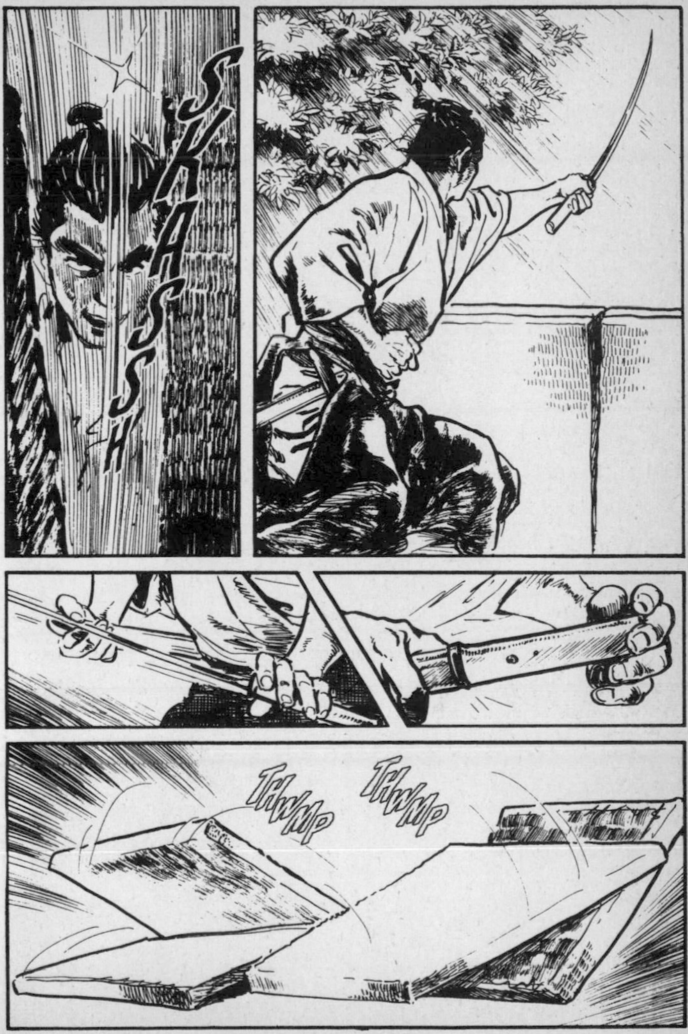
SKASSSH
THWMP
THWMP

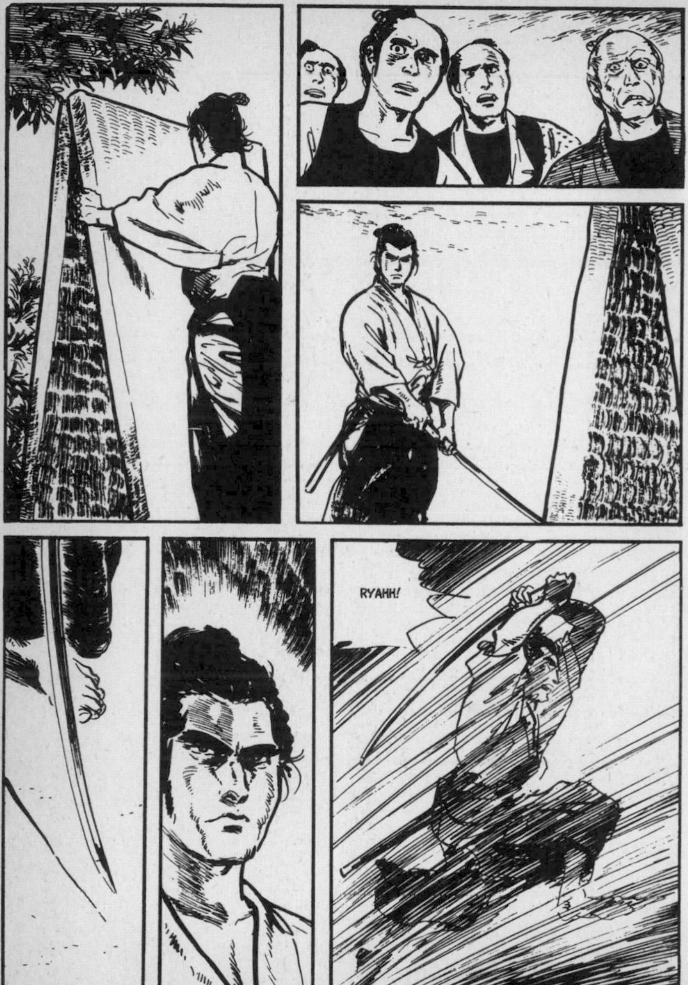
RYAHH!

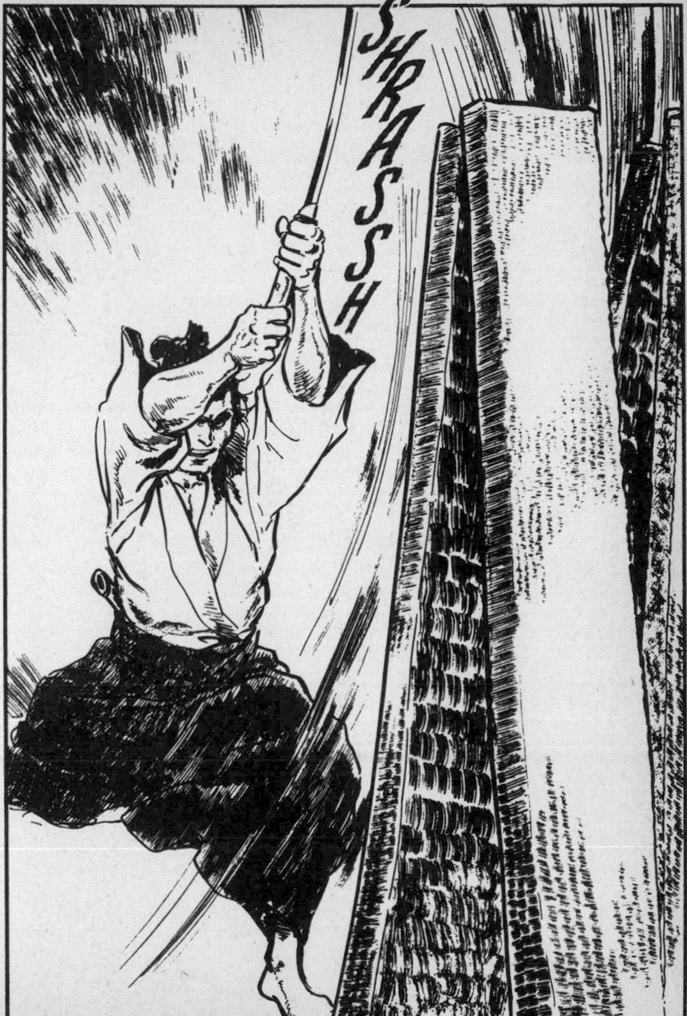
SHRASSSH

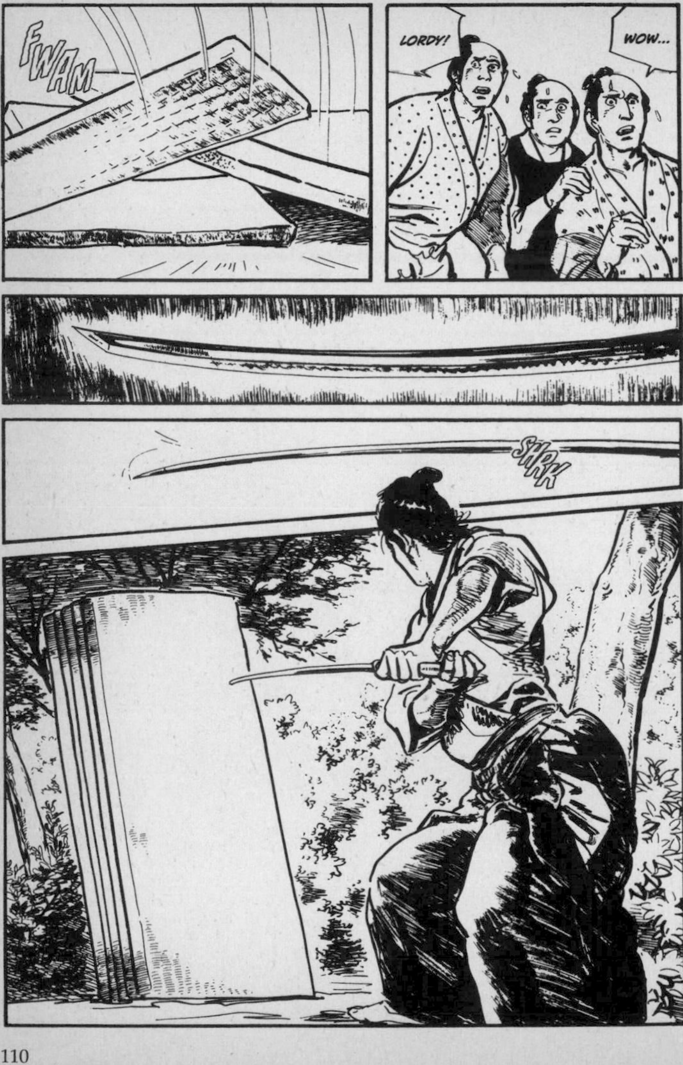
FWAM
LORDY!
WOW...
SHRK

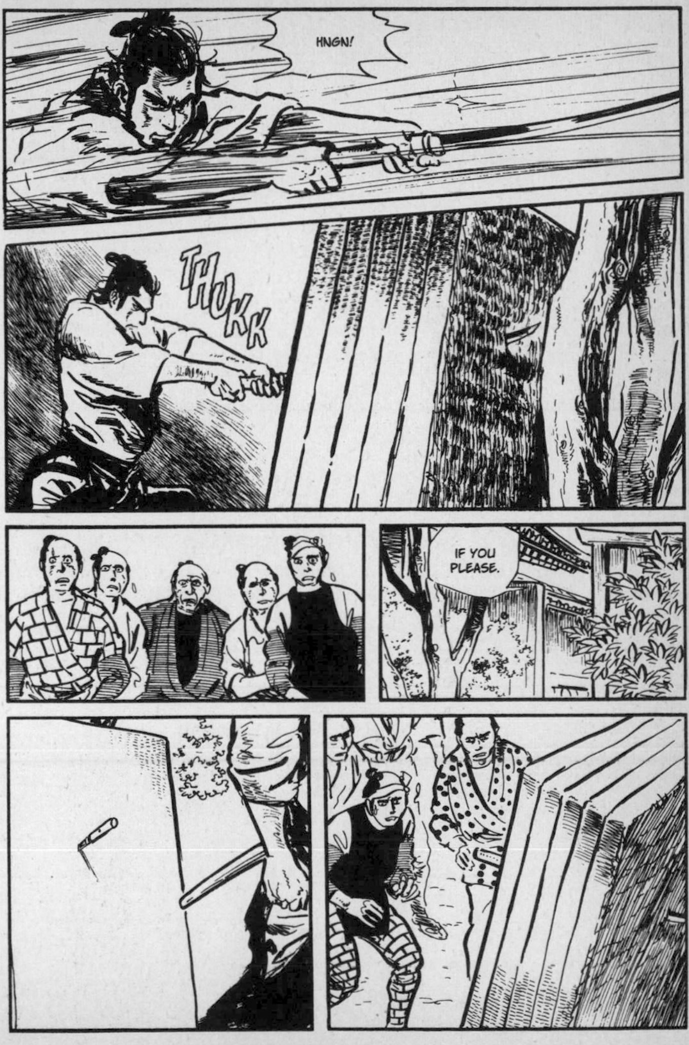
HNGN!
THUKK
IF YOU PLEASE.

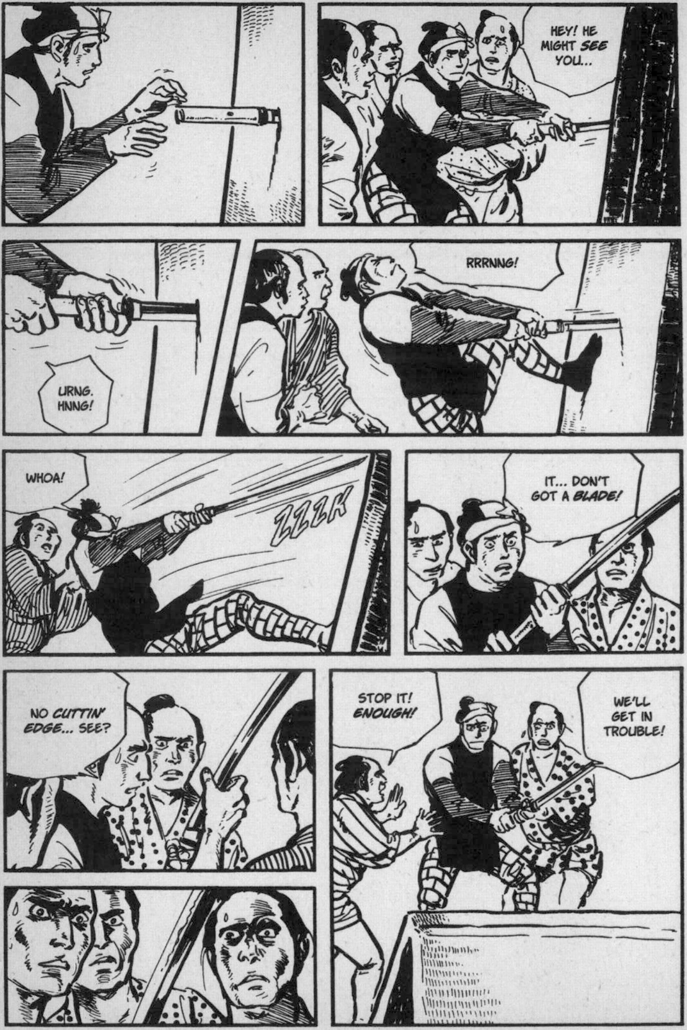
HEY! HE MIGHT SEE YOU...
URNG. HNNG!
RRRNNG!
WHOA!
ZZZK
IT... DON'T GOT A BLADE!
NO CUTTIN' EDGE... SEE?
STOP IT! ENOUGH!
WE'LL GET IN TROUBLE!

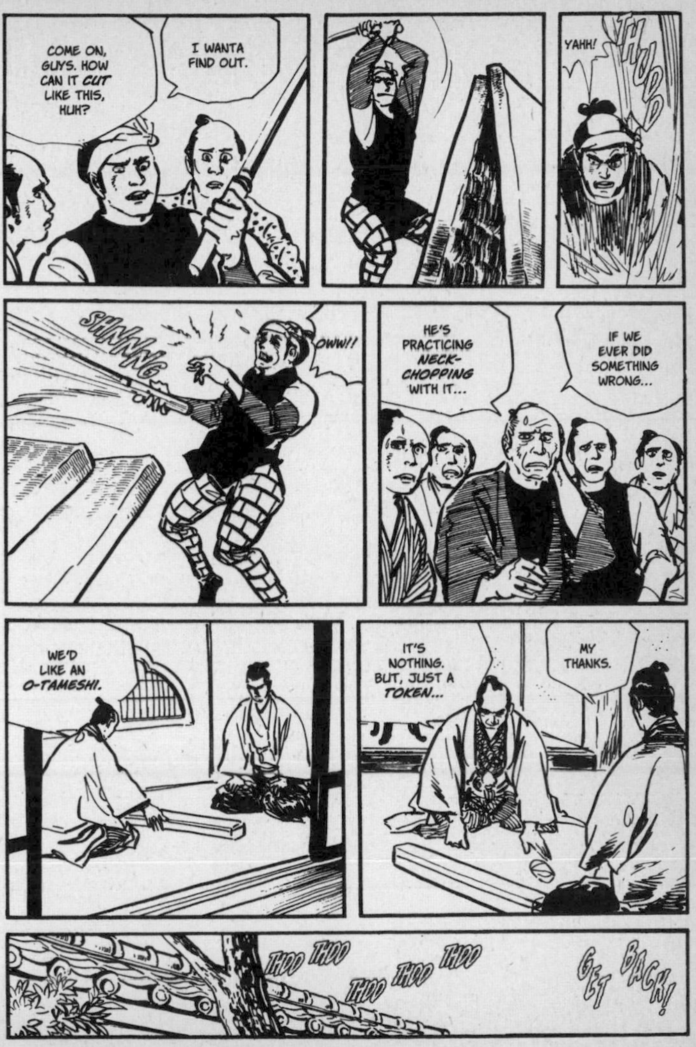
COME ON, GUYS. HOW CAN IT CUT LIKE THIS, HUH?
I WANTA FIND OUT.
YAHH!
THUDD
SHINNNG
OWW!!
HE'S PRACTICING NECK-CHOPPING WITH IT...
IF WE EVER DID SOMETHING WRONG...
WE'D LIKE AN O-TAMESHI.
IT'S NOTHING. BUT, JUST A TOKEN...
MY THANKS.
THOO THOO
THOO THOO THOO
GET BACK!

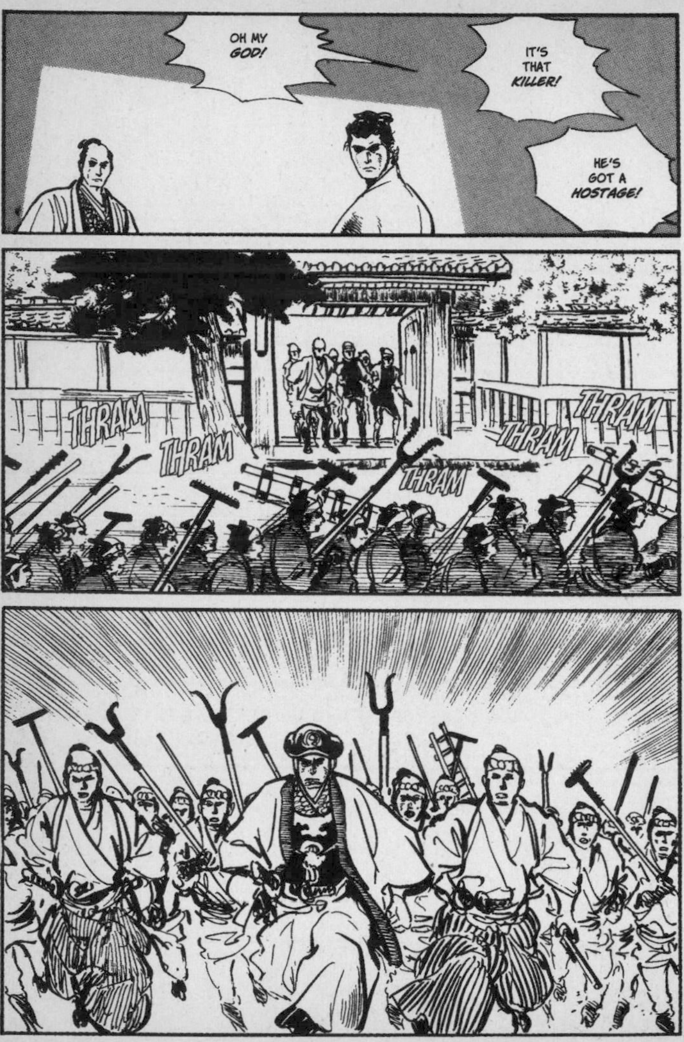
OH MY *GOD!*
IT'S THAT *KILLER!*
HE'S GOT A *HOSTAGE!*
THRAM
THRAM
THRAM
THRAM
THRAM

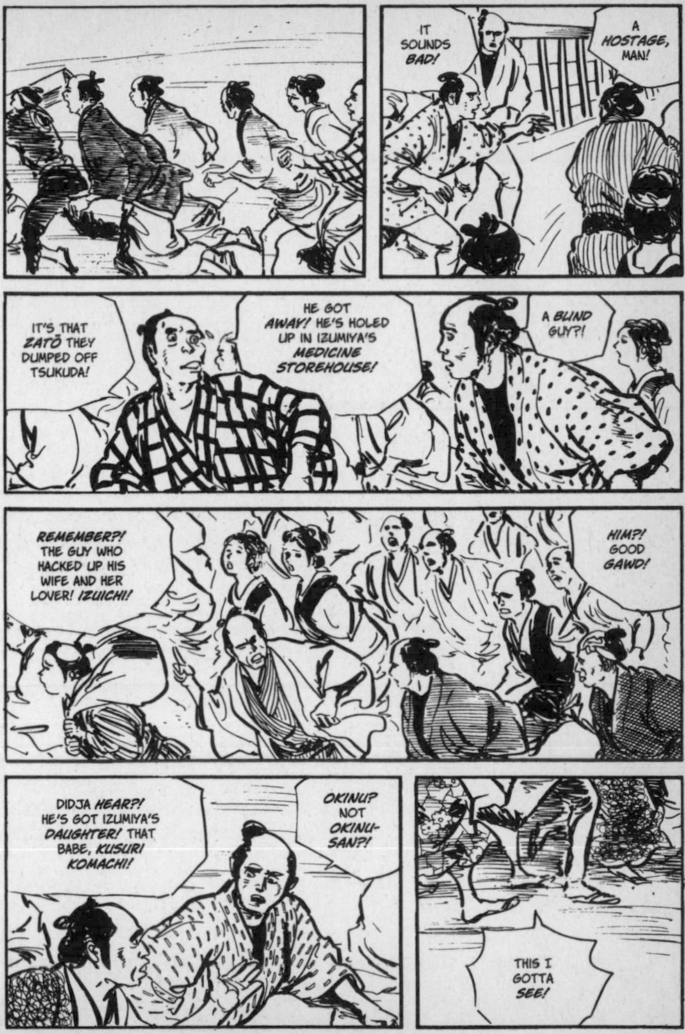
IT SOUNDS BAD!
A HOSTAGE, MAN!
IT'S THAT ZATŌ THEY DUMPED OFF TSUKUDA!
HE GOT AWAY! HE'S HOLED UP IN IZUMIYA'S MEDICINE STOREHOUSE!
A BLIND GUY?!
REMEMBER?! THE GUY WHO HACKED UP HIS WIFE AND HER LOVER! IZUICHI!
HIM?! GOOD GAWD!
DIDJA HEAR?! HE'S GOT IZUMIYA'S DAUGHTER! THAT BABE, KUSURI KOMACHI!
OKINU? NOT OKINU-SAN?!
THIS I GOTTA SEE!

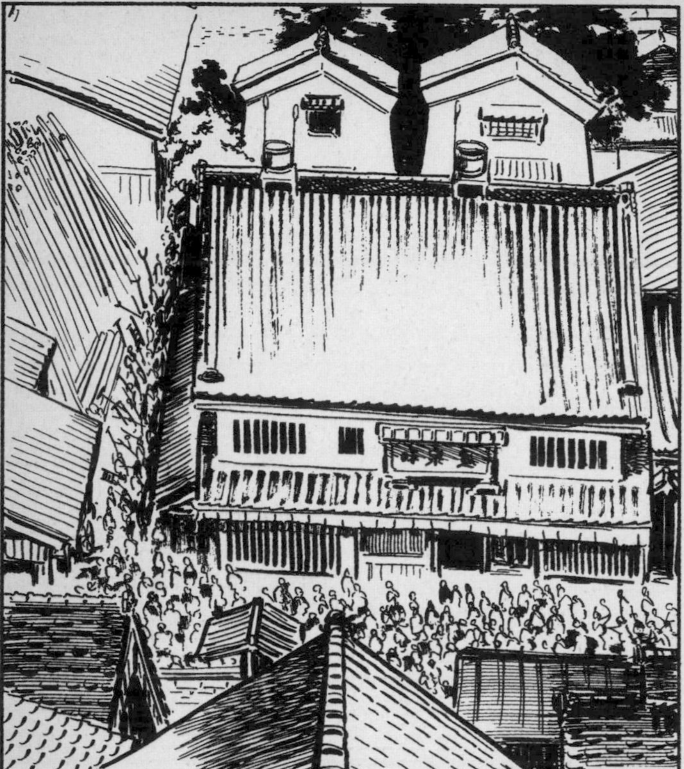
IZUMIYA
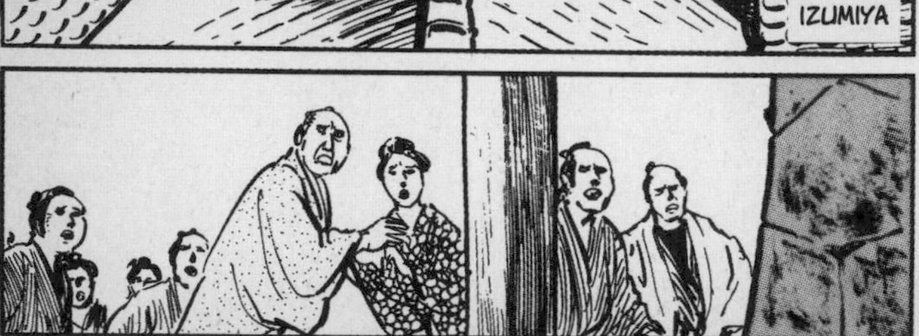

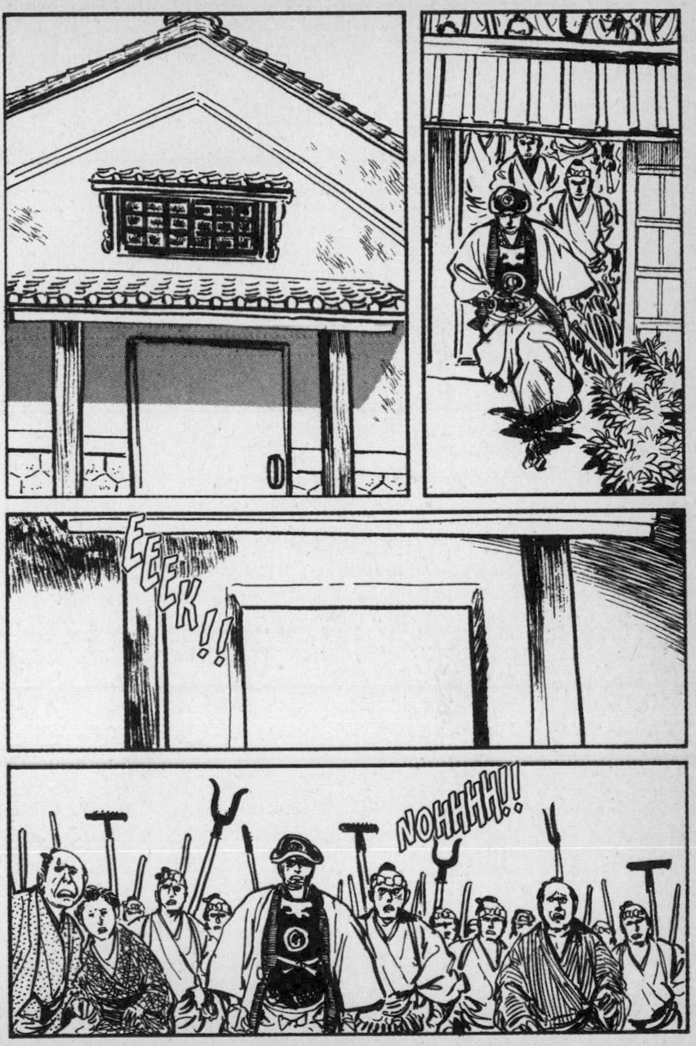
EEEK!!
NOHHHH!!

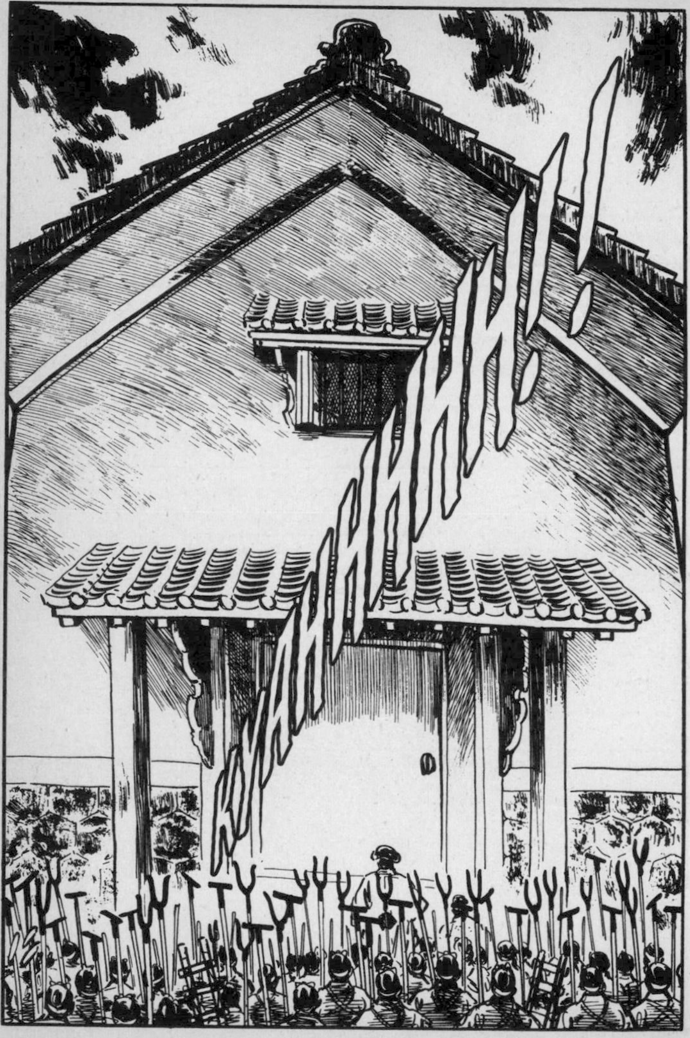
KYAAHHHHH!!

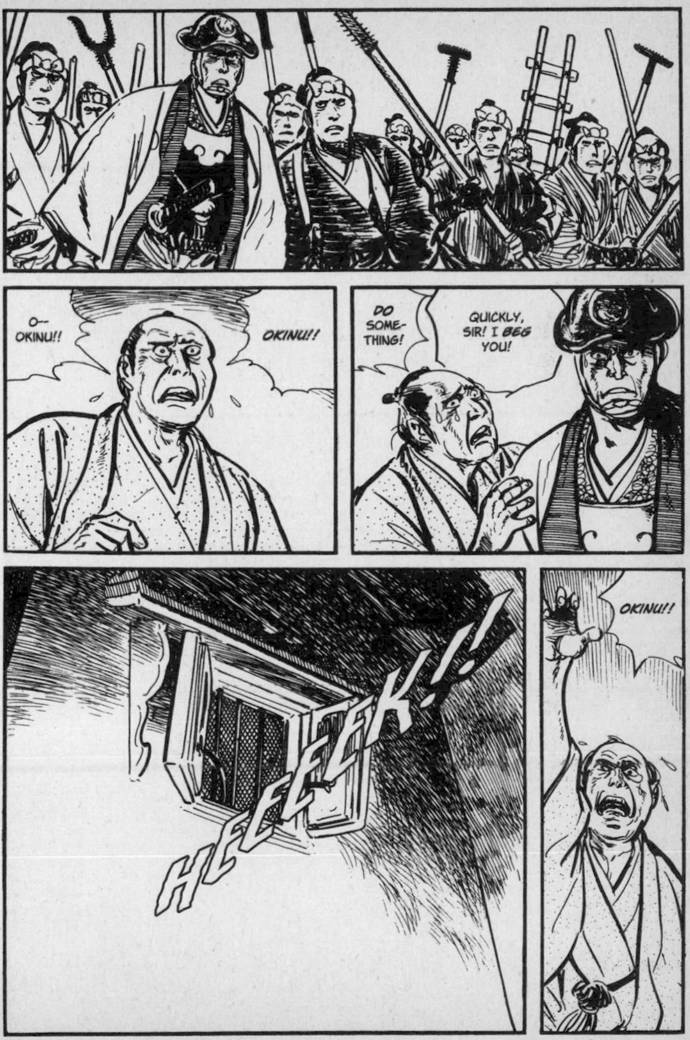
O-- OKINU!!
OKINU!!
DO SOME-THING!
QUICKLY, SIR! I BEG YOU!
HEEEEEK!!
OKINU!!

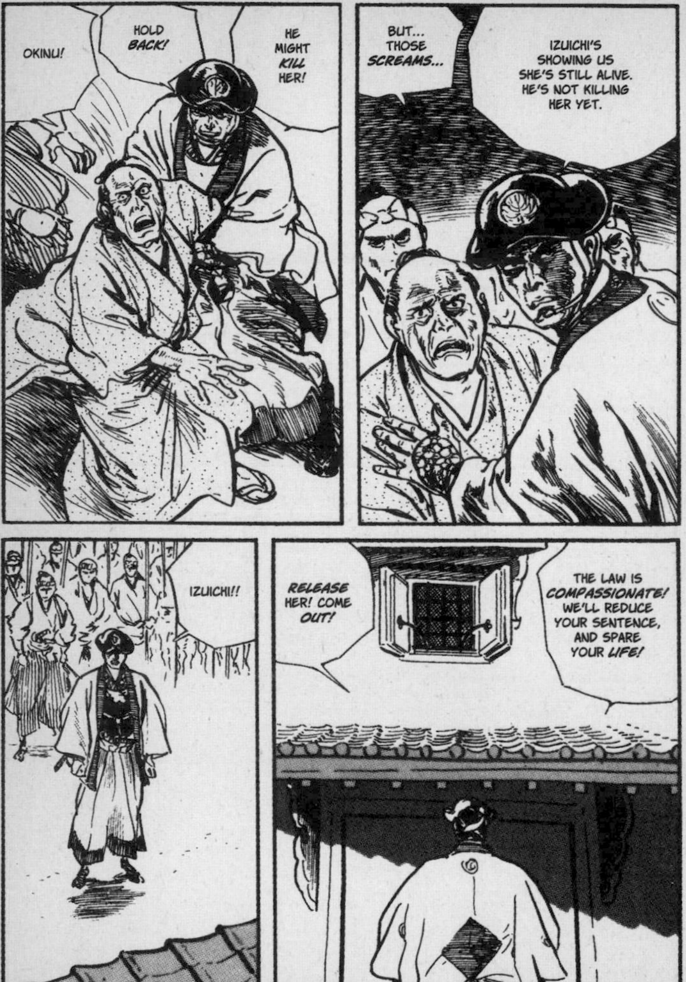
OKINU!
HOLD BACK!
HE MIGHT KILL HER!
BUT... THOSE SCREAMS...
IZUICHI'S SHOWING US SHE'S STILL ALIVE. HE'S NOT KILLING HER YET.
IZUICHI!!
RELEASE HER! COME OUT!
THE LAW IS COMPASSIONATE! WE'LL REDUCE YOUR SENTENCE, AND SPARE YOUR LIFE!

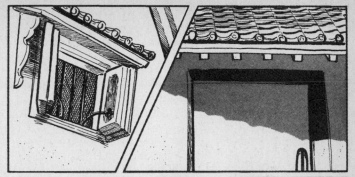

IZUICHI!

DO YOU *HEAR* ME?!

GRRN!

YOU DAMNED *ZATŌ!* WE'LL TEAR IT DOWN AND *DRAG* YOU OUT! CRUCIFIXION! *HEAD DOWN!*

KYAHHHHH!!

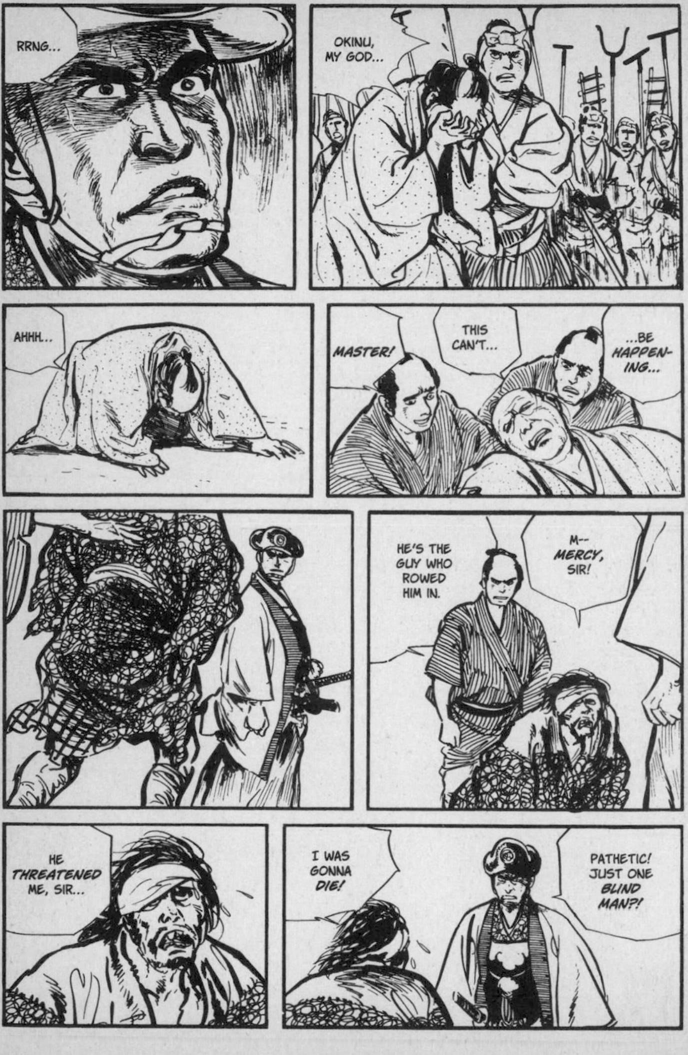
RRNG...
OKINU, MY GOD...
AHHH...
MASTER!
THIS CAN'T...
...BE HAPPEN-ING...
HE'S THE GUY WHO ROWED HIM IN.
M--MERCY, SIR!
HE THREATENED ME, SIR...
I WAS GONNA DIE!
PATHETIC! JUST ONE BLIND MAN?!

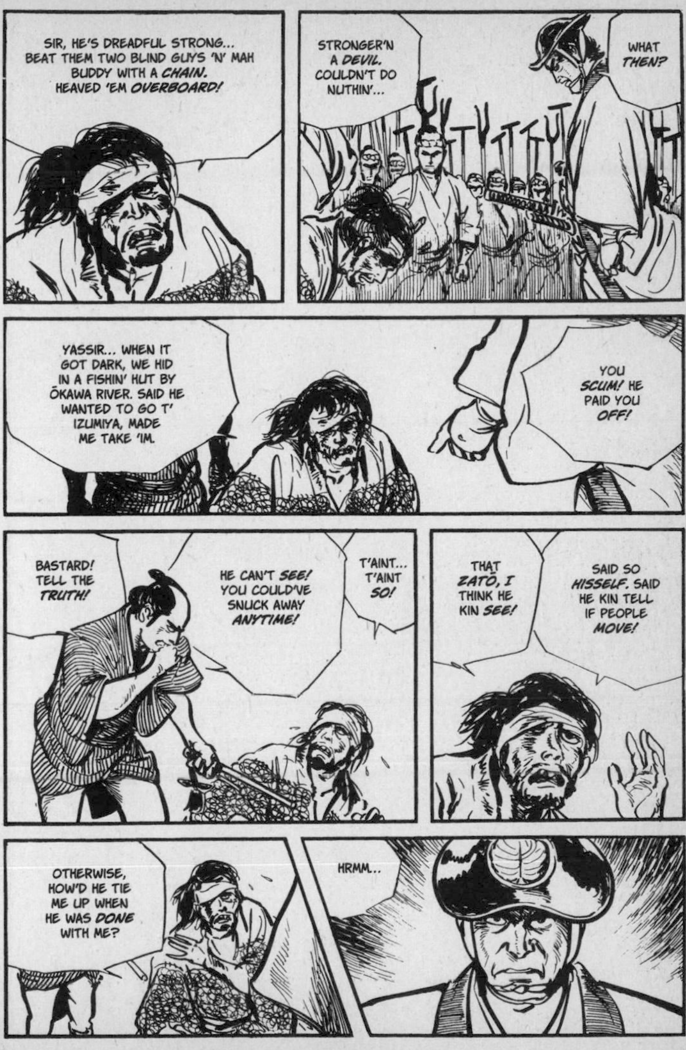
SIR, HE'S DREADFUL STRONG... BEAT THEM TWO BLIND GUYS 'N' MAH BUDDY WITH A *CHAIN.* HEAVED 'EM *OVERBOARD!*
STRONGER'N A *DEVIL.* COULDN'T DO NUTHIN'...
WHAT *THEN?*
YASSIR... WHEN IT GOT DARK, WE HID IN A FISHIN' HUT BY ŌKAWA RIVER. SAID HE WANTED TO GO T' IZUMIYA, MADE ME TAKE 'IM.
YOU *SCUM!* HE PAID YOU *OFF!*
BASTARD! TELL THE *TRUTH!*
HE CAN'T *SEE!* YOU COULD'VE SNUCK AWAY *ANYTIME!*
T'AINT... T'AINT *SO!*
THAT *ZATŌ,* I THINK HE KIN *SEE!*
SAID SO *HISSELF.* SAID HE KIN TELL IF PEOPLE *MOVE!*
OTHERWISE, HOW'D HE TIE ME UP WHEN HE WAS *DONE* WITH ME?
HRMM..

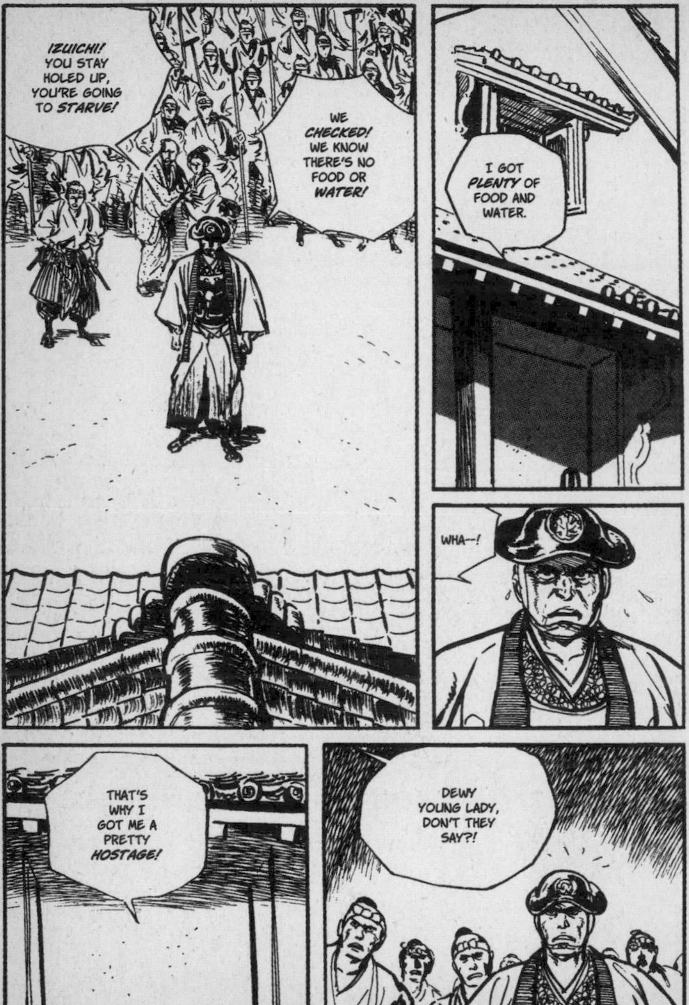
IZUICHI! YOU STAY HOLED UP, YOU'RE GOING TO STARVE!
WE CHECKED! WE KNOW THERE'S NO FOOD OR WATER!
I GOT PLENTY OF FOOD AND WATER.
WHA--!
THAT'S WHY I GOT ME A PRETTY HOSTAGE!
DEWY YOUNG LADY, DON'T THEY SAY?!

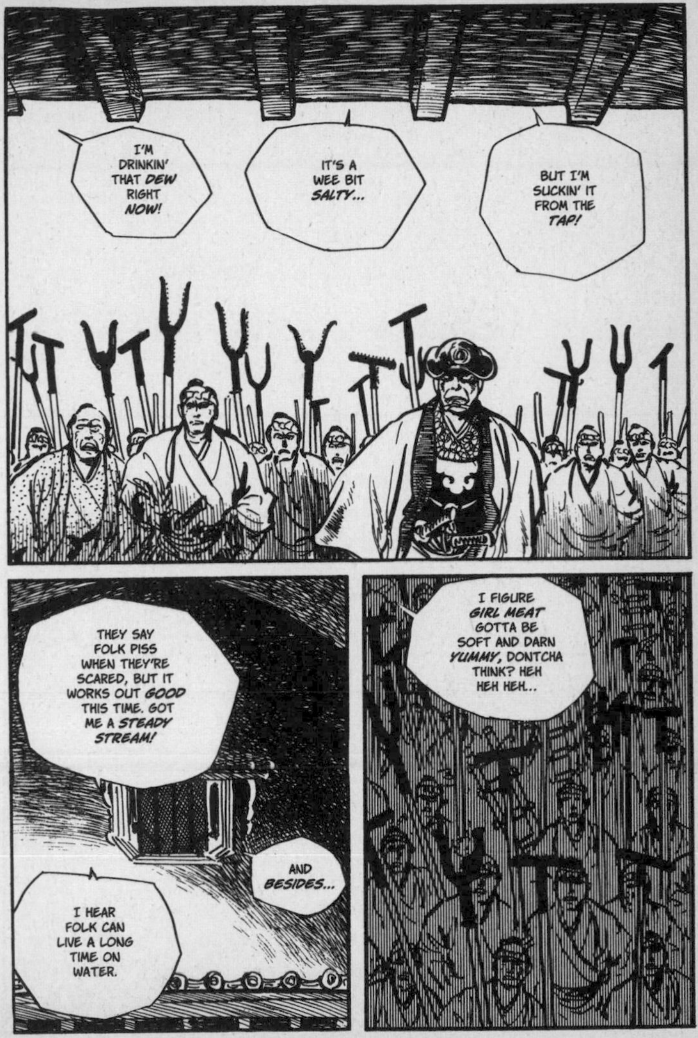

I'M DRINKIN' THAT *DEW* RIGHT *NOW!*
IT'S A WEE BIT *SALTY...*
BUT I'M SUCKIN' IT FROM THE *TAP!*
THEY SAY FOLK PISS WHEN THEY'RE SCARED, BUT IT WORKS OUT *GOOD* THIS TIME. GOT ME A *STEADY STREAM!*
I HEAR FOLK CAN LIVE A LONG TIME ON WATER.
AND *BESIDES...*
I FIGURE *GIRL MEAT* GOTTA BE SOFT AND DARN *YUMMY,* DONTCHA THINK? HEH HEH HEH...

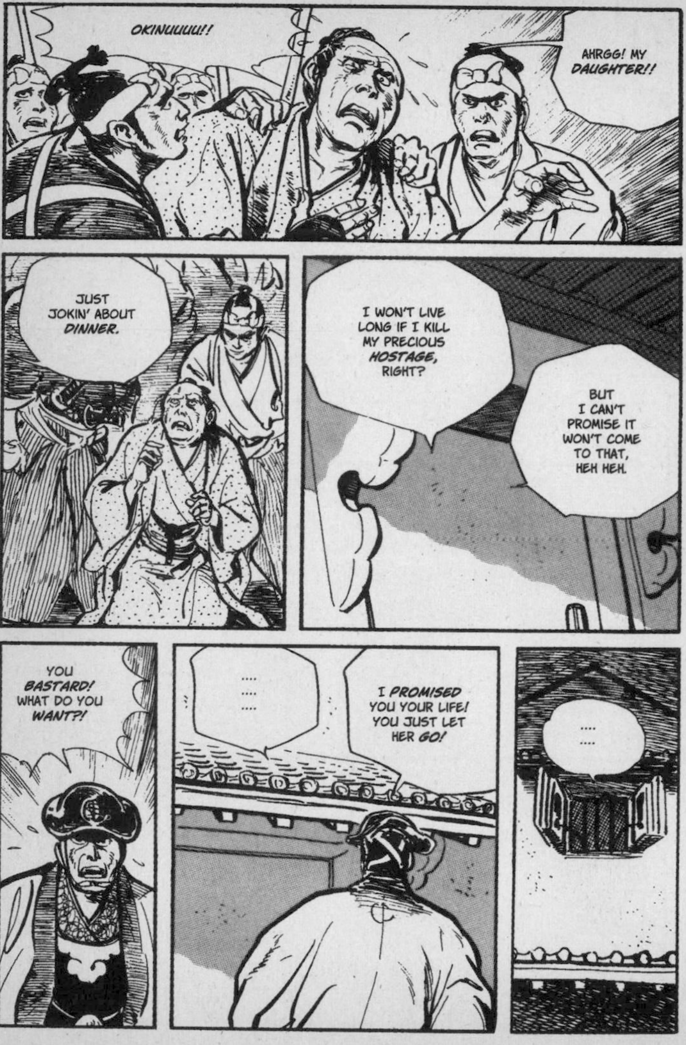

OKINUUUU!!
AHRGG! MY DAUGHTER!!
JUST JOKIN' ABOUT DINNER.
I WON'T LIVE LONG IF I KILL MY PRECIOUS HOSTAGE, RIGHT?
BUT I CAN'T PROMISE IT WON'T COME TO THAT, HEH HEH.
YOU BASTARD! WHAT DO YOU WANT?!
....
I PROMISED YOU YOUR LIFE! YOU JUST LET HER GO!
....

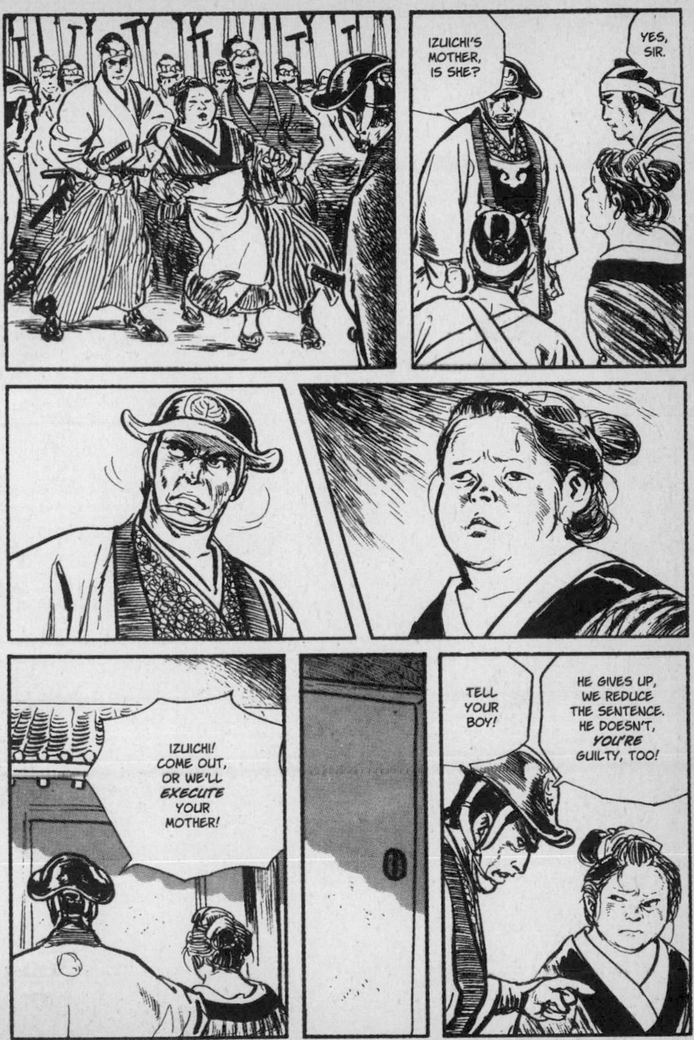
IZUICHI'S MOTHER, IS SHE?
YES, SIR.
IZUICHI! COME OUT, OR WE'LL EXECUTE YOUR MOTHER!
TELL YOUR BOY!
HE GIVES UP, WE REDUCE THE SENTENCE. HE DOESN'T, YOU'RE GUILTY, TOO!

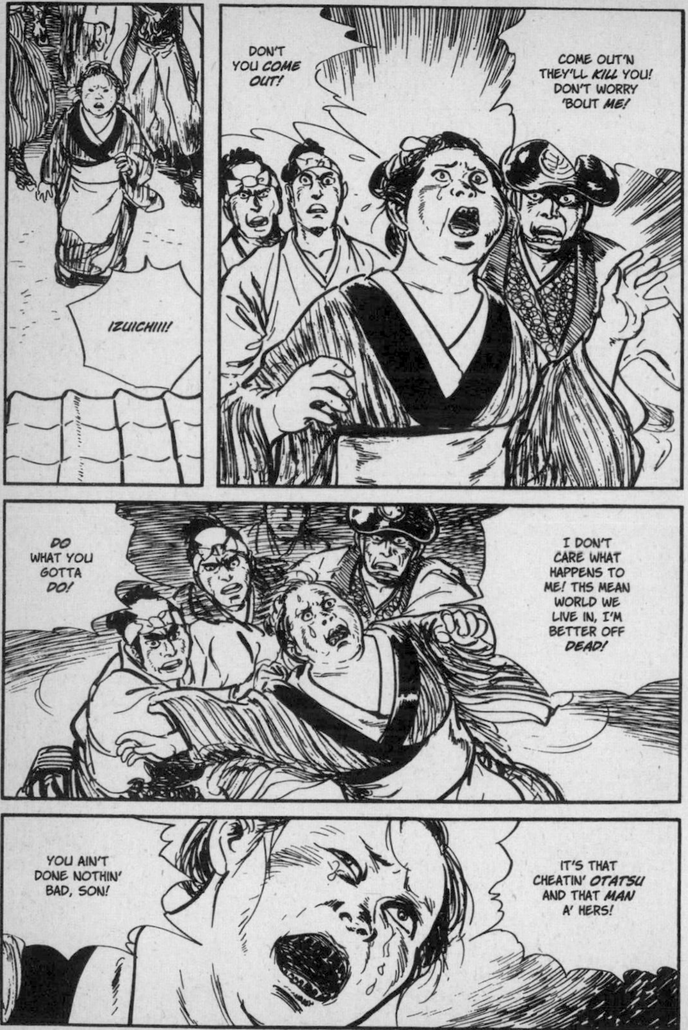
IZUICHI!!!
DON'T YOU COME OUT!
COME OUT'N THEY'LL KILL YOU! DON'T WORRY 'BOUT ME!
DO WHAT YOU GOTTA DO!
I DON'T CARE WHAT HAPPENS TO ME! THS MEAN WORLD WE LIVE IN, I'M BETTER OFF DEAD!
YOU AIN'T DONE NOTHIN' BAD, SON!
IT'S THAT CHEATIN' OTATSU AND THAT MAN A' HERS!

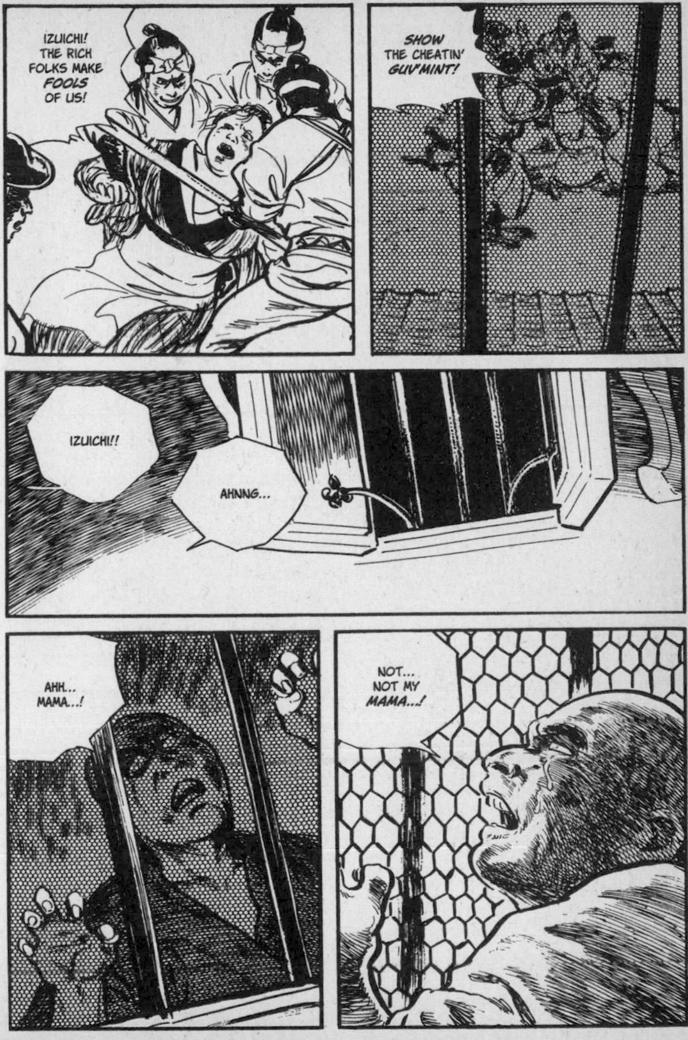
IZUICHI! THE RICH FOLKS MAKE FOOLS OF US!
SHOW THE CHEATIN' GUV'MINT!
IZUICHI!!
AHNNG...
AHH... MAMA...!
NOT... NOT MY MAMA...!

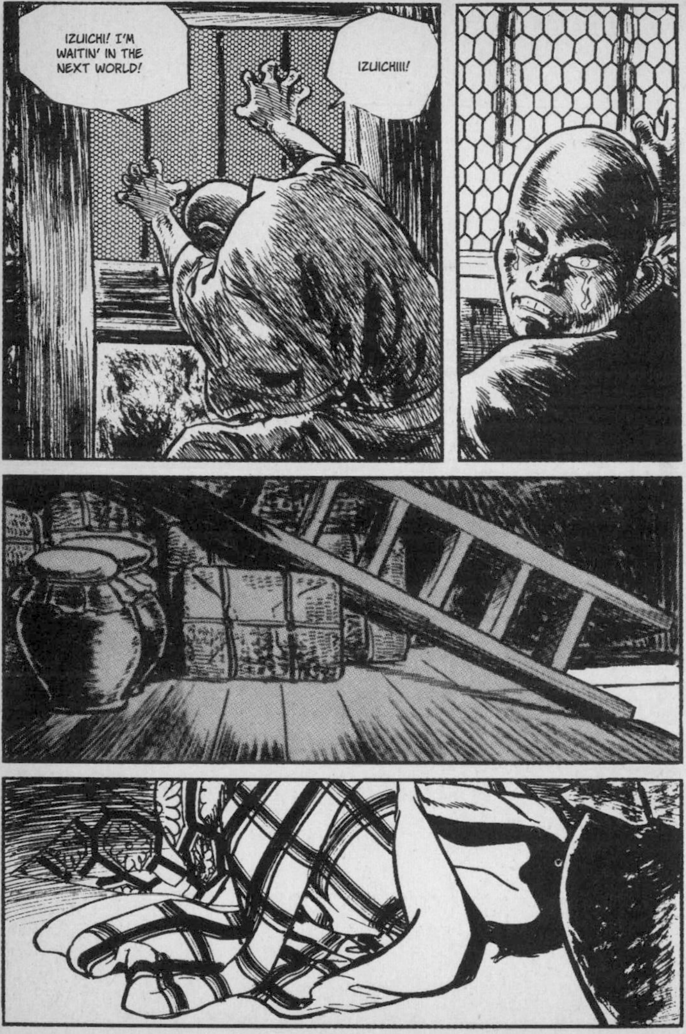
IZUICHI! I'M WAITIN' IN THE NEXT WORLD!
IZUICHIII!

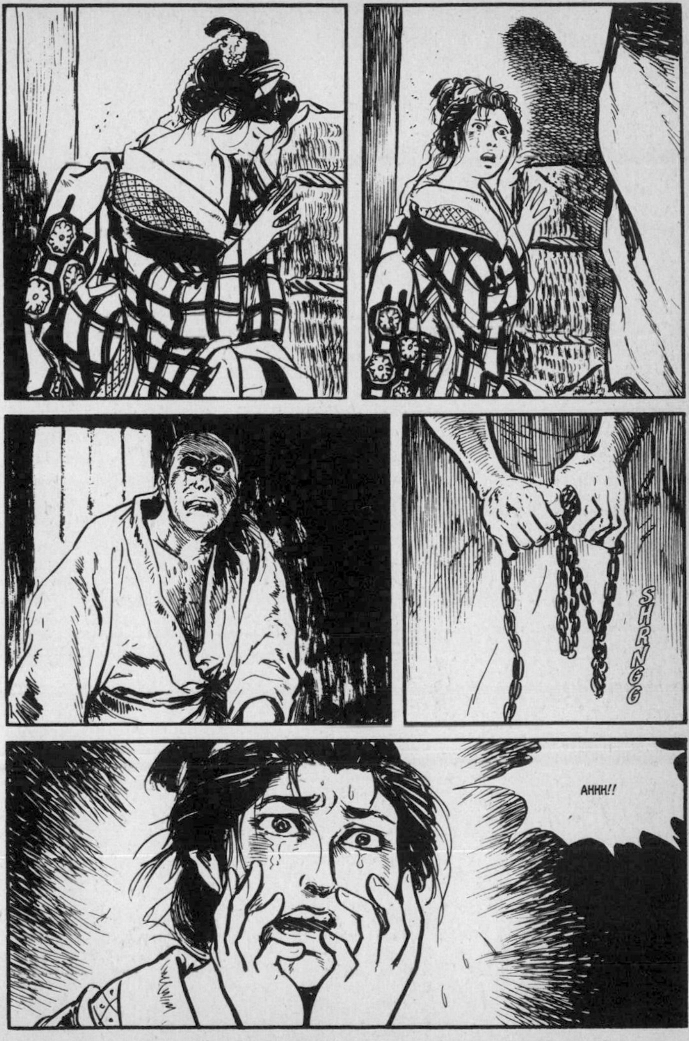
SHRNGG
AHHH!!

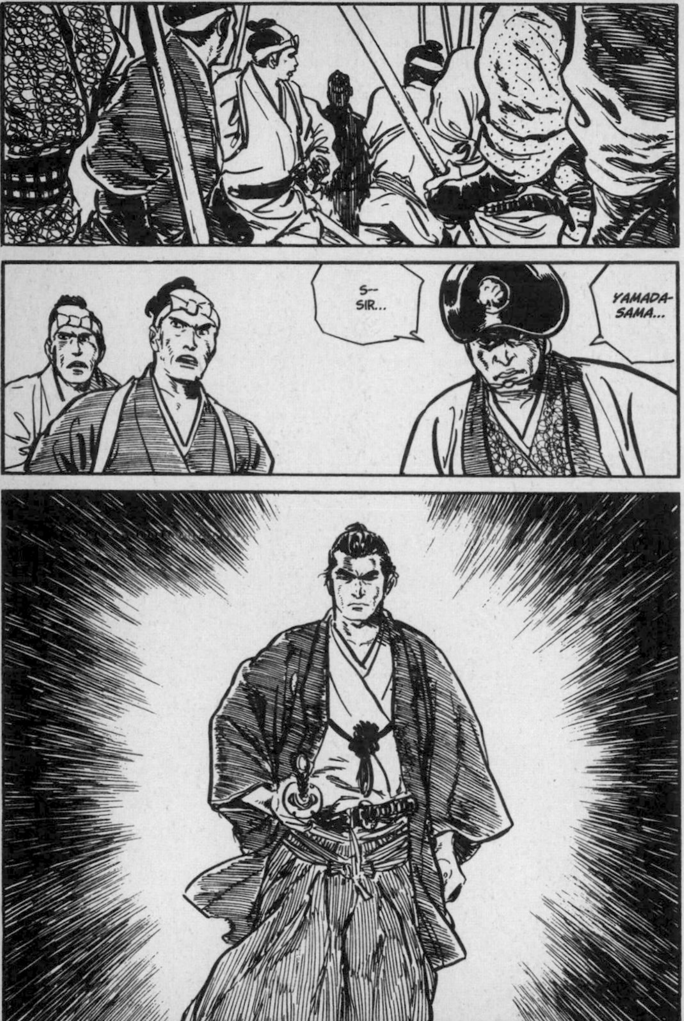
S--
SIR...
YAMADA-
SAMA...

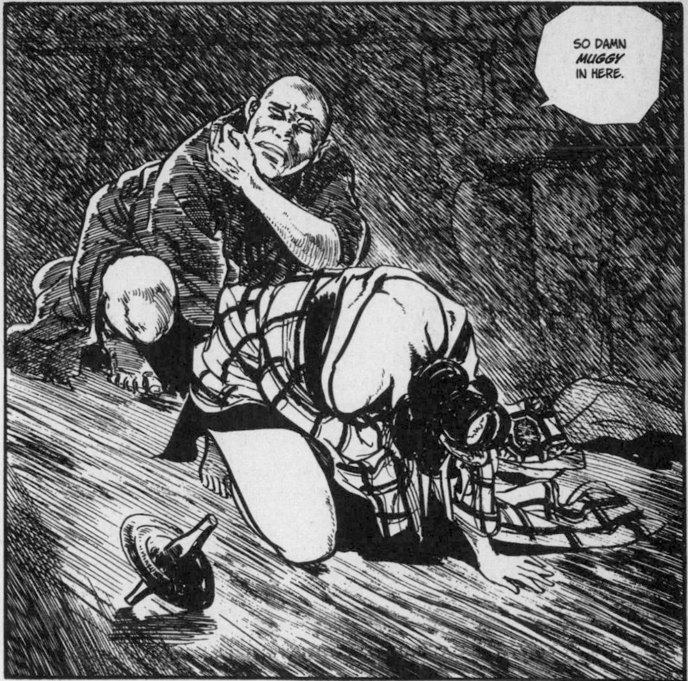
SO DAMN *MUGGY* IN HERE.
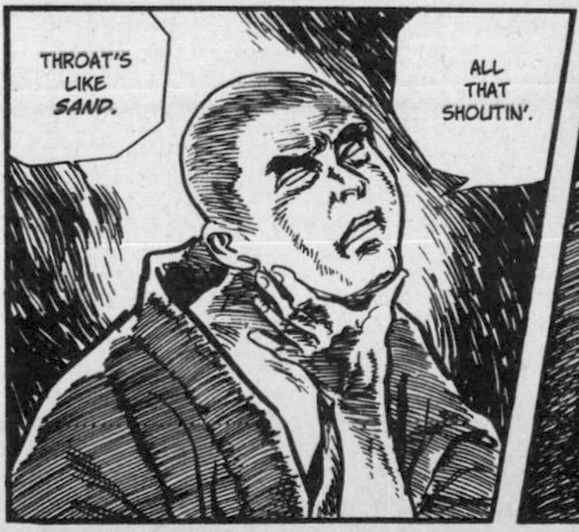
THROAT'S LIKE *SAND*.
ALL THAT SHOUTIN'.
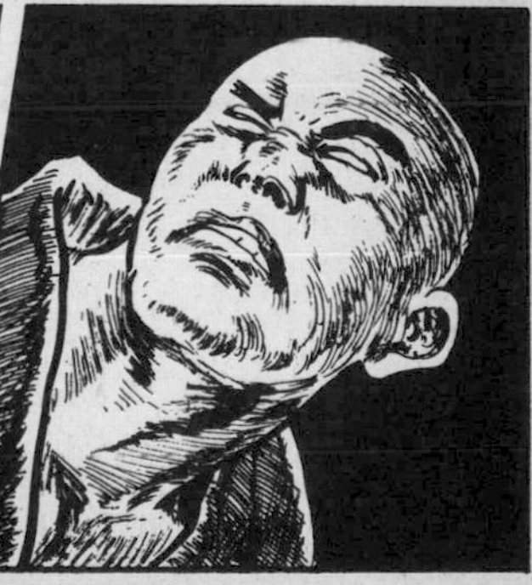

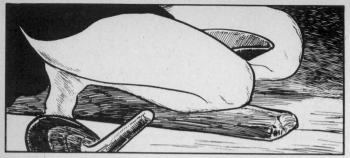

I DON'T *HEAR* NOTHIN'.

JUST A *DRIBBLE'S* FINE, MISSY.

AHH...

FOLK CAN LIVE *TEN DAYS* IF THEY GOT *WATER.* I'LL DRINK YOURS, AND YOU DRINK *MINE.*

DRINK TOGETHER, STAY TOGETHER, EH?

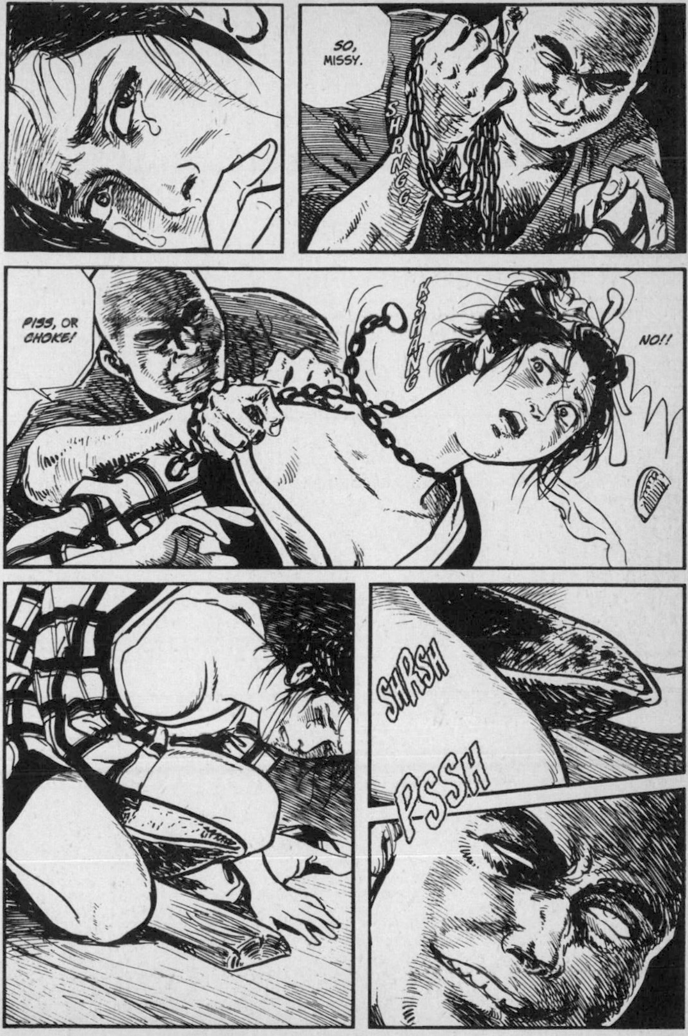
SO, MISSY.
SHRNGG
PISS, OR CHOKE!
KSHANG
NO!!
SHRSH
PSSH

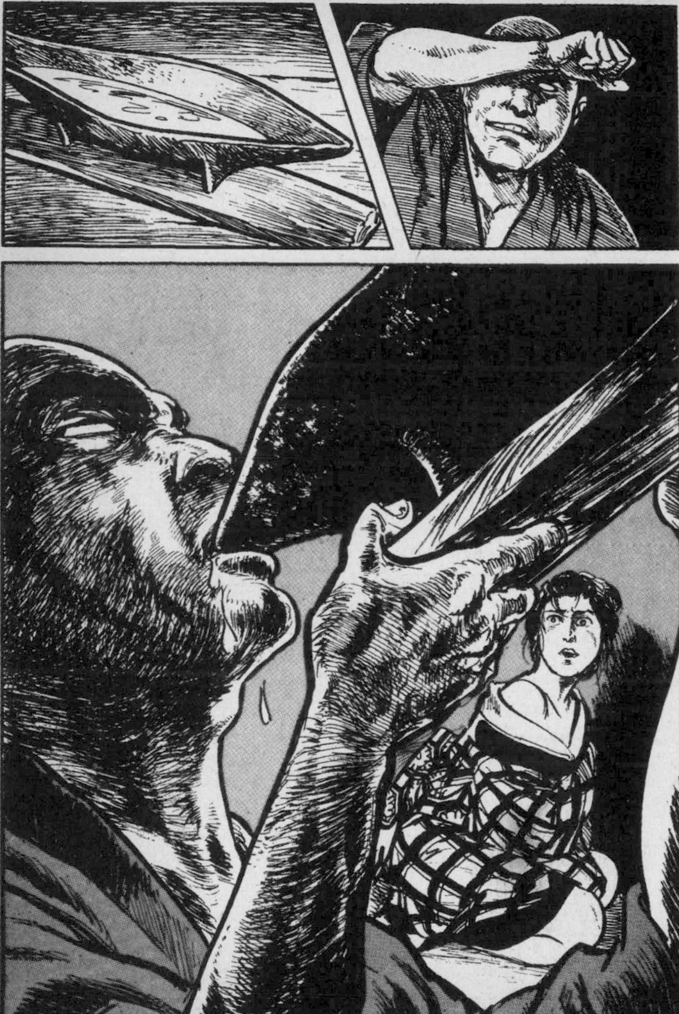

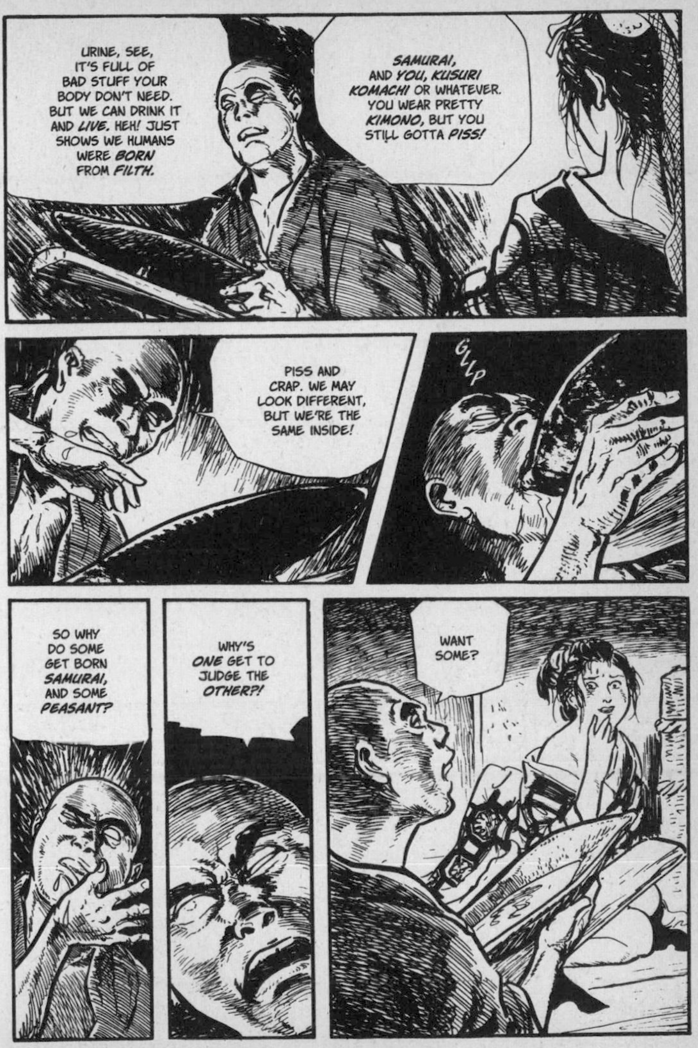
URINE, SEE, IT'S FULL OF BAD STUFF YOUR BODY DON'T NEED. BUT WE CAN DRINK IT AND *LIVE.* HEH! JUST SHOWS WE HUMANS WERE *BORN* FROM *FILTH.*
SAMURAI, AND *YOU, KUSURI KOMACHI* OR WHATEVER. YOU WEAR PRETTY *KIMONO,* BUT YOU STILL GOTTA *PISS!*
PISS AND CRAP. WE MAY LOOK DIFFERENT, BUT WE'RE THE SAME INSIDE!
GLLP
SO WHY DO SOME GET BORN *SAMURAI,* AND SOME *PEASANT?*
WHY'S *ONE* GET TO JUDGE THE *OTHER?!*
WANT SOME?

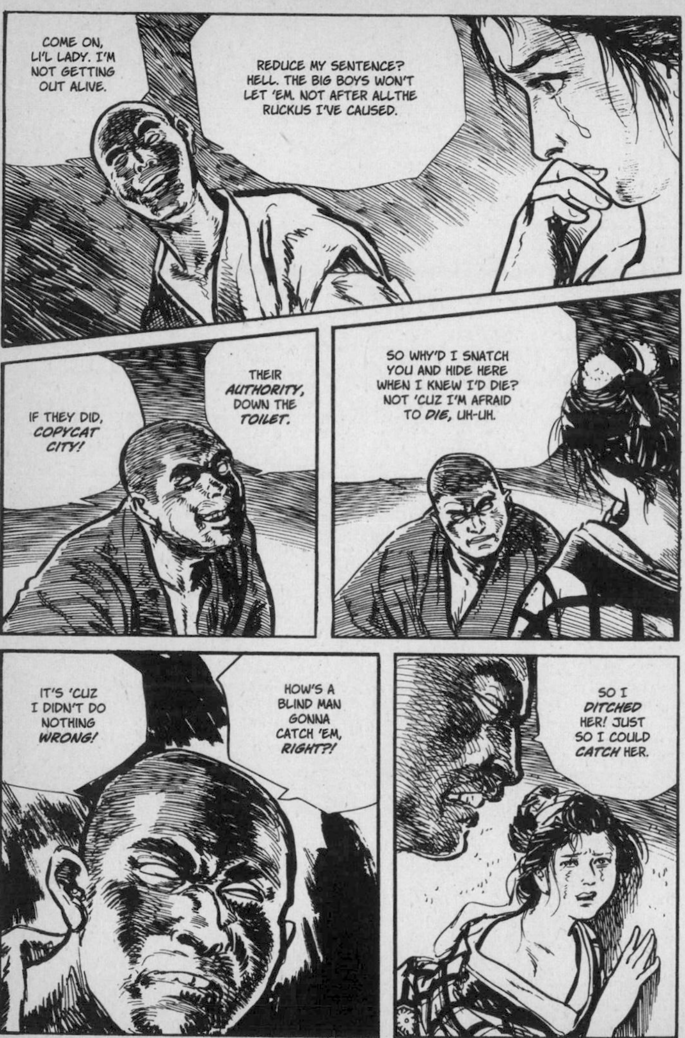
COME ON, LI'L LADY. I'M NOT GETTING OUT ALIVE.
REDUCE MY SENTENCE? HELL. THE BIG BOYS WON'T LET 'EM. NOT AFTER ALLTHE RUCKUS I'VE CAUSED.
IF THEY DID, *COPYCAT CITY!*
THEIR *AUTHORITY,* DOWN THE *TOILET.*
SO WHY'D I SNATCH YOU AND HIDE HERE WHEN I KNEW I'D DIE? NOT 'CUZ I'M AFRAID TO *DIE,* UH-UH.
IT'S 'CUZ I DIDN'T DO NOTHING *WRONG!*
HOW'S A BLIND MAN GONNA CATCH 'EM, *RIGHT?!*
SO I *DITCHED* HER! JUST SO I COULD *CATCH* HER.

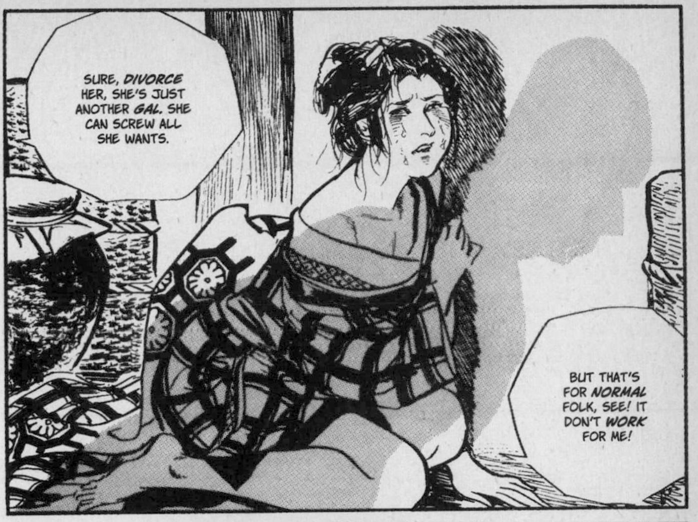
SURE, DIVORCE HER, SHE'S JUST ANOTHER GAL. SHE CAN SCREW ALL SHE WANTS.
BUT THAT'S FOR NORMAL FOLK, SEE! IT DON'T WORK FOR ME!
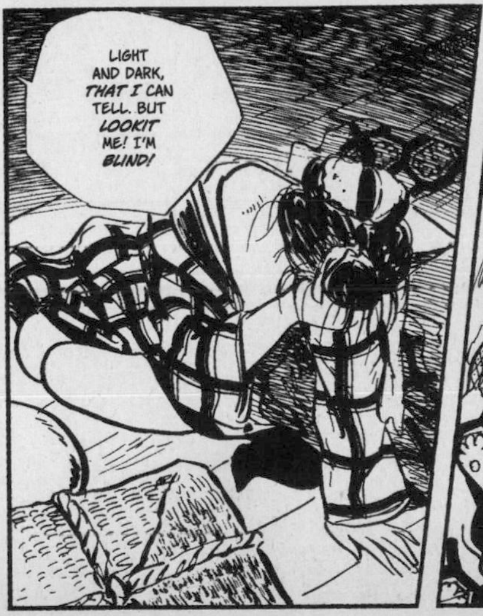
LIGHT AND DARK, THAT I CAN TELL. BUT LOOKIT ME! I'M BLIND!
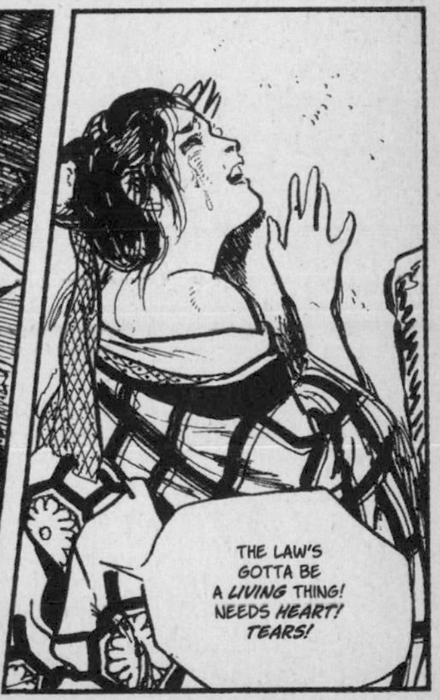
THE LAW'S GOTTA BE A LIVING THING! NEEDS HEART! TEARS!

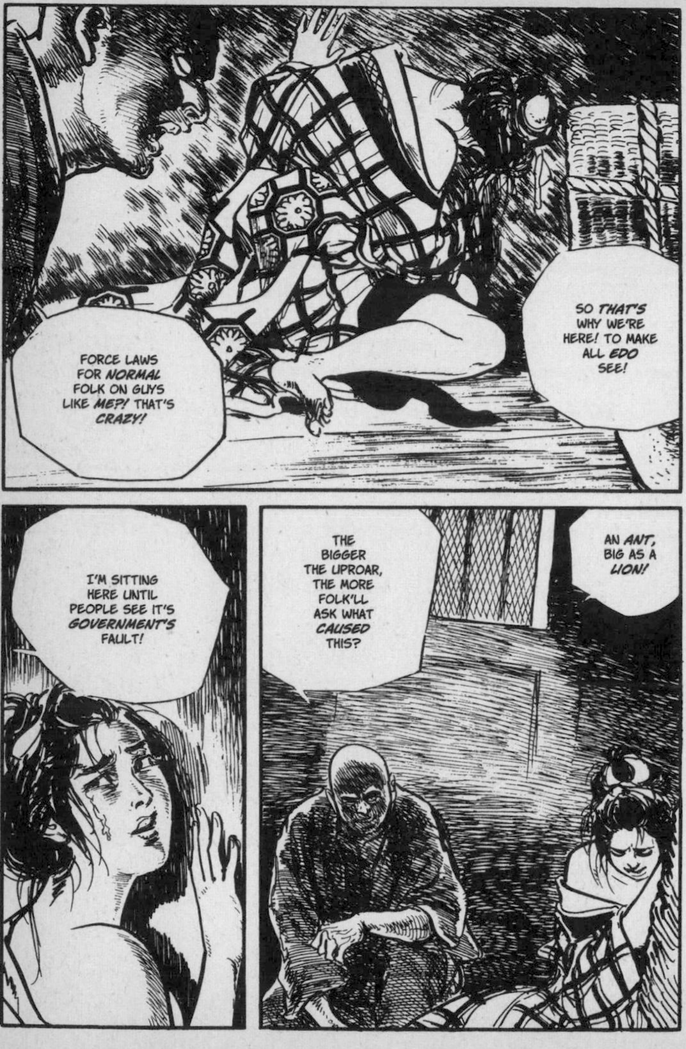
FORCE LAWS FOR NORMAL FOLK ON GUYS LIKE ME?! THAT'S CRAZY!
SO THAT'S WHY WE'RE HERE! TO MAKE ALL EDO SEE!
I'M SITTING HERE UNTIL PEOPLE SEE IT'S GOVERNMENT'S FAULT!
THE BIGGER THE UPROAR, THE MORE FOLK'LL ASK WHAT CAUSED THIS?
AN ANT, BIG AS A LION!

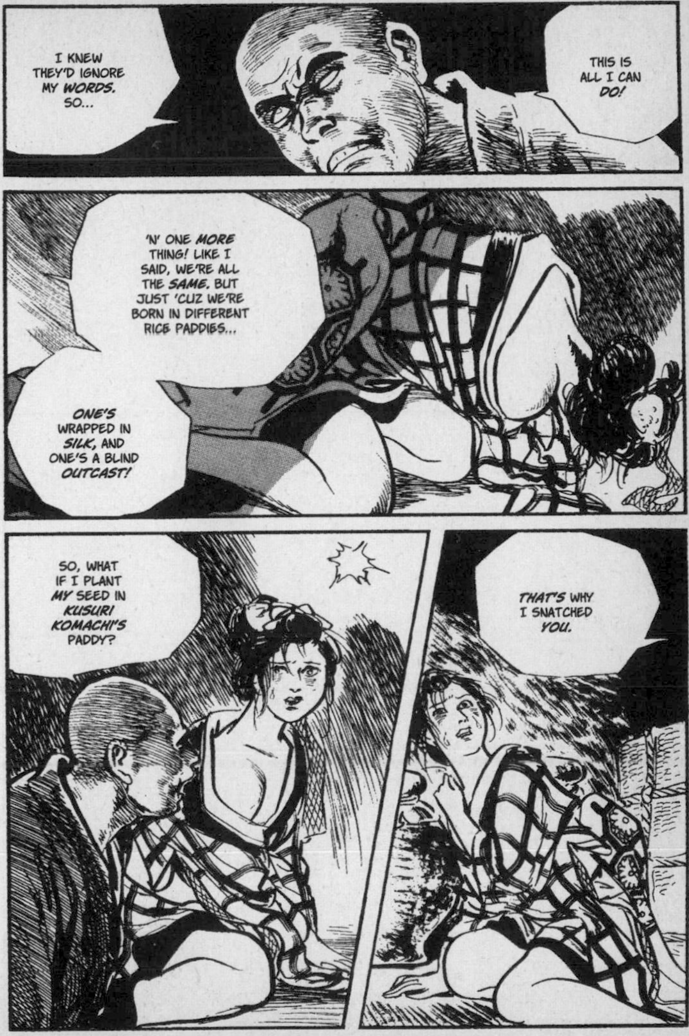
I KNEW THEY'D IGNORE MY WORDS. SO...
THIS IS ALL I CAN DO!
'N' ONE MORE THING! LIKE I SAID, WE'RE ALL THE SAME. BUT JUST 'CUZ WE'RE BORN IN DIFFERENT RICE PADDIES...
ONE'S WRAPPED IN SILK, AND ONE'S A BLIND OUTCAST!
SO, WHAT IF I PLANT MY SEED IN KUSURI KOMACHI'S PADDY?
THAT'S WHY I SNATCHED YOU.

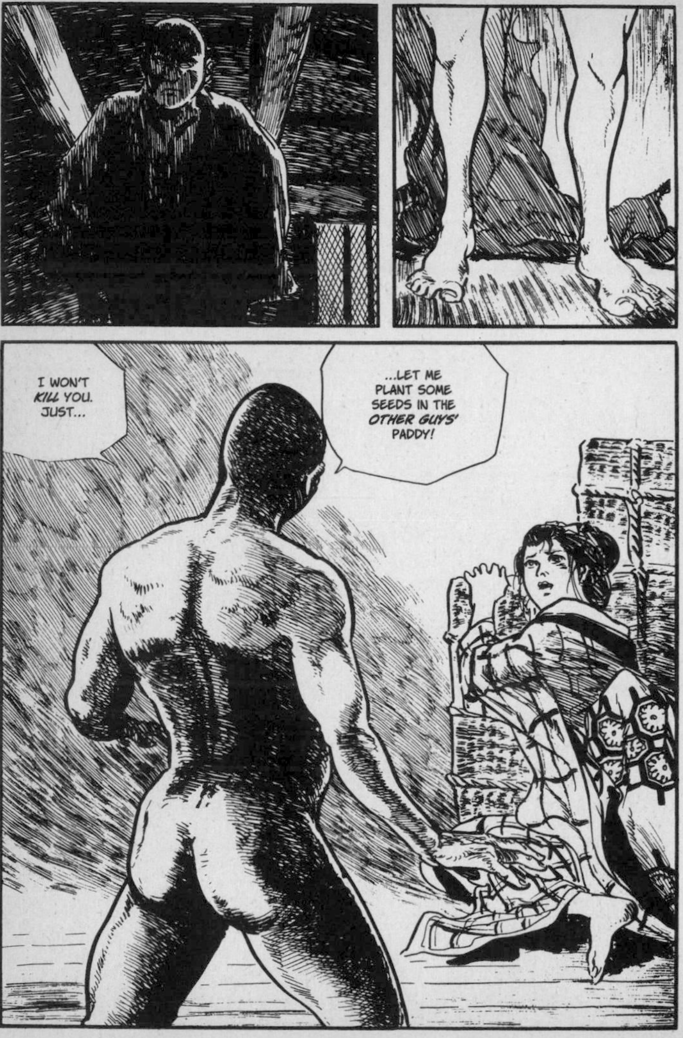
I WON'T *KILL* YOU. JUST...
...LET ME PLANT SOME SEEDS IN THE *OTHER GUYS'* PADDY!

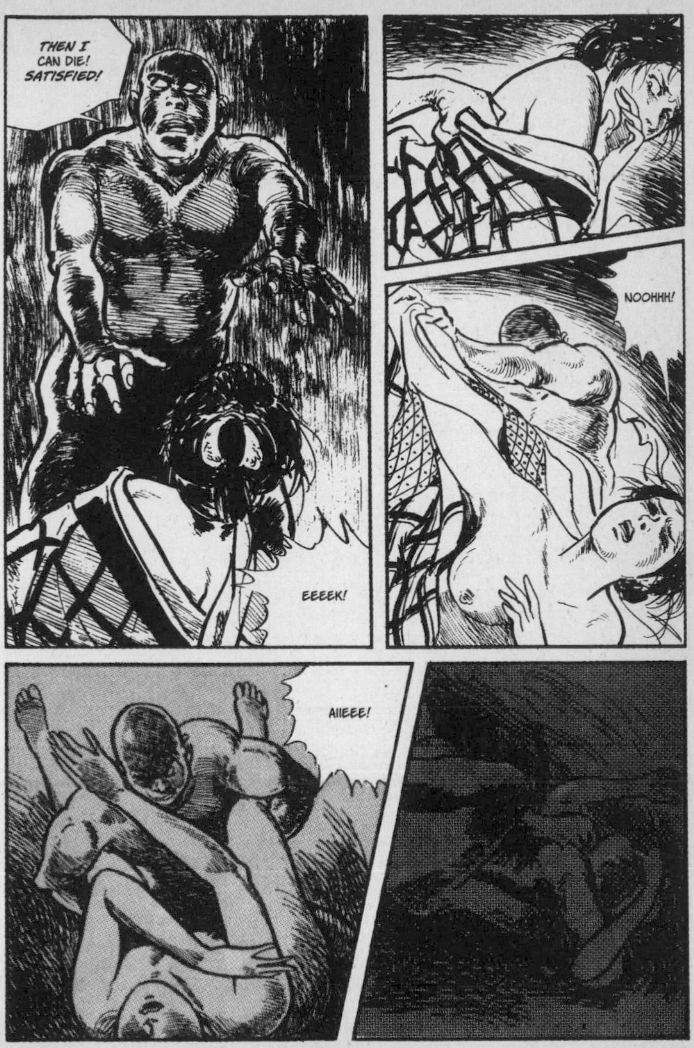
THEN I CAN DIE! SATISFIED!
EEEEK!
NOOHHH!
AIIEEE!

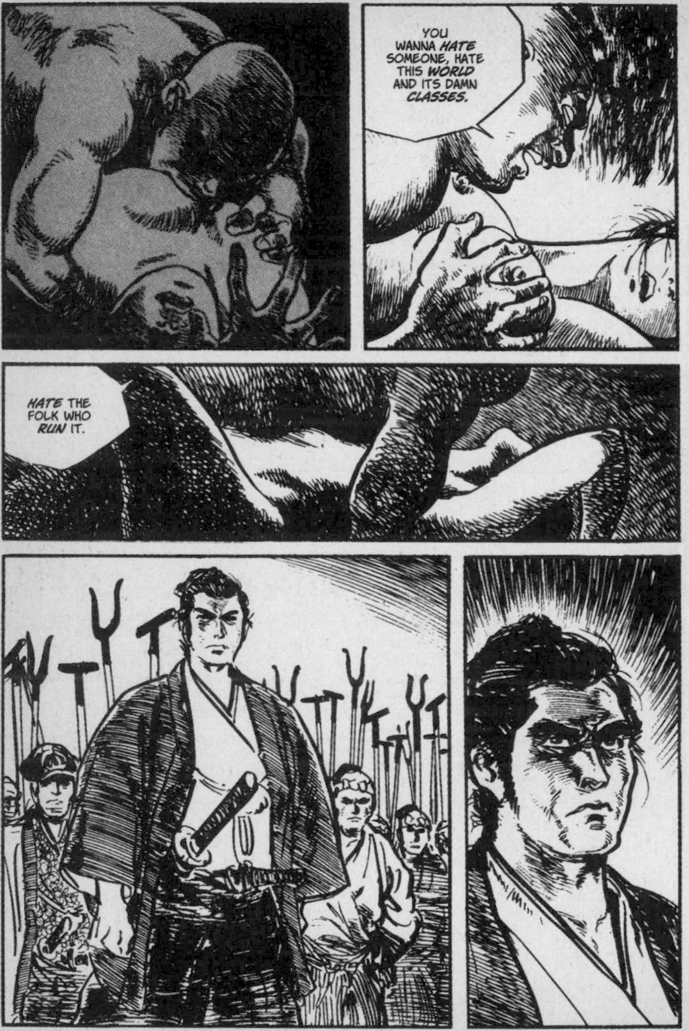
YOU WANNA *HATE* SOMEONE, HATE THIS *WORLD* AND ITS DAMN *CLASSES.*
HATE THE FOLK WHO *RUN* IT.

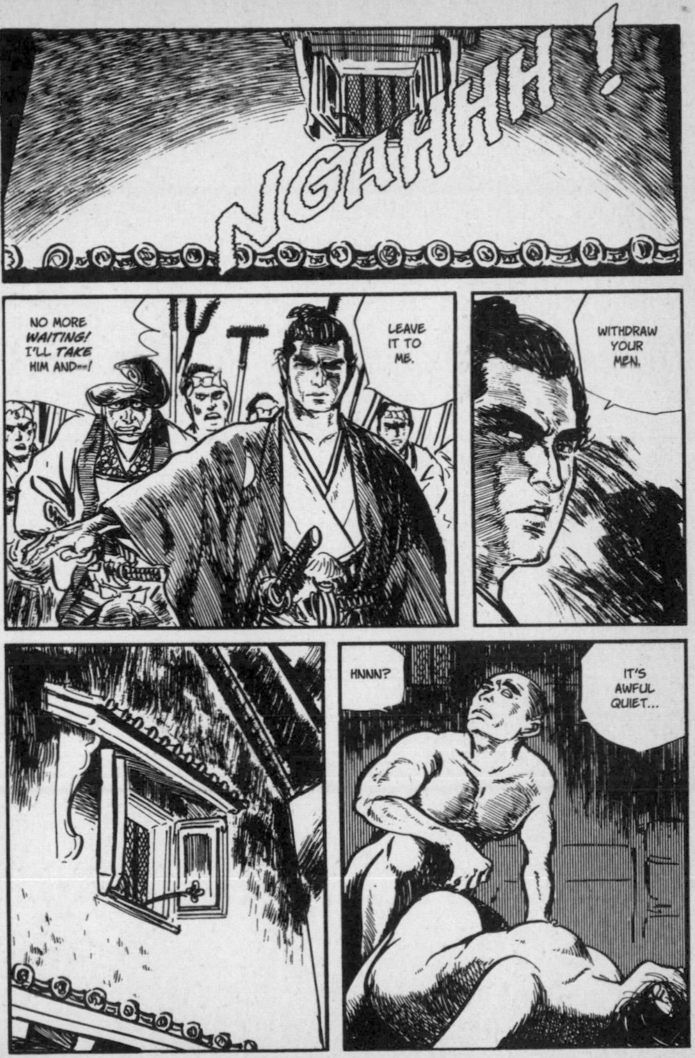
NGAHHH!
NO MORE WAITING! I'LL TAKE HIM AND--!
LEAVE IT TO ME.
WITHDRAW YOUR MEN.
HNNN?
IT'S AWFUL QUIET...

CAN'T FEEL ANY PEOPLE!

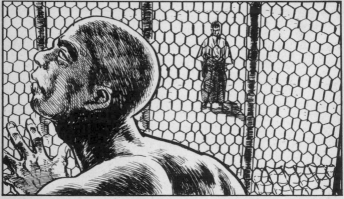

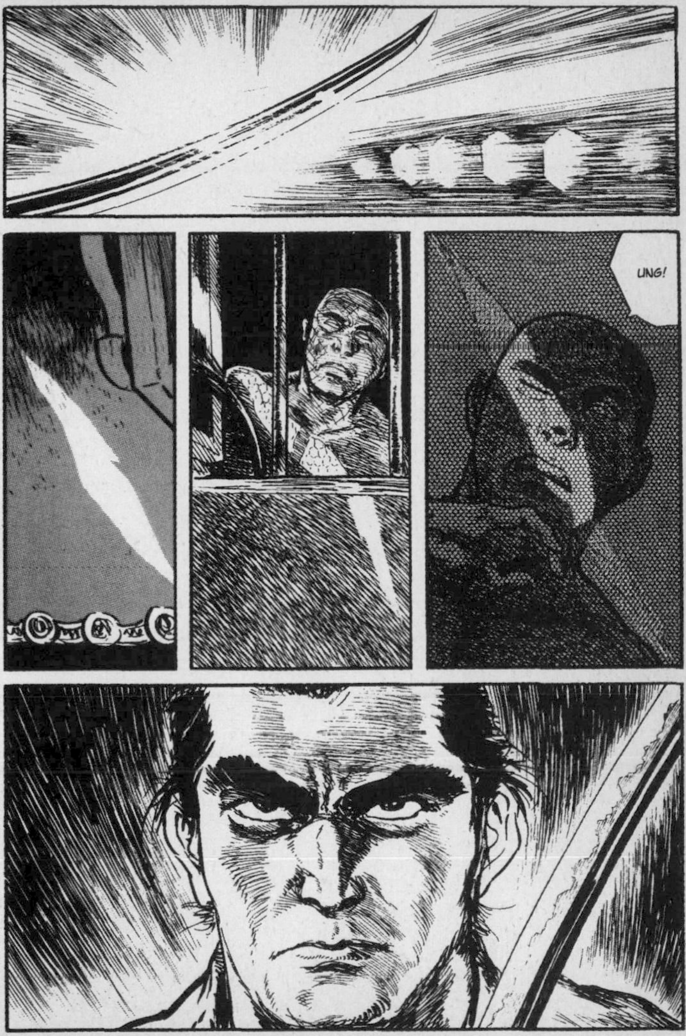
UNG!

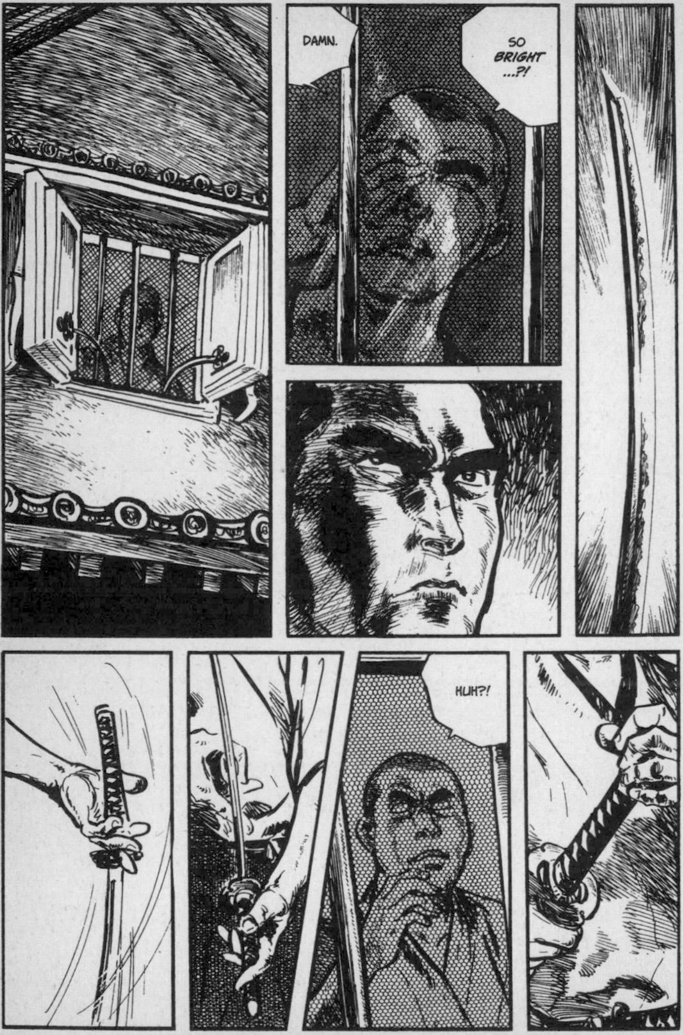
DAMN.
SO BRIGHT ...?!
HUH?!

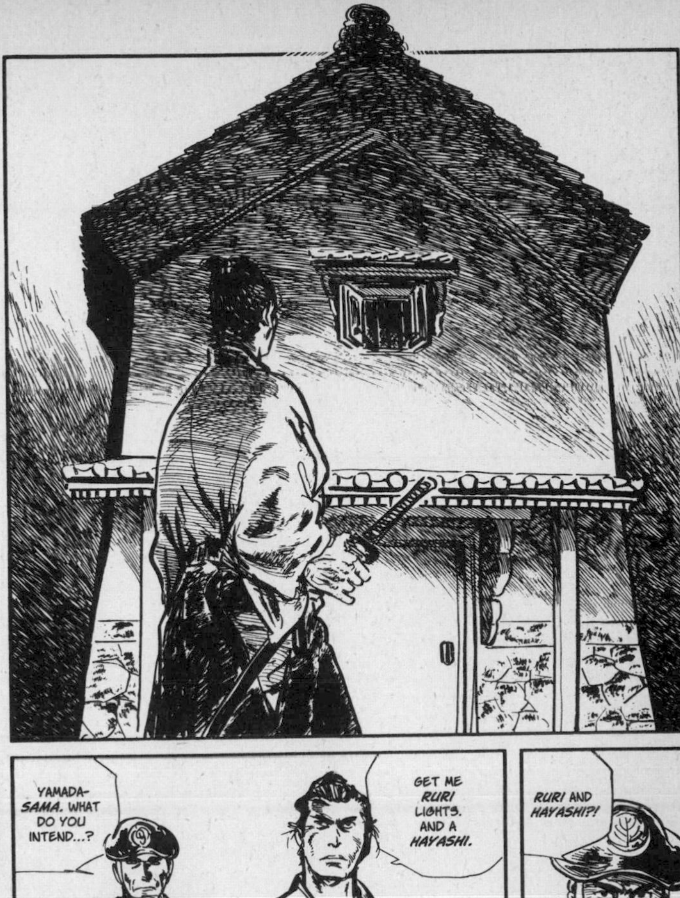

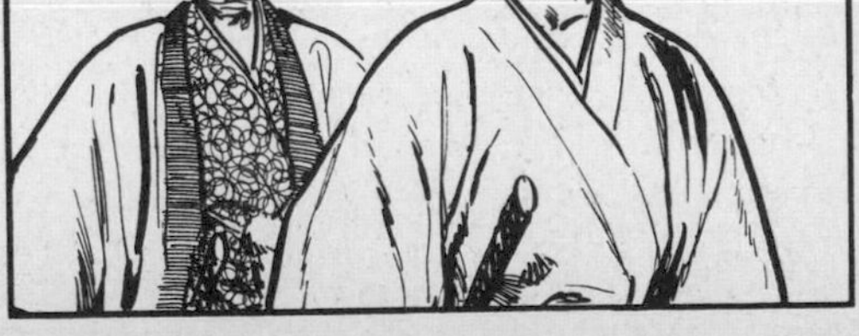
YAMADA-*SAMA.* WHAT DO YOU INTEND...?
GET ME *RURI* LIGHTS. AND A *HAYASHI.*

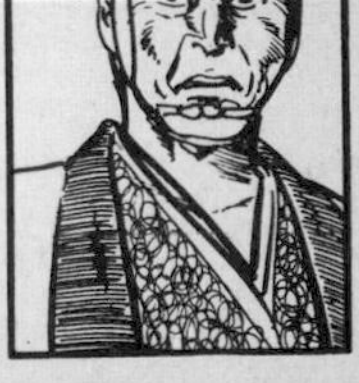
RURI AND *HAYASHI?!*

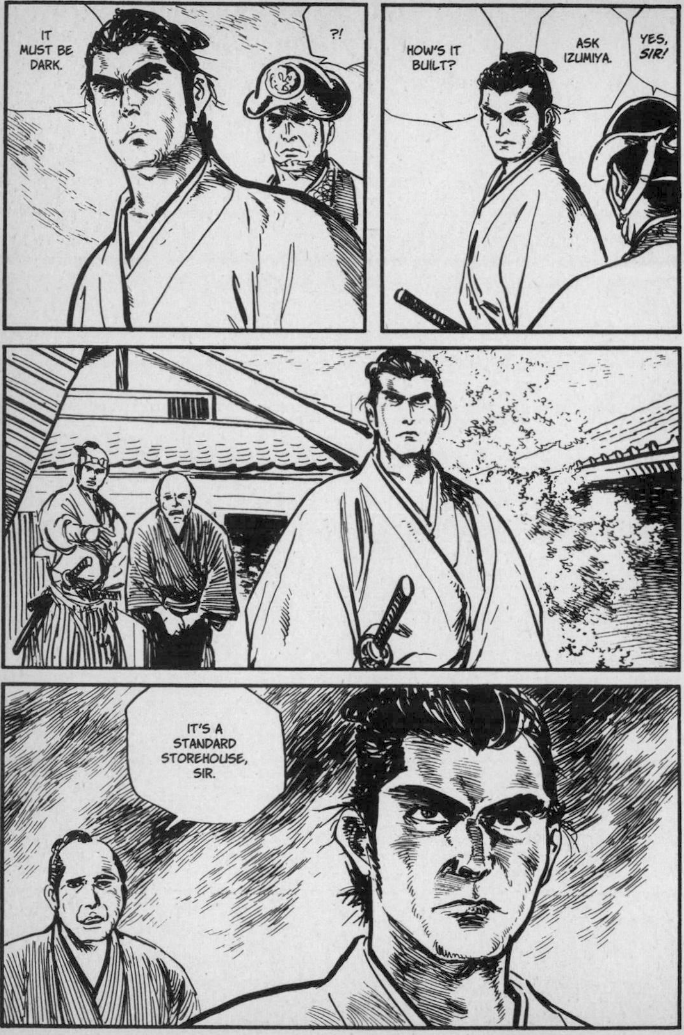
IT MUST BE DARK.
?!
HOW'S IT BUILT?
ASK IZUMIYA.
YES, *SIR!*
IT'S A STANDARD STOREHOUSE, SIR.

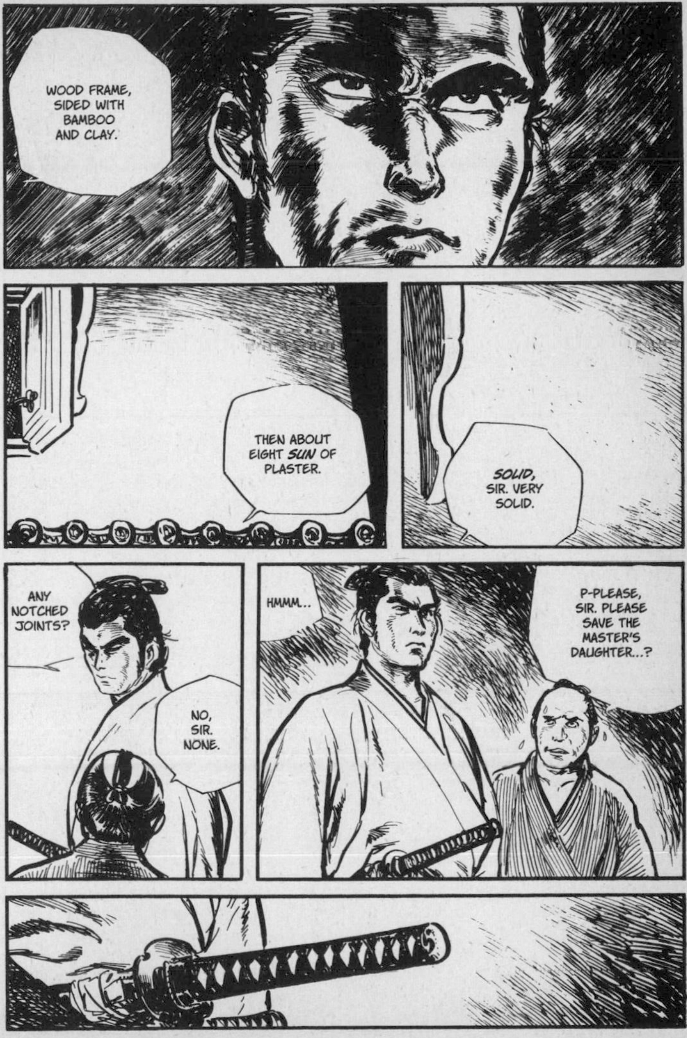
WOOD FRAME, SIDED WITH BAMBOO AND CLAY.
THEN ABOUT EIGHT *SUN* OF PLASTER.
SOLID, SIR. VERY SOLID.
ANY NOTCHED JOINTS?
NO, SIR. NONE.
HMMM..
P-PLEASE, SIR. PLEASE SAVE THE MASTER'S DAUGHTER...?

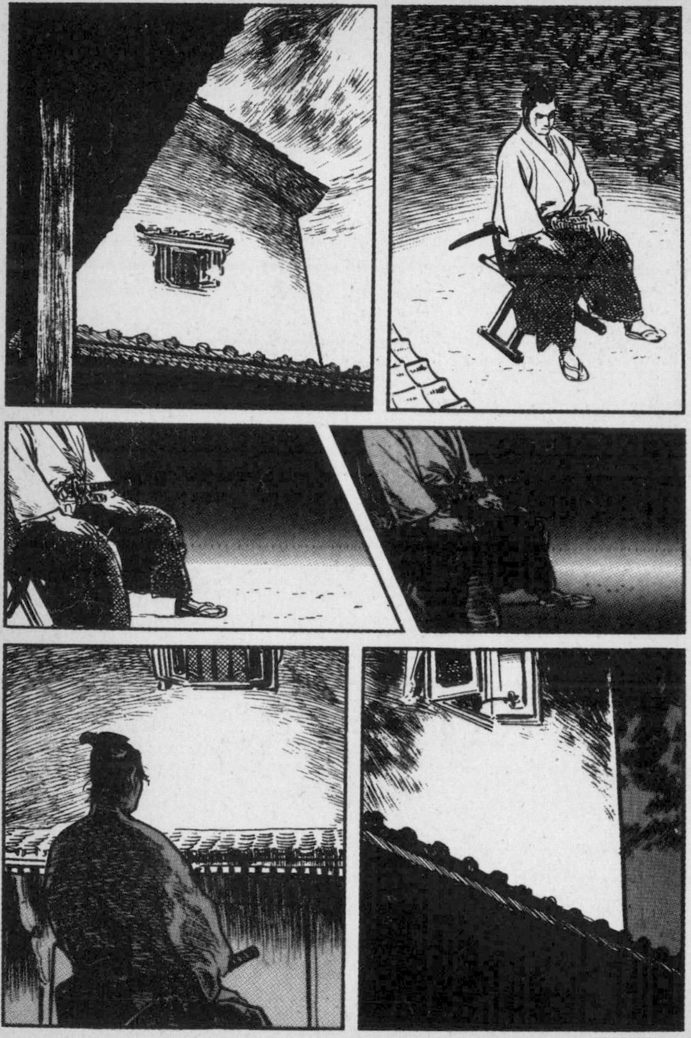

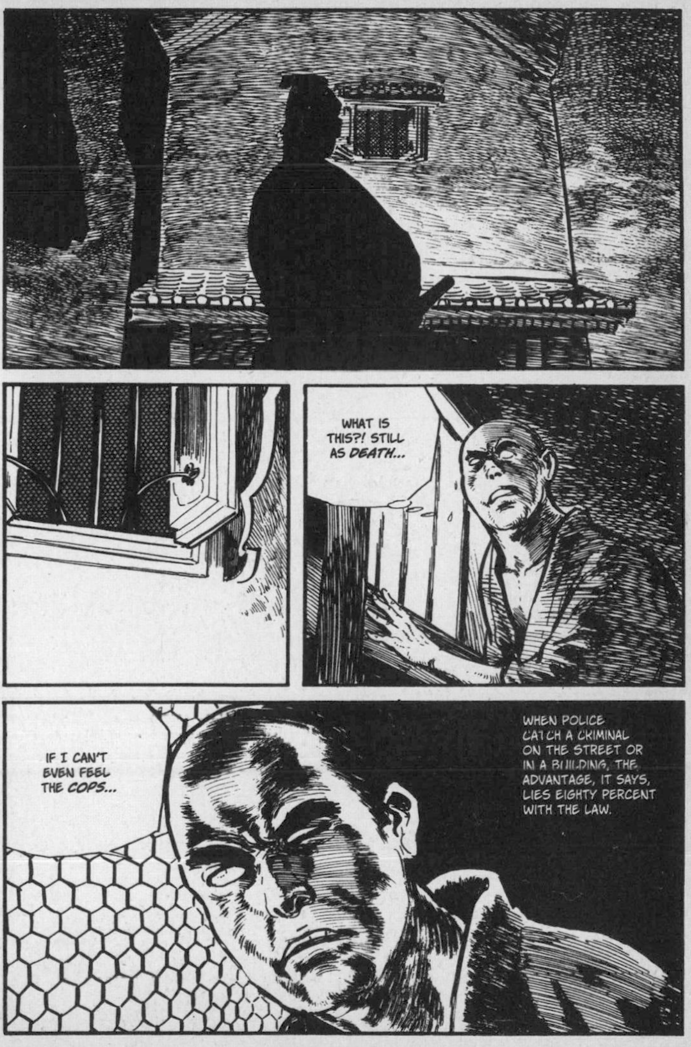
WHAT IS THIS?! STILL AS *DEATH*...
IF I CAN'T EVEN FEEL THE *COPS*...
WHEN POLICE CATCH A CRIMINAL ON THE STREET OR IN A BUILDING, THE ADVANTAGE, IT SAYS, LIES EIGHTY PERCENT WITH THE LAW.

AND WHEN POLICE SURPRISE A CRIMINAL AT HOME OR ASLEEP, THEY CAN LURE HIM OUT BY SAYING THEY JUST WANT A WORD WITH HIM.

EVEN IF THE SUSPECT RESISTS, ADVANTAGE ONE-HUNDRED PERCENT FOR THE LAW.

BUT BY HOLING UP, A SUSPECT TURNS THE TABLES. EIGHTY PERCENT AND MORE TO *HIS* ADVANTAGE.

THAT CALCULATION EXPLAINS THE WAVE OF SIMILAR INCIDENTS THAT SWEPT THE OLD CAPITAL OF *EDO*, TODAY'S *TOKYO*, AND OTHER CITIES ACROSS JAPAN FROM THE *TENSHŌ* (1573-1542) THROUGH THE *MEIWA* (1764-1772) ERAS.

THE DEFENDER'S *ACHILLE'S HEEL* IS HIS INABILITY TO TELL WHAT'S GOING ON OUTSIDE. SOME DESCEND INTO CLAUSTROPHOBIA AND NAMELESS FEAR.

CONSEQUENTLY, THE MORE NOISE HIS PURSUERS MAKE, THE MORE COMFORT TO THE CRIMINAL. IT FEEDS HIS SENSE OF SUPERIORITY. MAYBE THE AUTHORITIES SHOULD REMEMBER CRIMINAL PSYCHOLOGY AND THE LESSONS OF THE PAST WHEN FACING SIMILAR SITUATIONS TODAY...

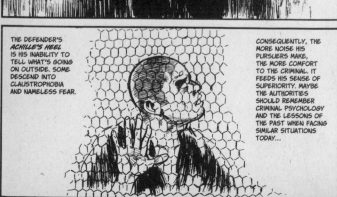

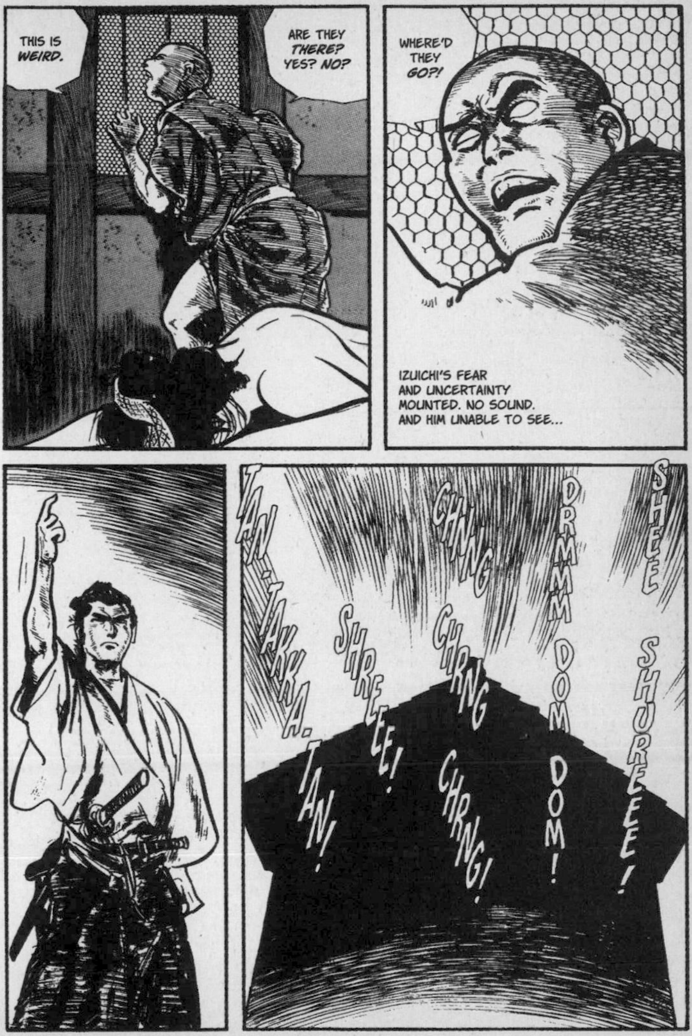
THIS IS *WEIRD.*
ARE THEY *THERE?* YES? *NO?*
WHERE'D THEY *GO?!*
IZUICHI'S FEAR AND UNCERTAINTY MOUNTED. NO SOUND. AND HIM UNABLE TO SEE...
TAN-TAKKA-TAN!
SHREEEE!
CHRNG CHRNG
CHRNG CHRNG!
DRMMM DOM DOM DOM!
SHEE SHUREEEE!

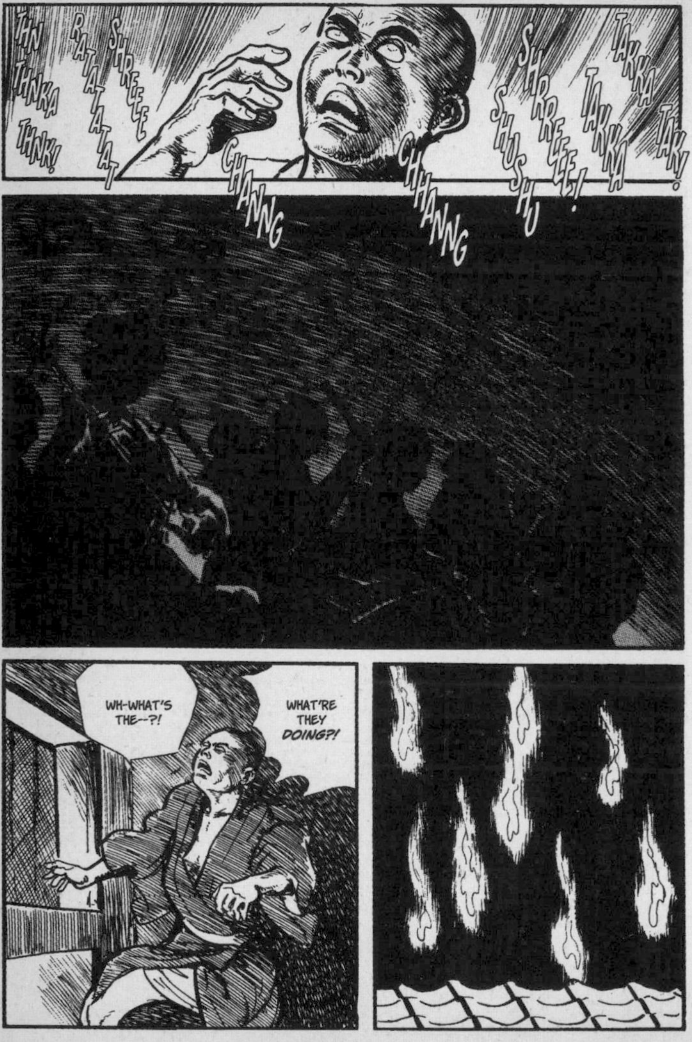
THN THNKA THNK!
RATATATATAT
SHREEE
CHANNG
CHHANNG
SHUSHU
SHREEEE!
TAKKA TAKKA
TAKKA TAK!
WH-WHAT'S THE--?!
WHAT'RE THEY DOING?!

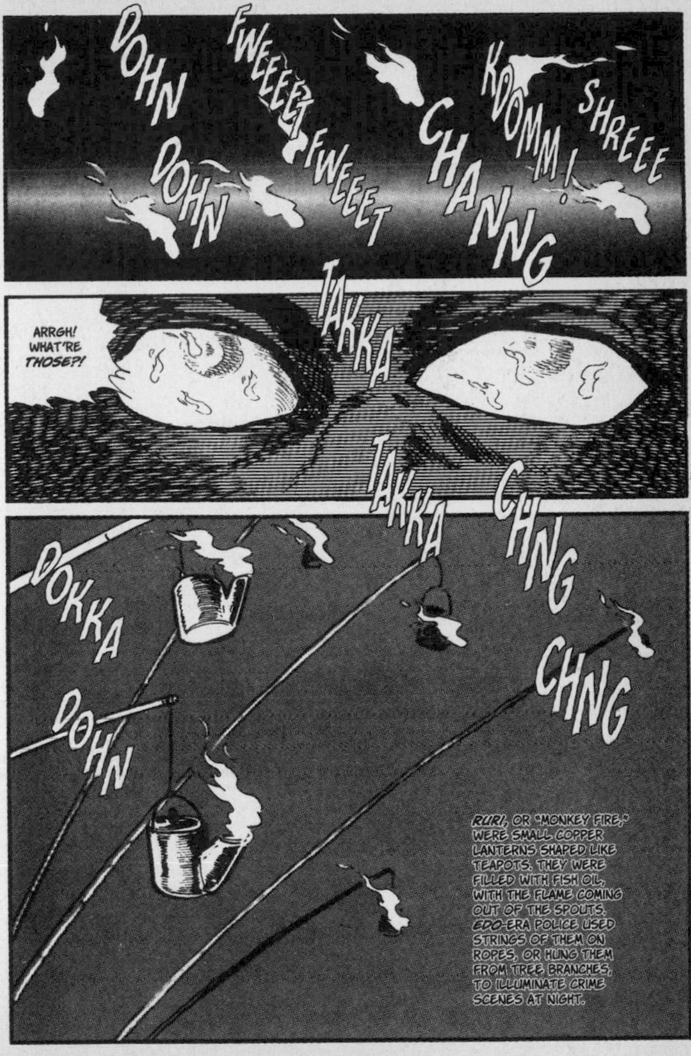
DOHN DOHN
FWEEEET FWEEEET
KOOMM!
CHANNG
SHREEE
ARRGH! WHAT'RE *THOSE?!*
TAKKA TAKKA
CHNG CHNG
DOKKA DOHN
RURI, OR "MONKEY FIRE," WERE SMALL COPPER LANTERNS SHAPED LIKE TEAPOTS. THEY WERE FILLED WITH FISH OIL, WITH THE FLAME COMING OUT OF THE SPOUTS. *EDO*-ERA POLICE USED STRINGS OF THEM ON ROPES, OR HUNG THEM FROM TREE BRANCHES, TO ILLUMINATE CRIME SCENES AT NIGHT.

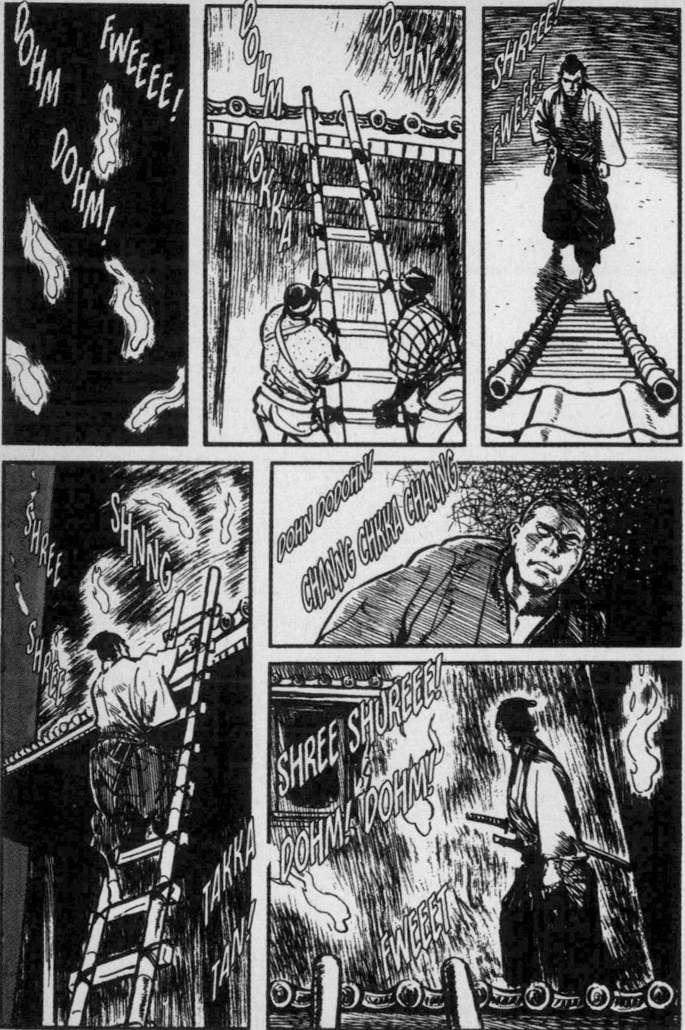
DOHM
FWEEEEE!
DOHM DOHM!
DOHM
DOHN!
DOKKA
SHREEE!
FWEEE!
SHREE
SHNNG
SHREE
SHREE
TAKKA
TAN!
DOHN DODOHN!
CHANNG CHKKA CHANNG
SHREE SHUREEE!
DOHM! DOHM!
FWEEET

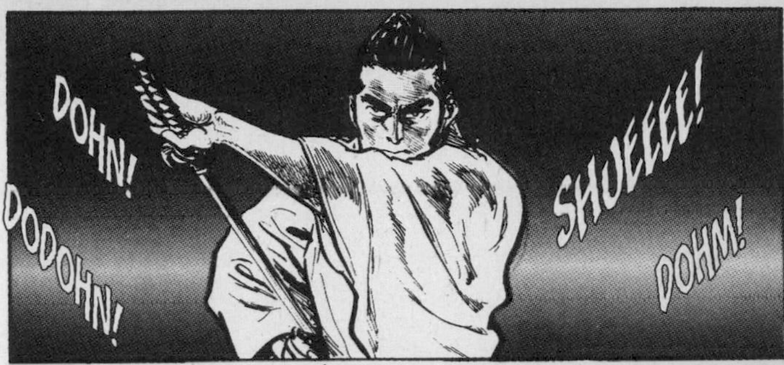
DOHN!
DODOHN!
SHUEEEE!
DOHM!

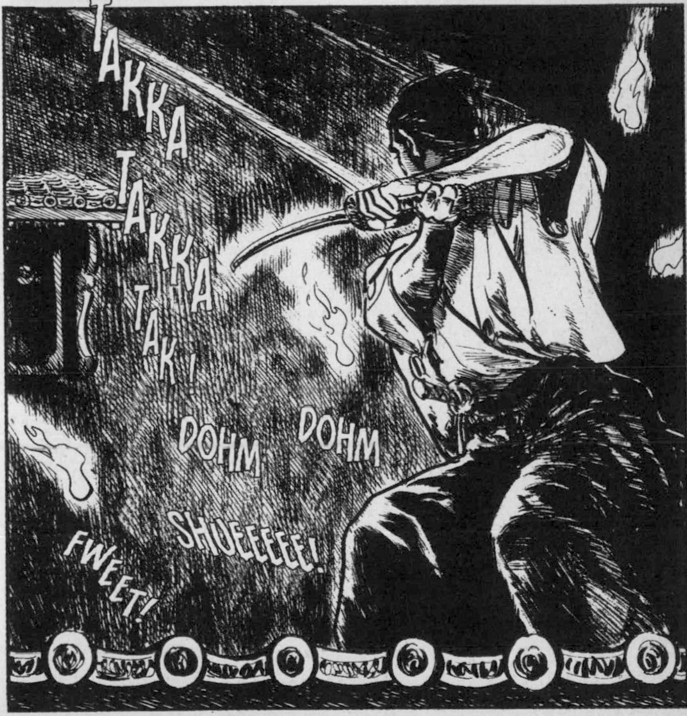
TAKKA TAKKA TAK!
DOHM
DOHM
SHUEEEEEE!
FWEET!

F w s s s s

AH?!

....
....

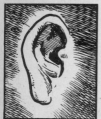

SOMEONE'S *THERE!* ON THE *ROOF!*

SLAMM!!

K'SHAK

CAN'T FOOL ME! I *FEEL* YOU!

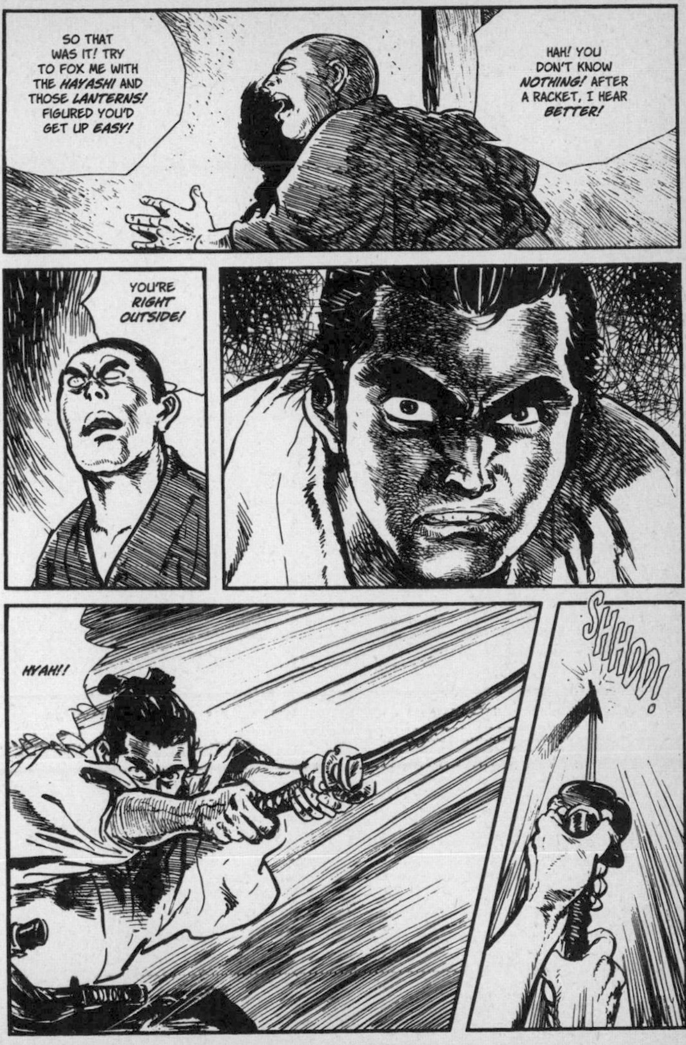
SO THAT WAS IT! TRY TO FOX ME WITH THE *HAYASHI* AND THOSE *LANTERNS!* FIGURED YOU'D GET UP *EASY!*
HAH! YOU DON'T KNOW *NOTHING!* AFTER A RACKET, I HEAR *BETTER!*
YOU'RE *RIGHT OUTSIDE!*
HYAH!!
SHHOO!

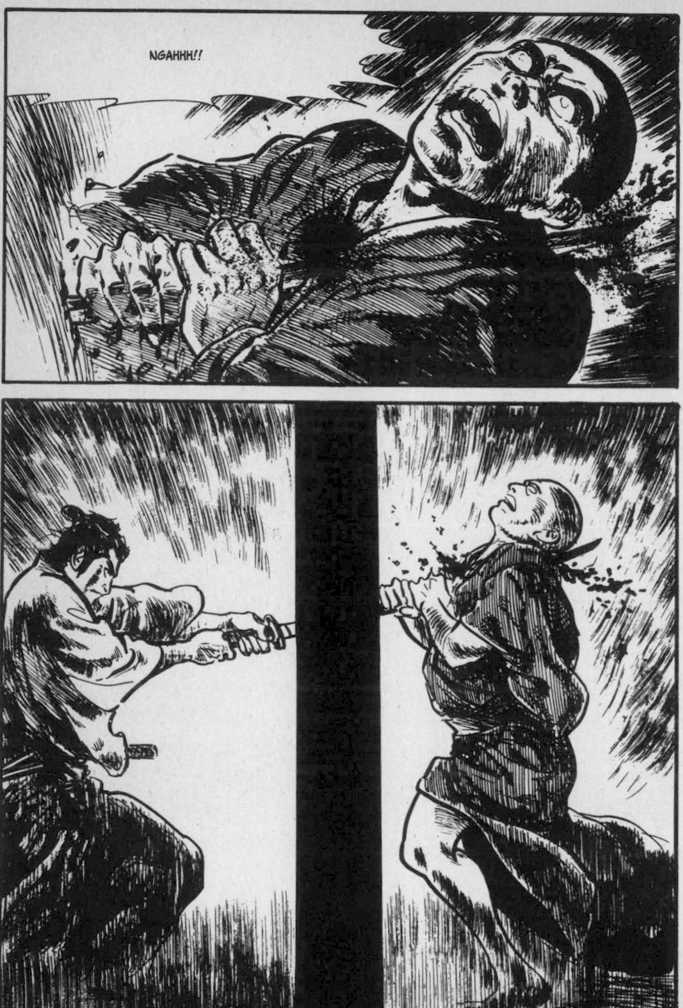
NGAHHH!!

the fourth

Tōshū
Daigongen

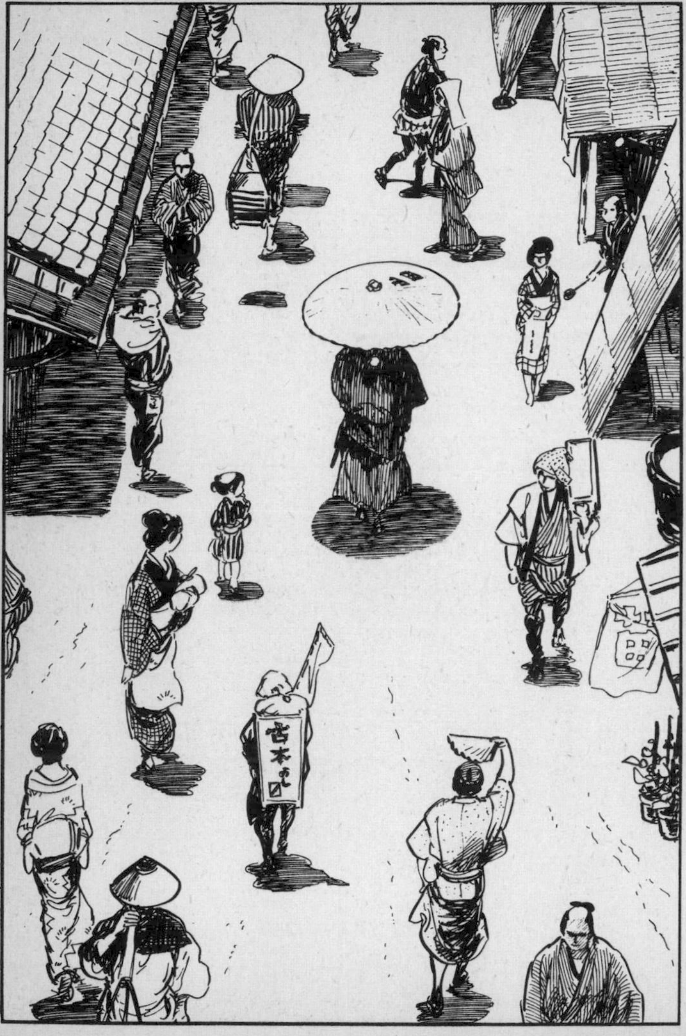

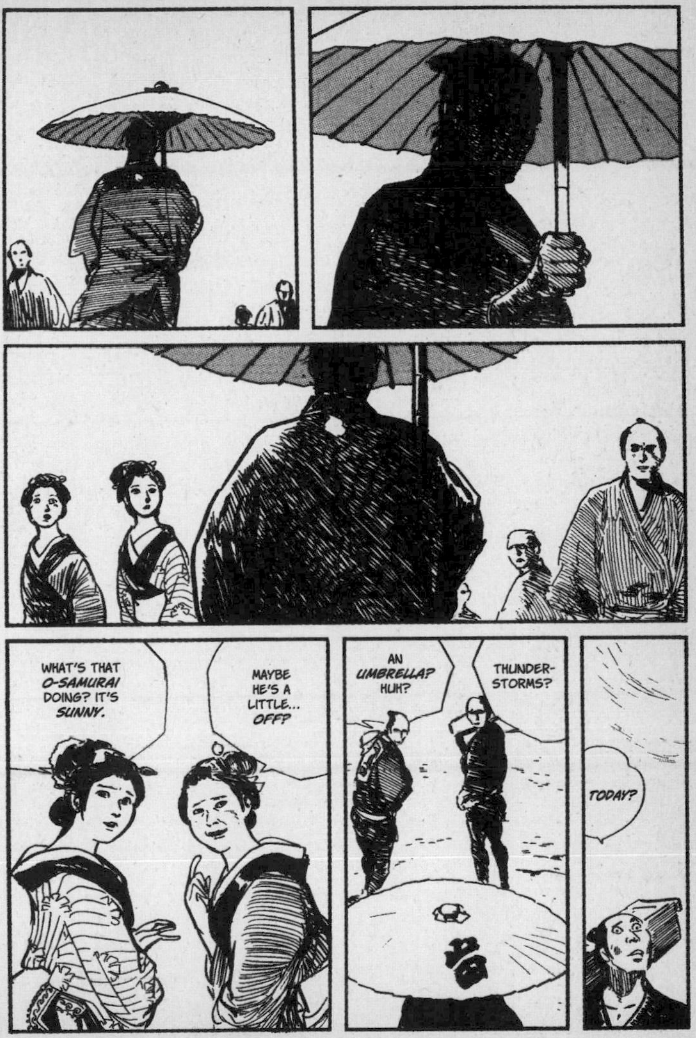
WHAT'S THAT *O-SAMURAI* DOING? IT'S *SUNNY*.
MAYBE HE'S A LITTLE... *OFF?*
AN *UMBRELLA?* HUH?
THUNDER-STORMS?
TODAY?

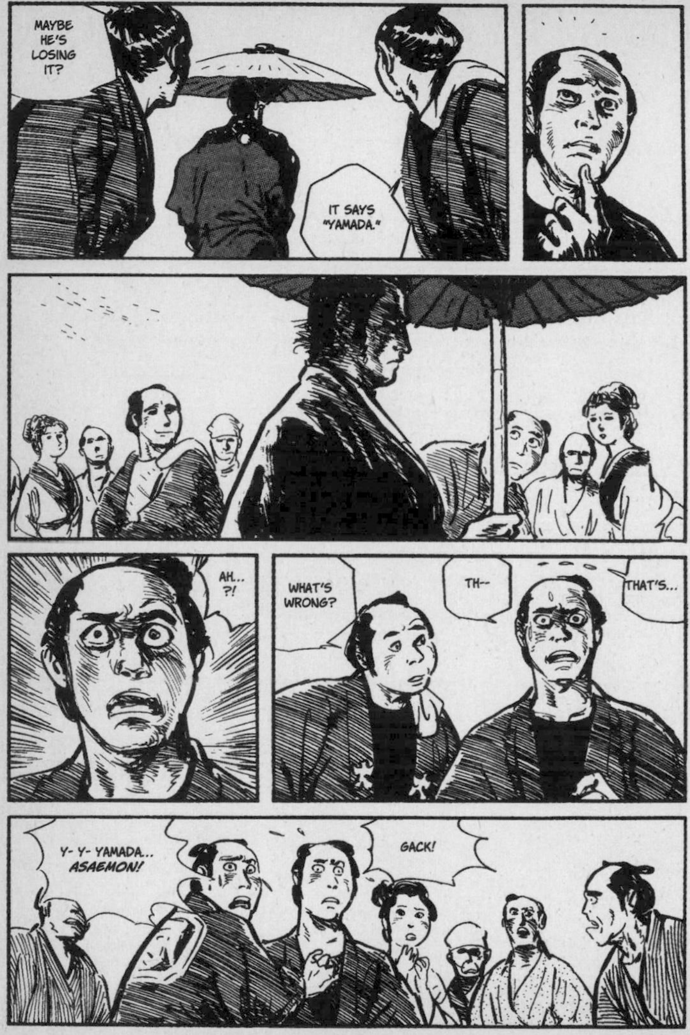
MAYBE HE'S LOSING IT?
IT SAYS "YAMADA."
AH... ?!
WHAT'S WRONG?
TH--
THAT'S...
Y- Y- YAMADA... ***ASAEMON!***
GACK!

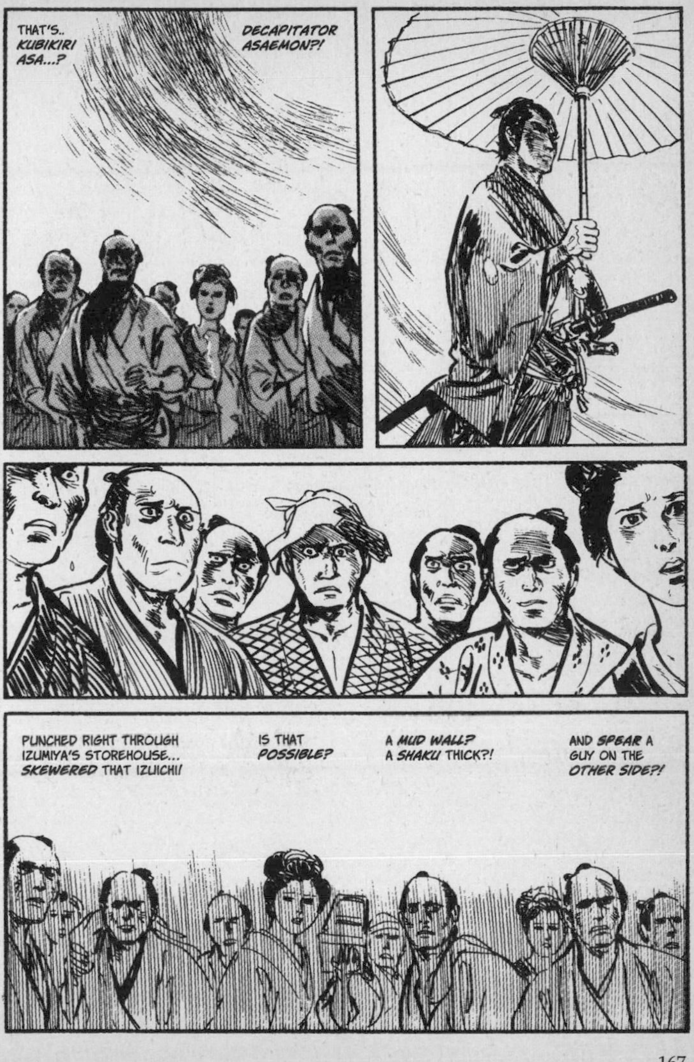
THAT'S.. KUBIKIRI ASA...?
DECAPITATOR ASAEMON?!
PUNCHED RIGHT THROUGH IZUMIYA'S STOREHOUSE... SKEWERED THAT IZUICHI!
IS THAT POSSIBLE?
A MUD WALL? A SHAKU THICK?!
AND SPEAR A GUY ON THE OTHER SIDE?!

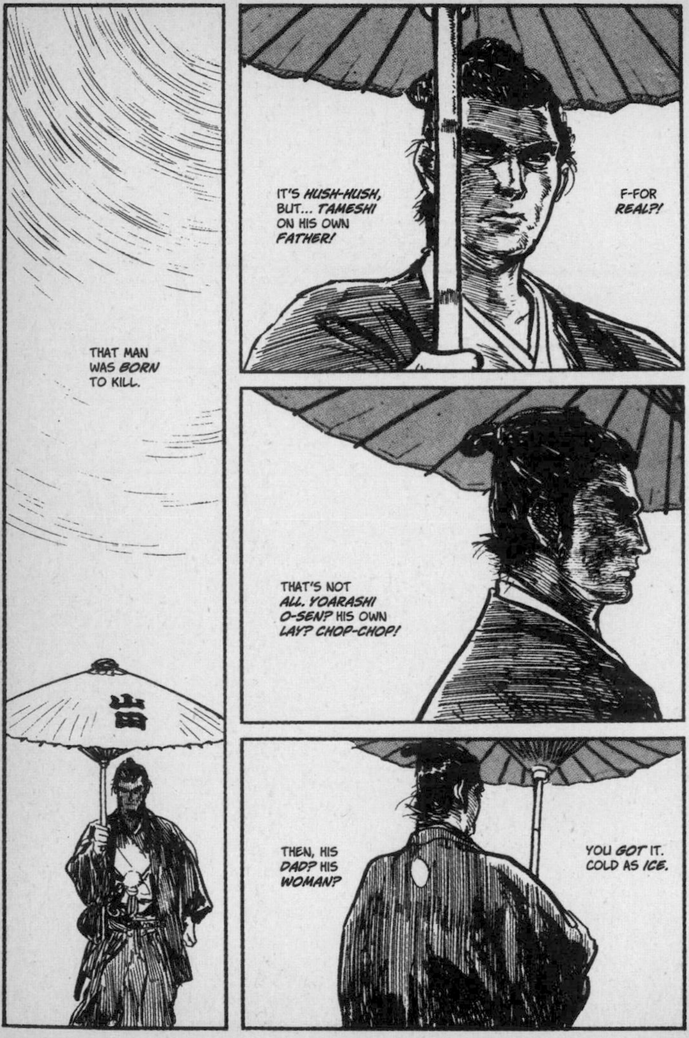
THAT MAN WAS *BORN* TO KILL.
山田
IT'S *HUSH-HUSH*, BUT... *TAMESHI* ON HIS OWN *FATHER!*
F-FOR *REAL?!*
THAT'S NOT *ALL. YOARASHI O-SEN?* HIS OWN *LAY? CHOP-CHOP!*
THEN, HIS *DAD?* HIS *WOMAN?*
YOU *GOT* IT. COLD AS *ICE.*

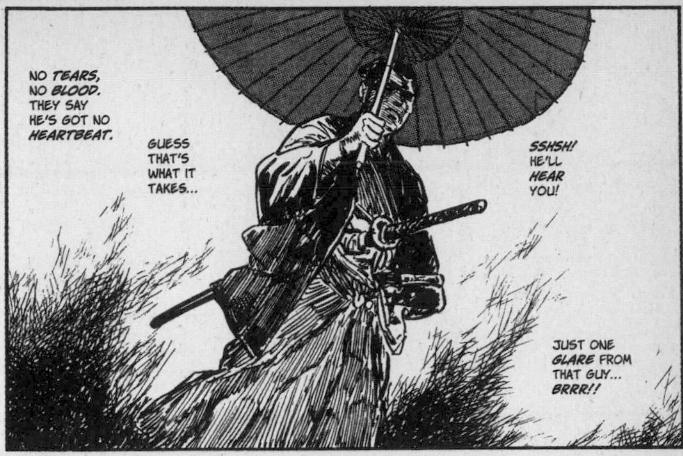
NO *TEARS,* NO *BLOOD.* THEY SAY HE'S GOT NO *HEARTBEAT.*
GUESS THAT'S WHAT IT TAKES...
SSHSH! HE'LL *HEAR* YOU!
JUST ONE *GLARE* FROM THAT GUY... *BRRR!!*

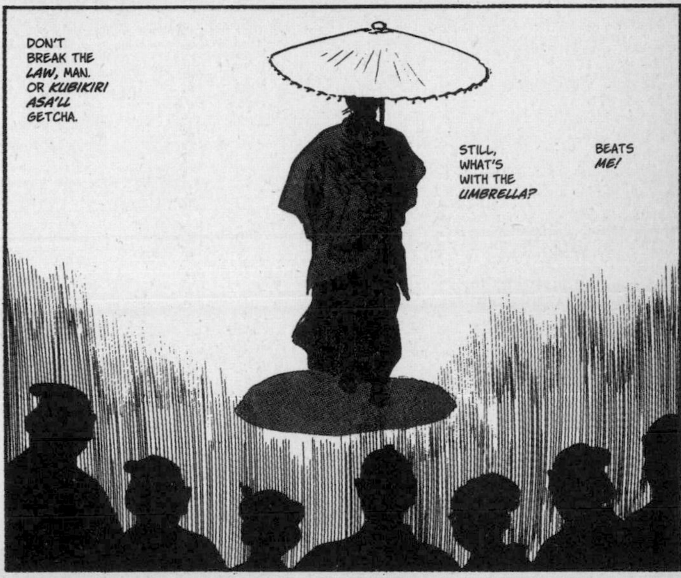
DON'T BREAK THE *LAW,* MAN. OR *KUBIKIRI ASA'LL* GETCHA.
STILL, WHAT'S WITH THE *UMBRELLA?*
BEATS *ME!*

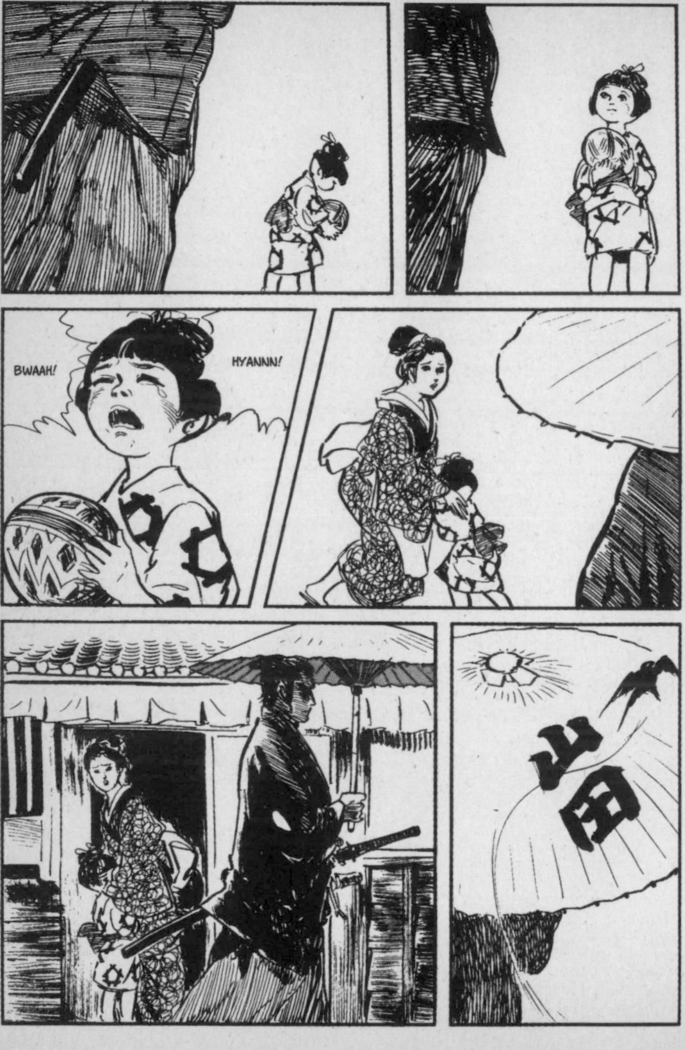
BWAAH!
HYANNN!
山田

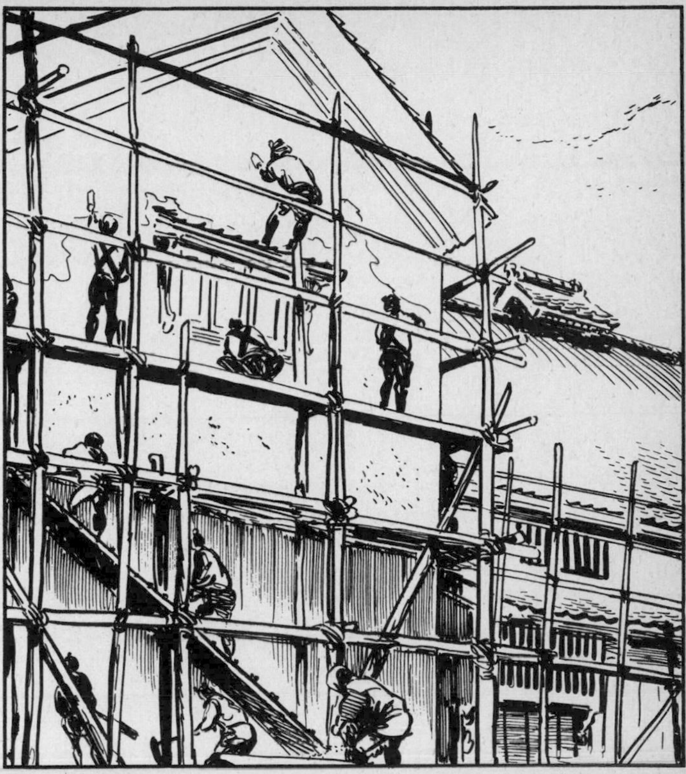
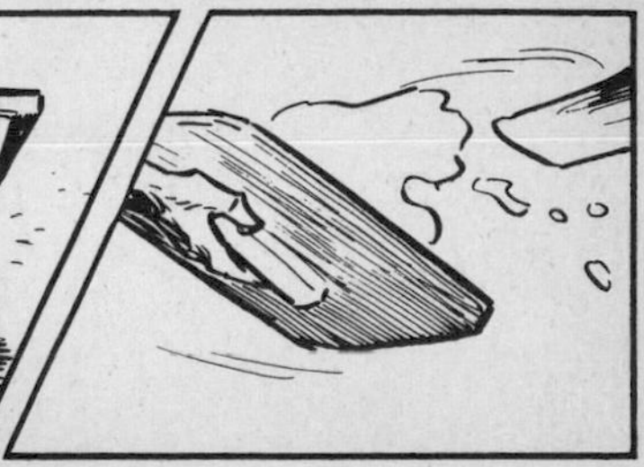
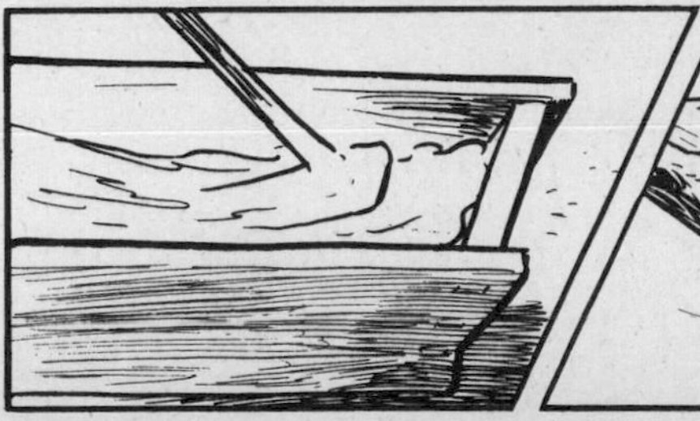

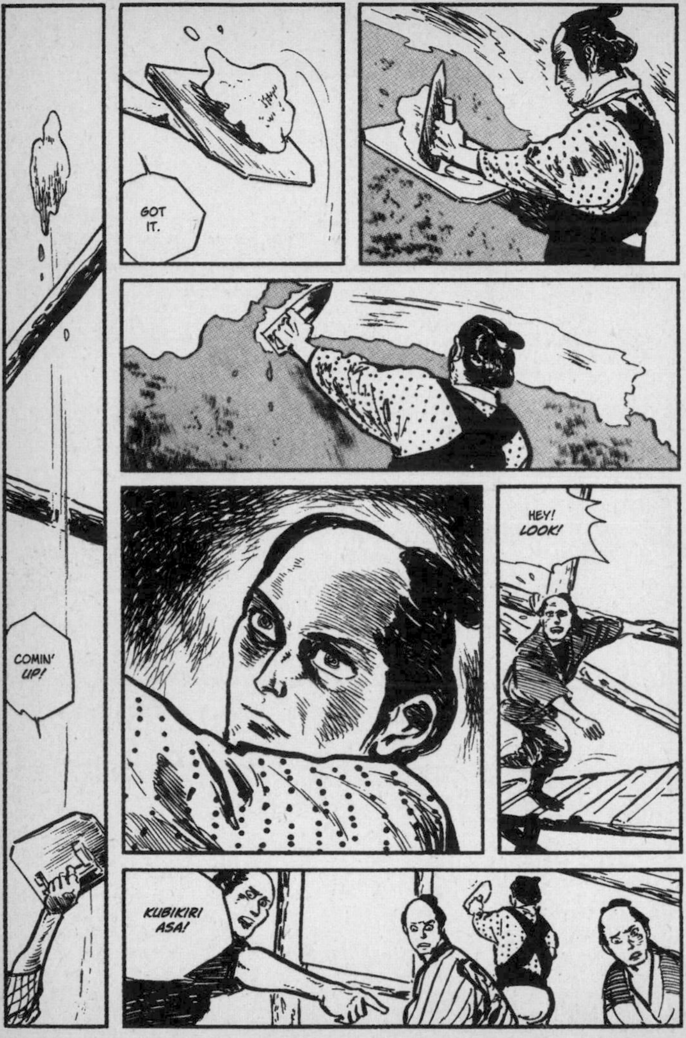
COMIN' UP!
GOT IT.
HEY! LOOK!
KUBIKIRI ASA!

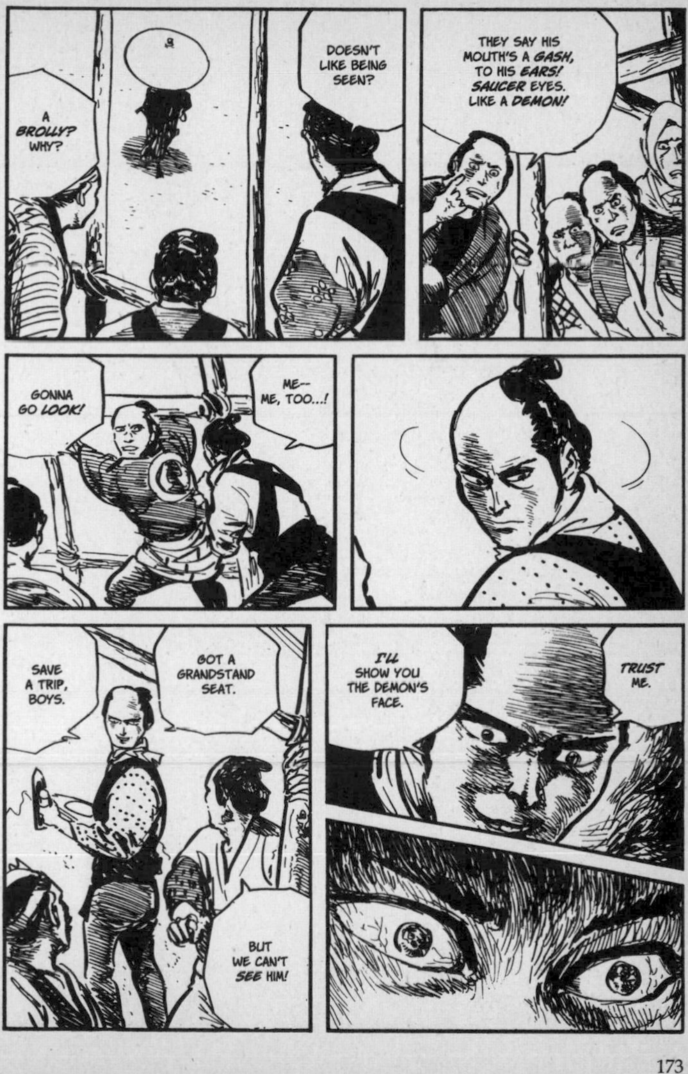
A BROLLY? WHY?
DOESN'T LIKE BEING SEEN?
THEY SAY HIS MOUTH'S A GASH, TO HIS EARS! SAUCER EYES. LIKE A DEMON!
GONNA GO LOOK!
ME-- ME, TOO...!
SAVE A TRIP, BOYS.
GOT A GRANDSTAND SEAT.
BUT WE CAN'T SEE HIM!
I'LL SHOW YOU THE DEMON'S FACE.
TRUST ME.

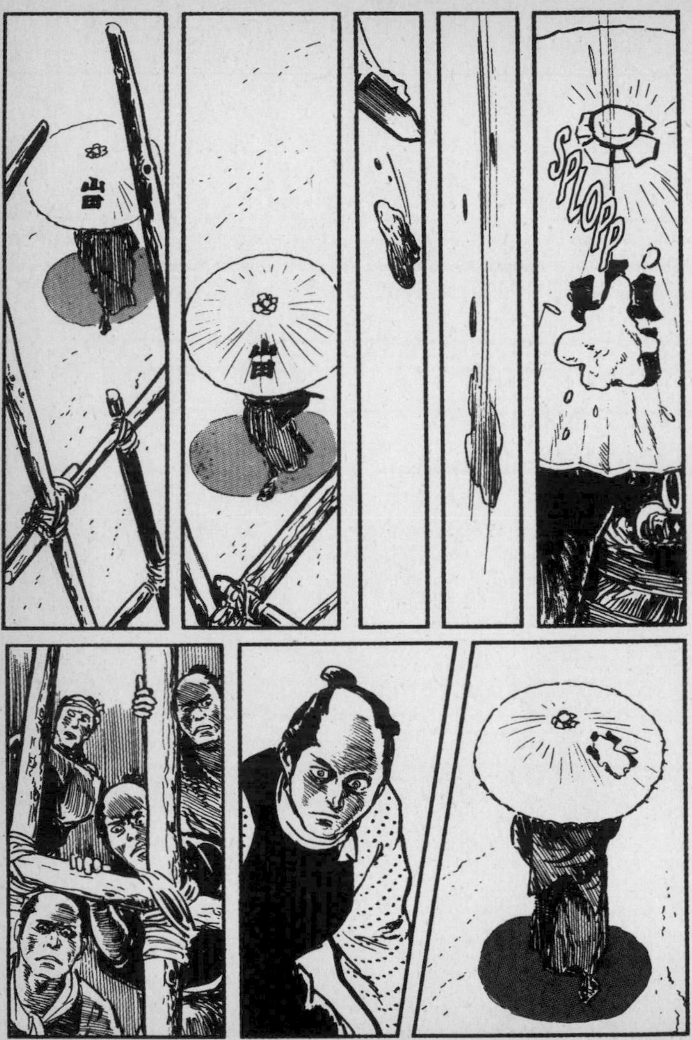
SPLOPP

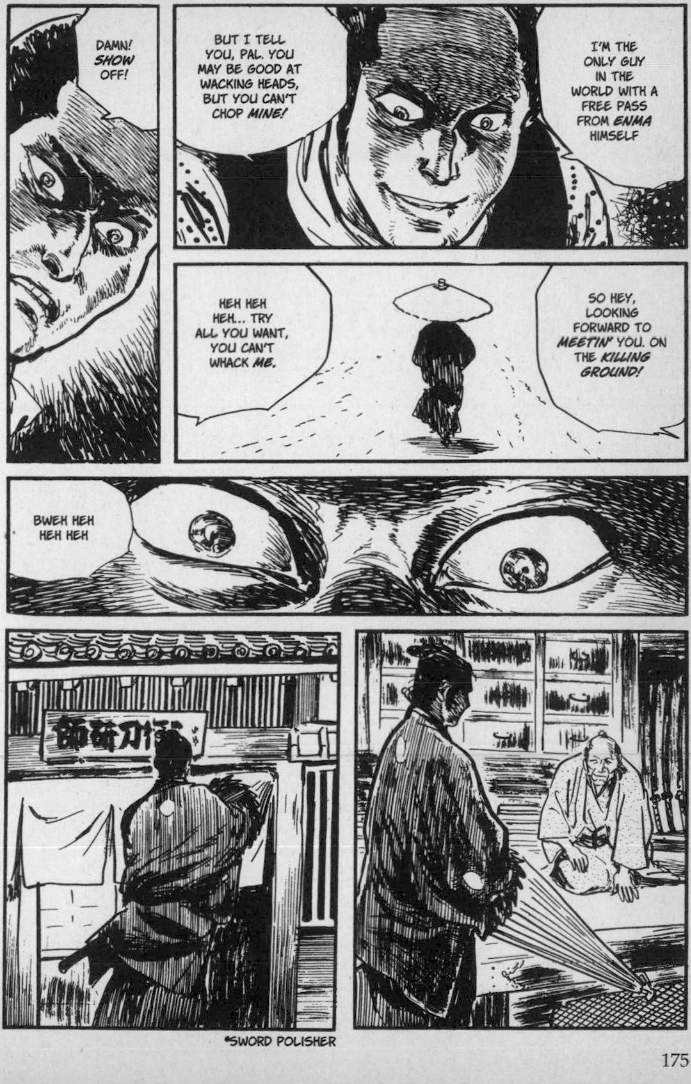
DAMN! *SHOW* OFF!
BUT I TELL YOU, PAL. YOU MAY BE GOOD AT WACKING HEADS, BUT YOU CAN'T CHOP *MINE!*
I'M THE ONLY GUY IN THE WORLD WITH A FREE PASS FROM *ENMA* HIMSELF
HEH HEH HEH... TRY ALL YOU WANT, YOU CAN'T WHACK *ME.*
SO HEY, LOOKING FORWARD TO *MEETIN'* YOU. ON THE *KILLING GROUND!*
BWEH HEH HEH HEH

*SWORD POLISHER

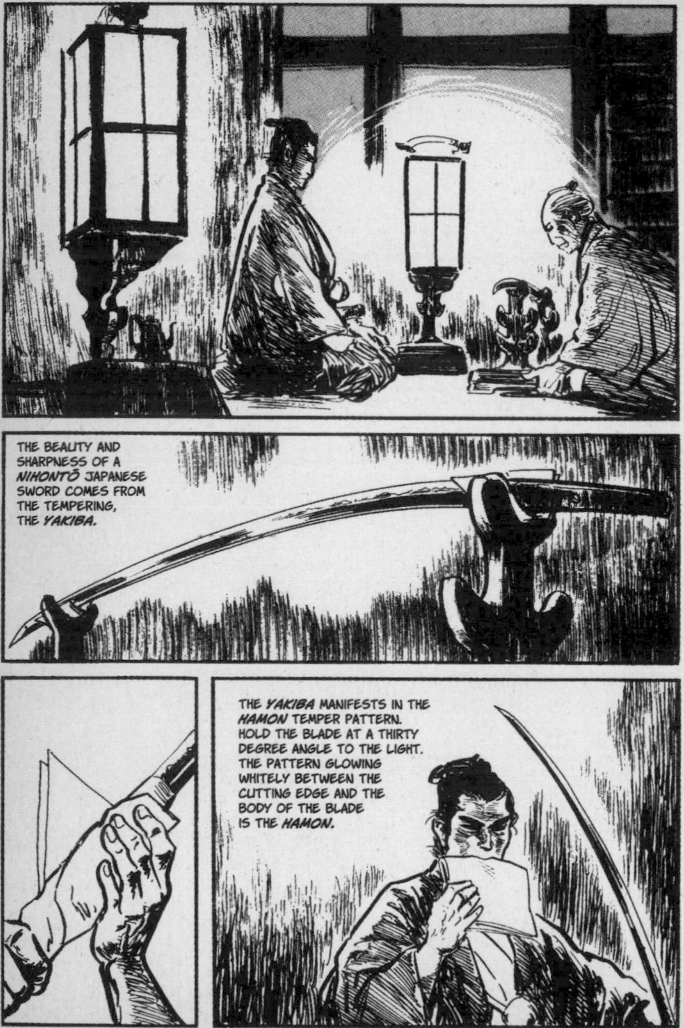
THE BEAUTY AND SHARPNESS OF A *NIHONTŌ* JAPANESE SWORD COMES FROM THE TEMPERING, THE *YAKIBA.*
THE *YAKIBA* MANIFESTS IN THE *HAMON* TEMPER PATTERN. HOLD THE BLADE AT A THIRTY DEGREE ANGLE TO THE LIGHT. THE PATTERN GLOWING WHITELY BETWEEN THE CUTTING EDGE AND THE BODY OF THE BLADE IS THE *HAMON.*

WERE YOU TO ENLARGE THE *HAMON* 150 TIMES OVER, YOU WOULD SEE IT'S MADE UP OF LARGE AND SMALL GRAINS.

THE LARGE GRAINS, *NIE,* CAN BE SEEN WITH THE NAKED EYE. THOSE TOO SMALL TO SEE ARE *NIOI.* THE GLOWING SECTION IS MARTENSITE STEEL, THE DARK PORTION TROOSTITE.

MARTENSITE IS HARD, TROOSTITE COMPARATIVELY SOFT. WHEN A SWORD IS POLISHED, RUBBED HUNDREDS OF TIMES, THE TROOSTITE WEARS AWAY, BUT THE MARTENSITE REMAINS.

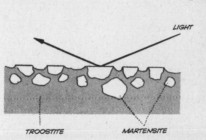

LIGHT

TROOSTITE

MARTENSITE

THIS DEFRACTS THE LIGHT, CAUSING THAT GLOW, CREATING THE *HAMON.*

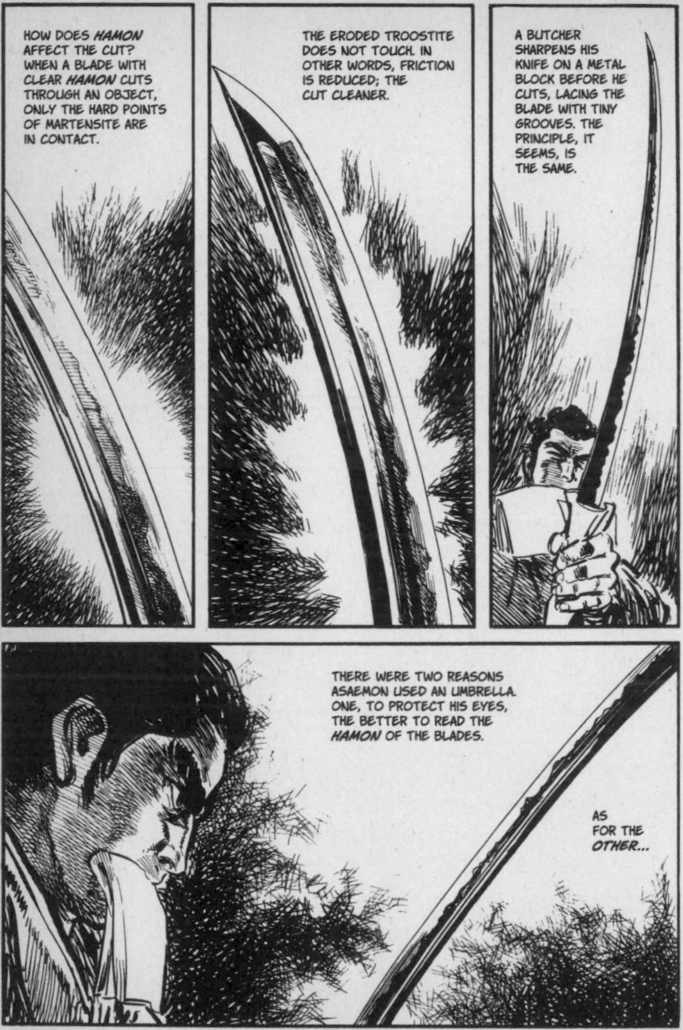
HOW DOES *HAMON* AFFECT THE CUT? WHEN A BLADE WITH CLEAR *HAMON* CUTS THROUGH AN OBJECT, ONLY THE HARD POINTS OF MARTENSITE ARE IN CONTACT.
THE ERODED TROOSTITE DOES NOT TOUCH. IN OTHER WORDS, FRICTION IS REDUCED; THE CUT CLEANER.
A BUTCHER SHARPENS HIS KNIFE ON A METAL BLOCK BEFORE HE CUTS, LACING THE BLADE WITH TINY GROOVES. THE PRINCIPLE, IT SEEMS, IS THE SAME.
THERE WERE TWO REASONS ASAEMON USED AN UMBRELLA. ONE, TO PROTECT HIS EYES, THE BETTER TO READ THE *HAMON* OF THE BLADES.
AS FOR THE *OTHER*...

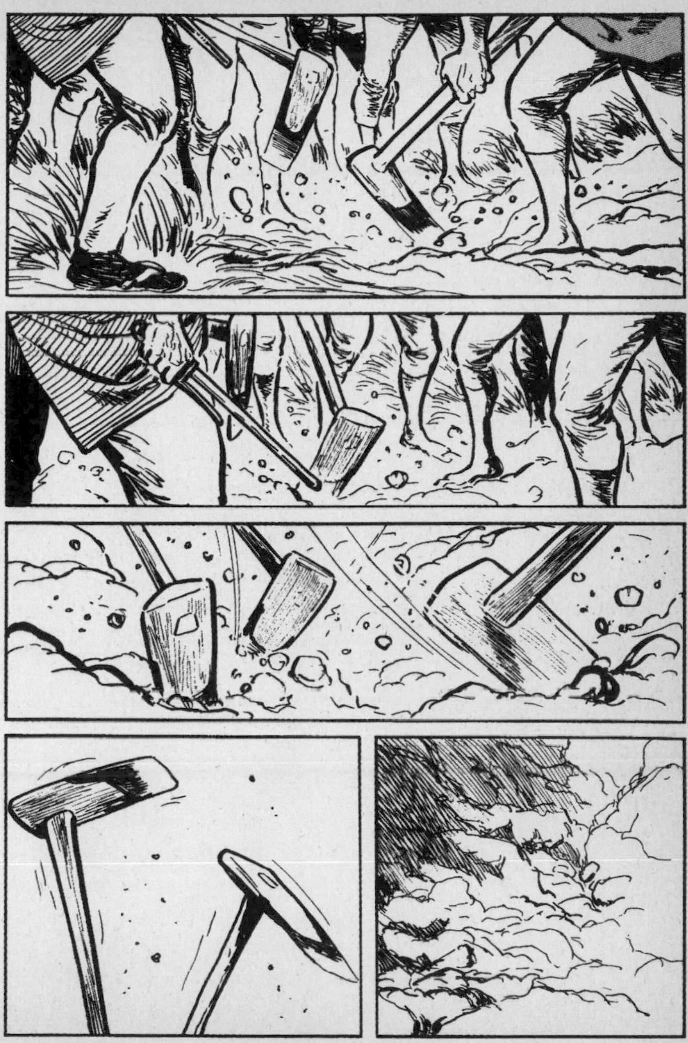

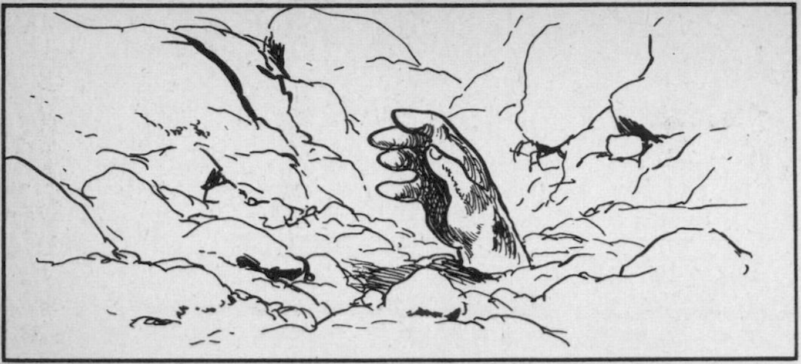

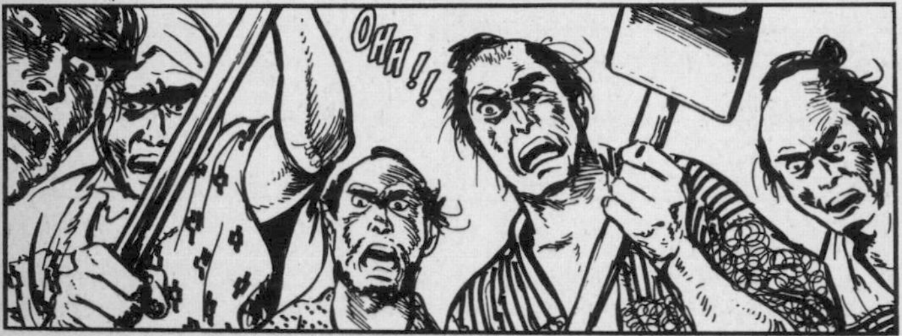
OHH!!

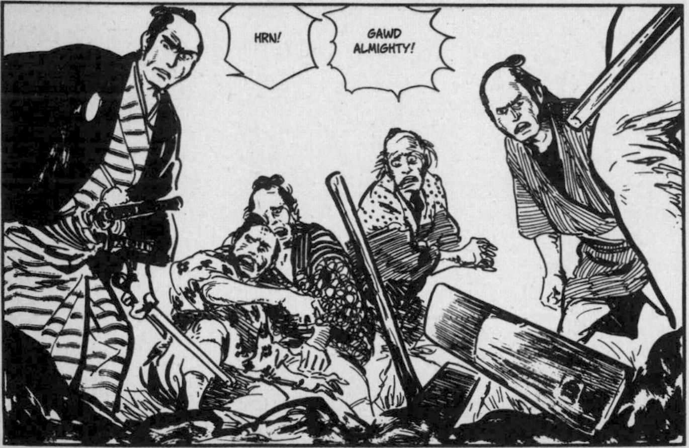
HRN!
GAWD ALMIGHTY!

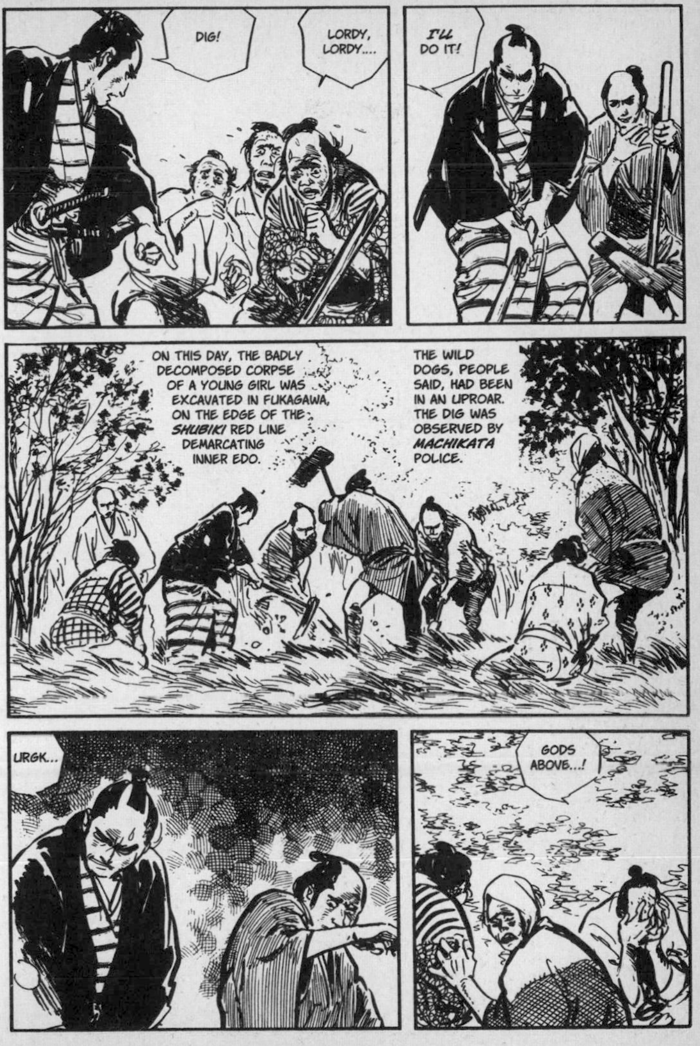
DIG!
LORDY, LORDY....
I'LL DO IT!
ON THIS DAY, THE BADLY DECOMPOSED CORPSE OF A YOUNG GIRL WAS EXCAVATED IN FUKAGAWA, ON THE EDGE OF THE *SHUBIKI* RED LINE DEMARCATING INNER EDO.
THE WILD DOGS, PEOPLE SAID, HAD BEEN IN AN UPROAR. THE DIG WAS OBSERVED BY *MACHIKATA* POLICE.
URGK...
GODS ABOVE...!

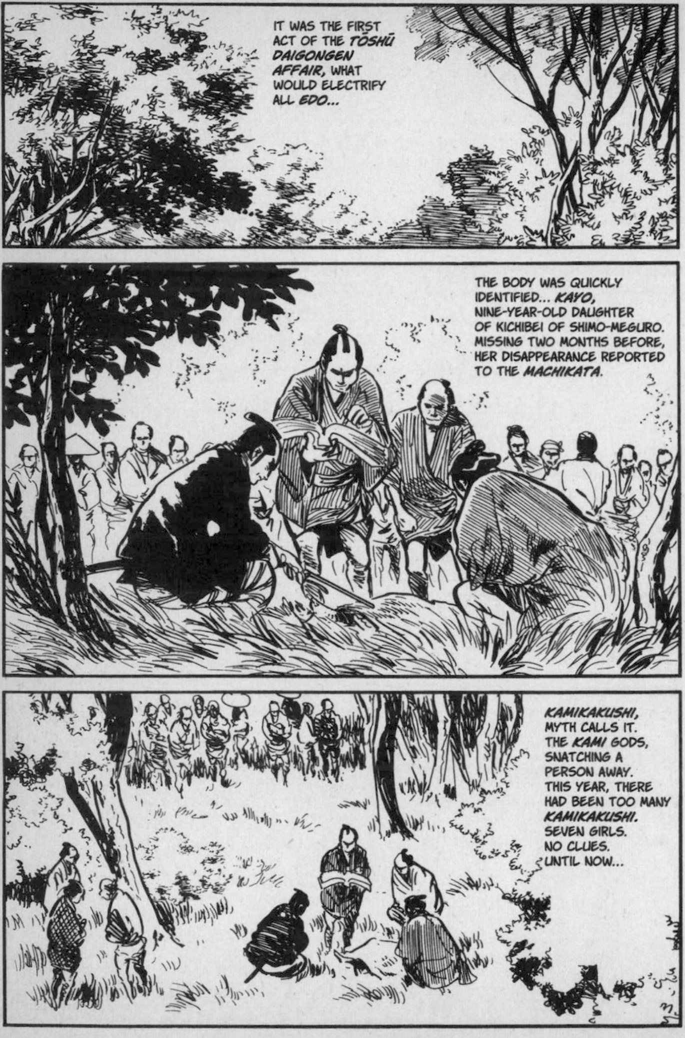
IT WAS THE FIRST ACT OF THE *TŌSHŪ DAIGONGEN AFFAIR,* WHAT WOULD ELECTRIFY ALL *EDO...*
THE BODY WAS QUICKLY IDENTIFIED... *KAYO,* NINE-YEAR-OLD DAUGHTER OF KICHIBEI OF SHIMO-MEGURO. MISSING TWO MONTHS BEFORE, HER DISAPPEARANCE REPORTED TO THE *MACHIKATA.*
KAMIKAKUSHI, MYTH CALLS IT. THE *KAMI* GODS, SNATCHING A PERSON AWAY. THIS YEAR, THERE HAD BEEN TOO MANY *KAMIKAKUSHI.* SEVEN GIRLS. NO CLUES. UNTIL NOW...

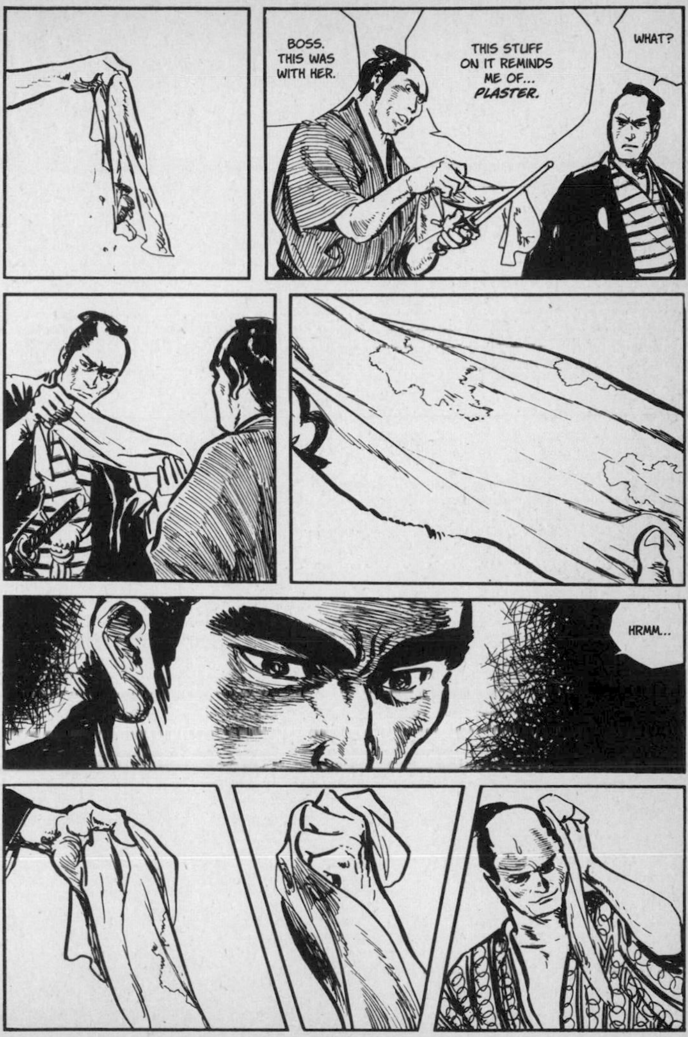
BOSS. THIS WAS WITH HER.
THIS STUFF ON IT REMINDS ME OF... *PLASTER.*
WHAT?
HRMM...

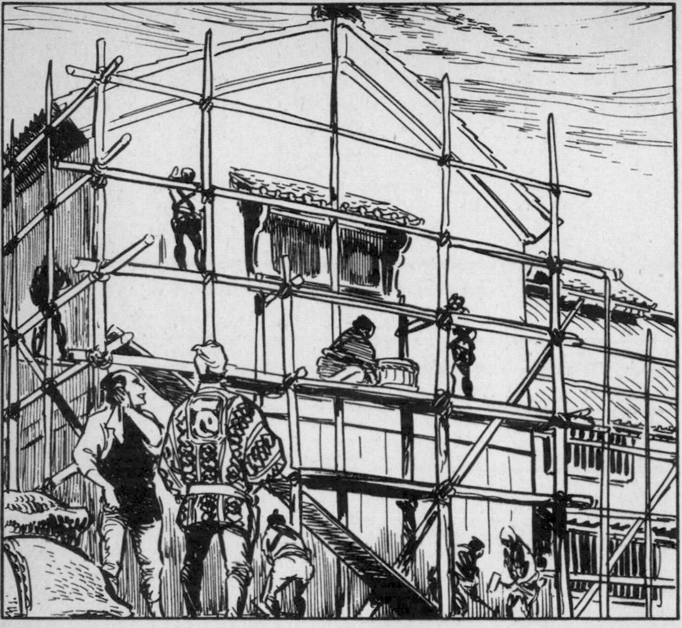

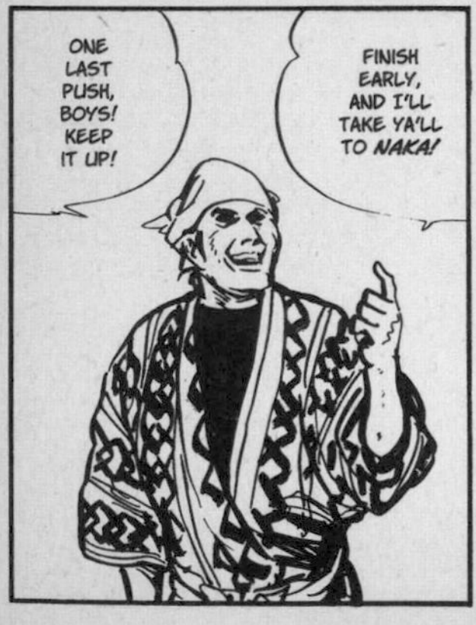
ONE LAST PUSH, BOYS! KEEP IT UP!
FINISH EARLY, AND I'LL TAKE YA'LL TO *NAKA!*

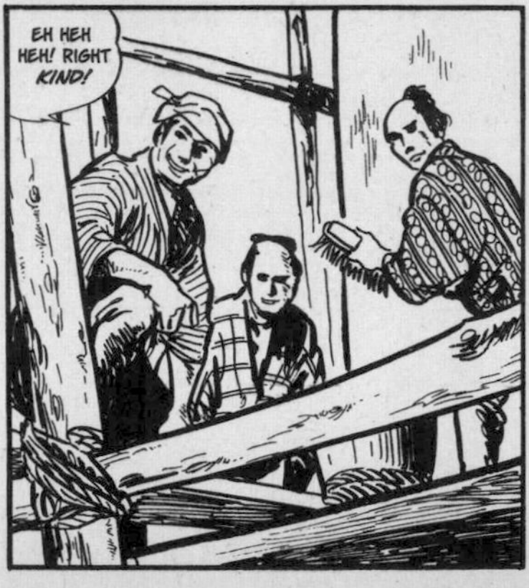
EH HEH HEH! RIGHT *KIND!*

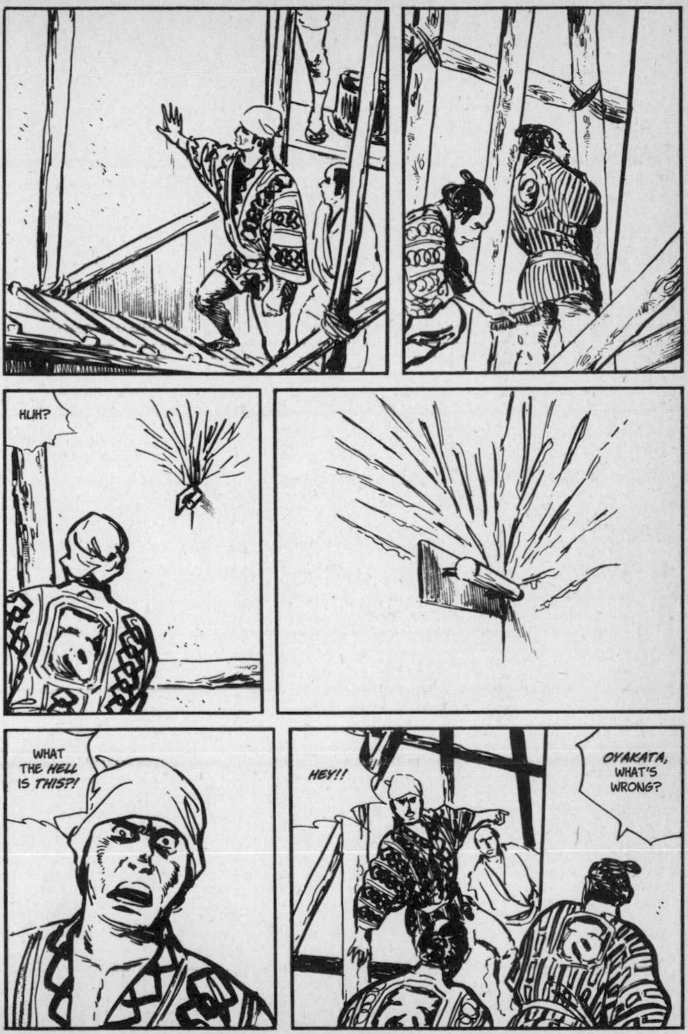
HUH?
WHAT THE *HELL* IS *THIS?!*
HEY!!
OYAKATA, WHAT'S WRONG?

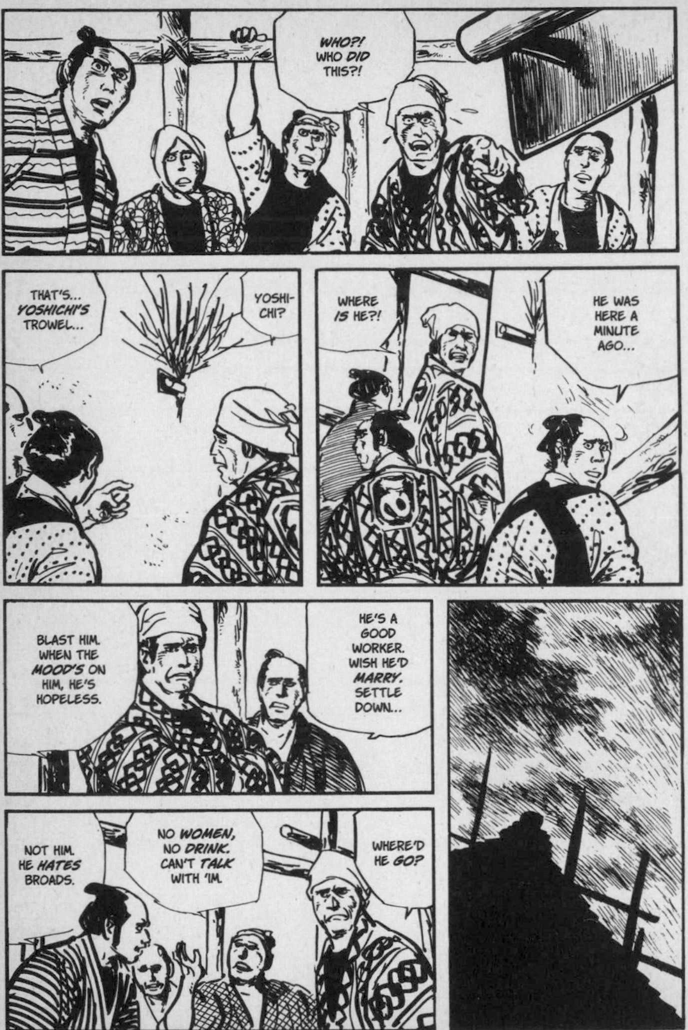
WHO?! WHO DID THIS?!
THAT'S... YOSHICHI'S TROWEL...
YOSHI-CHI?
WHERE IS HE?!
HE WAS HERE A MINUTE AGO...
BLAST HIM. WHEN THE MOOD'S ON HIM, HE'S HOPELESS.
HE'S A GOOD WORKER. WISH HE'D MARRY. SETTLE DOWN...
NOT HIM. HE HATES BROADS.
NO WOMEN, NO DRINK. CAN'T TALK WITH 'IM.
WHERE'D HE GO?

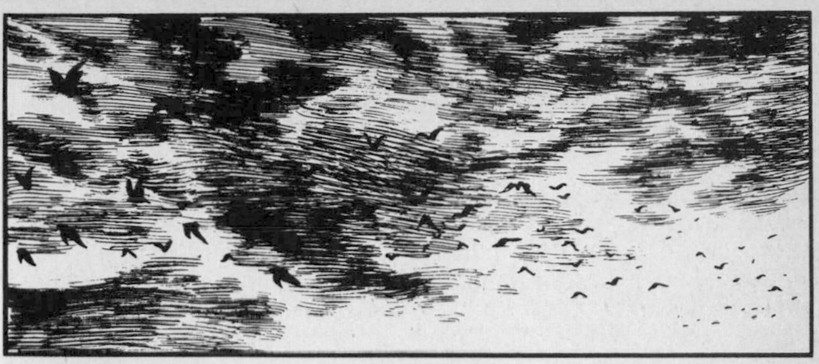

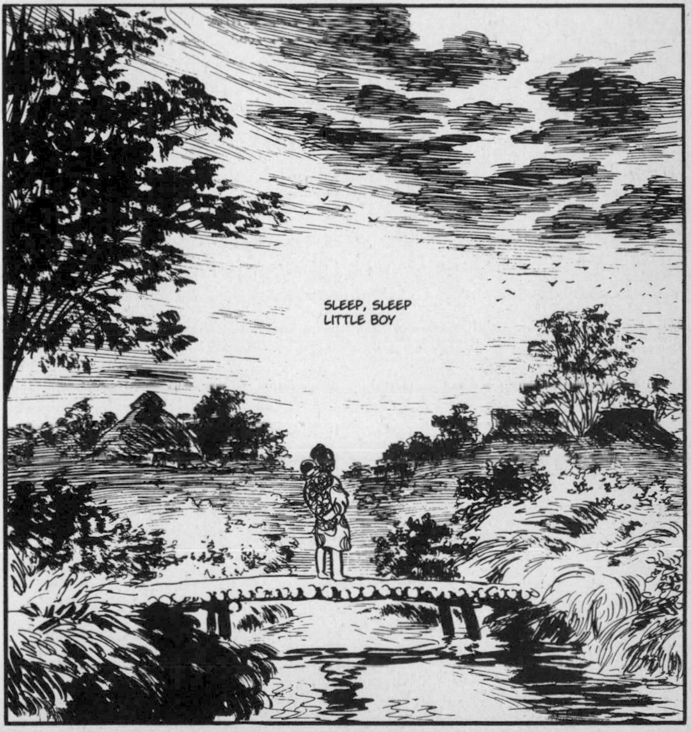
SLEEP, SLEEP
LITTLE BOY

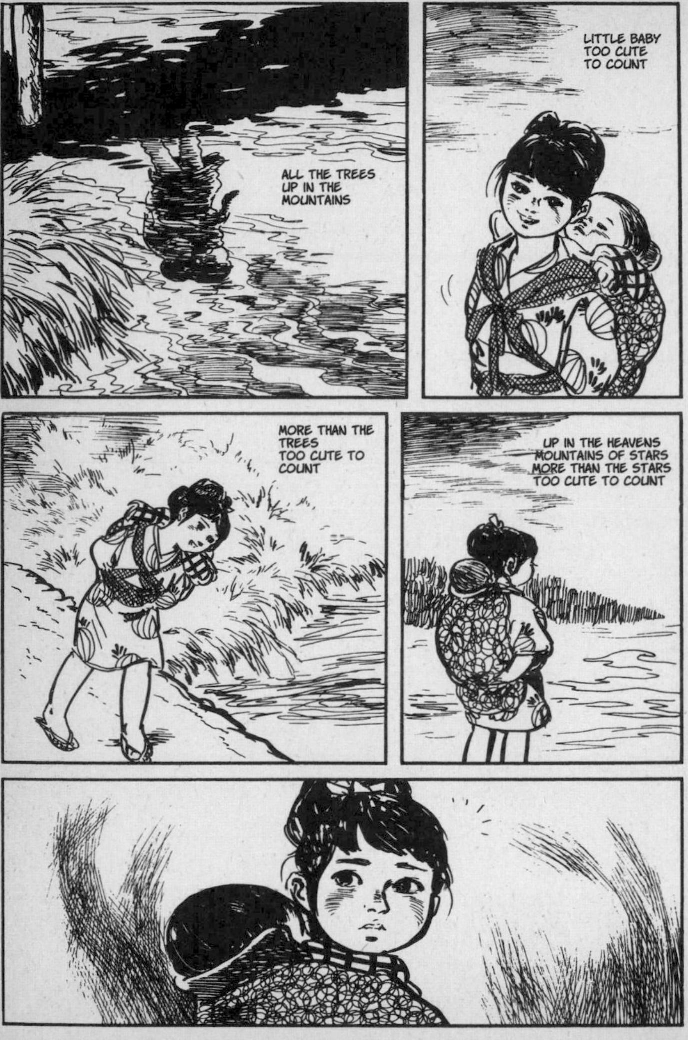
ALL THE TREES
UP IN THE
MOUNTAINS
LITTLE BABY
TOO CUTE
TO COUNT
MORE THAN THE
TREES
TOO CUTE TO
COUNT
UP IN THE HEAVENS
MOUNTAINS OF STARS
MORE THAN THE STARS
TOO CUTE TO COUNT

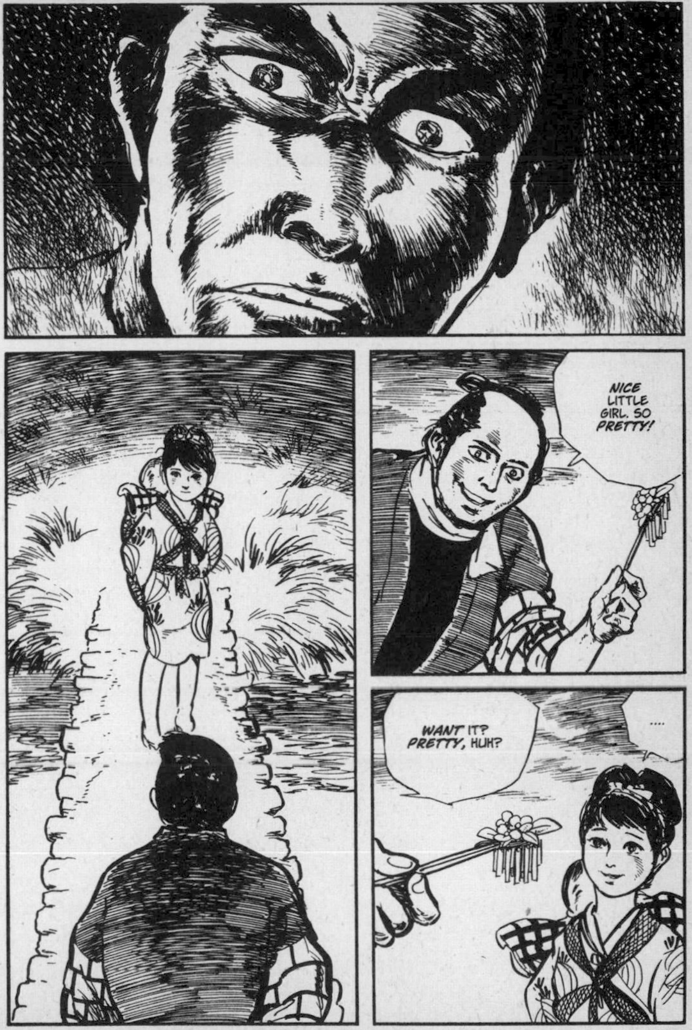
NICE LITTLE GIRL. SO PRETTY!
WANT IT? PRETTY, HUH?
....

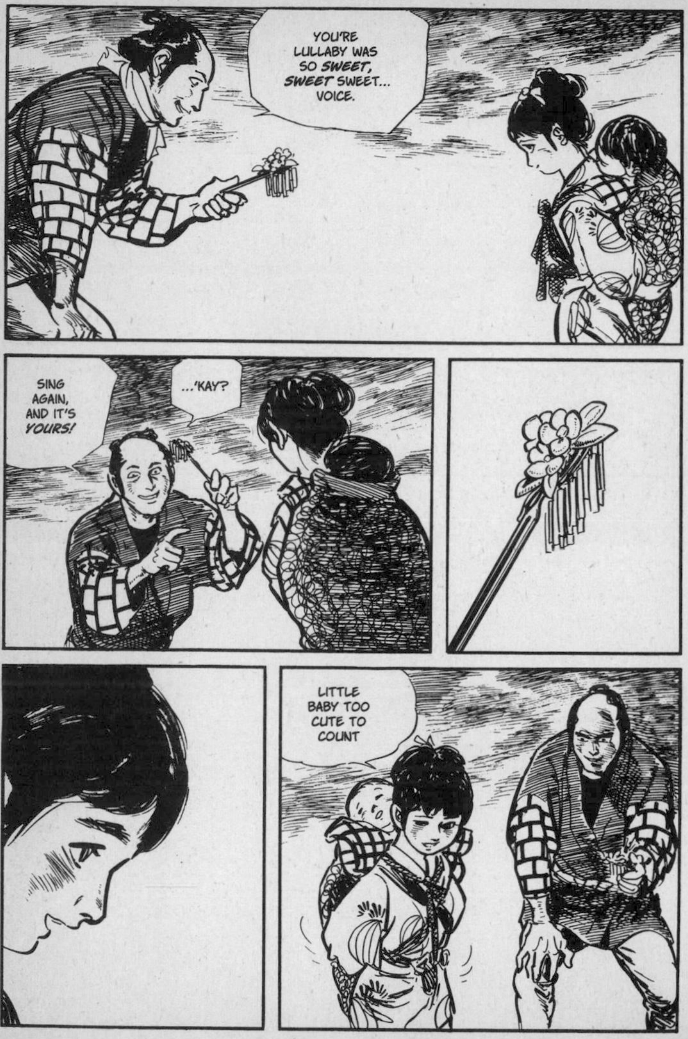
YOU'RE LULLABY WAS SO *SWEET*, *SWEET* SWEET... VOICE.
SING AGAIN, AND IT'S *YOURS!*
...'KAY?
LITTLE BABY TOO CUTE TO COUNT

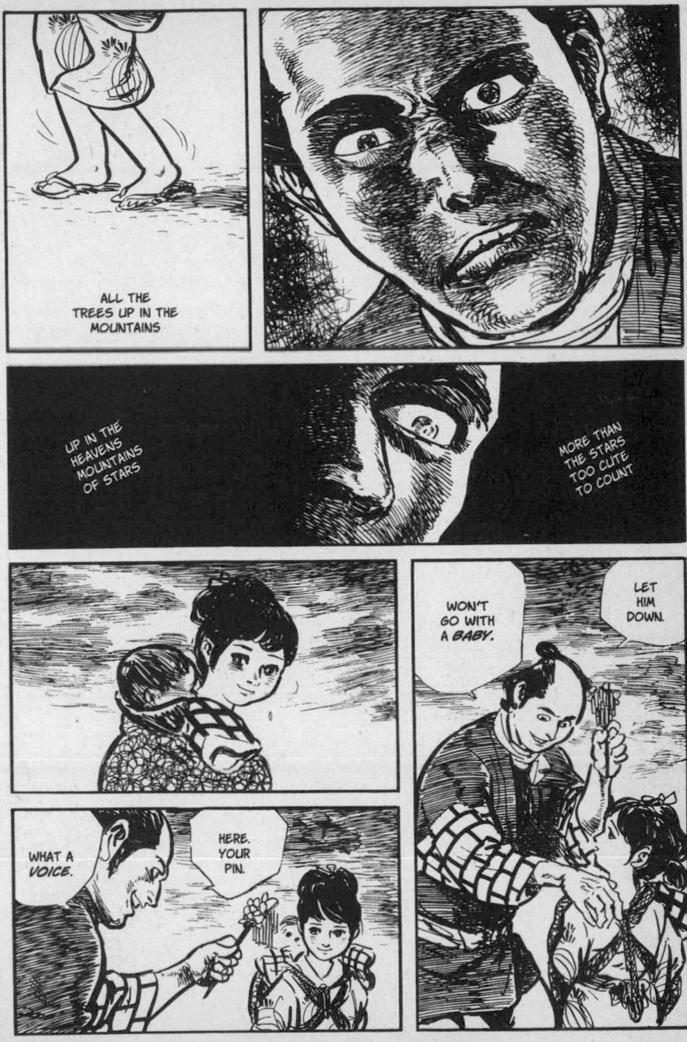
ALL THE TREES UP IN THE MOUNTAINS
UP IN THE HEAVENS MOUNTAINS OF STARS
MORE THAN THE STARS TOO CUTE TO COUNT
WHAT A *VOICE.*
HERE. YOUR PIN.
WON'T GO WITH A *BABY.*
LET HIM DOWN.

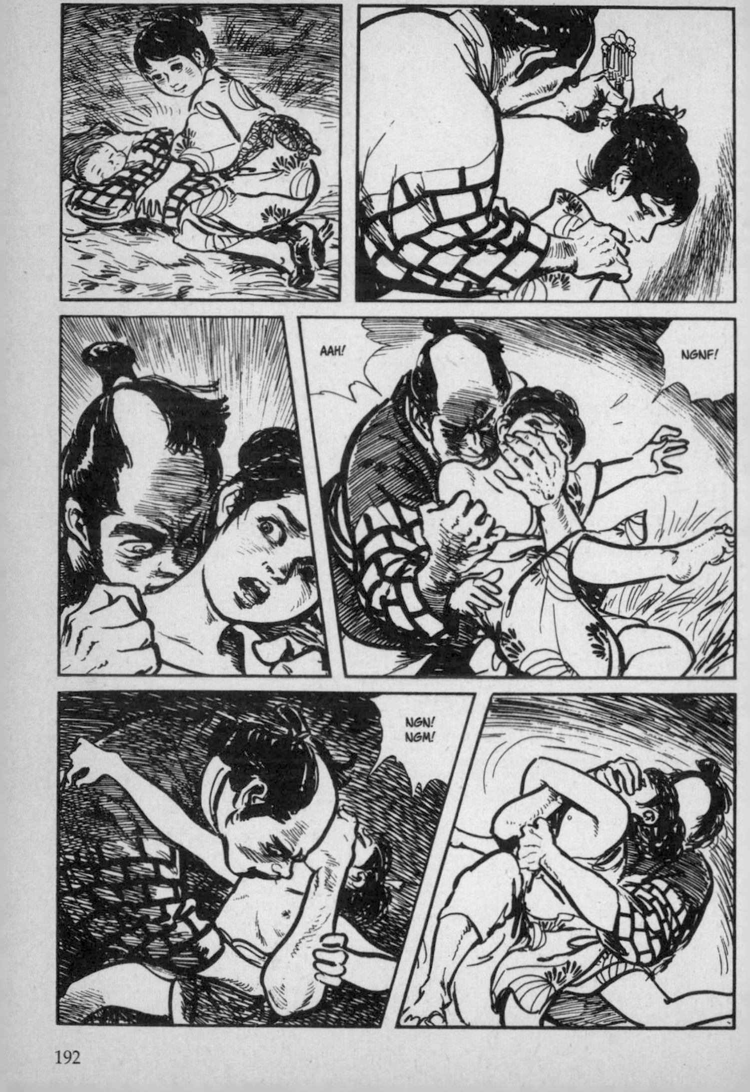
AAH!
NGNF!
NGN!
NGM!

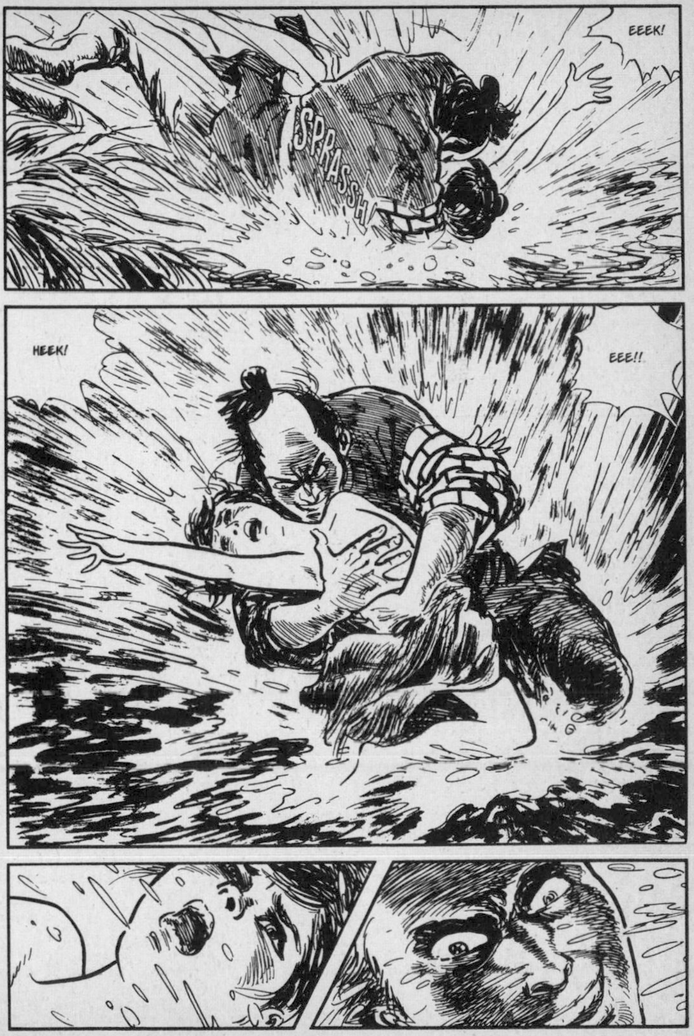

SPRASSH!
EEEK!
HEEK!
EEE!!

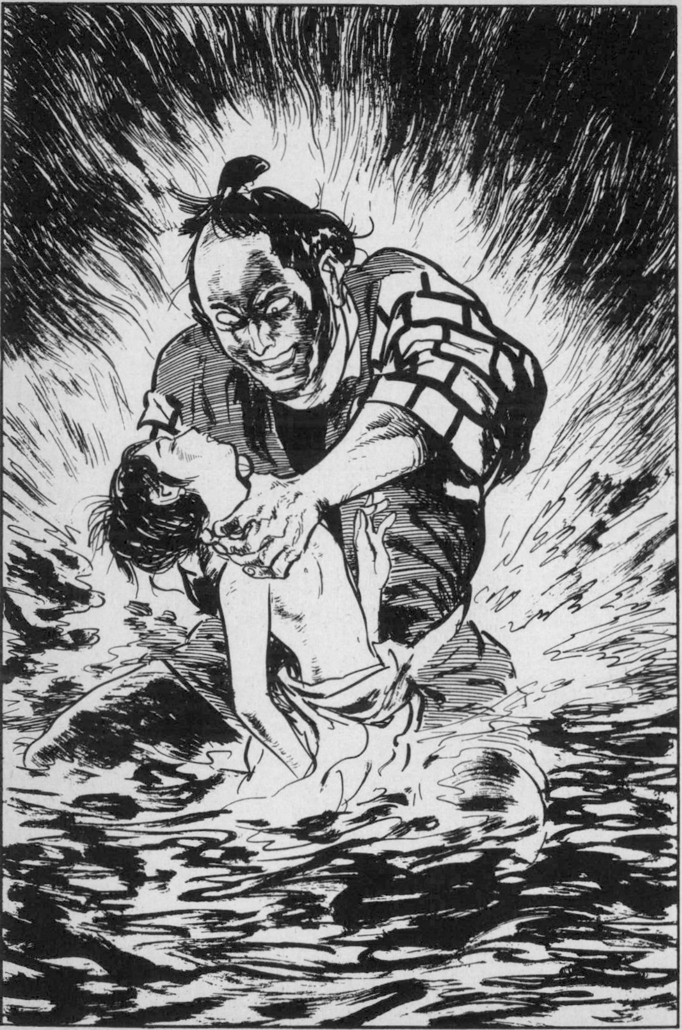

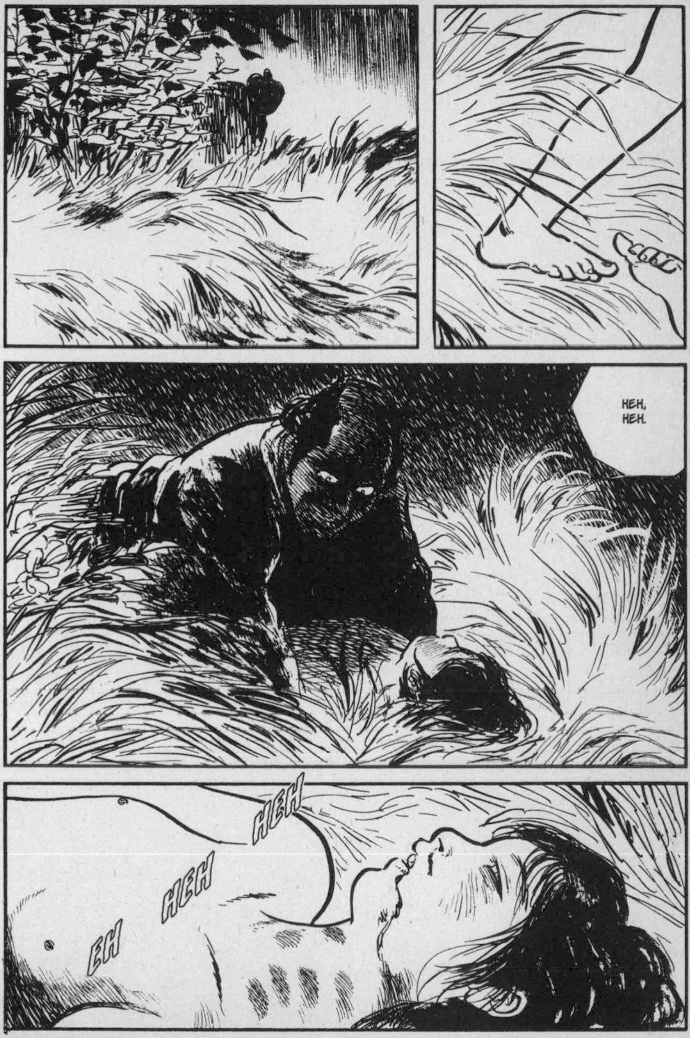
HEH, HEH.
HEH
HEH
EH

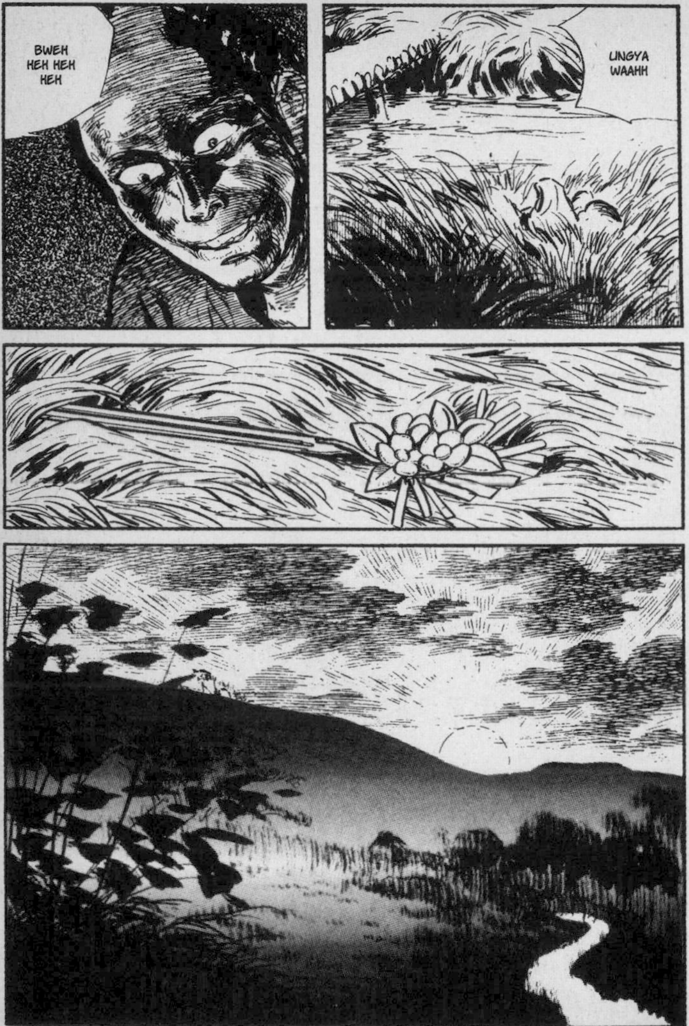
BWEH HEH HEH HEH
UNGYA WAAHH

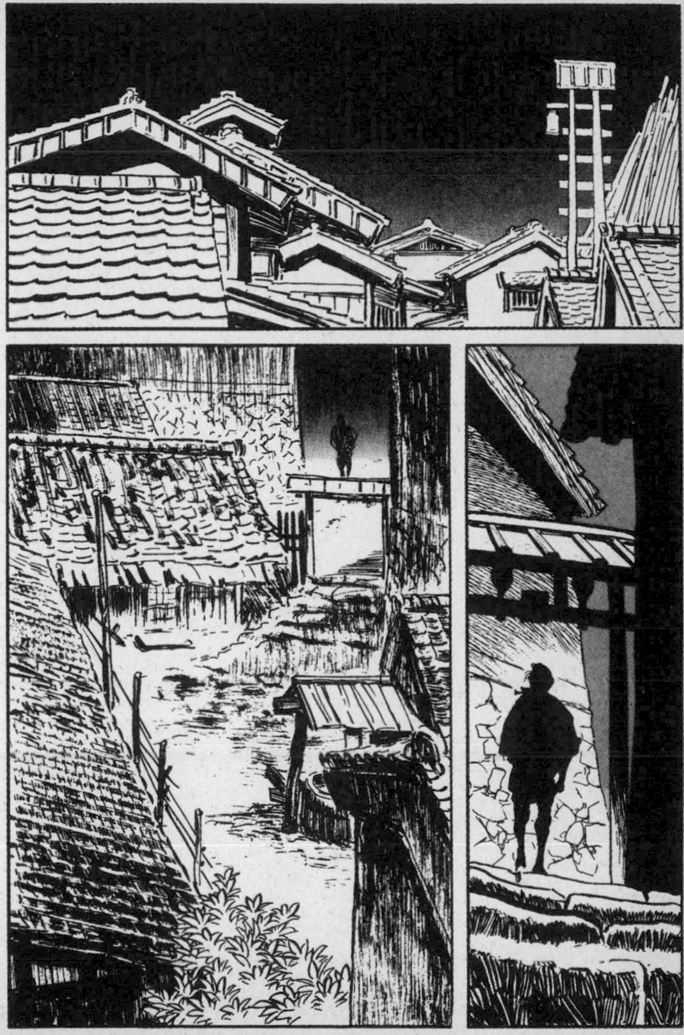

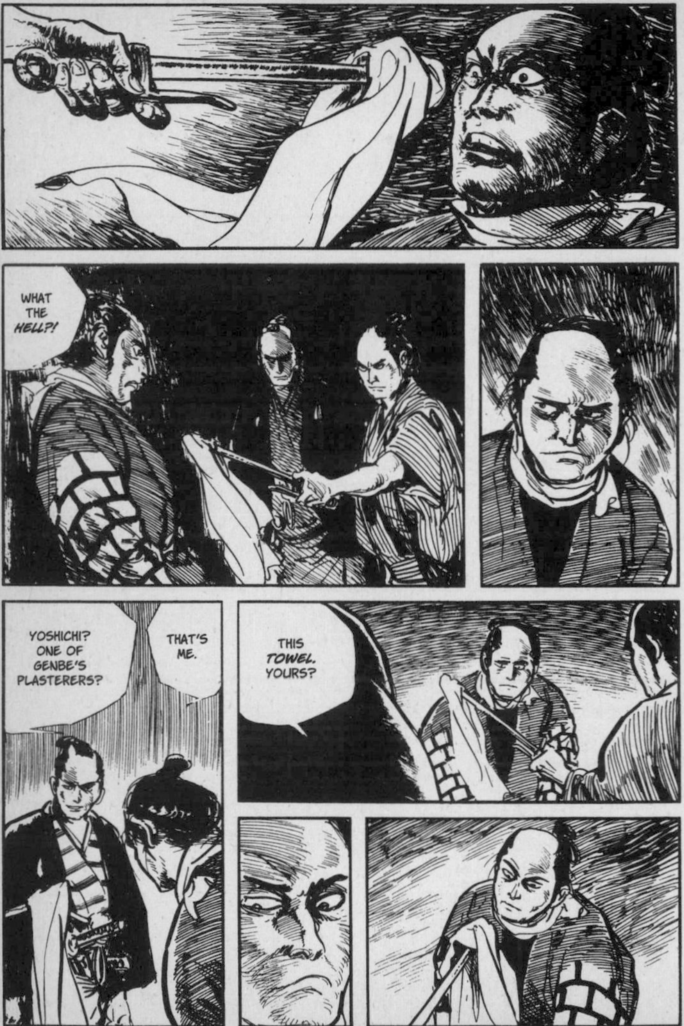
WHAT THE HELL?!
YOSHICHI? ONE OF GENBE'S PLASTERERS?
THAT'S ME.
THIS TOWEL. YOURS?

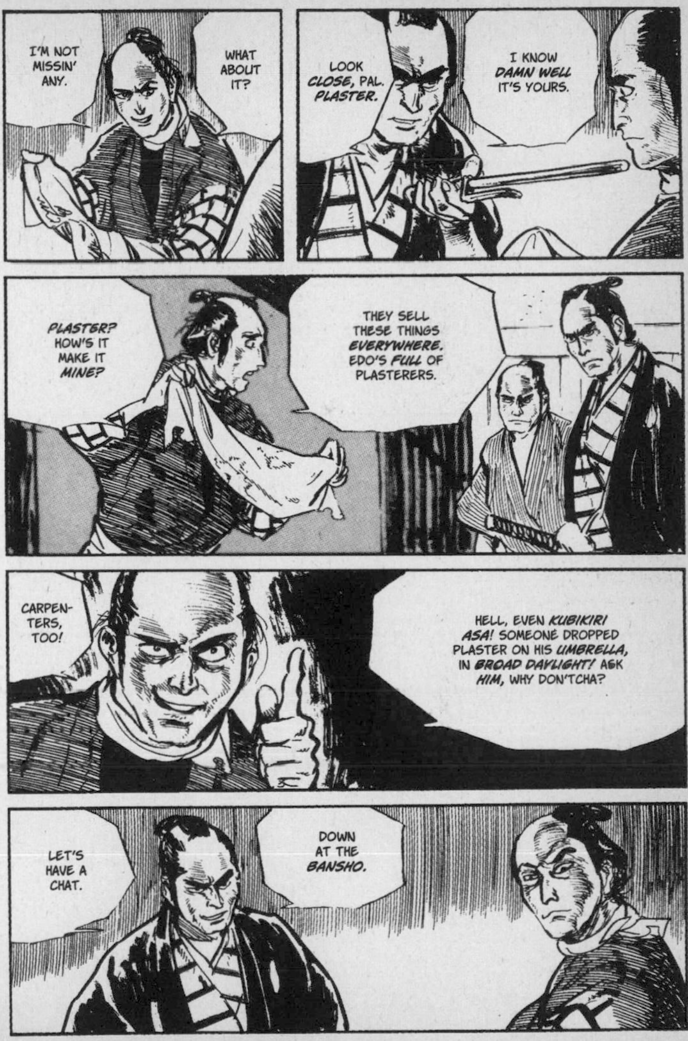
I'M NOT MISSIN' ANY.
WHAT ABOUT IT?
LOOK CLOSE, PAL. PLASTER.
I KNOW DAMN WELL IT'S YOURS.
PLASTER? HOW'S IT MAKE IT MINE?
THEY SELL THESE THINGS EVERYWHERE. EDO'S FULL OF PLASTERERS.
CARPEN-TERS, TOO!
HELL, EVEN KUBIKIRI ASA! SOMEONE DROPPED PLASTER ON HIS UMBRELLA, IN BROAD DAYLIGHT! ASK HIM, WHY DON'TCHA?
LET'S HAVE A CHAT.
DOWN AT THE BANSHO.

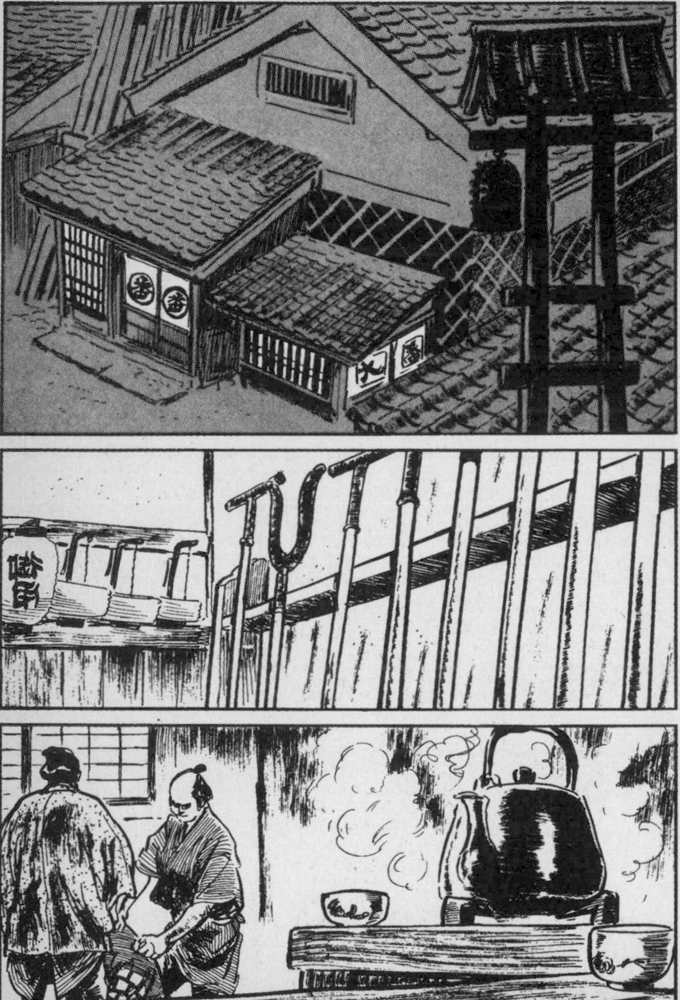

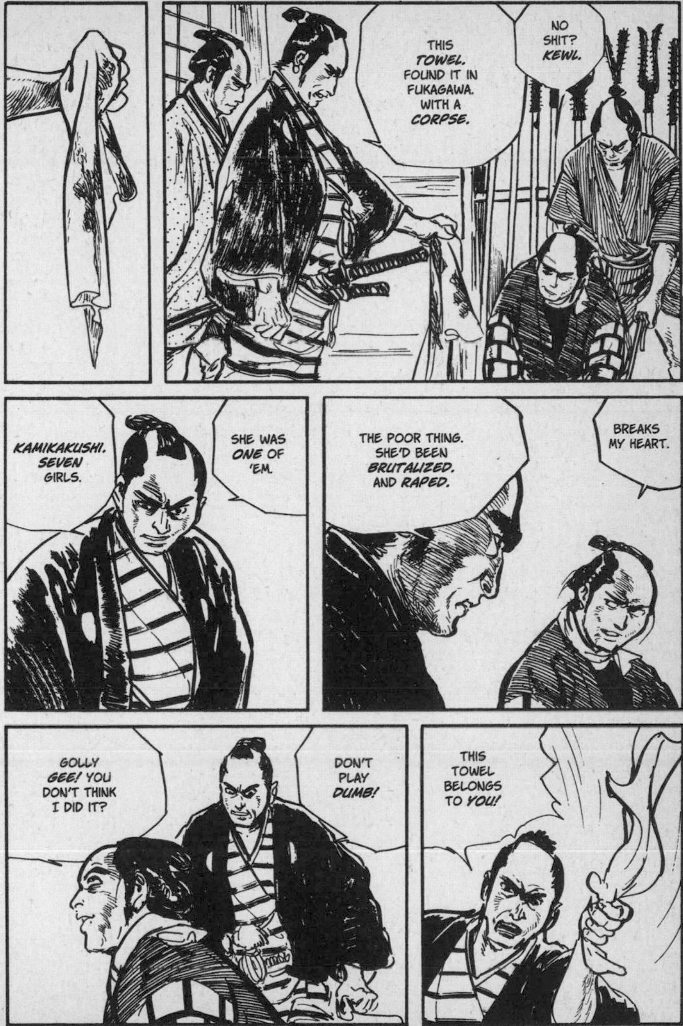
THIS TOWEL. FOUND IT IN FUKAGAWA. WITH A CORPSE.
NO SHIT? KEWL.
KAMIKAKUSHI. SEVEN GIRLS.
SHE WAS ONE OF 'EM.
THE POOR THING. SHE'D BEEN BRUTALIZED. AND RAPED.
BREAKS MY HEART.
GOLLY GEE! YOU DON'T THINK I DID IT?
DON'T PLAY DUMB!
THIS TOWEL BELONGS TO YOU!

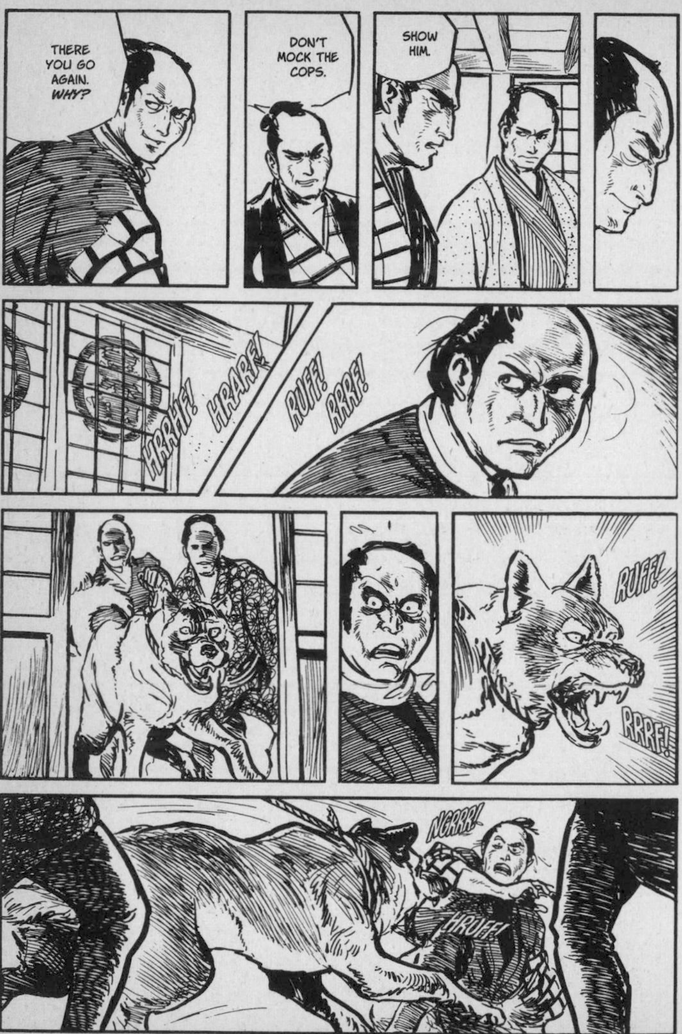
THERE YOU GO AGAIN. *WHY?*
DON'T MOCK THE COPS.
SHOW HIM.
HRRHF!
HRARF!
RUFF!
RRRF!
RUFF!
RRRF!
NGRRR!
HRUFF!

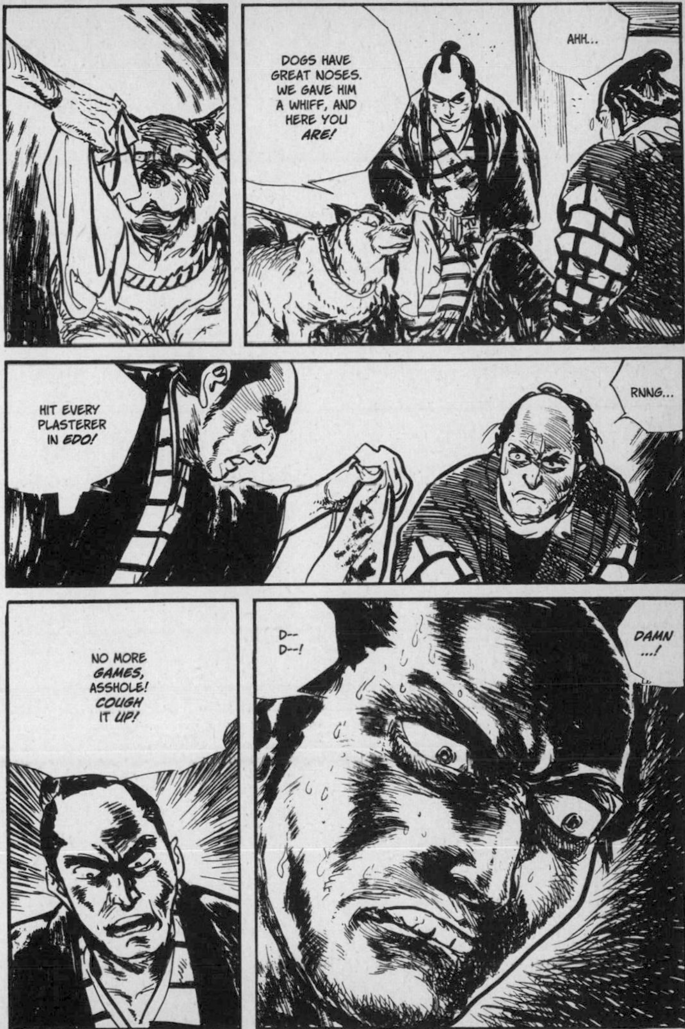
DOGS HAVE GREAT NOSES. WE GAVE HIM A WHIFF, AND HERE YOU *ARE!*
AHH...
HIT EVERY PLASTERER IN *EDO!*
RNNG...
NO MORE *GAMES,* ASSHOLE! *COUGH* IT *UP!*
D-- D--!
DAMN ...!

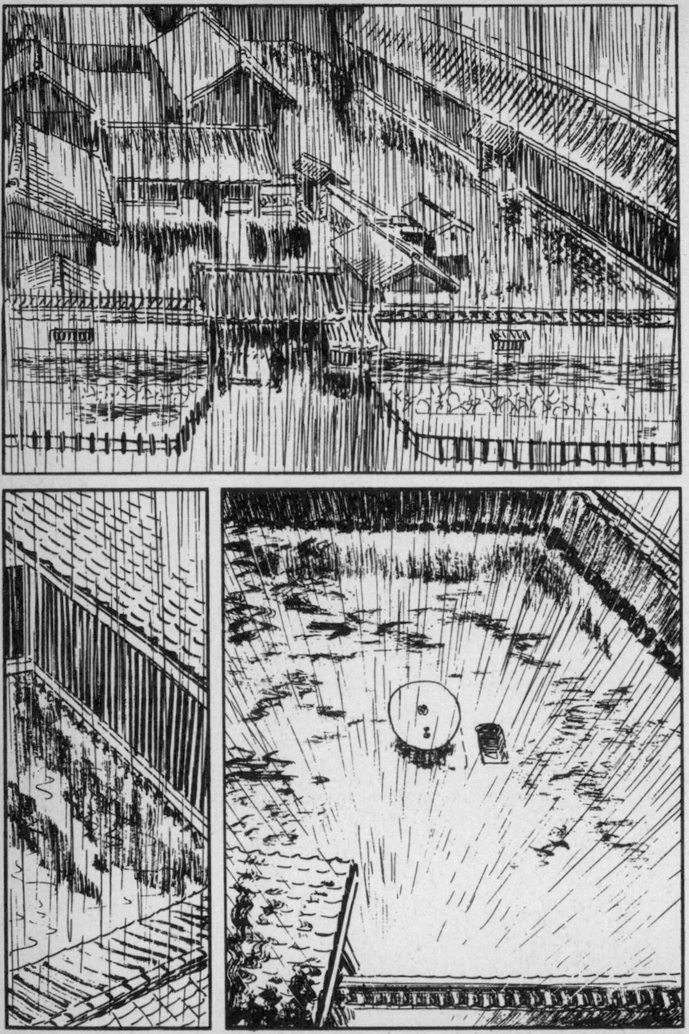

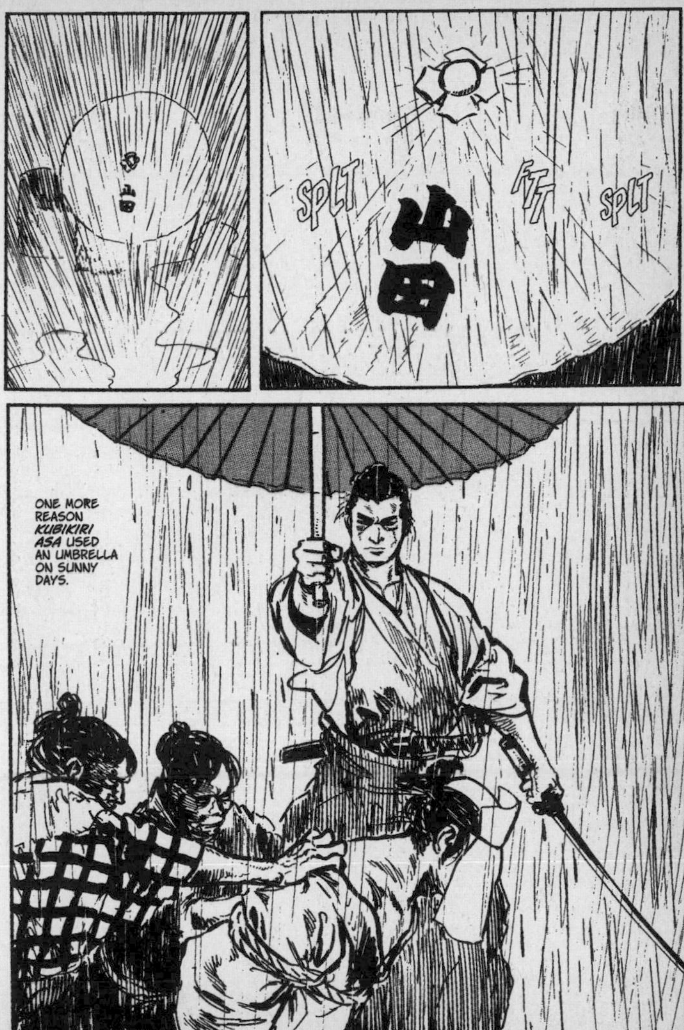
SPLT
山田
FTT
SPLT
ONE MORE REASON *KUBIKIRI ASA* USED AN UMBRELLA ON SUNNY DAYS.

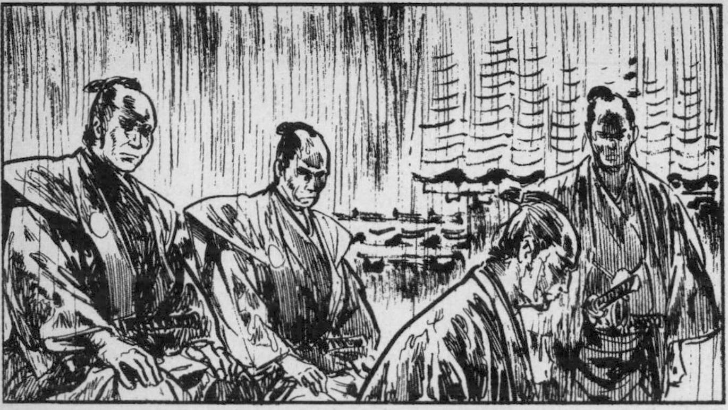

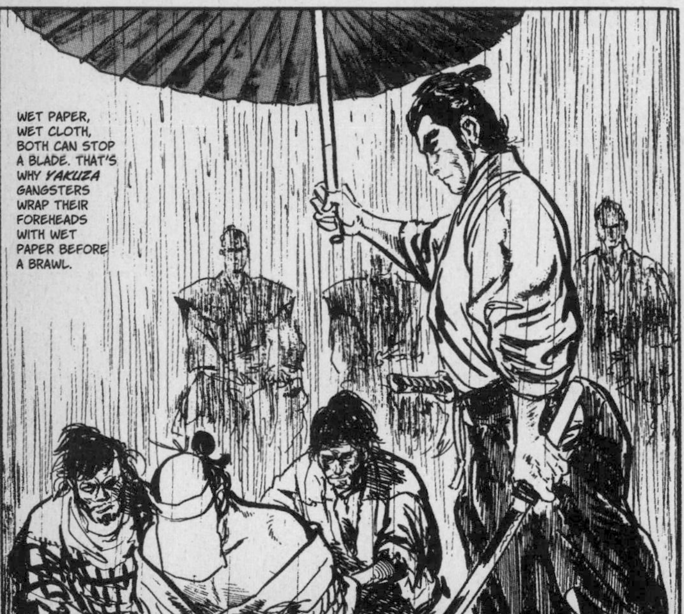
WET PAPER, WET CLOTH, BOTH CAN STOP A BLADE. THAT'S WHY *YAKUZA* GANGSTERS WRAP THEIR FOREHEADS WITH WET PAPER BEFORE A BRAWL.

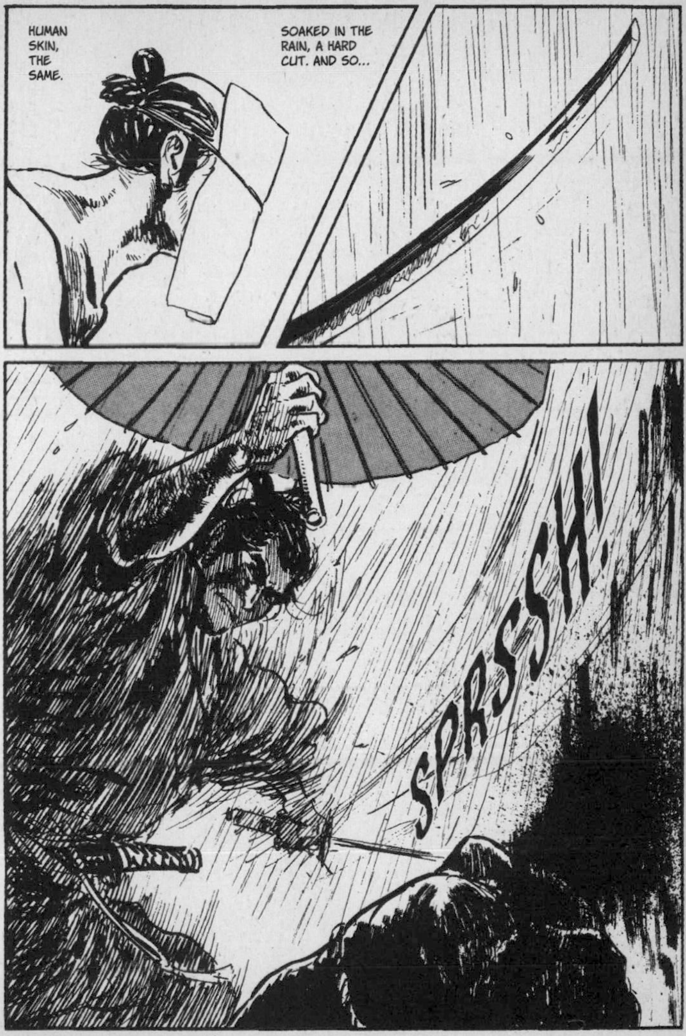
HUMAN SKIN, THE SAME.
SOAKED IN THE RAIN, A HARD CUT. AND SO...
SPRSSH!

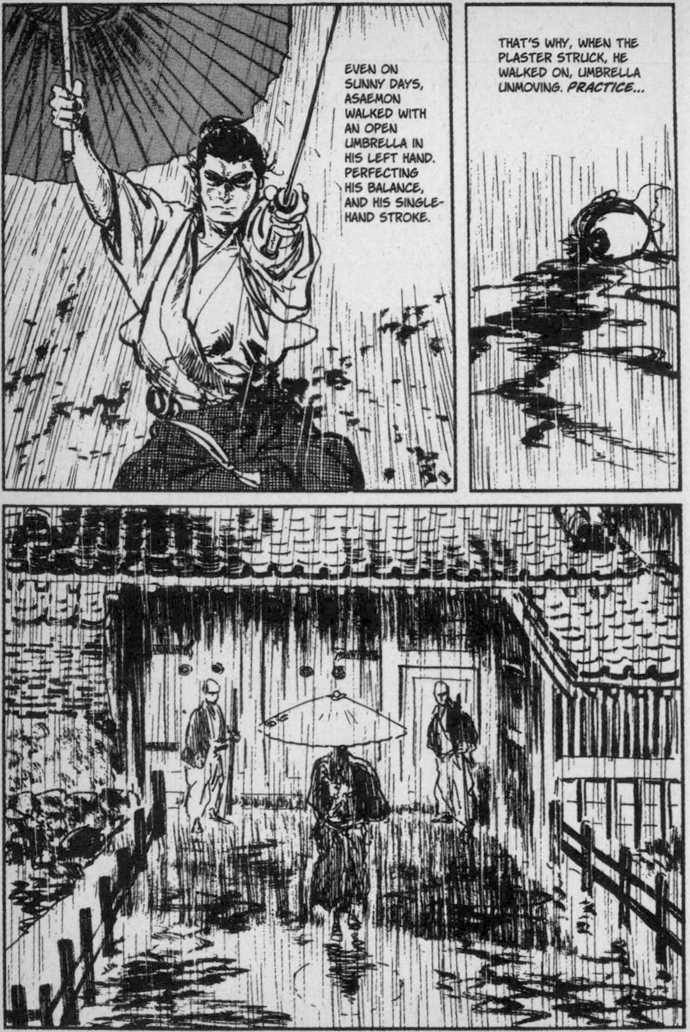
EVEN ON SUNNY DAYS, ASAEMON WALKED WITH AN OPEN UMBRELLA IN HIS LEFT HAND. PERFECTING HIS BALANCE, AND HIS SINGLE-HAND STROKE.
THAT'S WHY, WHEN THE PLASTER STRUCK, HE WALKED ON, UMBRELLA UNMOVING. *PRACTICE...*

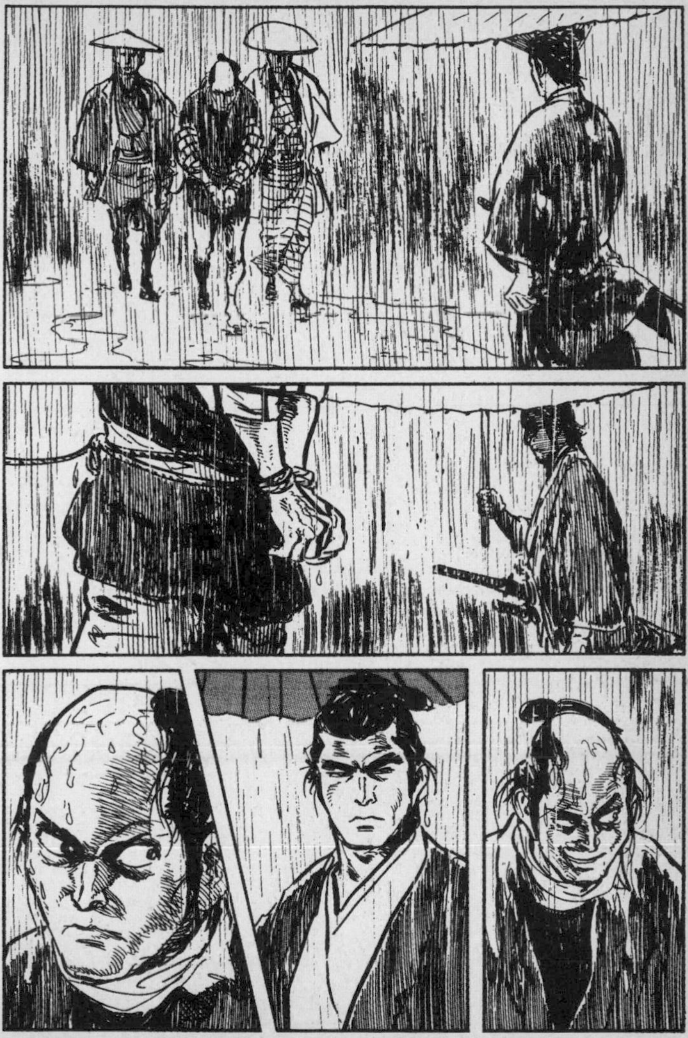

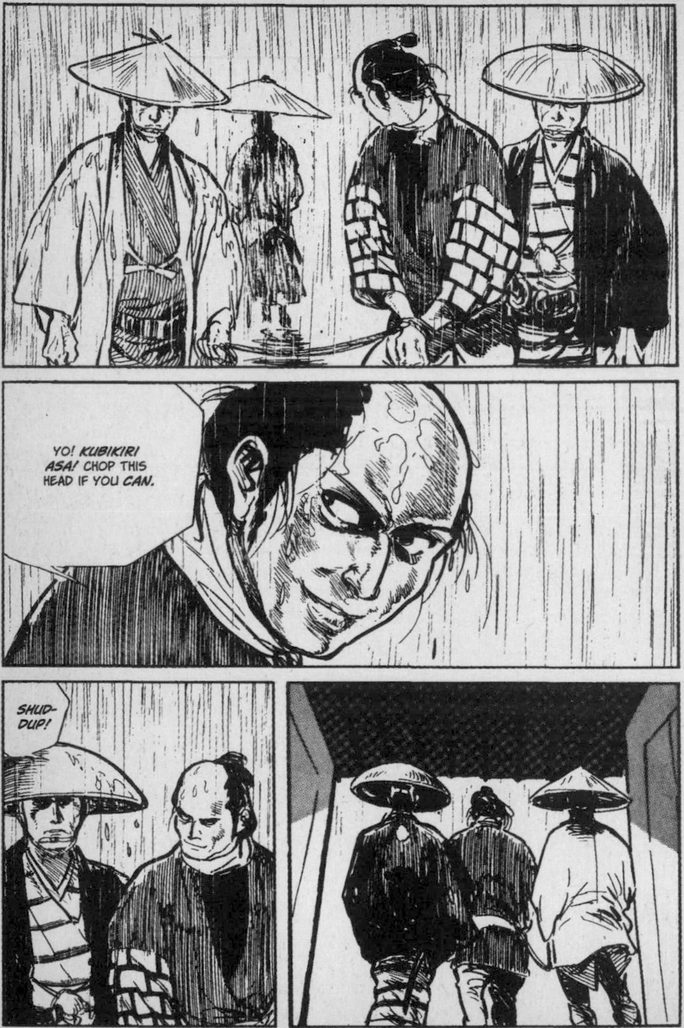
YO! KUBIKIRI ASA! CHOP THIS HEAD IF YOU CAN.
SHUD-DUP!

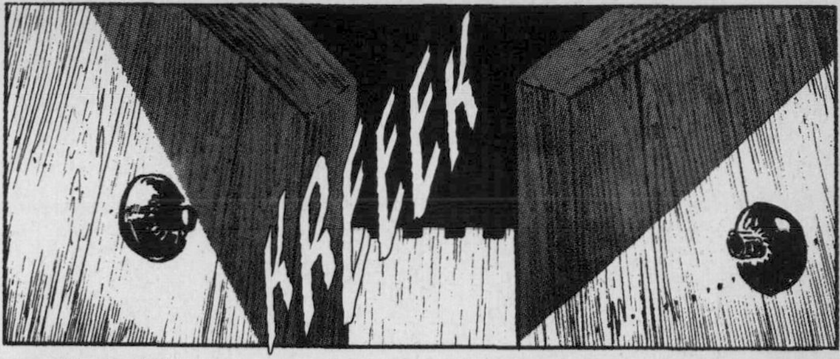
KREEEK
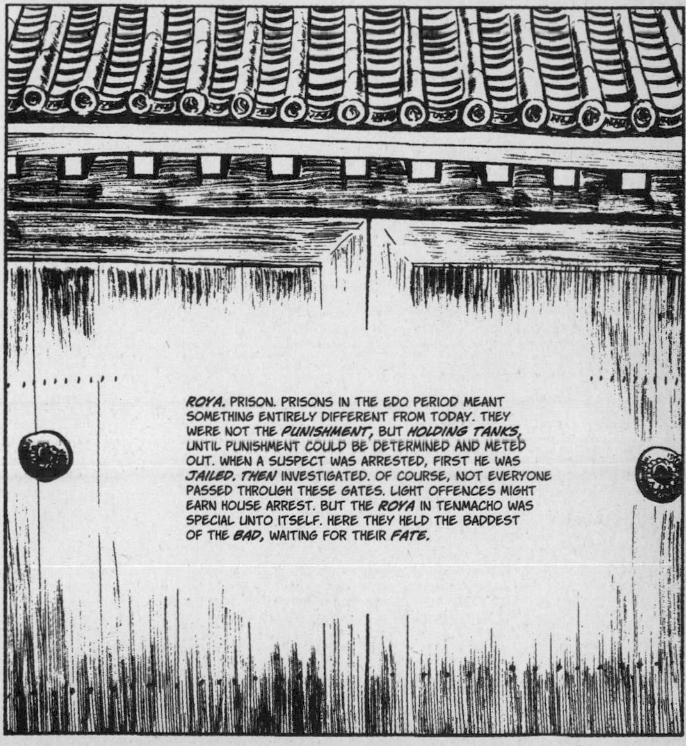
ROYA. PRISON. PRISONS IN THE EDO PERIOD MEANT SOMETHING ENTIRELY DIFFERENT FROM TODAY. THEY WERE NOT THE PUNISHMENT, BUT HOLDING TANKS, UNTIL PUNISHMENT COULD BE DETERMINED AND METED OUT. WHEN A SUSPECT WAS ARRESTED, FIRST HE WAS JAILED. THEN INVESTIGATED. OF COURSE, NOT EVERYONE PASSED THROUGH THESE GATES. LIGHT OFFENCES MIGHT EARN HOUSE ARREST. BUT THE ROYA IN TENMACHO WAS SPECIAL UNTO ITSELF. HERE THEY HELD THE BADDEST OF THE BAD, WAITING FOR THEIR FATE.

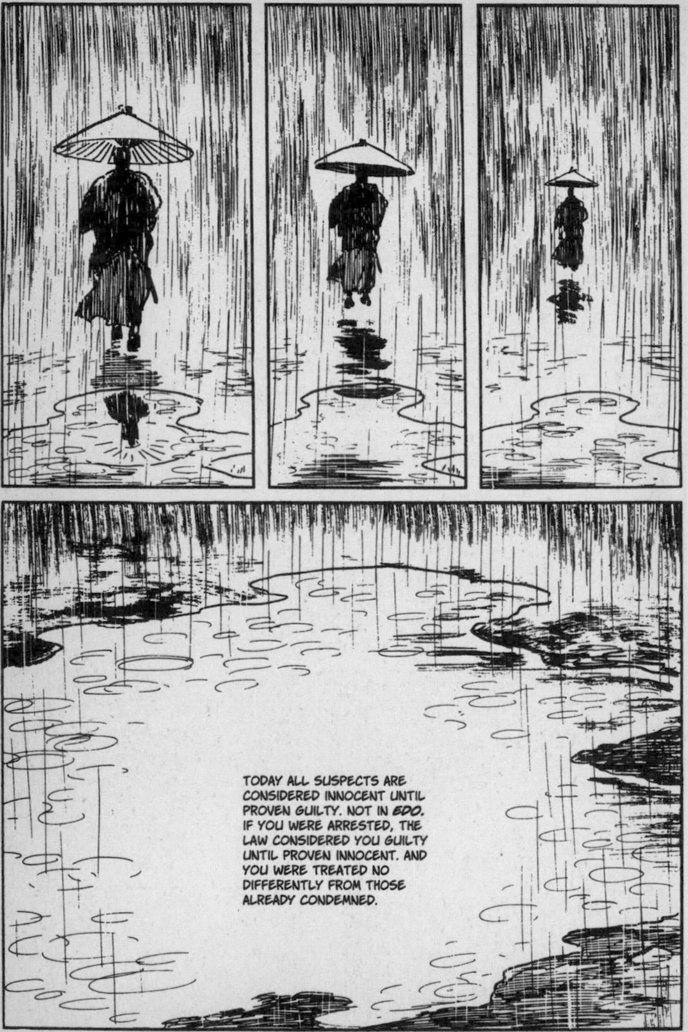
TODAY ALL SUSPECTS ARE CONSIDERED INNOCENT UNTIL PROVEN GUILTY. NOT IN *EDO.* IF YOU WERE ARRESTED, THE LAW CONSIDERED YOU GUILTY UNTIL PROVEN INNOCENT. AND YOU WERE TREATED NO DIFFERENTLY FROM THOSE ALREADY CONDEMNED.

THE SUSPECT WAS BROUGHT THROUGH THE FRONT GATE TO THE *KAGIYAKU DŌSHIN*, THE CONSTABLES WHO RAN THE PRISON.

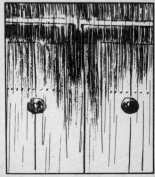

213

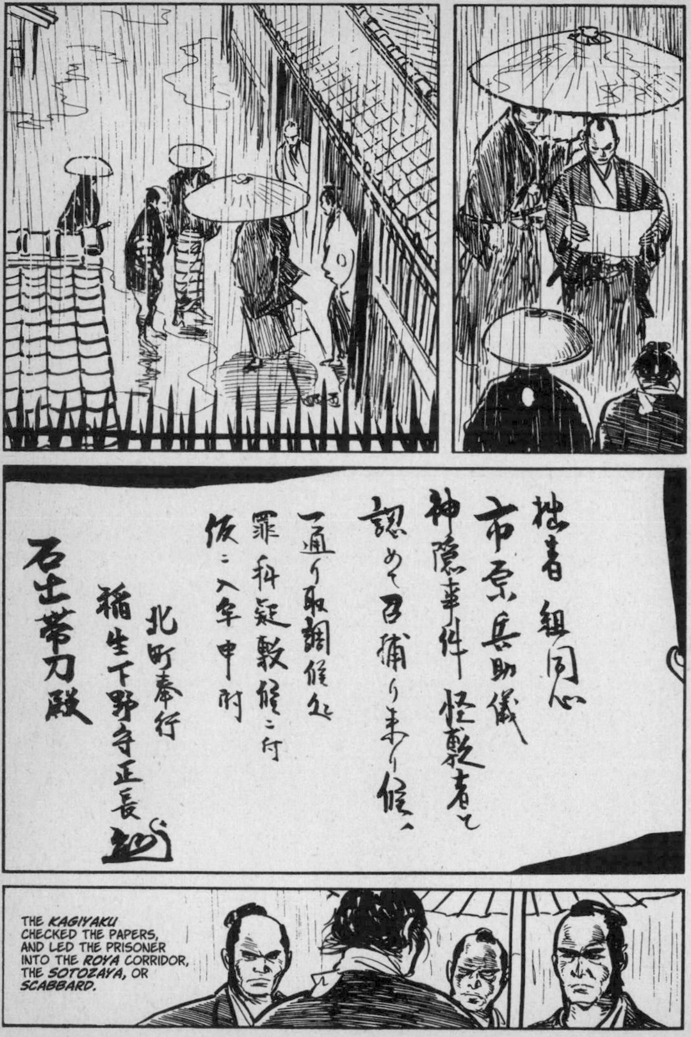
拙者 組同心
市京兵助儀
神隠事件 怪敷者と
認め召捕り来り候へ
一通り取調候処
罪科疑敷候に付
仮に入牢申附
北町奉行
稲生下野守正長
石出帯刀殿
THE *KAGIYAKU* CHECKED THE PAPERS, AND LED THE PRISONER INTO THE *ROYA* CORRIDOR, THE *SOTOZAYA*, OR *SCABBARD*.

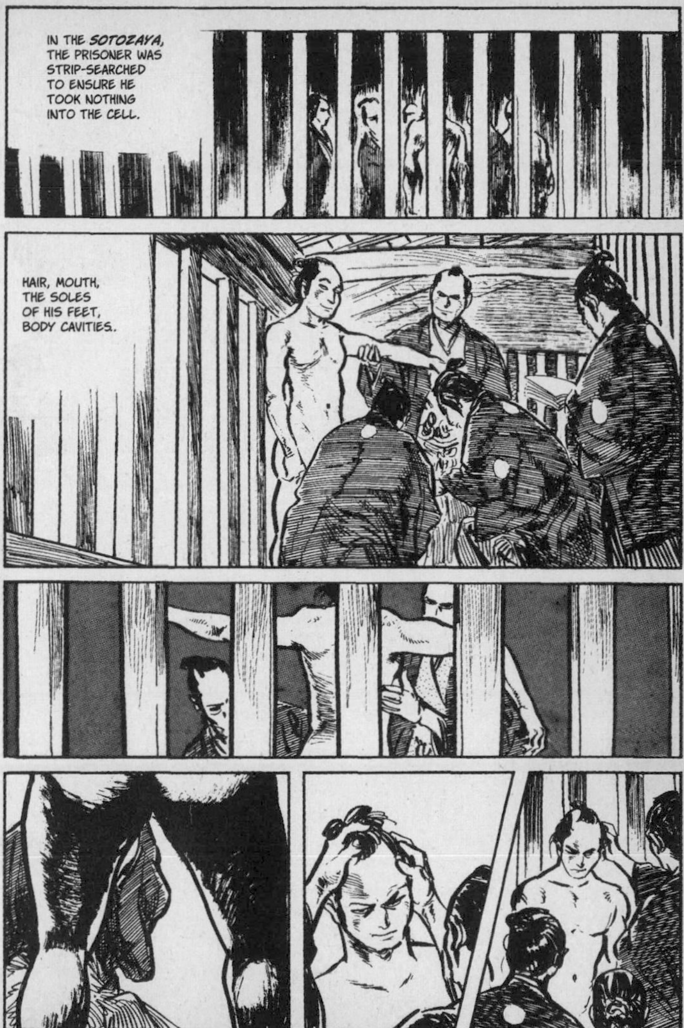
IN THE SOTOZAYA, THE PRISONER WAS STRIP-SEARCHED TO ENSURE HE TOOK NOTHING INTO THE CELL.
HAIR, MOUTH, THE SOLES OF HIS FEET, BODY CAVITIES.

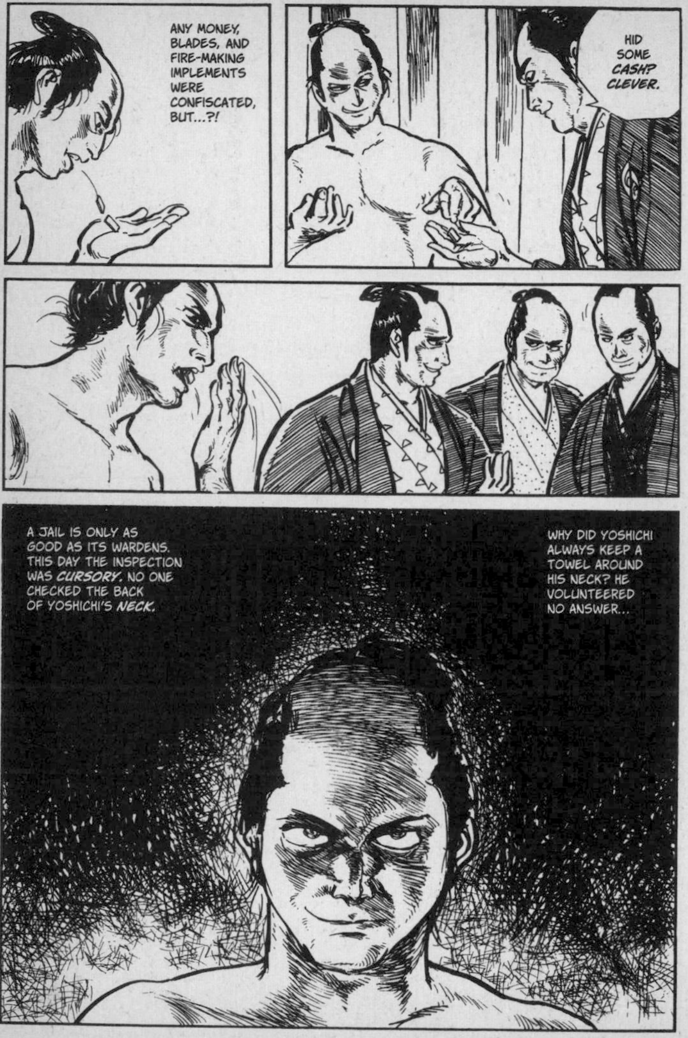
ANY MONEY, BLADES, AND FIRE-MAKING IMPLEMENTS WERE CONFISCATED, BUT...?!
HID SOME CASH? CLEVER.
A JAIL IS ONLY AS GOOD AS ITS WARDENS. THIS DAY THE INSPECTION WAS CURSORY. NO ONE CHECKED THE BACK OF YOSHICHI'S NECK.
WHY DID YOSHICHI ALWAYS KEEP A TOWEL AROUND HIS NECK? HE VOLUNTEERED NO ANSWER...

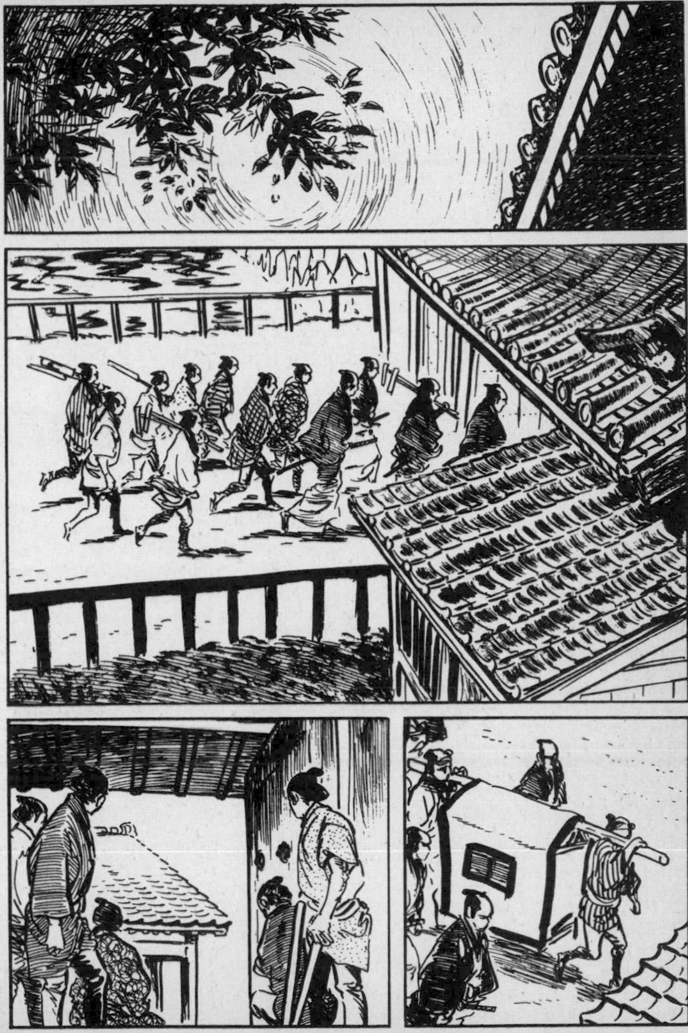

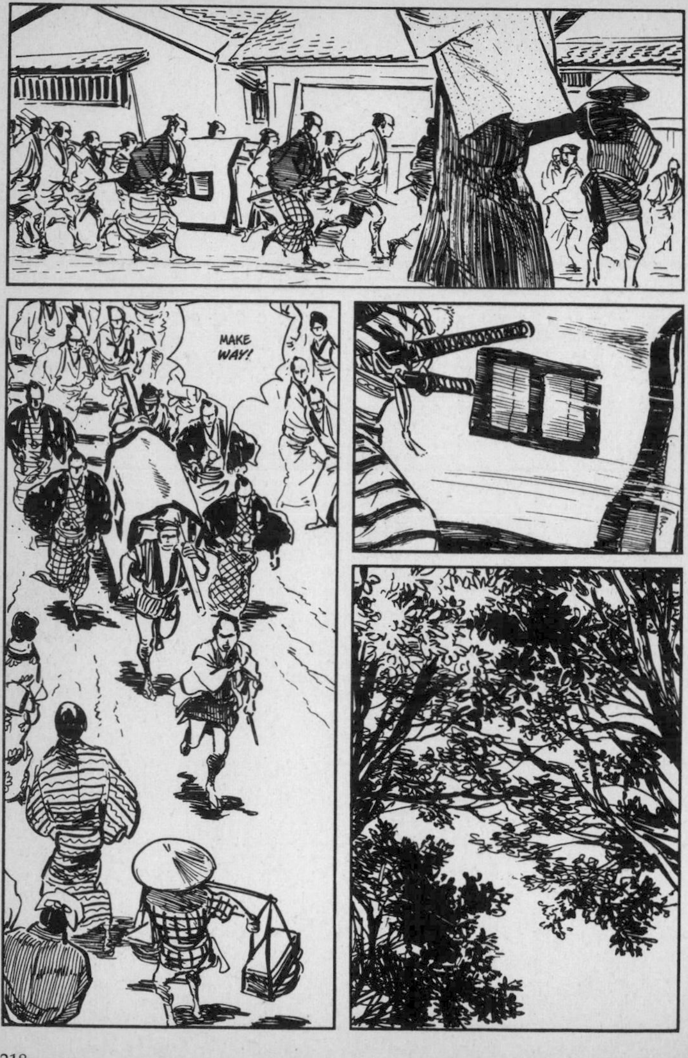
MAKE WAY!

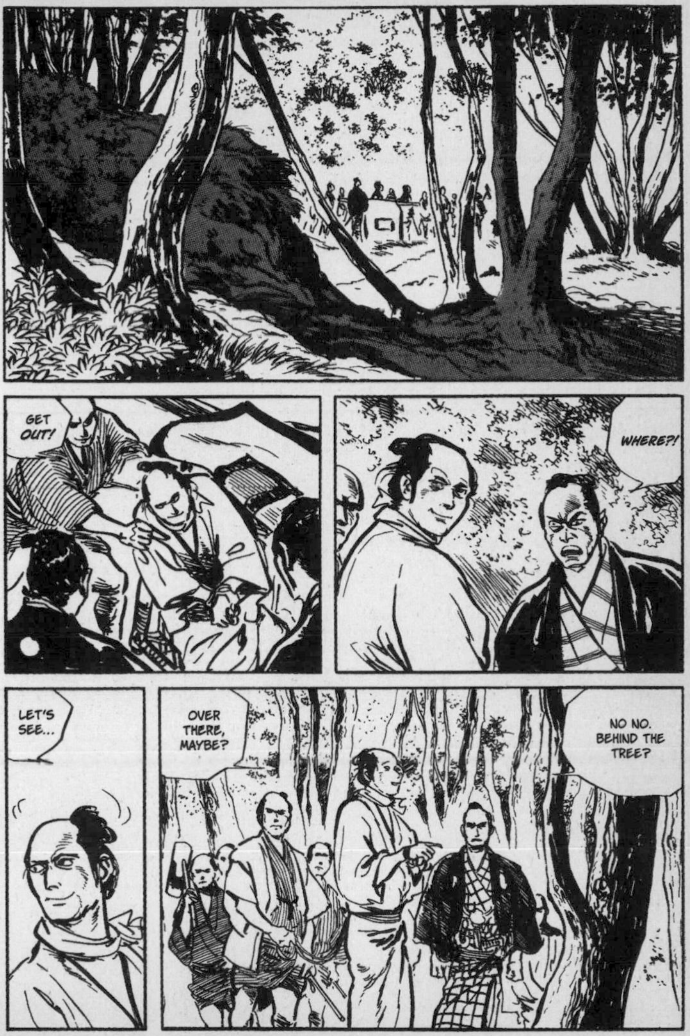
GET OUT!
WHERE?!
LET'S SEE...
OVER THERE, MAYBE?
NO NO. BEHIND THE TREE?

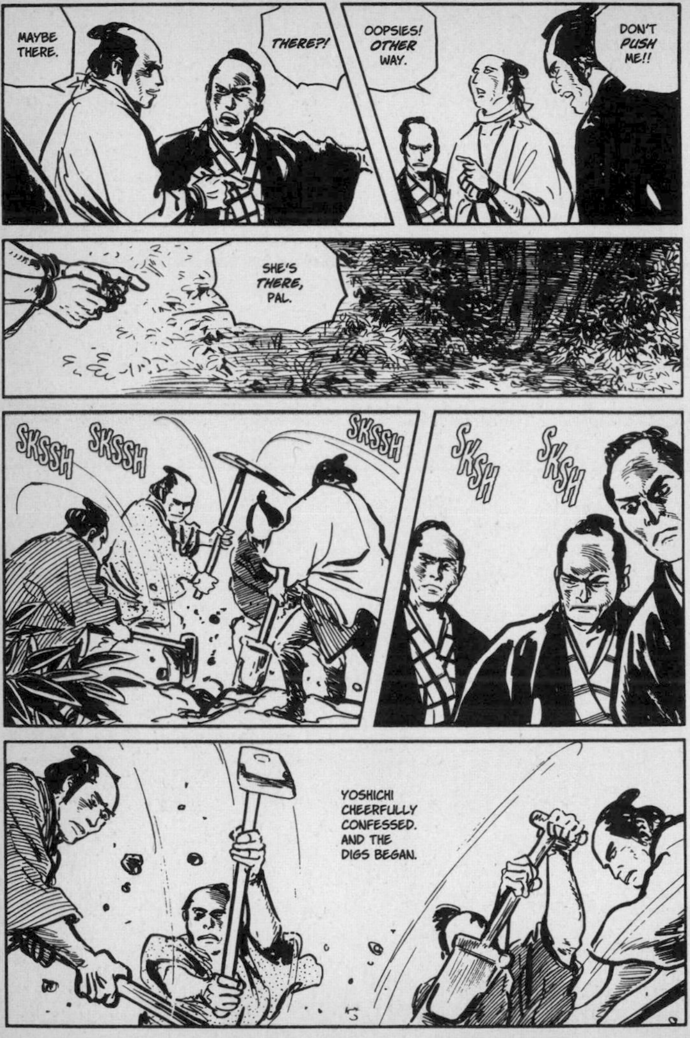
MAYBE THERE.
THERE?!
OOPSIES! OTHER WAY.
DON'T PUSH ME!!
SHE'S THERE, PAL.
SKSSH
SKSSH
SKSSH
SKSH
SKSH
YOSHICHI CHEERFULLY CONFESSED. AND THE DIGS BEGAN.

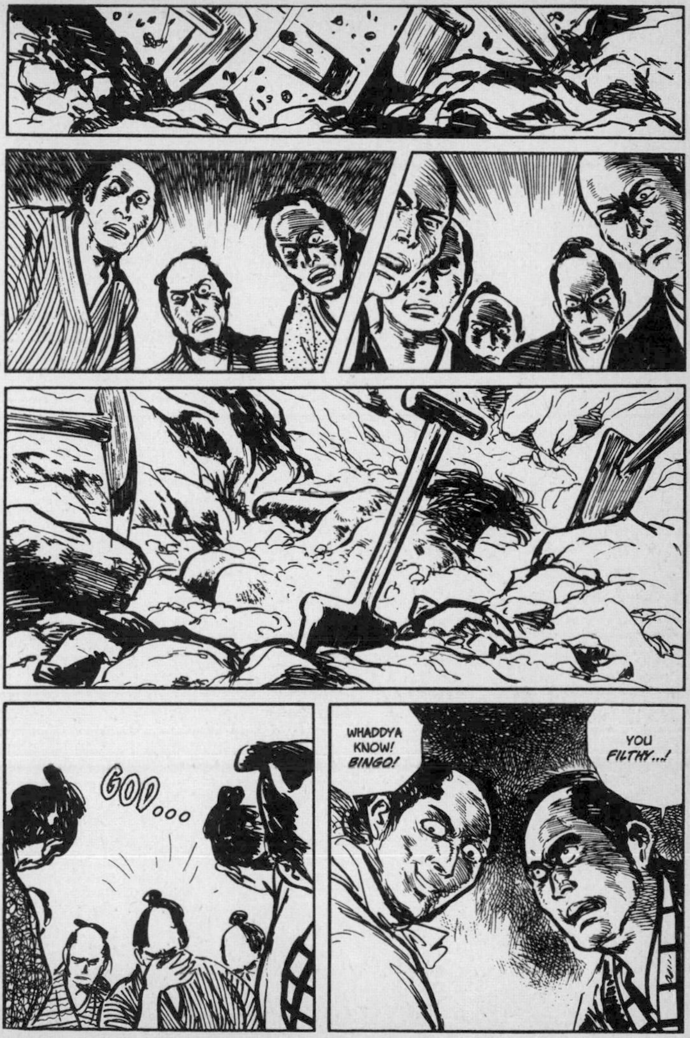
GOD...
WHADDYA KNOW! BINGO!
YOU FILTHY...!

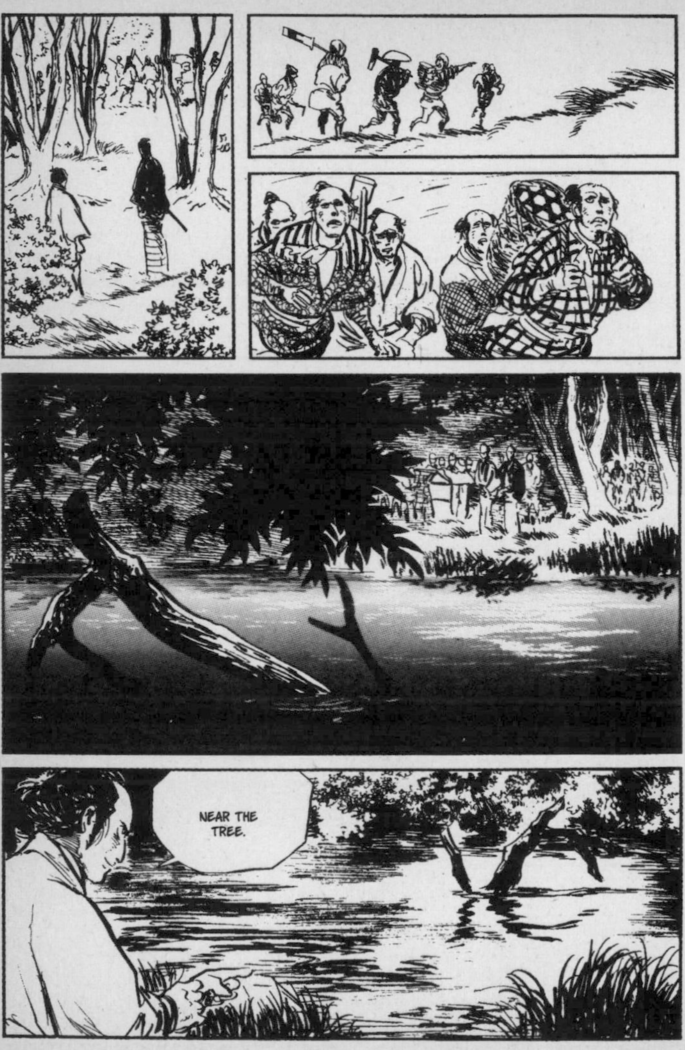
NEAR THE TREE.

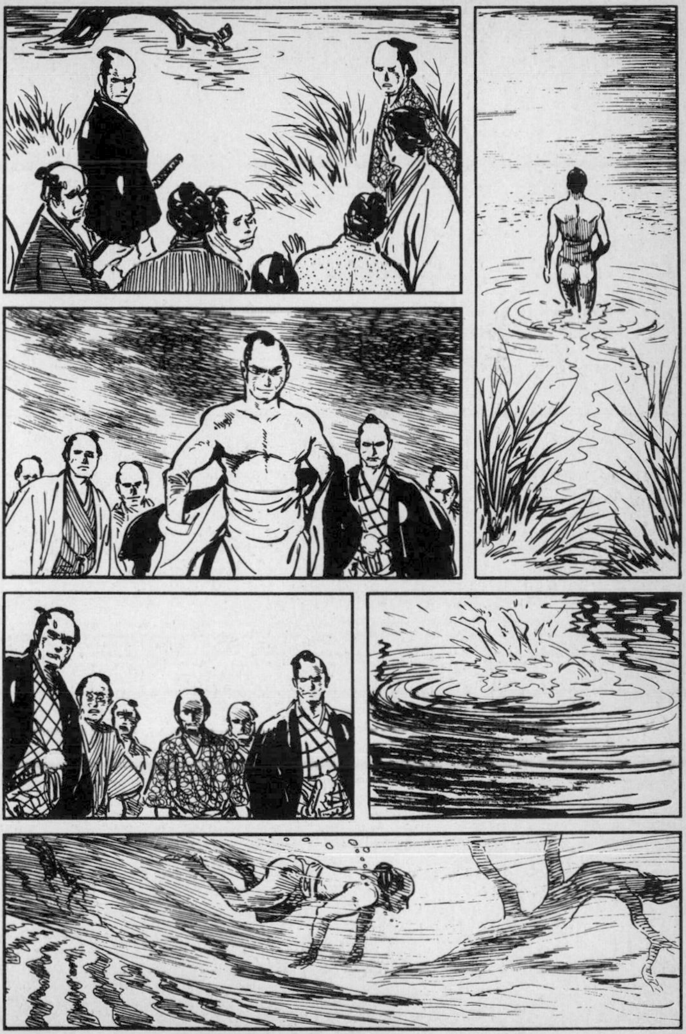

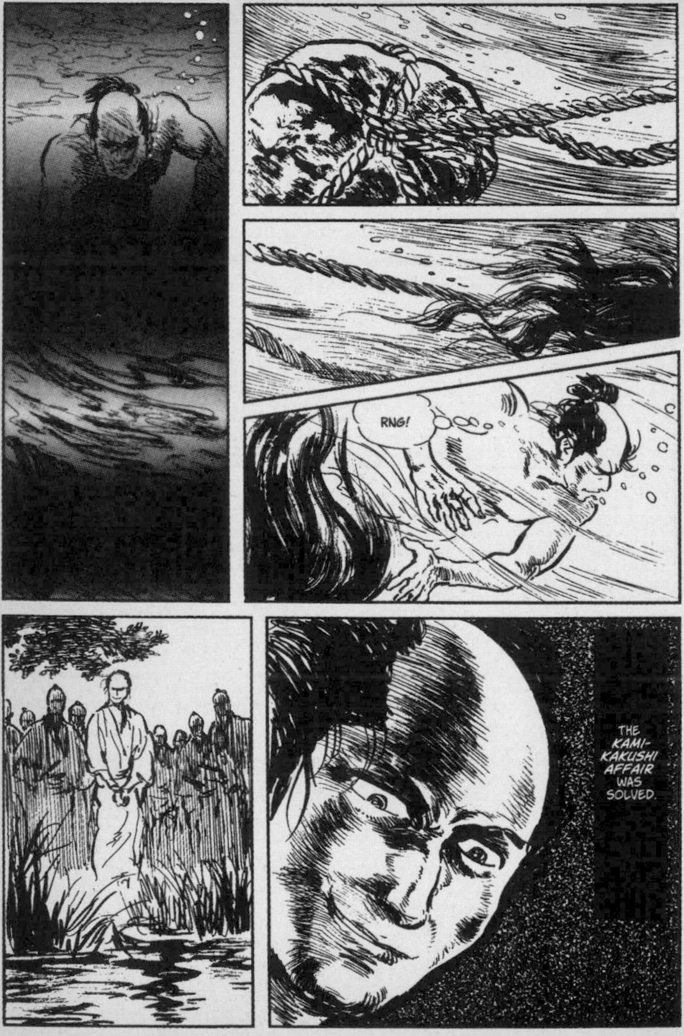
RNG!
THE KAMI-KAKUSHI AFFAIR WAS SOLVED.

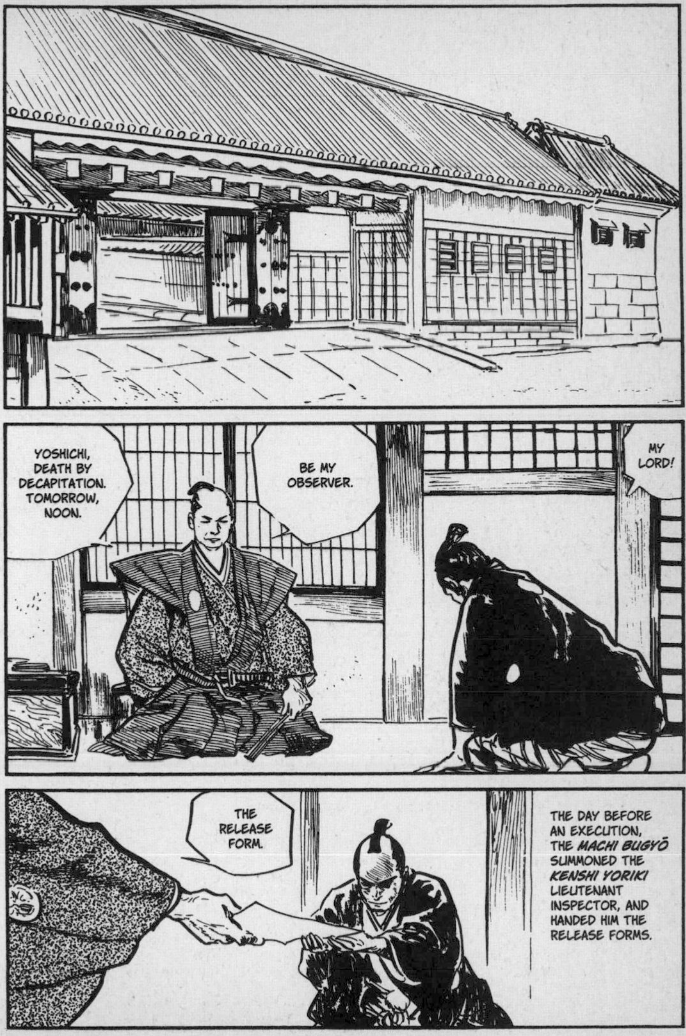
YOSHICHI, DEATH BY DECAPITATION. TOMORROW, NOON.
BE MY OBSERVER.
MY LORD!
THE RELEASE FORM.
THE DAY BEFORE AN EXECUTION, THE *MACHI BUGYŌ* SUMMONED THE *KENSHI YORIKI* LIEUTENANT INSPECTOR, AND HANDED HIM THE RELEASE FORMS.

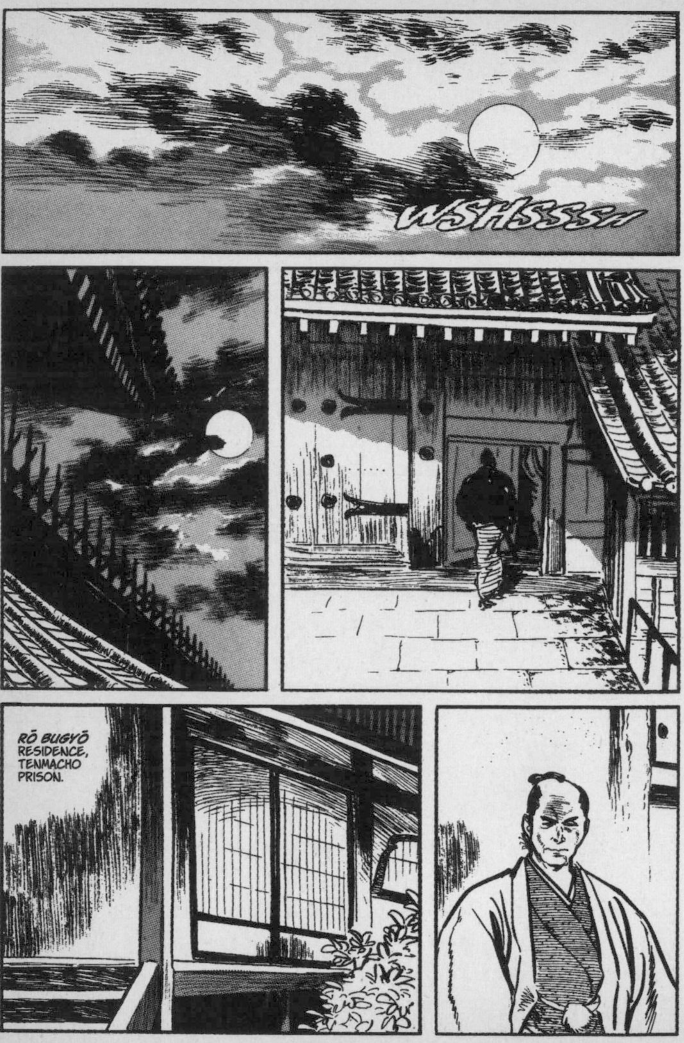
WSHSSSS..
RŌ BUGYŌ RESIDENCE, TENMACHO PRISON.

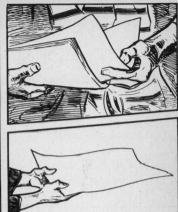

THE DIRECTIVE WENT TO ISHIDE TATEWAKI, THE *RO BUGYO.*

ONE BEHEADING, ONE FOLDED SHEET. TWO BEHEADINGS, TWO SHEETS.

JUST ONE TOMORROW, YOSHICHI.

YES, SIR.

CHING CHING

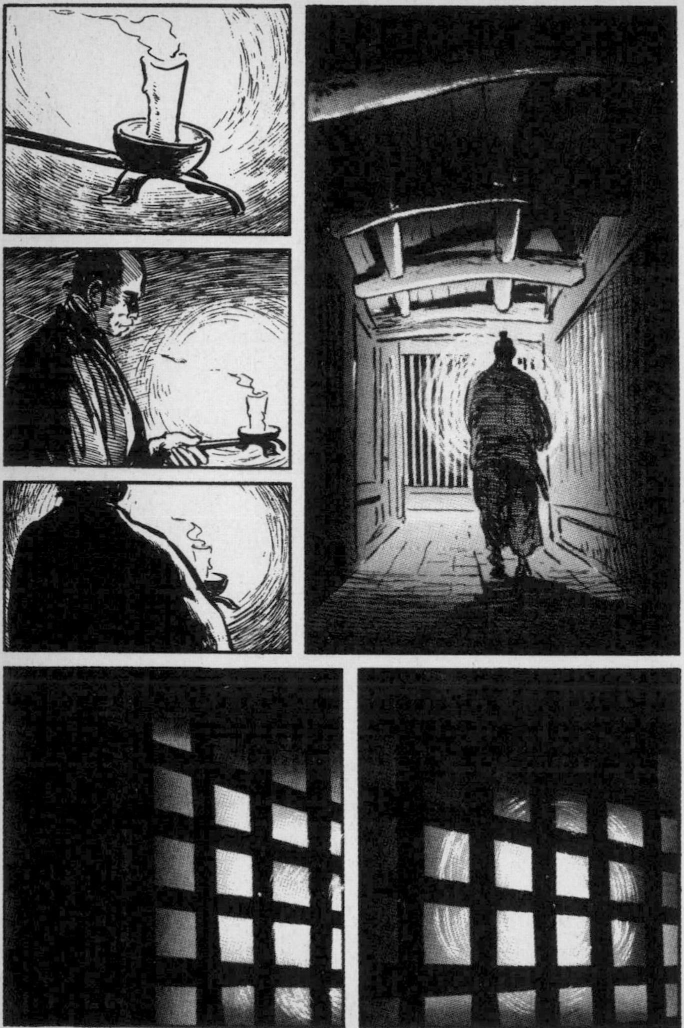

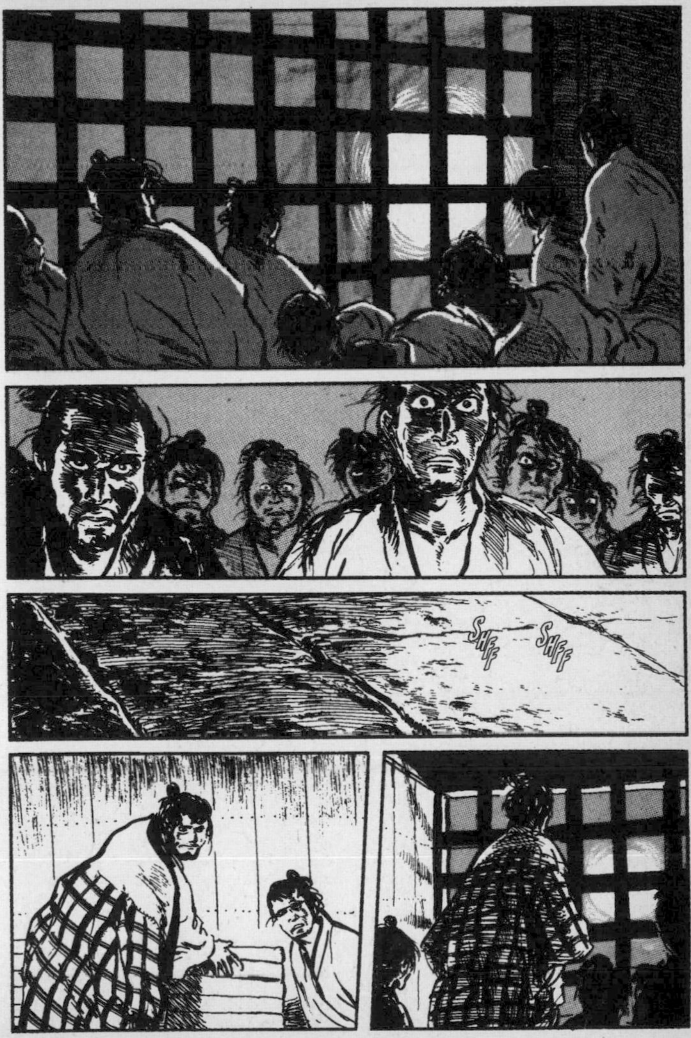
SHFF
SHFF

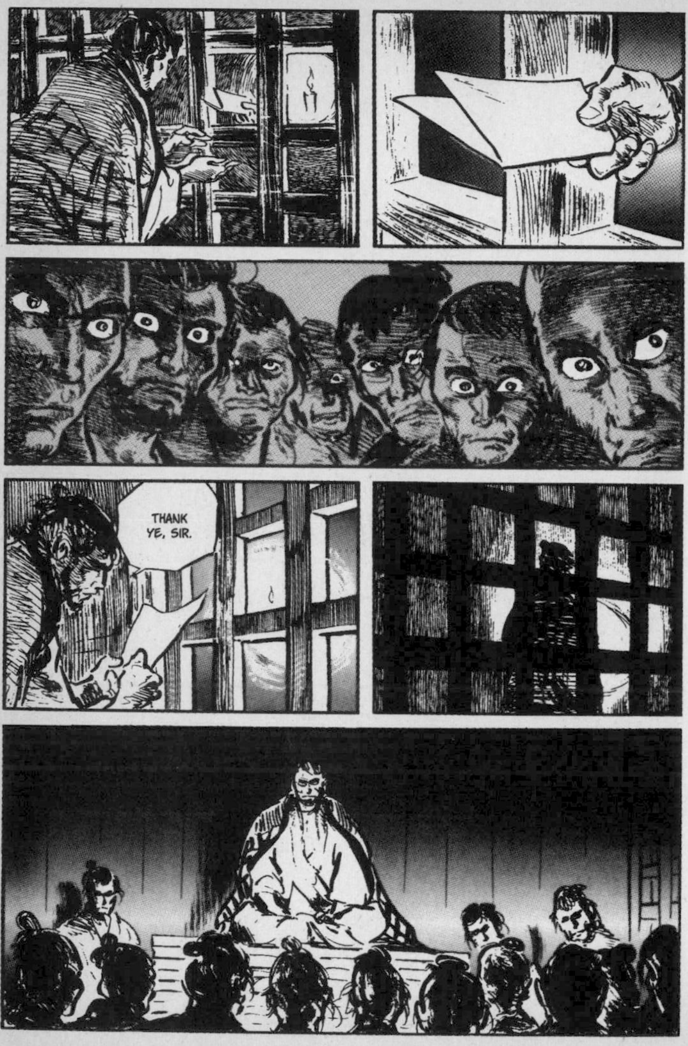
THANK YE, SIR.

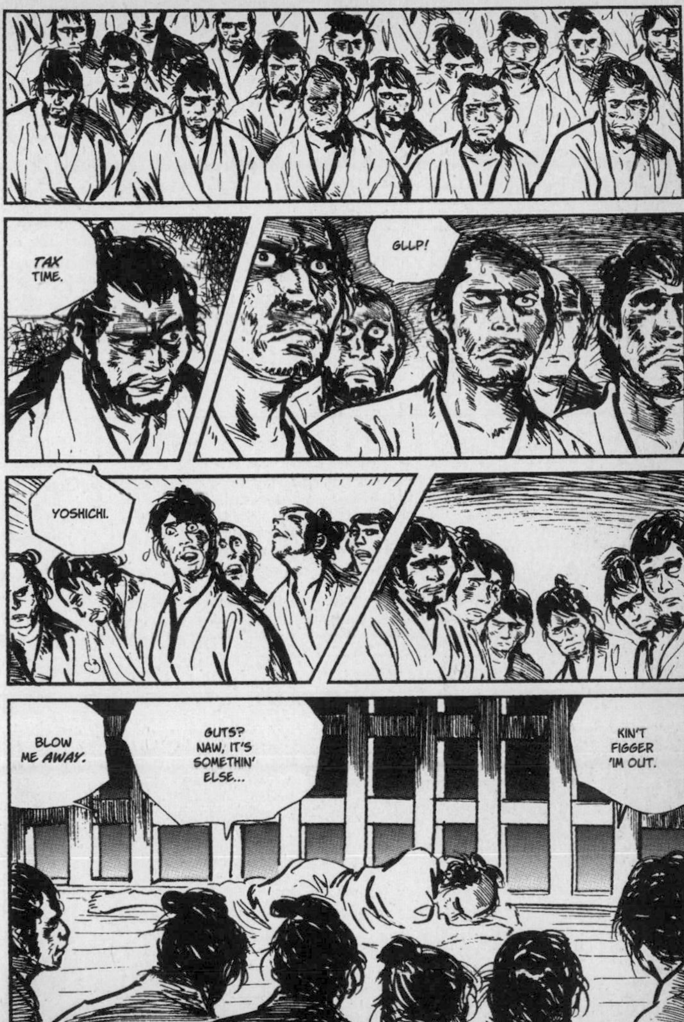
TAX TIME.
GLLP!
YOSHICHI.
BLOW ME AWAY.
GUTS? NAW, IT'S SOMETHIN' ELSE...
KIN'T FIGGER 'IM OUT.

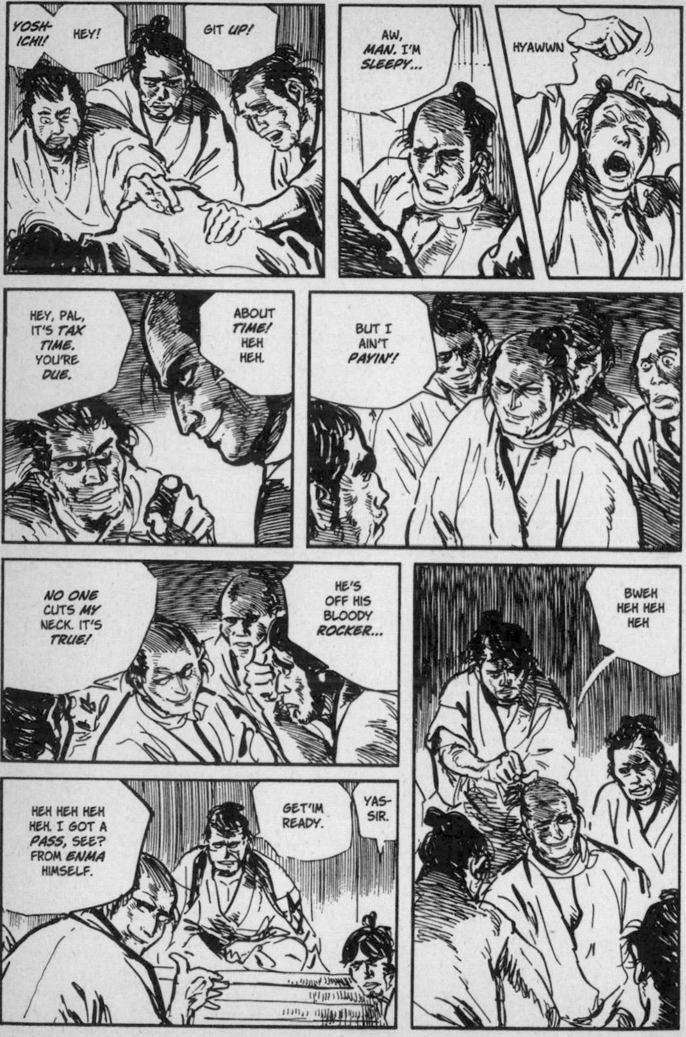
YOSH-ICHI!
HEY!
GIT UP!
AW, MAN. I'M SLEEPY...
HYAWWN
HEY, PAL, IT'S TAX TIME. YOU'RE DUE.
ABOUT TIME! HEH HEH.
BUT I AIN'T PAYIN'!
NO ONE CUTS MY NECK. IT'S TRUE!
HE'S OFF HIS BLOODY ROCKER...
HEH HEH HEH HEH. I GOT A PASS, SEE? FROM ENMA HIMSELF.
GET'IM READY.
YAS-SIR.
BWEH HEH HEH HEH

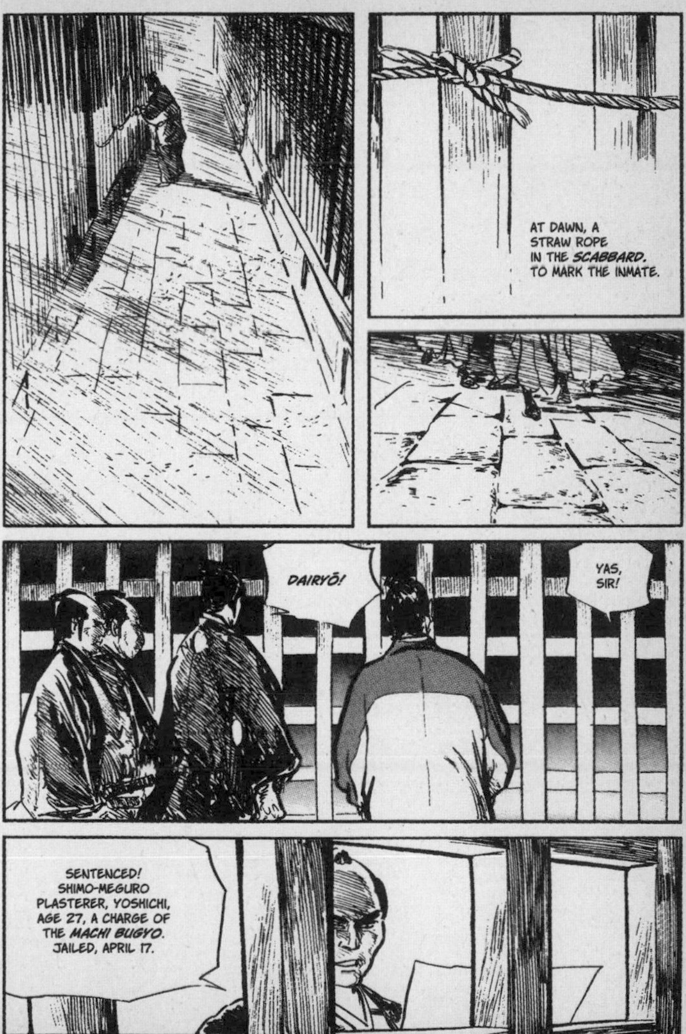
AT DAWN, A STRAW ROPE IN THE *SCABBARD.* TO MARK THE INMATE.
DAIRYŌ!
YAS, SIR!
SENTENCED! SHIMO-MEGURO PLASTERER, YOSHICHI, AGE 27, A CHARGE OF THE *MACHI BUGYO.* JAILED, APRIL 17.

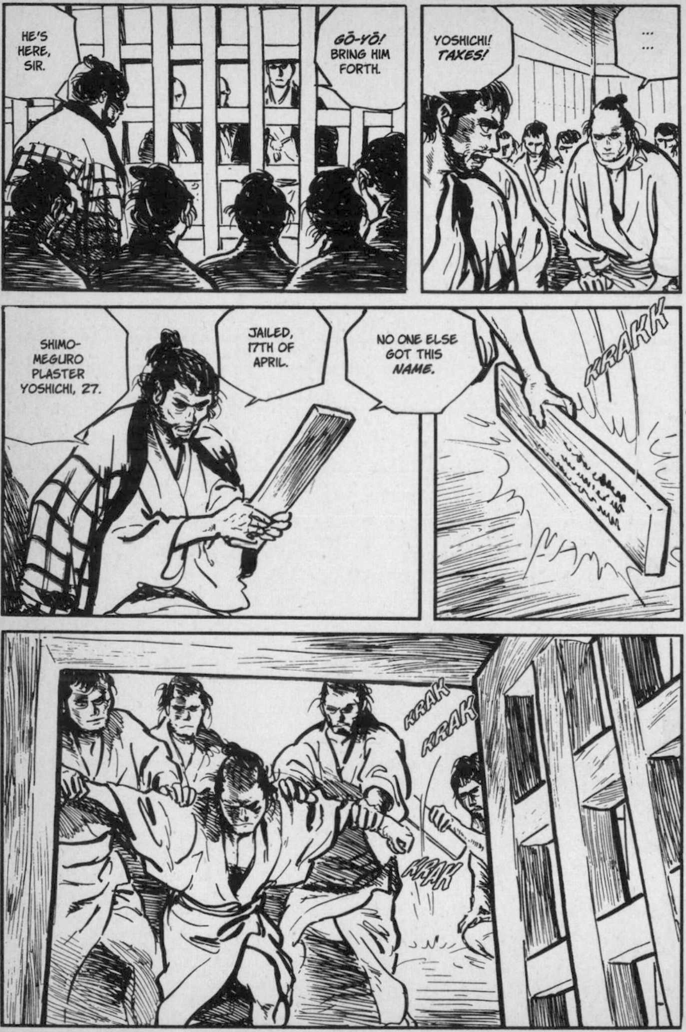
HE'S HERE, SIR.
GŌ-YŌ! BRING HIM FORTH.
YOSHICHI! TAXES!
... ...
SHIMO-MEGURO PLASTER YOSHICHI, 27.
JAILED, 17TH OF APRIL.
NO ONE ELSE GOT THIS NAME.
KRAKK
KRAK
KRAK
KRAK

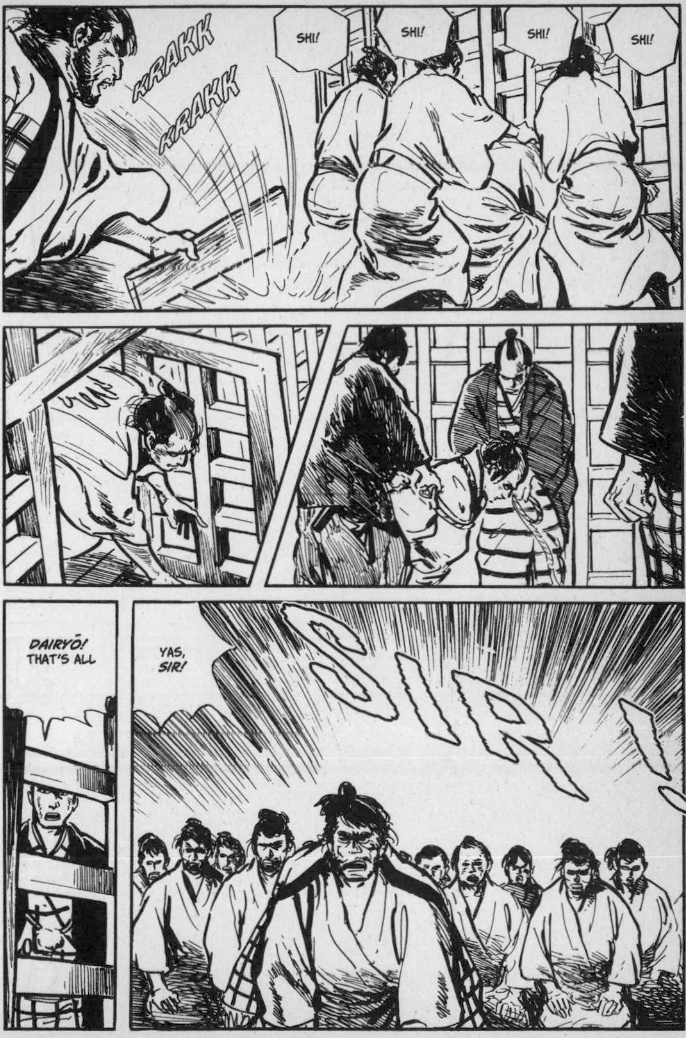
KRAKK
KRAKK
SHI!
SHI!
SHI!
SHI!
DAIRYŌ! THAT'S ALL
YAS, SIR!
SIR!

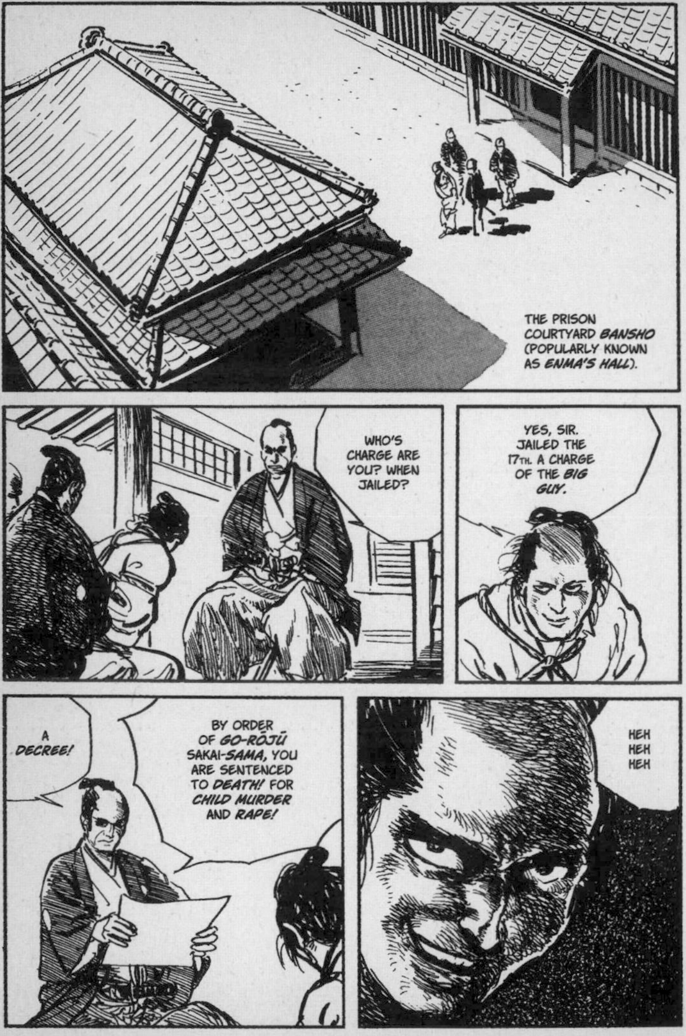
THE PRISON COURTYARD BANSHO (POPULARLY KNOWN AS ENMA'S HALL).
WHO'S CHARGE ARE YOU? WHEN JAILED?
YES, SIR. JAILED THE 17TH. A CHARGE OF THE BIG GUY.
A DECREE!
BY ORDER OF GO-RŌJŪ SAKAI-SAMA, YOU ARE SENTENCED TO DEATH! FOR CHILD MURDER AND RAPE!
HEH HEH HEH

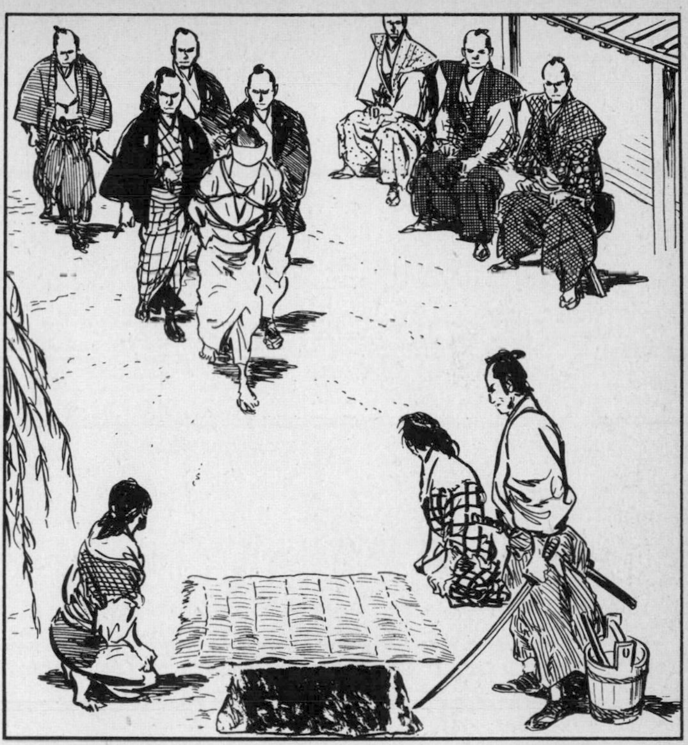

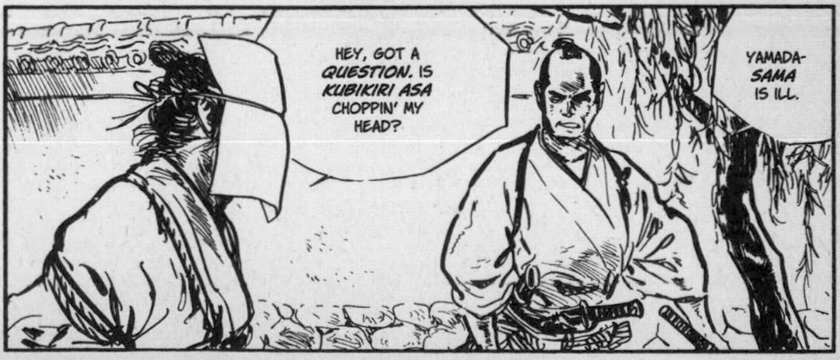
HEY, GOT A QUESTION. IS KUBIKIRI ASA CHOPPIN' MY HEAD?
YAMADA-SAMA IS ILL.

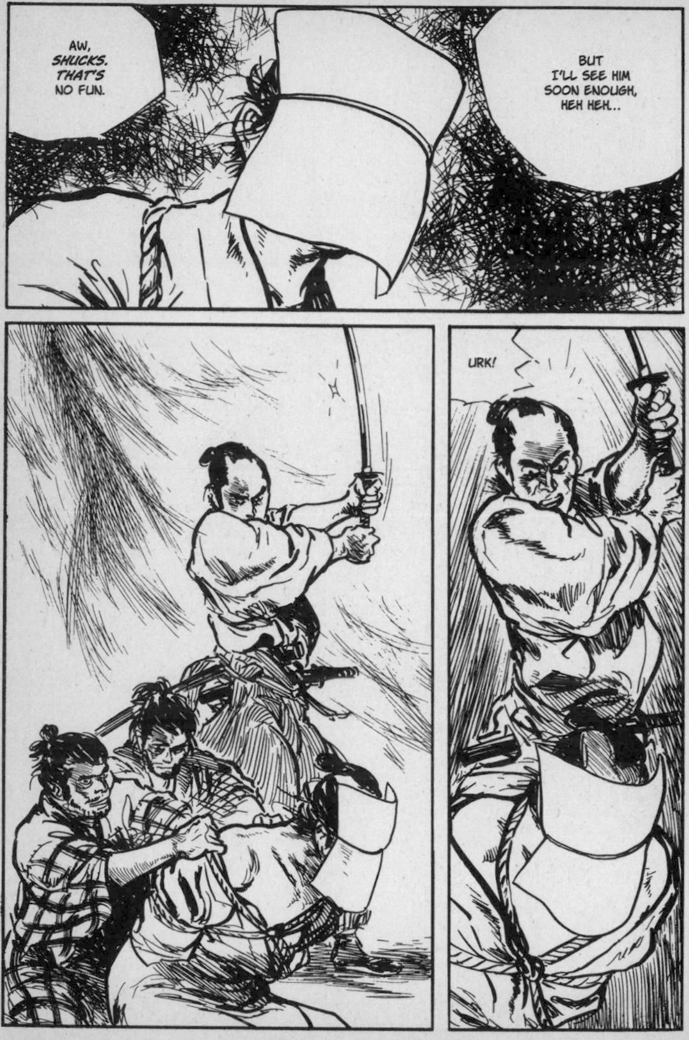
AW, *SHUCKS.* *THAT'S* NO FUN.
BUT I'LL SEE HIM SOON ENOUGH, HEH HEH...
URK!

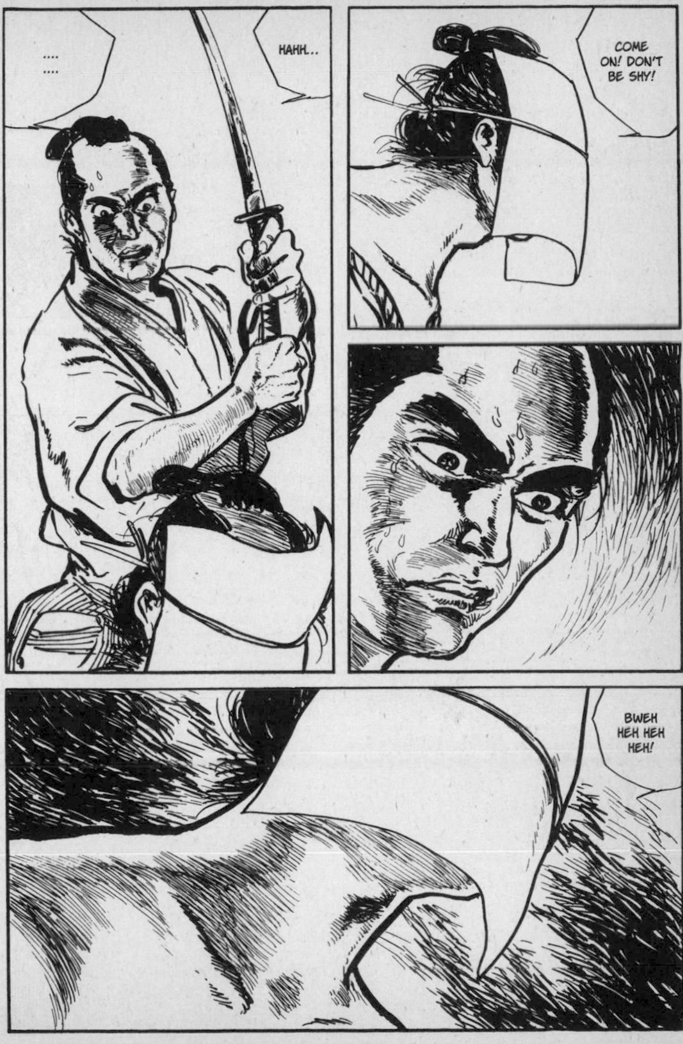
....
....
HAHH...
COME ON! DON'T BE SHY!
BWEH HEH HEH HEH!

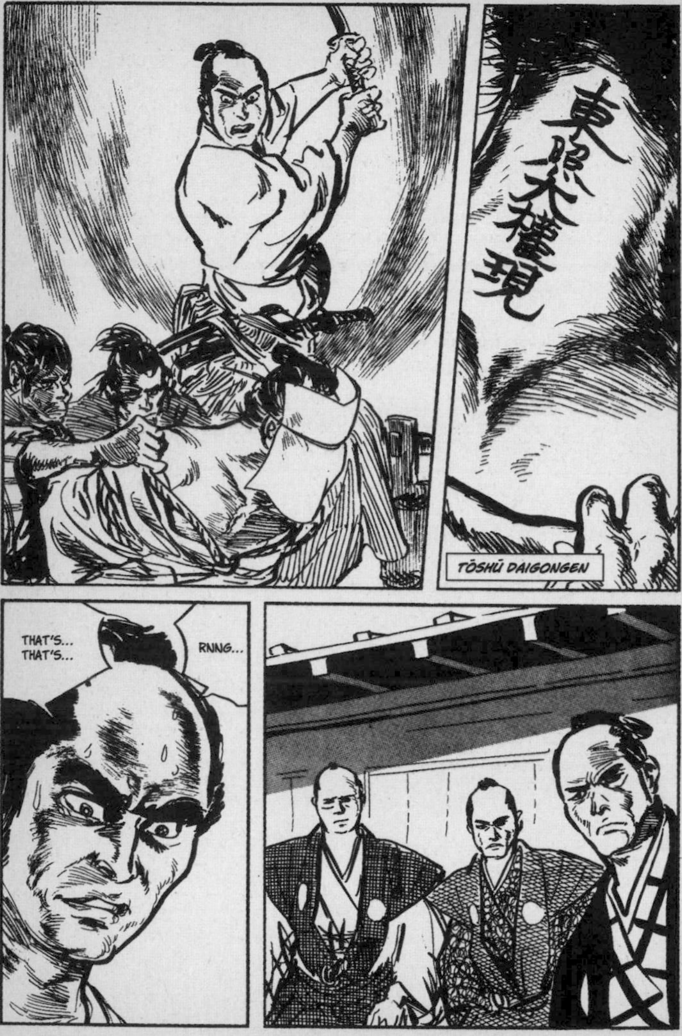

東照大權現
TŌSHŪ DAIGONGEN
THAT'S...
THAT'S...
RNNG...

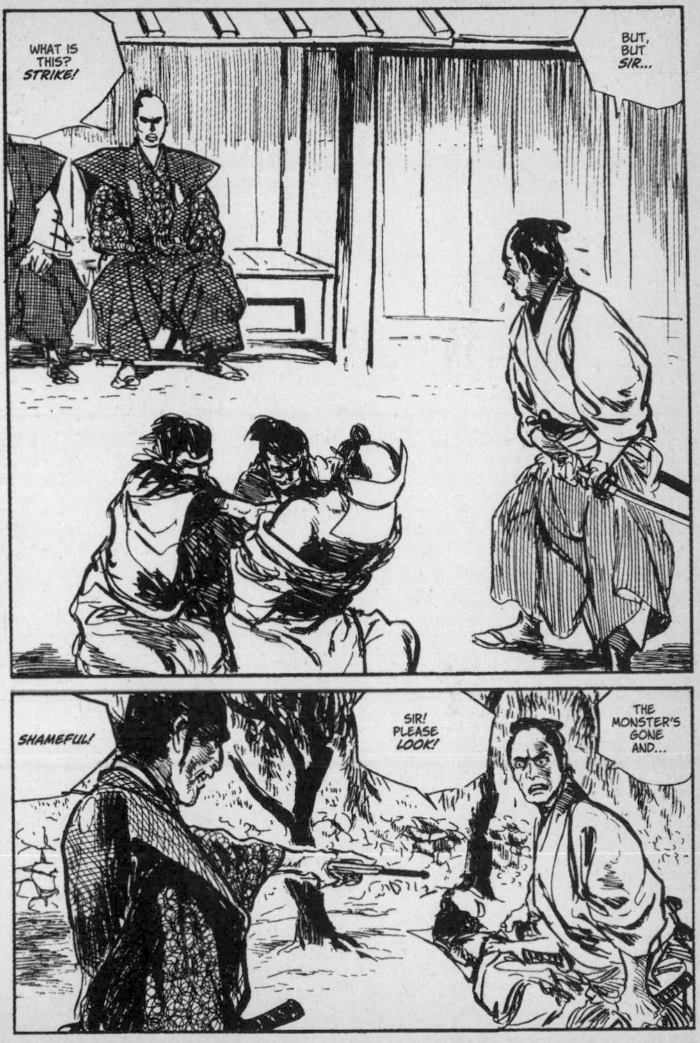
WHAT IS THIS? STRIKE!
BUT, BUT SIR...
SHAMEFUL!
SIR! PLEASE LOOK!
THE MONSTER'S GONE AND...

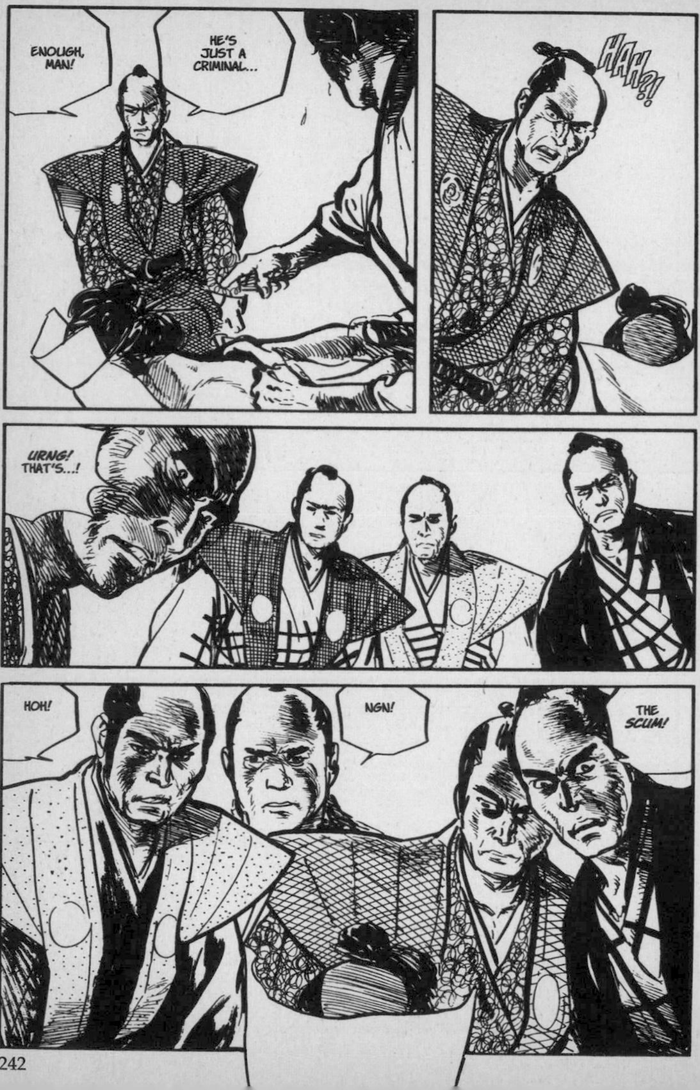
ENOUGH, MAN!
HE'S JUST A CRIMINAL...
HAH?!
URNG! THAT'S...!
HOH!
NGN!
THE SCUM!

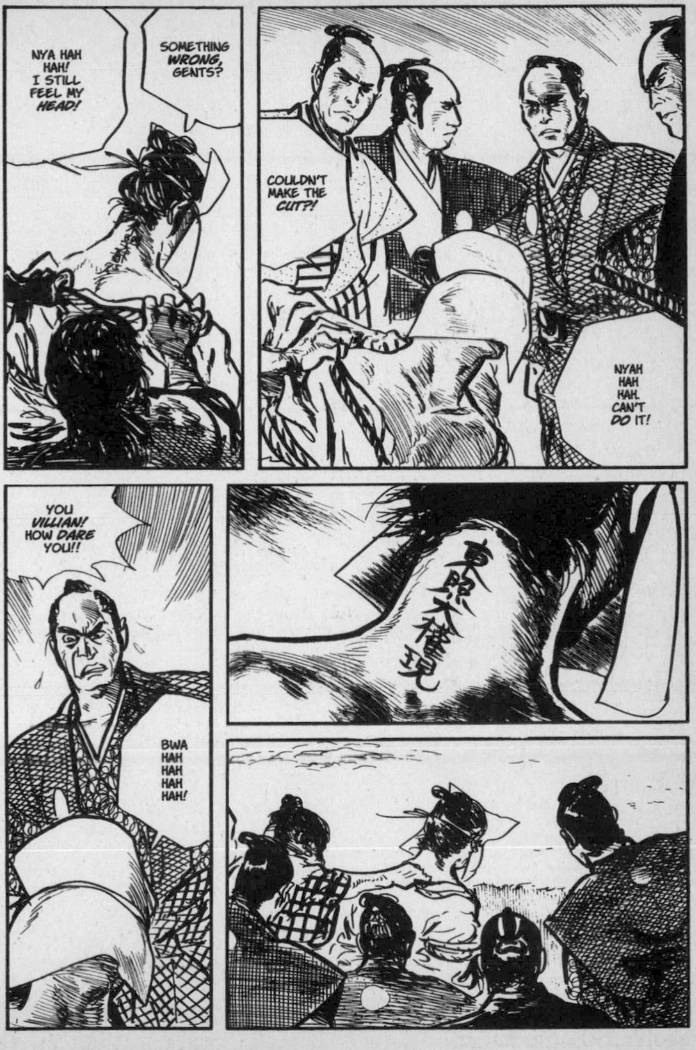
NYA HAH HAH! I STILL FEEL MY *HEAD!*
SOMETHING *WRONG,* GENTS?
COULDN'T MAKE THE *CUT?!*
NYAH HAH HAH. CAN'T *DO* IT!
YOU *VILLIAN!* HOW *DARE* YOU!!
BWA HAH HAH HAH HAH!
東照大權現

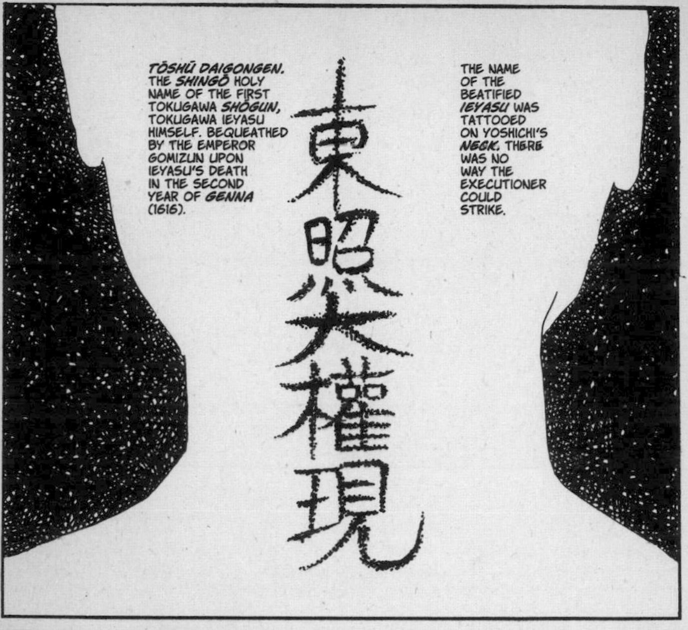
TŌSHŪ DAIGONGEN. THE SHINGŌ HOLY NAME OF THE FIRST TOKUGAWA SHŌGUN, TOKUGAWA IEYASU HIMSELF. BEQUEATHED BY THE EMPEROR GOMIZUN UPON IEYASU'S DEATH IN THE SECOND YEAR OF GENNA (1616).
東照大權現
THE NAME OF THE BEATIFIED IEYASU WAS TATTOOED ON YOSHICHI'S NECK. THERE WAS NO WAY THE EXECUTIONER COULD STRIKE.

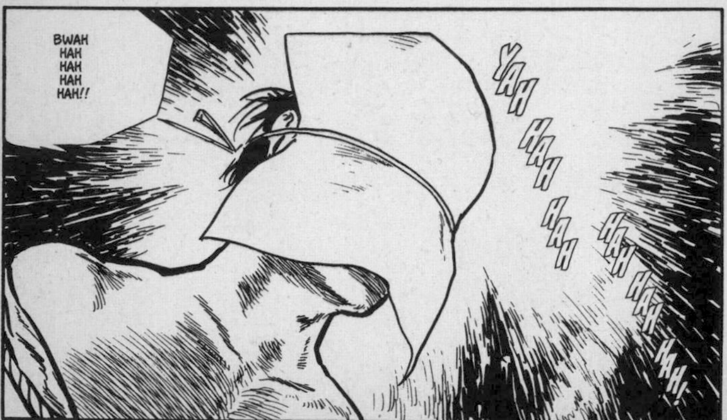
BWAH HAH HAH HAH HAH!!
YAH HAH HAH HAH HAH HAH!

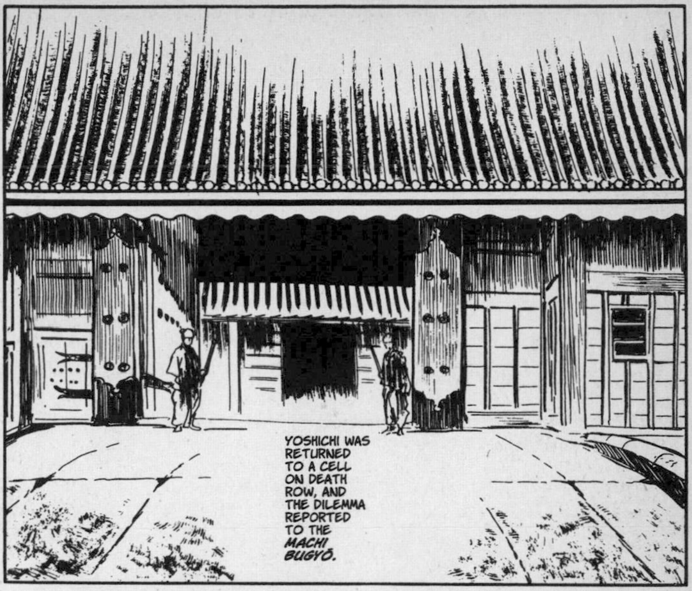
YOSHICHI WAS RETURNED TO A CELL ON DEATH ROW, AND THE DILEMMA REPORTED TO THE *MACHI BUGYŌ*.

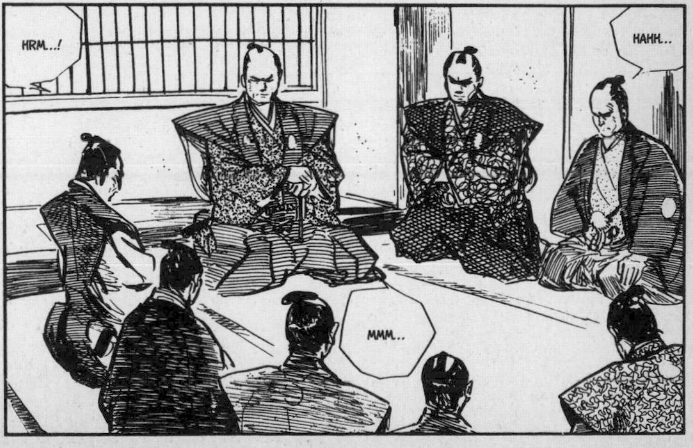
HRM..!
HAHH..
MMM..

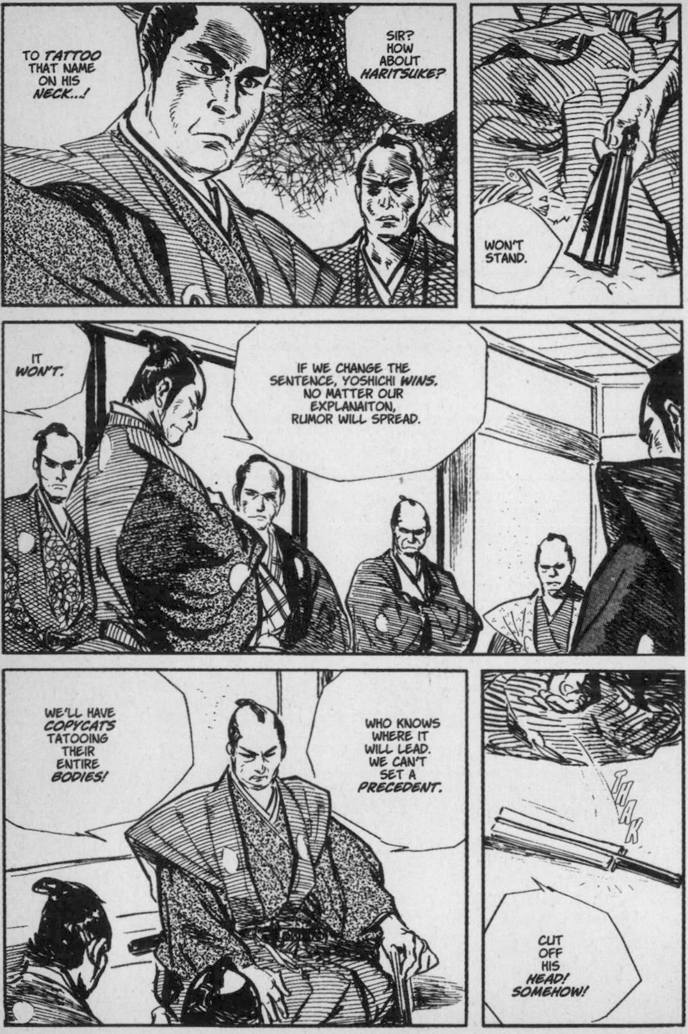
TO TATTOO THAT NAME ON HIS NECK...!
SIR? HOW ABOUT HARITSUKE?
WON'T STAND.
IT WON'T.
IF WE CHANGE THE SENTENCE, YOSHICHI WINS. NO MATTER OUR EXPLANAITON, RUMOR WILL SPREAD.
WE'LL HAVE COPYCATS TATOOING THEIR ENTIRE BODIES!
WHO KNOWS WHERE IT WILL LEAD. WE CAN'T SET A PRECEDENT.
THAK
CUT OFF HIS HEAD! SOMEHOW!

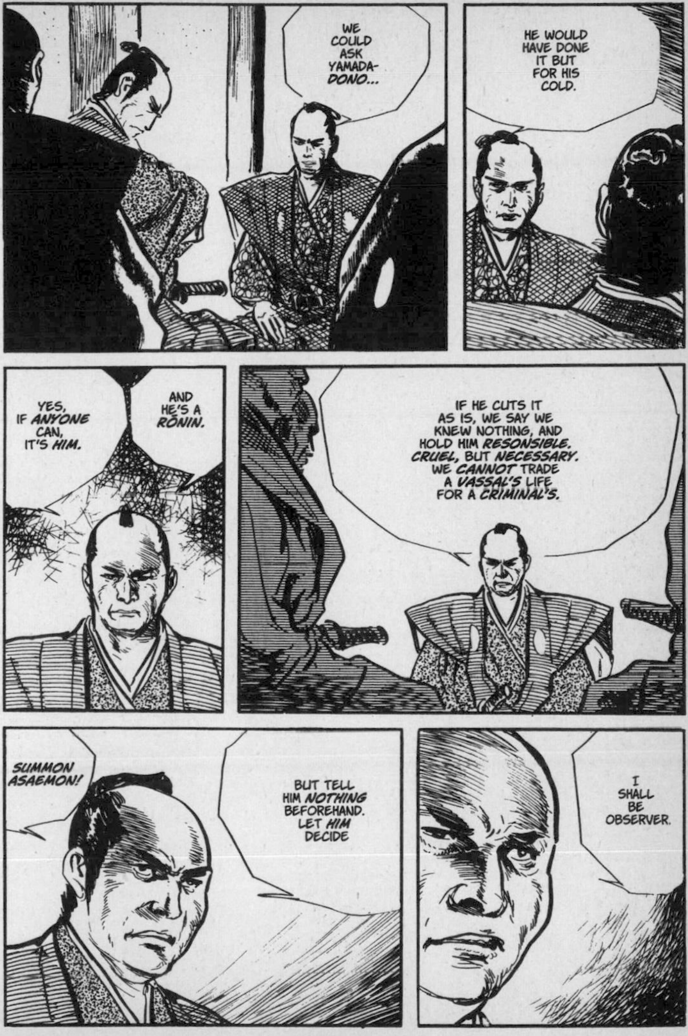

WE COULD ASK YAMADA-*DONO...*
HE WOULD HAVE DONE IT BUT FOR HIS COLD.
YES, IF *ANYONE* CAN, IT'S *HIM.*
AND HE'S A *RŌNIN.*
IF HE CUTS IT AS IS, WE SAY WE KNEW NOTHING, AND HOLD HIM *RESONSIBLE. CRUEL,* BUT *NECESSARY.* WE *CANNOT* TRADE A *VASSAL'S* LIFE FOR A *CRIMINAL'S.*
SUMMON ASAEMON!
BUT TELL HIM *NOTHING* BEFOREHAND. LET *HIM* DECIDE
I SHALL BE OBSERVER.

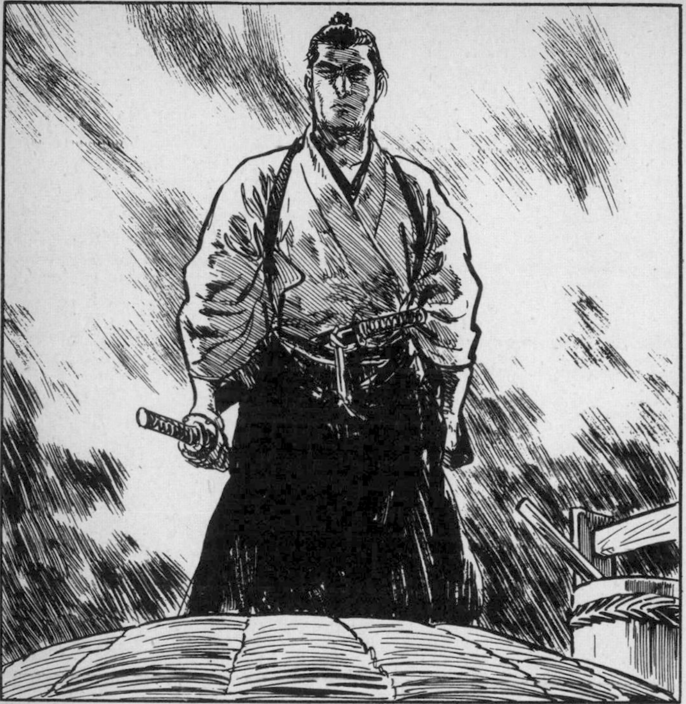

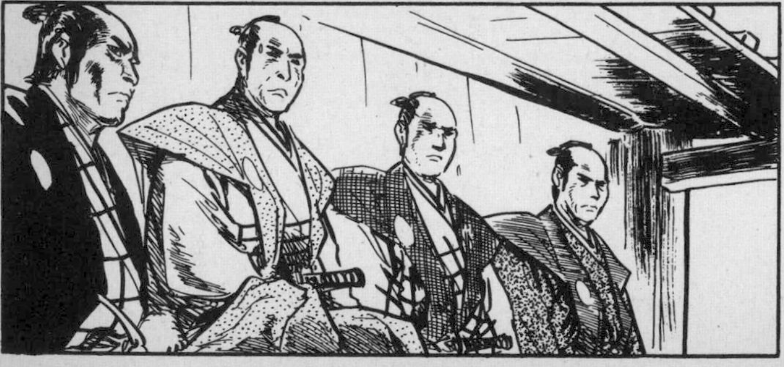

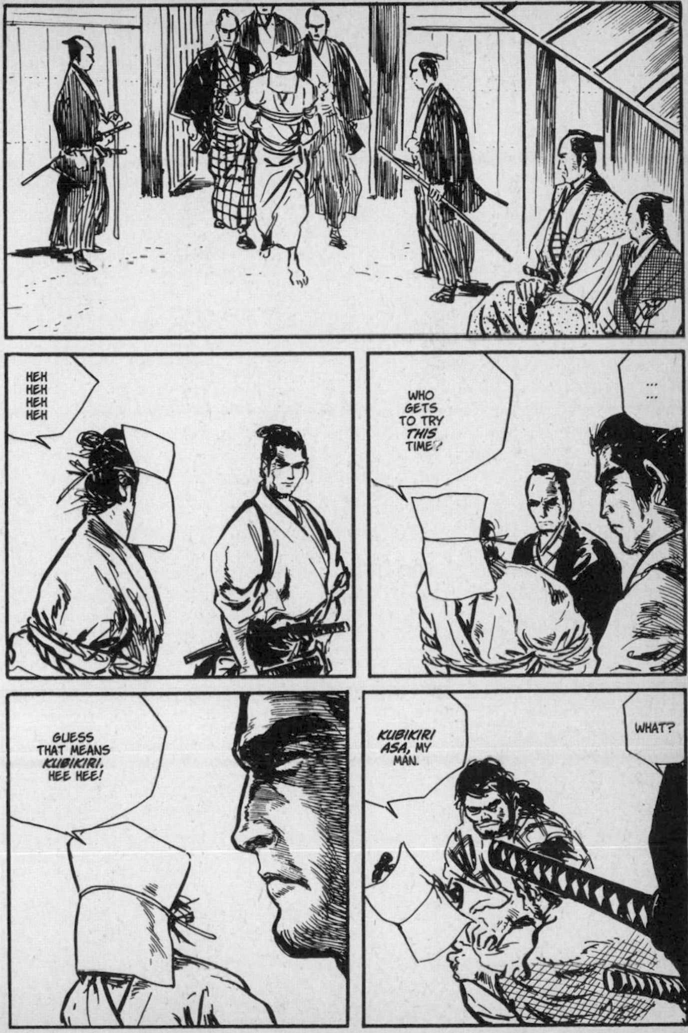
HEH HEH HEH HEH
WHO GETS TO TRY *THIS* TIME?
... ...
GUESS THAT MEANS *KUBIKIRI.* HEE HEE!
KUBIKIRI ASA, MY MAN.
WHAT?

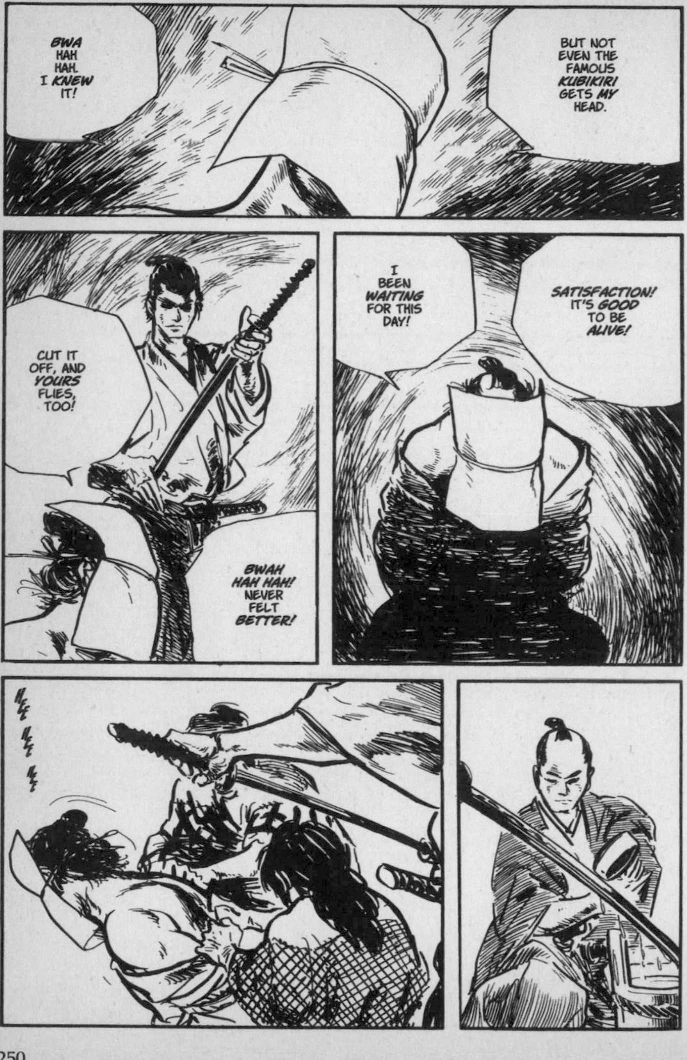
BWA HAH HAH. I KNEW IT!
BUT NOT EVEN THE FAMOUS KUBIKIRI GETS MY HEAD.
CUT IT OFF, AND YOURS FLIES, TOO!
BWAH HAH HAH! NEVER FELT BETTER!
I BEEN WAITING FOR THIS DAY!
SATISFACTION! IT'S GOOD TO BE ALIVE!

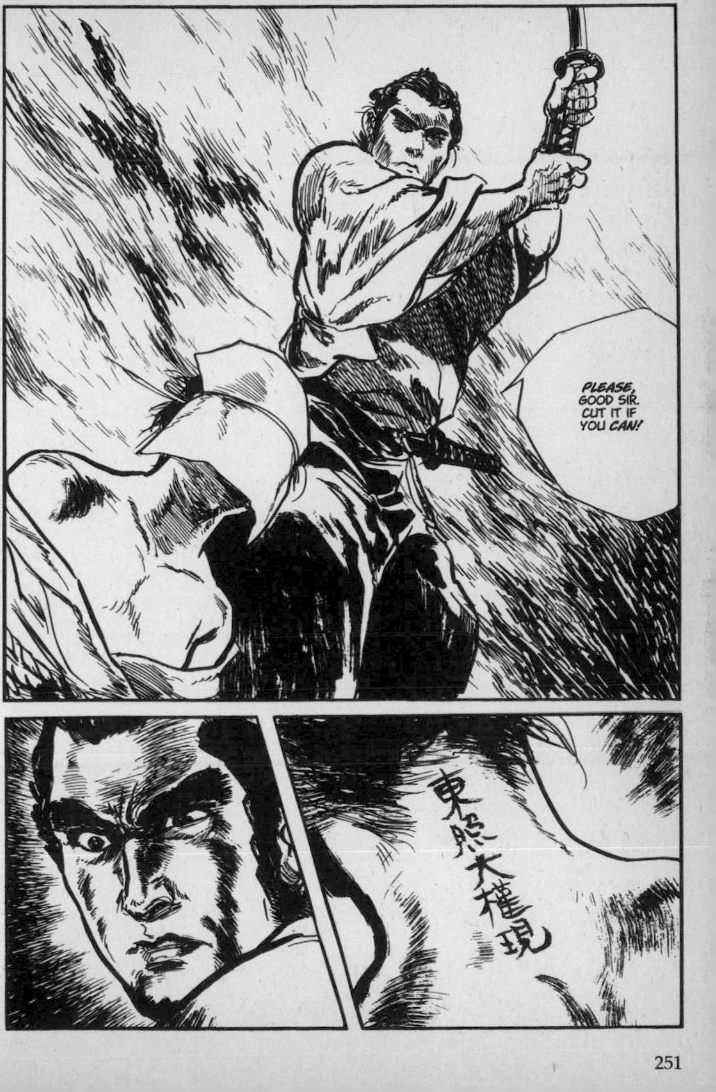
PLEASE, GOOD SIR. CUT IT IF YOU CAN!
東照大權現

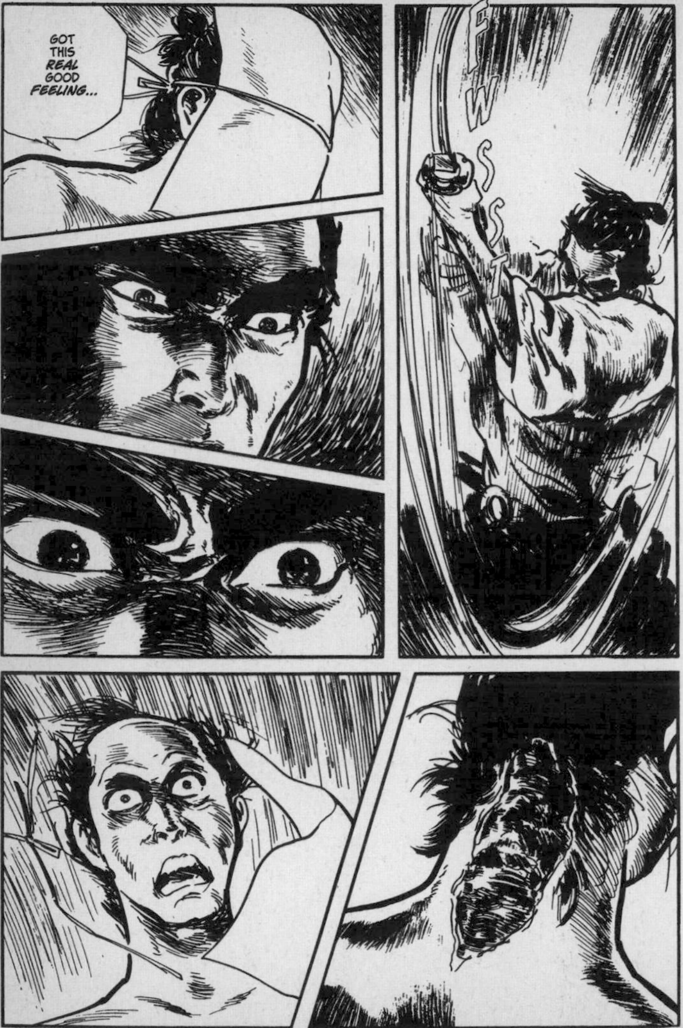
GOT THIS REAL GOOD FEELING...
FWSSST

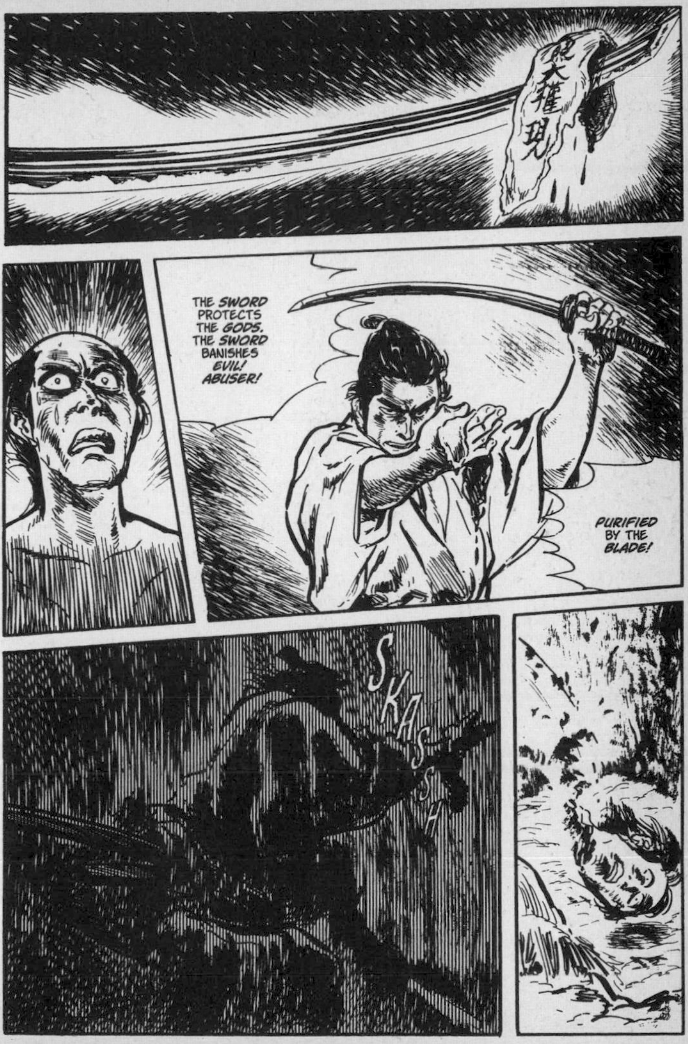
大権現
THE *SWORD* PROTECTS THE *GODS.* THE *SWORD* BANISHES *EVIL! ABUSER!*
PURIFIED BY THE *BLADE!*
SKASSH

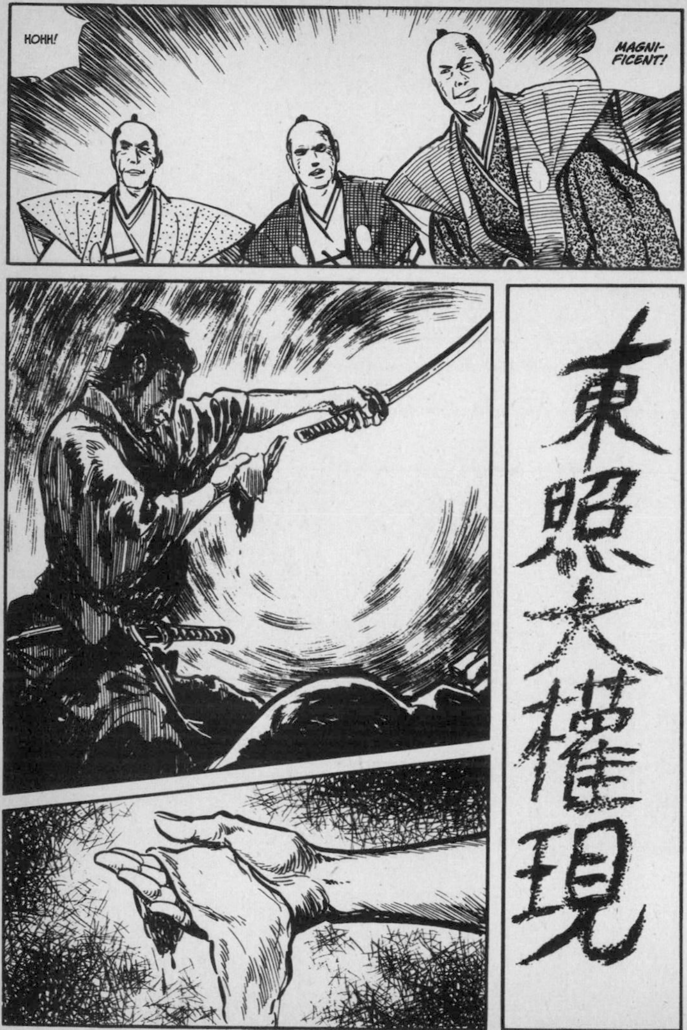
HOHH!
MAGNI-
FICENT!
東照大権現

the fifth

Asaji

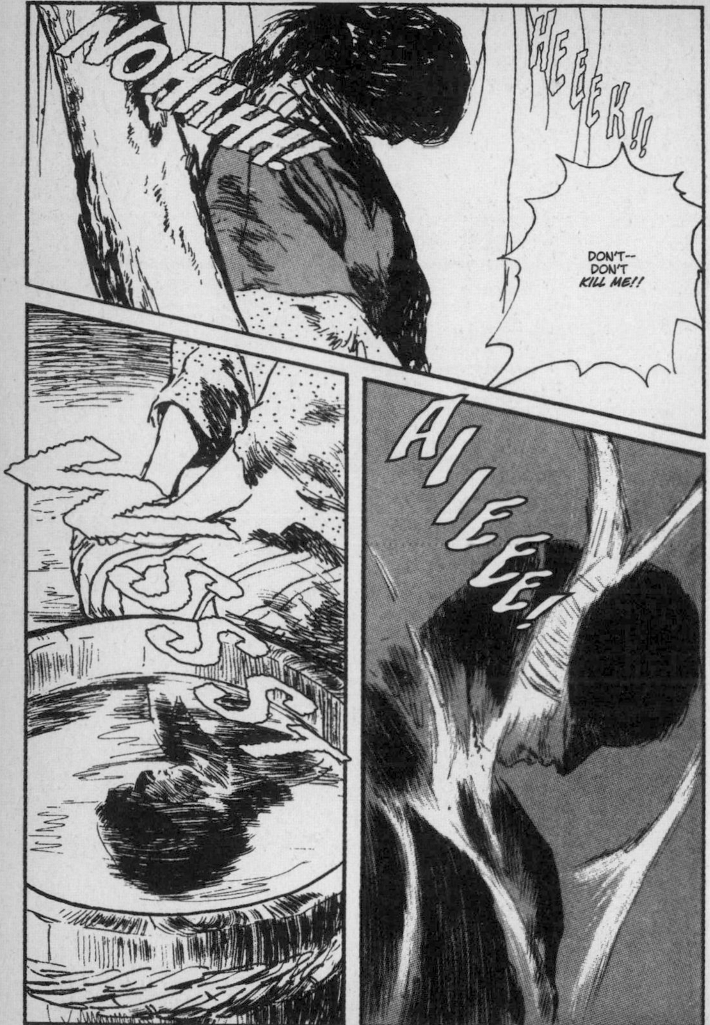
NOEEEH!!
HEEEK!!
DON'T--
DON'T
KILL ME!!
SSSS
AIIEEE!

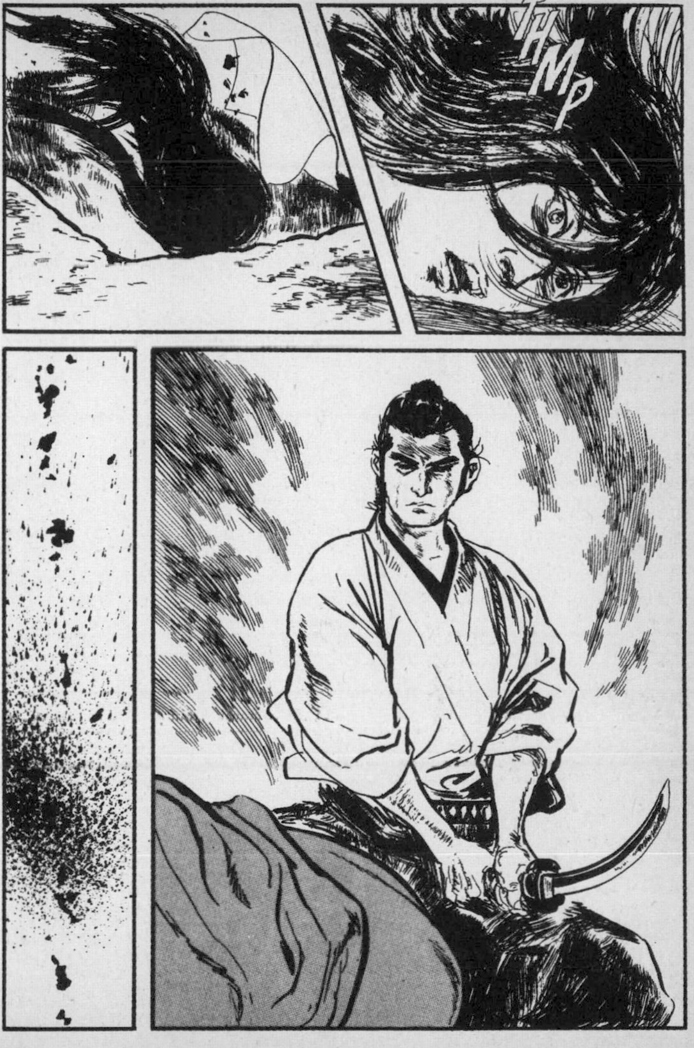
THMP

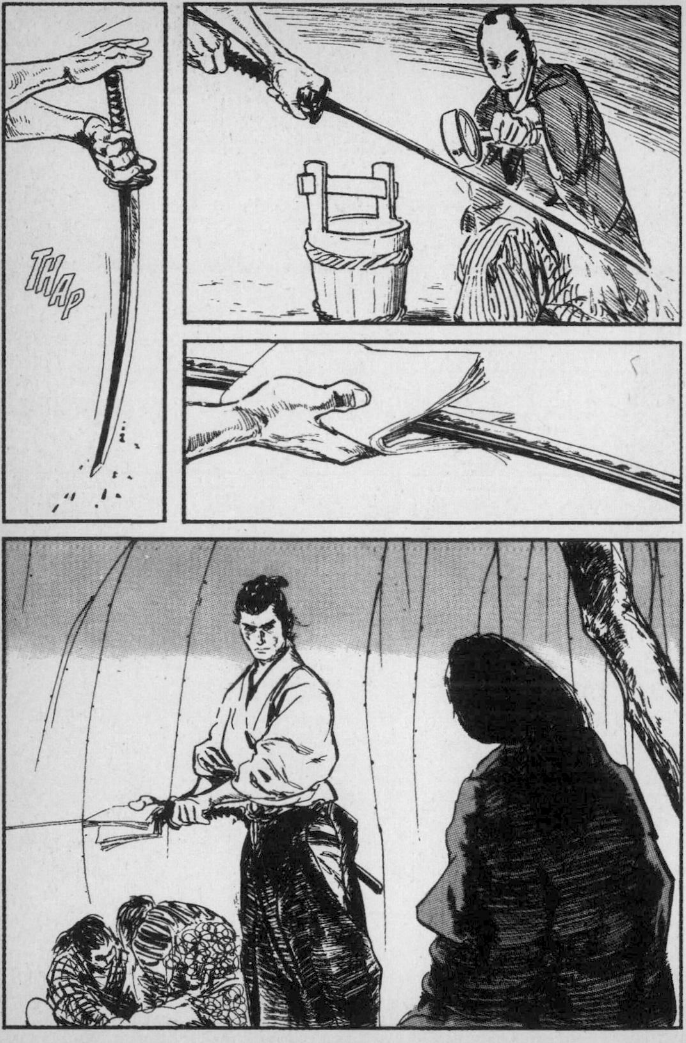
THAP

CHNG!

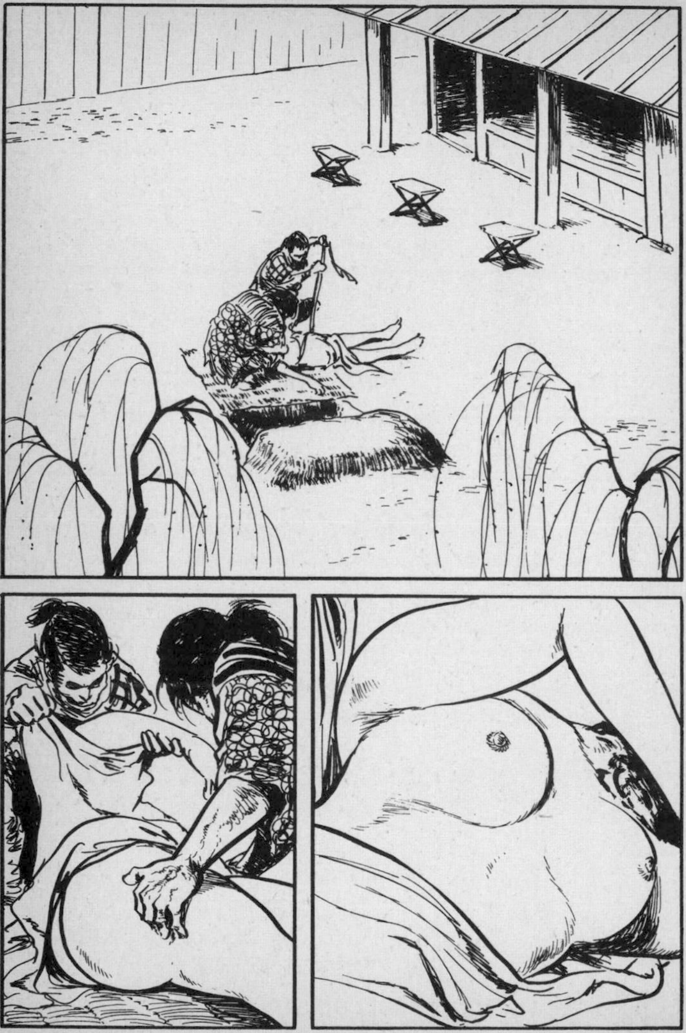

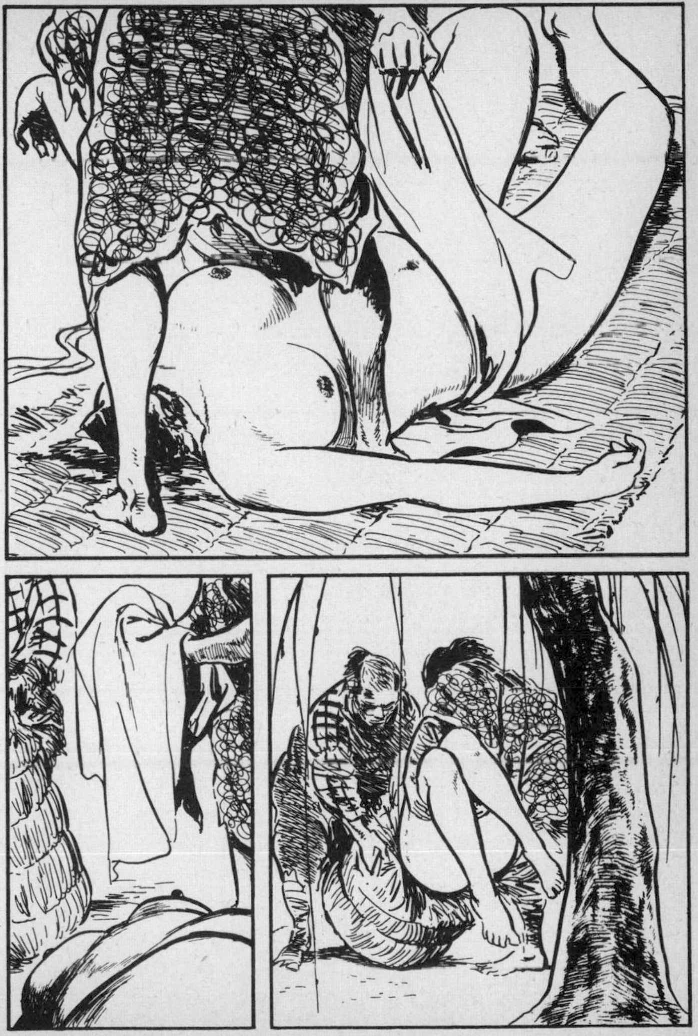

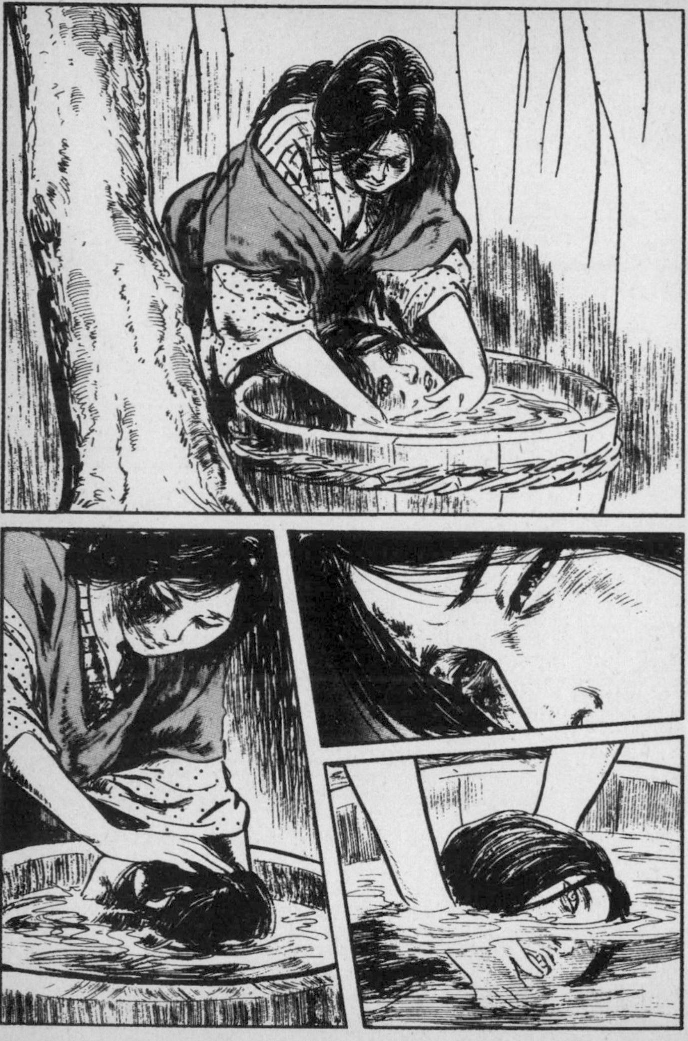

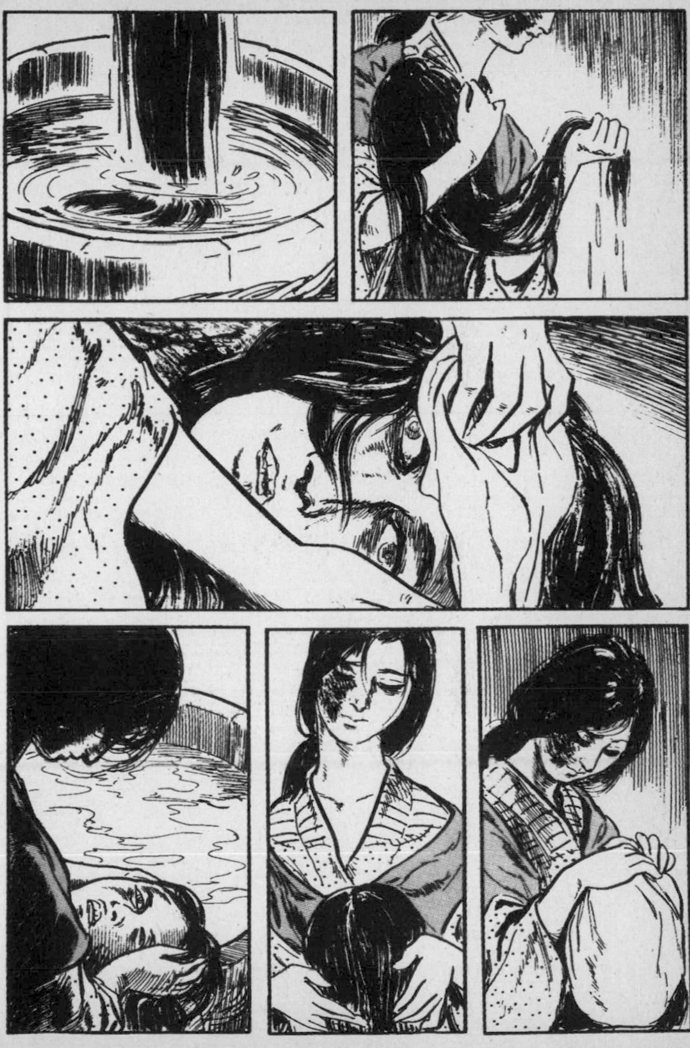

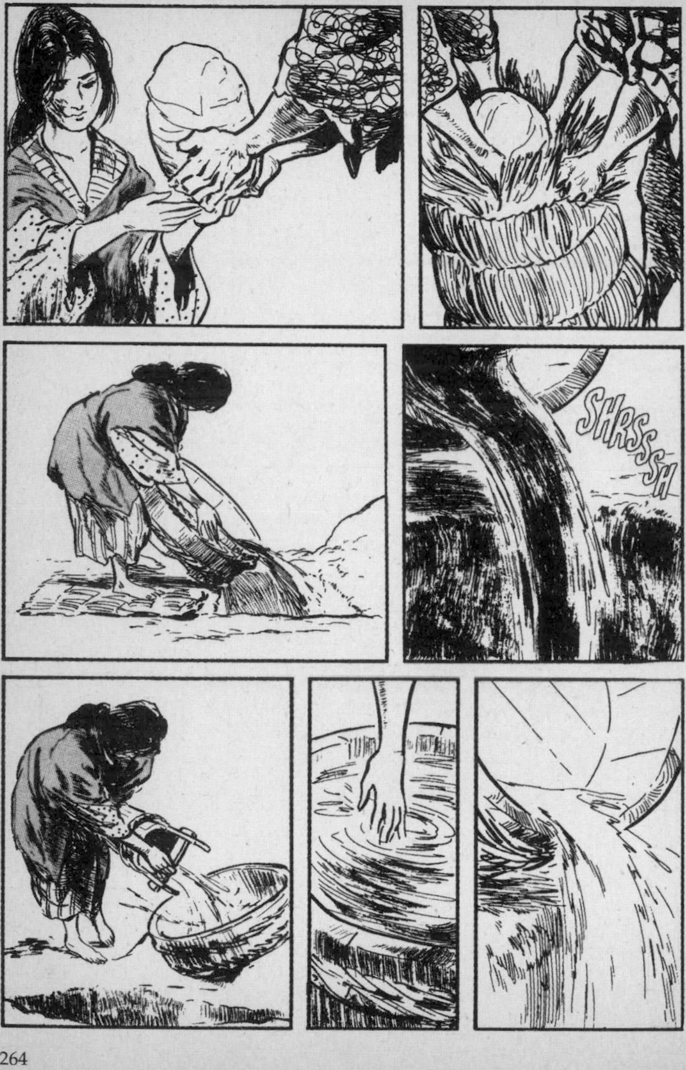
SHRSSSH

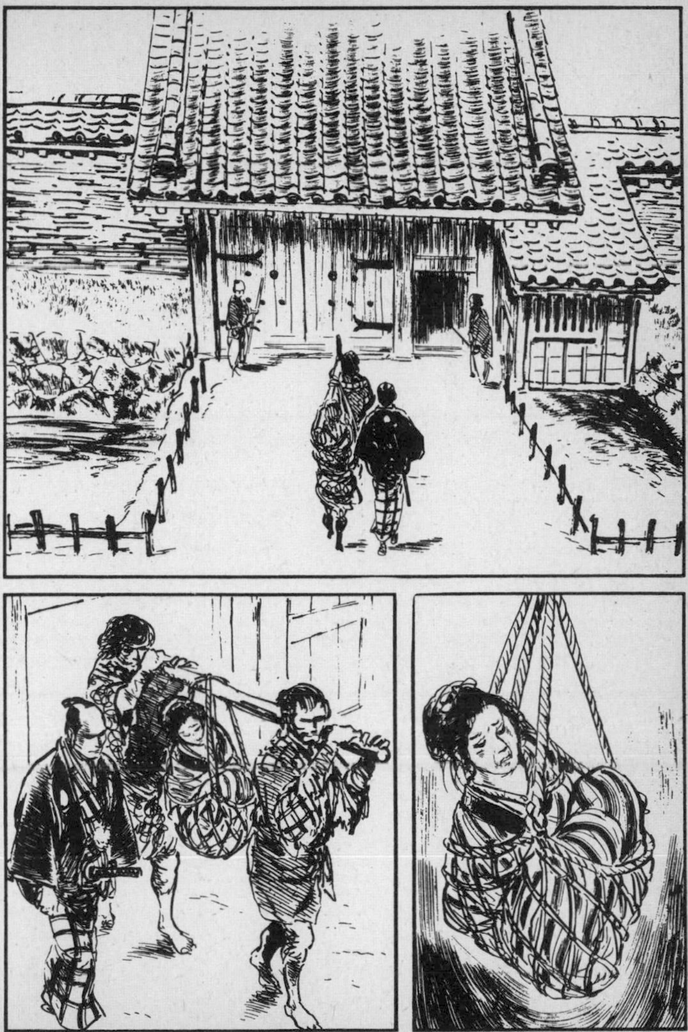

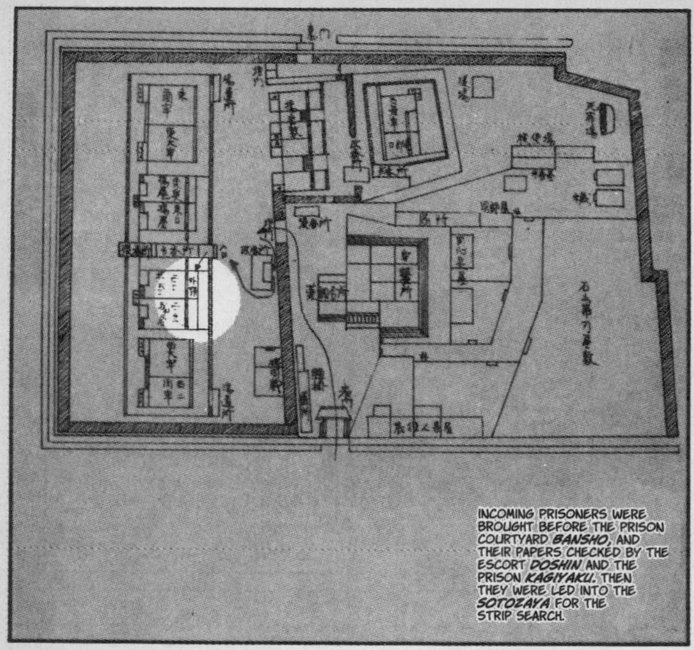
INCOMING PRISONERS WERE BROUGHT BEFORE THE PRISON COURTYARD BANSHO, AND THEIR PAPERS CHECKED BY THE ESCORT DOSHIN AND THE PRISON KAGIYAKU. THEN THEY WERE LED INTO THE SOTOZAYA FOR THE STRIP SEARCH.

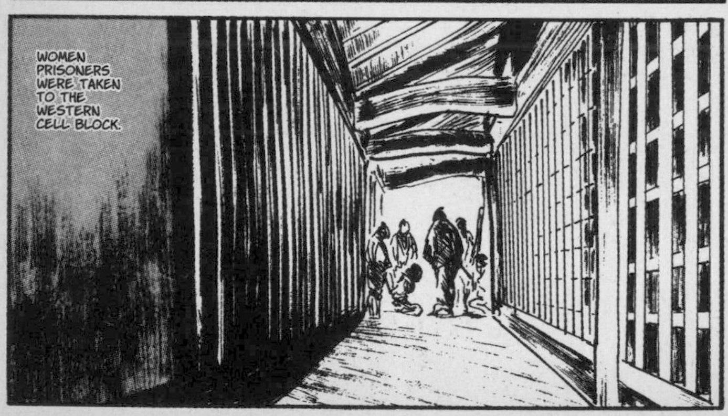
WOMEN PRISONERS WERE TAKEN TO THE WESTERN CELL BLOCK.

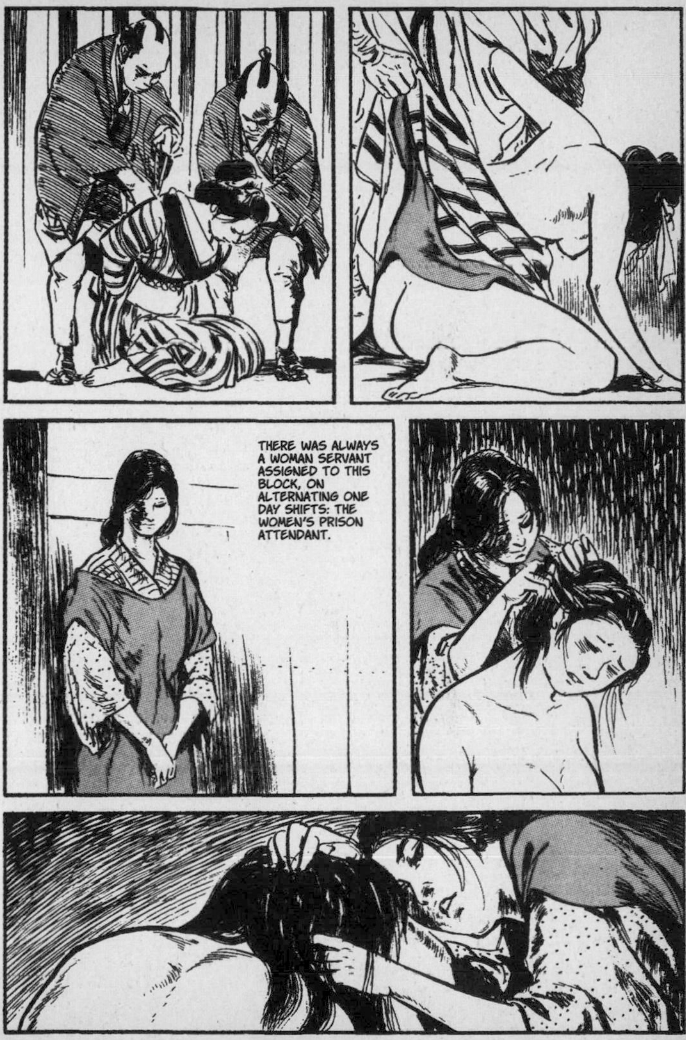
THERE WAS ALWAYS A WOMAN SERVANT ASSIGNED TO THIS BLOCK, ON ALTERNATING ONE DAY SHIFTS: THE WOMEN'S PRISON ATTENDANT.

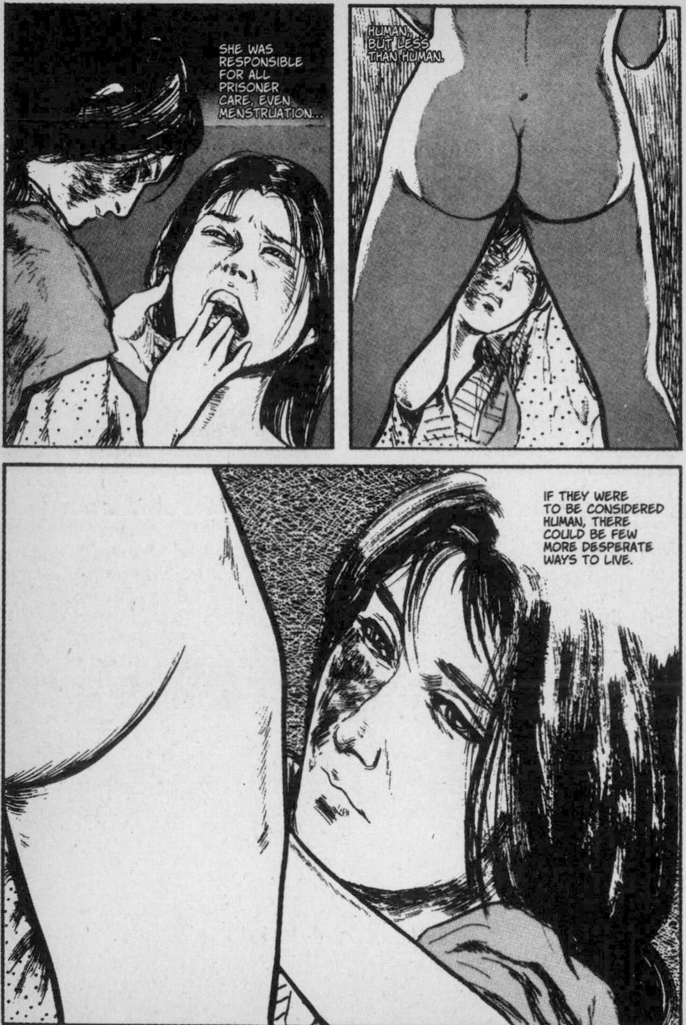
SHE WAS RESPONSIBLE FOR ALL PRISONER CARE, EVEN MENSTRUATION...
HUMAN, BUT LESS THAN HUMAN.
IF THEY WERE TO BE CONSIDERED HUMAN, THERE COULD BE FEW MORE DESPERATE WAYS TO LIVE.

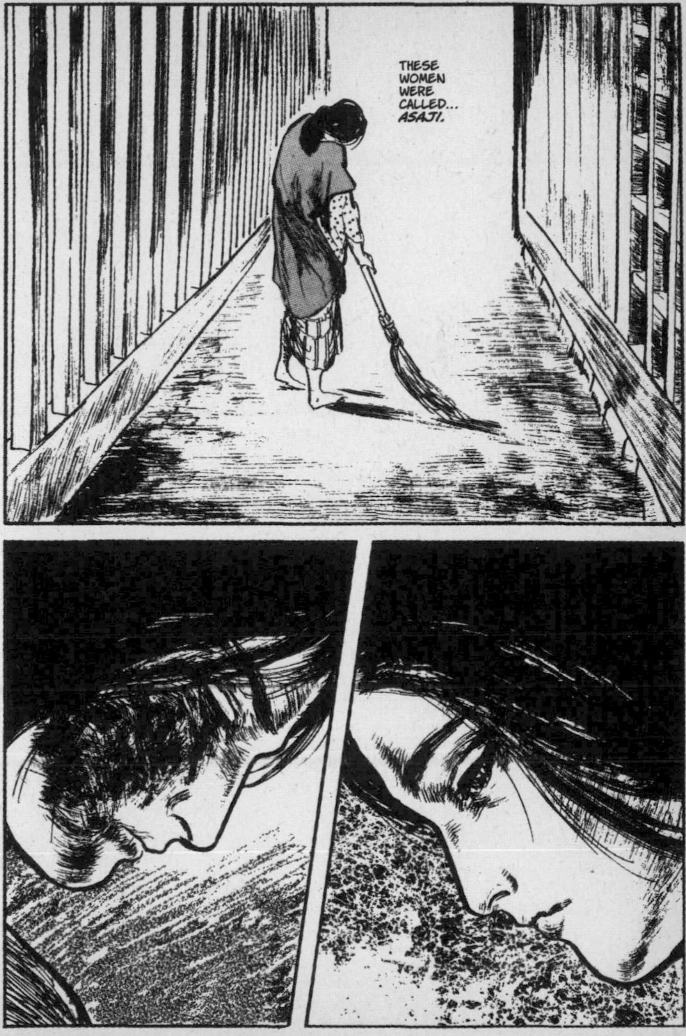
THESE WOMEN WERE CALLED... ASAJI.

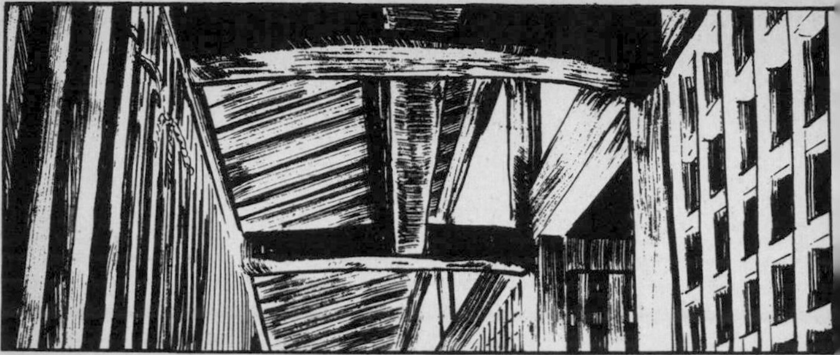

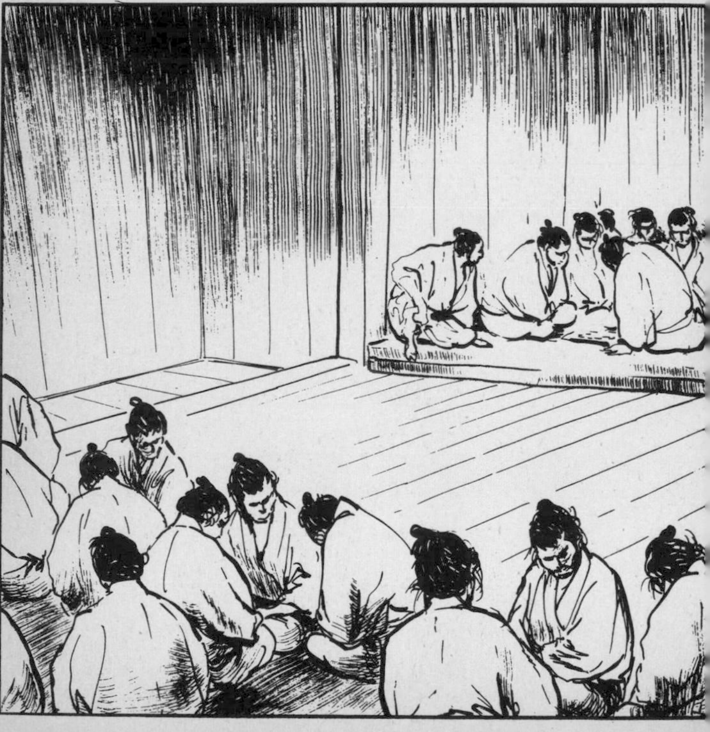

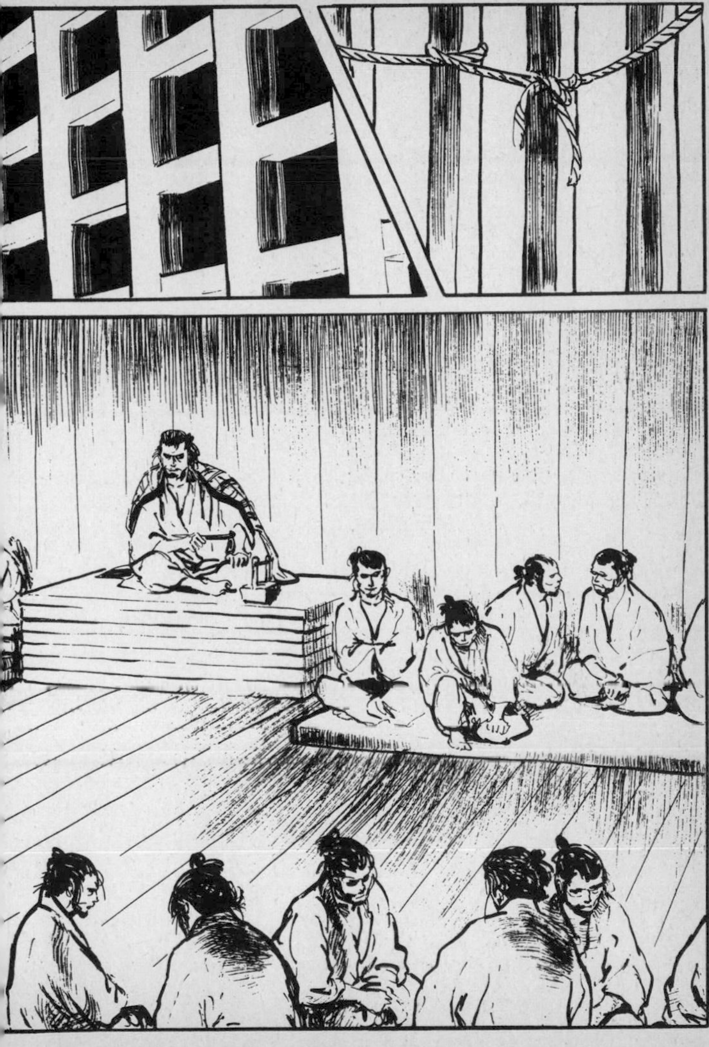

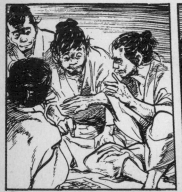

272

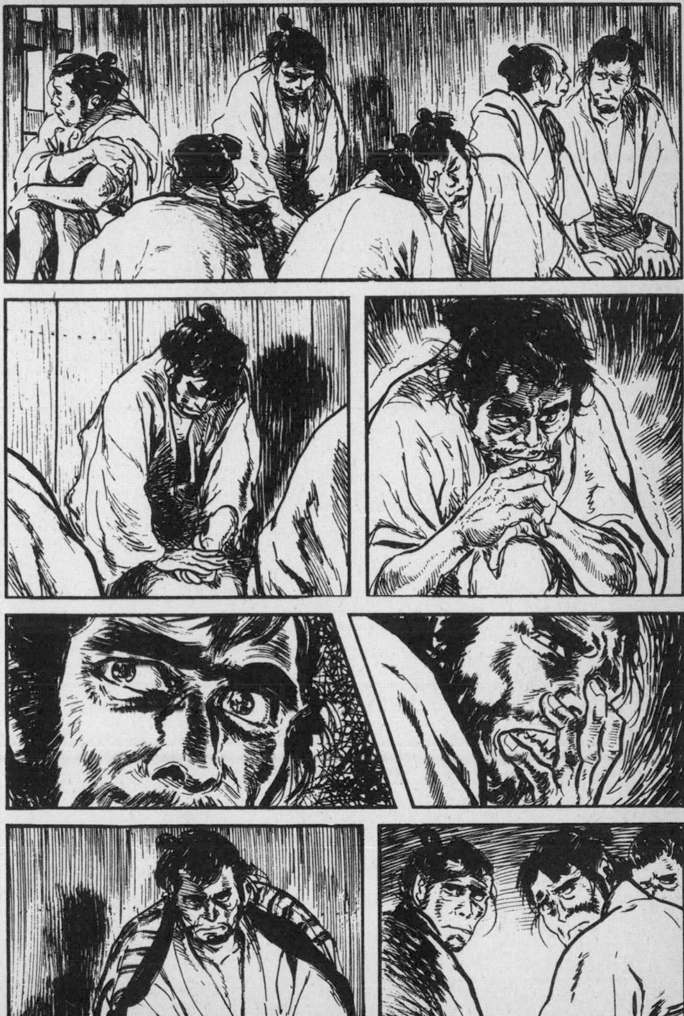

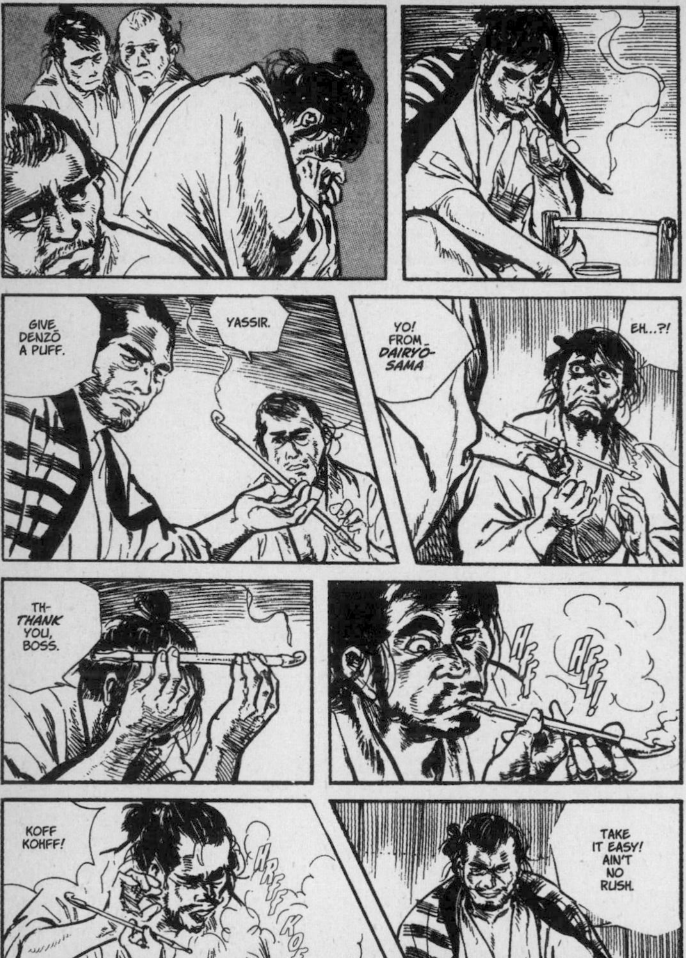
GIVE DENZŌ A PUFF.
YASSIR.
YO! FROM *DAIRYŌ-SAMA*
EH...?!
TH- *THANK* YOU, BOSS.
HFF
HFF!
KOFF KOHFF!
HRFF
KOFF
TAKE IT EASY! AIN'T NO RUSH.

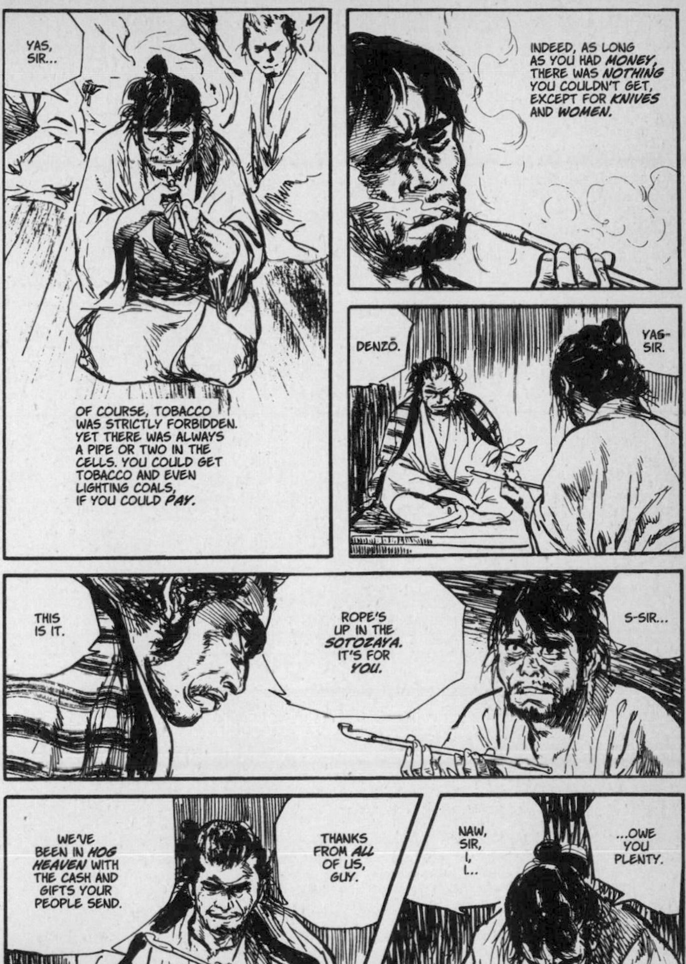
YAS, SIR...
OF COURSE, TOBACCO WAS STRICTLY FORBIDDEN. YET THERE WAS ALWAYS A PIPE OR TWO IN THE CELLS. YOU COULD GET TOBACCO AND EVEN LIGHTING COALS, IF YOU COULD *PAY.*
INDEED, AS LONG AS YOU HAD *MONEY,* THERE WAS *NOTHING* YOU COULDN'T GET, EXCEPT FOR *KNIVES* AND *WOMEN.*
DENZŌ.
YAS-SIR.
THIS IS IT.
ROPE'S UP IN THE *SOTOZAYA.* IT'S FOR *YOU.*
S-SIR...
WE'VE BEEN IN *HOG HEAVEN* WITH THE CASH AND GIFTS YOUR PEOPLE SEND.
THANKS FROM *ALL* OF US, GUY.
NAW, SIR, I, I...
...OWE YOU PLENTY.

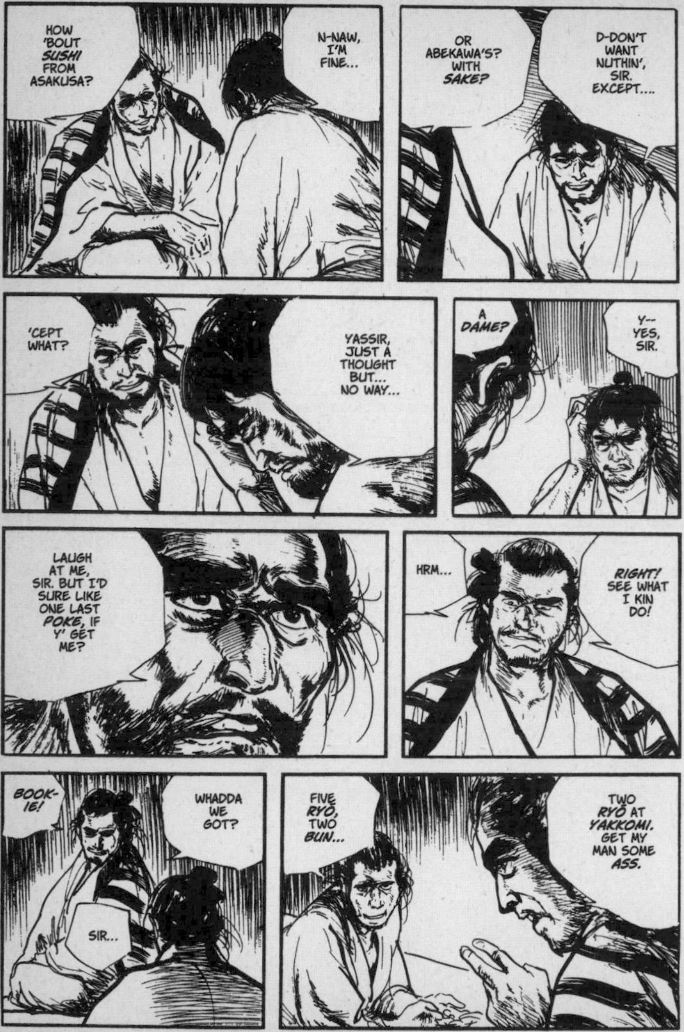
HOW 'BOUT SUSHI FROM ASAKUSA?
N-NAW, I'M FINE...
OR ABEKAWA'S? WITH SAKE?
D-DON'T WANT NUTHIN', SIR. EXCEPT....
'CEPT WHAT?
YASSIR, JUST A THOUGHT BUT... NO WAY...
A DAME?
Y-- YES, SIR.
LAUGH AT ME, SIR. BUT I'D SURE LIKE ONE LAST POKE, IF Y' GET ME?
HRM...
RIGHT! SEE WHAT I KIN DO!
BOOK-IE!
WHADDA WE GOT?
SIR...
FIVE RYŌ, TWO BUN...
TWO RYŌ AT YAKKOMI. GET MY MAN SOME ASS.

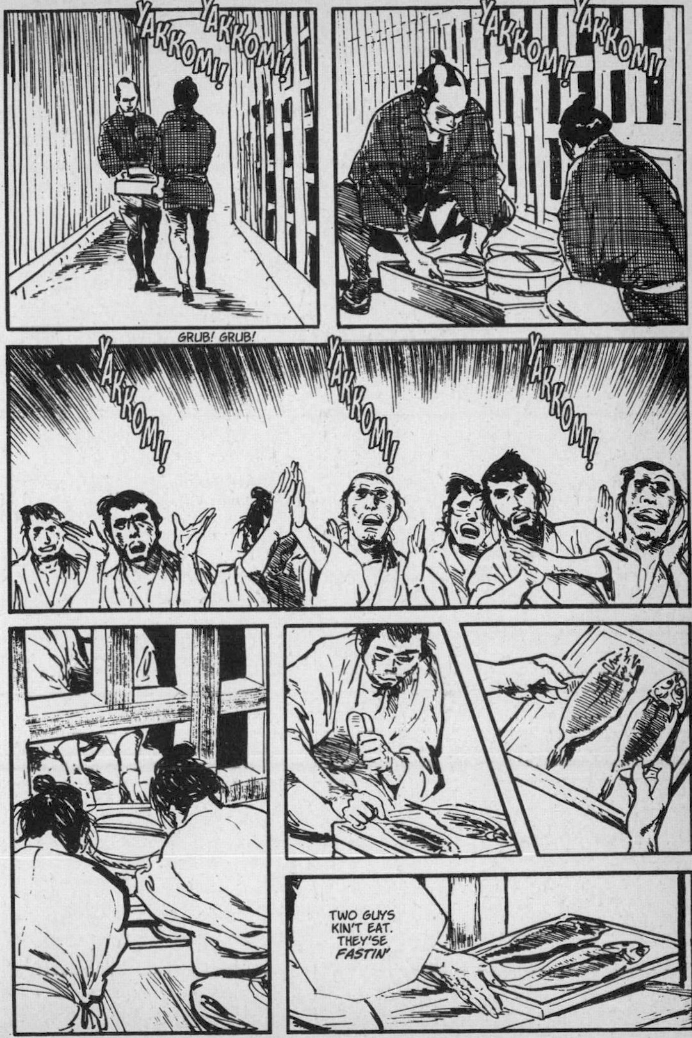
YAKKOMI!!
YAKKOMI!!
YAKKOMI!!
YAKKOMI!!
GRUB! GRUB!
YAKKOMI!
YAKKOMI!
YAKKOMI!
TWO GUYS KIN'T EAT. THEY'SE *FASTIN'*

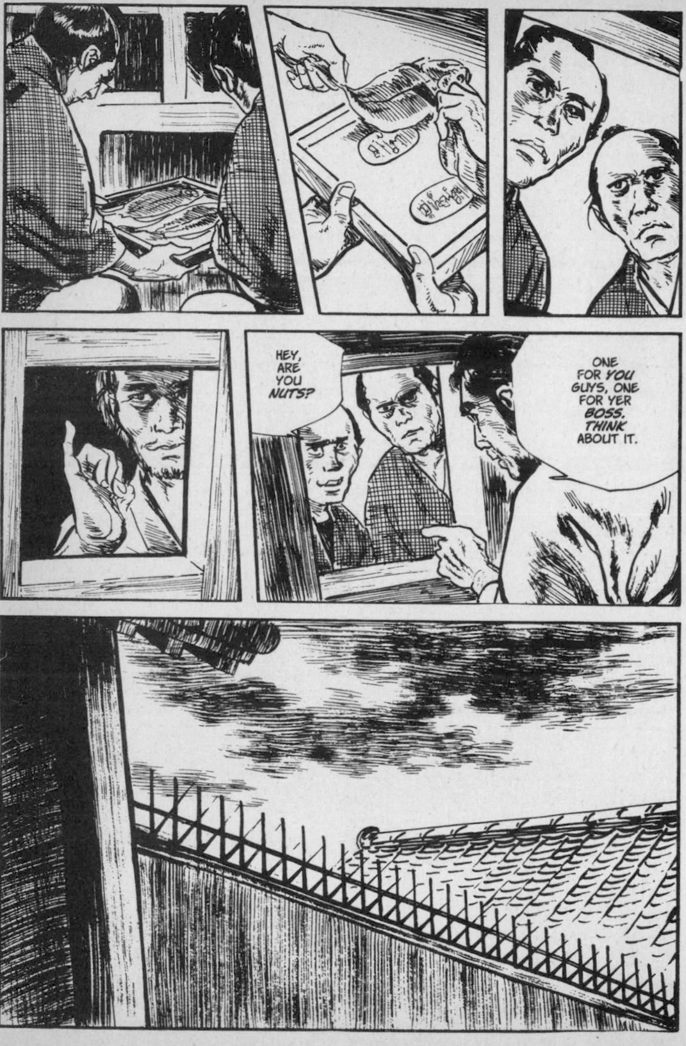
HEY, ARE YOU NUTS?
ONE FOR YOU GUYS, ONE FOR YER BOSS. THINK ABOUT IT.

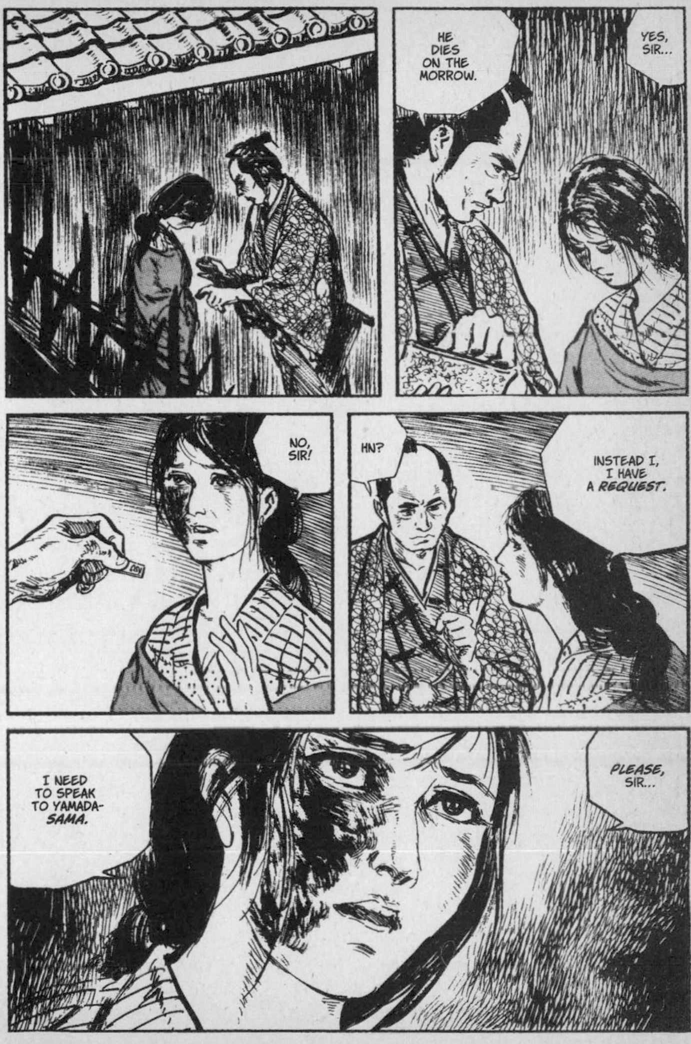
HE DIES ON THE MORROW.
YES, SIR...
NO, SIR!
HN?
INSTEAD I, I HAVE A *REQUEST*.
I NEED TO SPEAK TO YAMADA-*SAMA*.
PLEASE, SIR...

PLEASE, CAN YOU ASK?

WHAT DOES AN *ASAJI* WANT WITH YAMADA-*SAMA*?

PLEASE, SIR. I'LL DO *ANYTHING*.

I *BEG* OF YOU!

HMM...

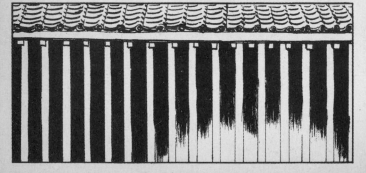

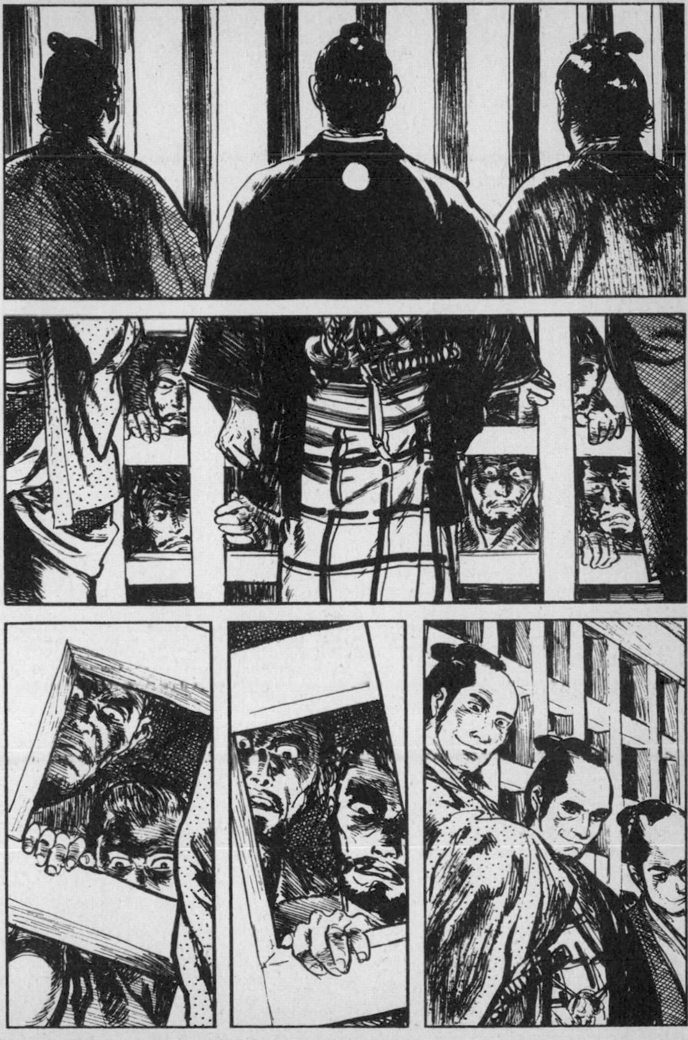

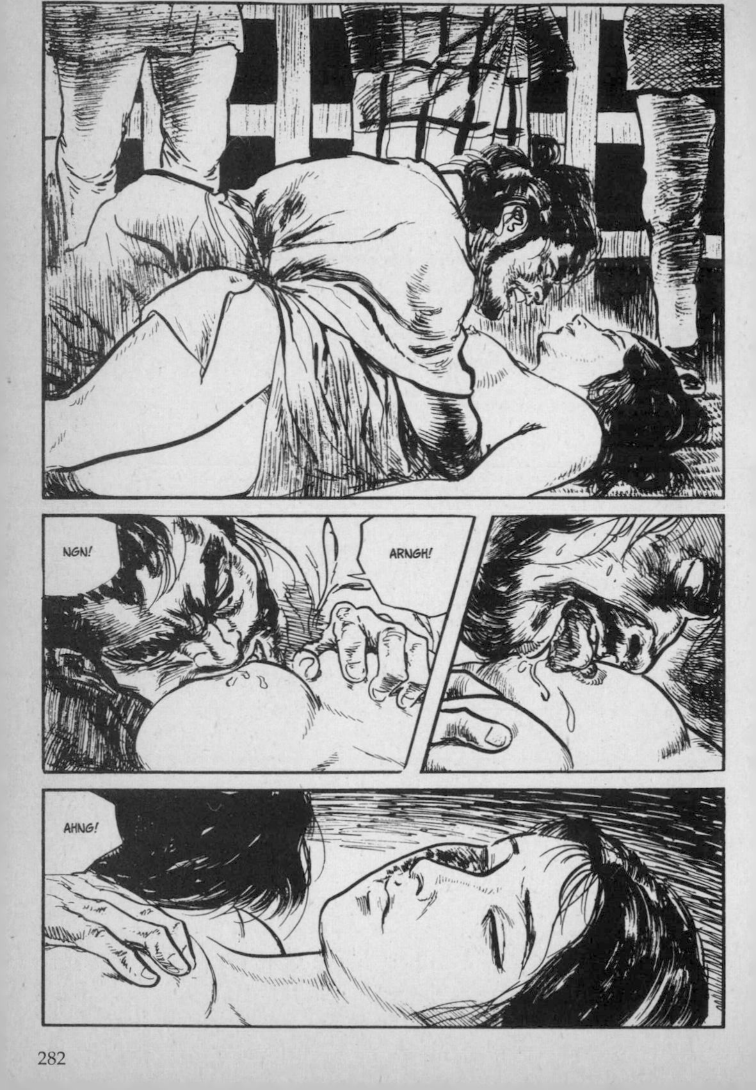
NGN!
ARNGH!
AHNG!

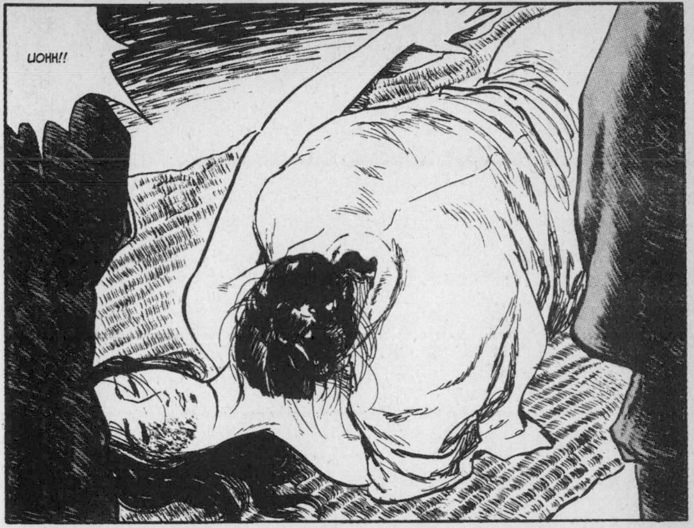
UOHH!!

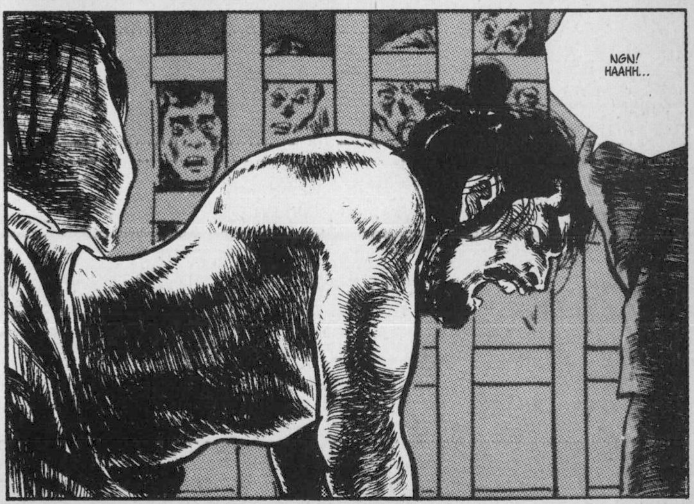
NGN!
HAAHH...

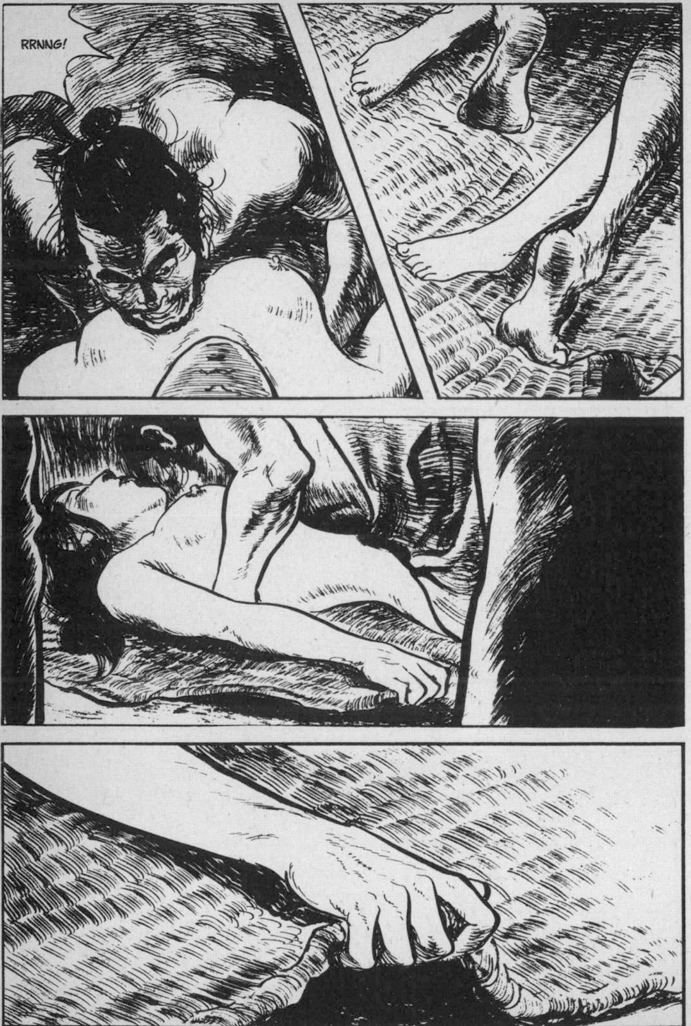
RRNNG!

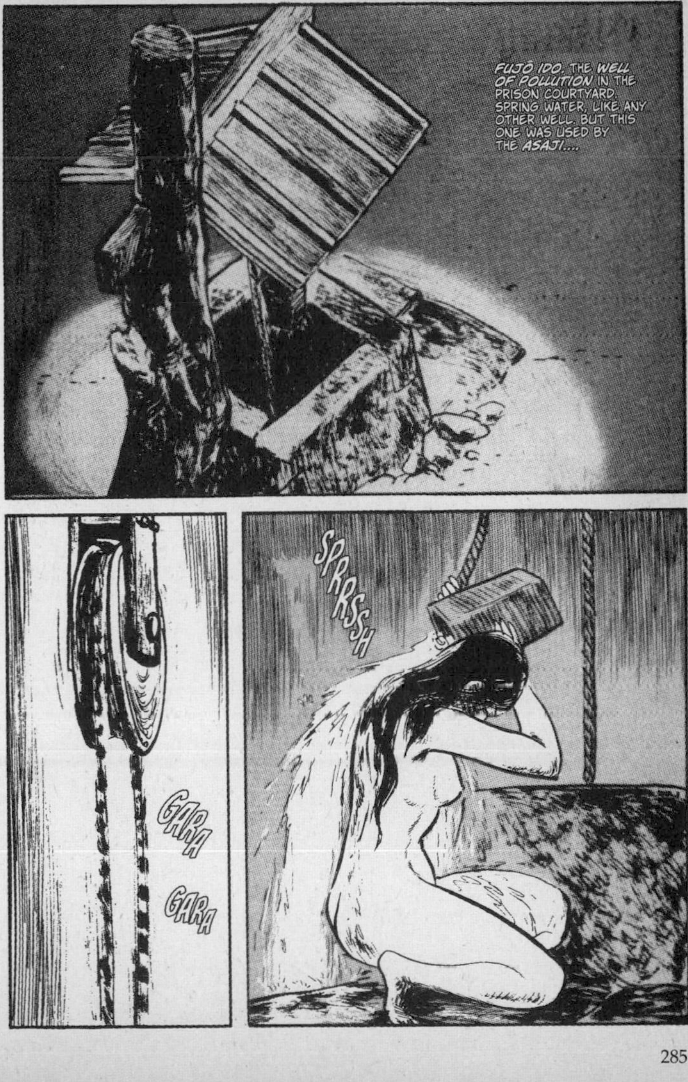
FUJŌ IDO, THE WELL OF POLLUTION IN THE PRISON COURTYARD. SPRING WATER, LIKE ANY OTHER WELL. BUT THIS ONE WAS USED BY THE ASAJI....
GARA
GARA
SPRRSSH

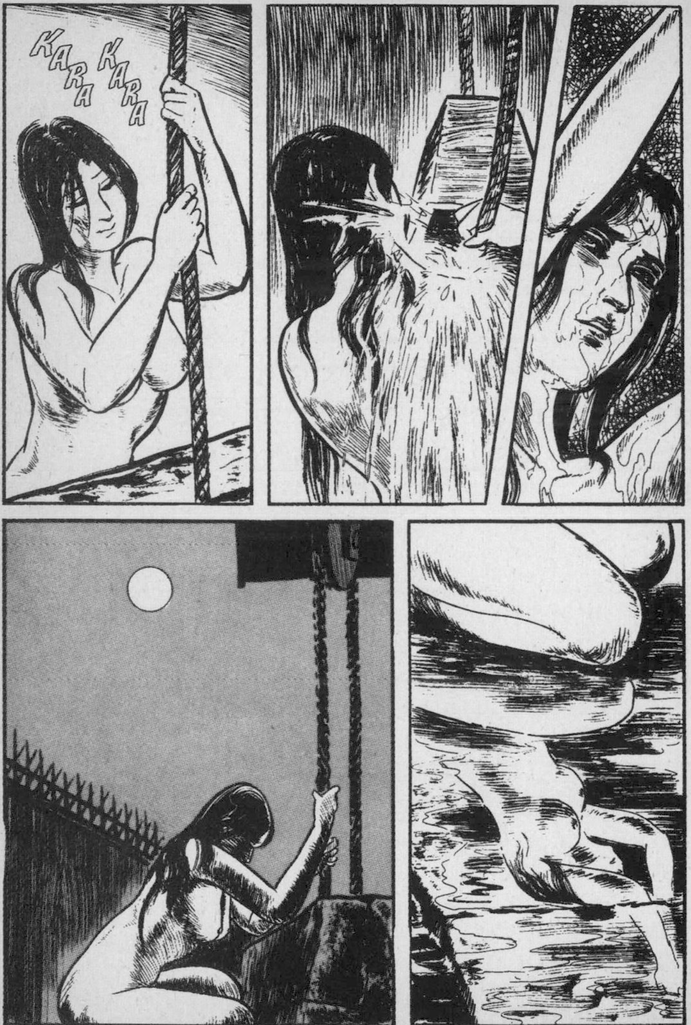
KARA KARA

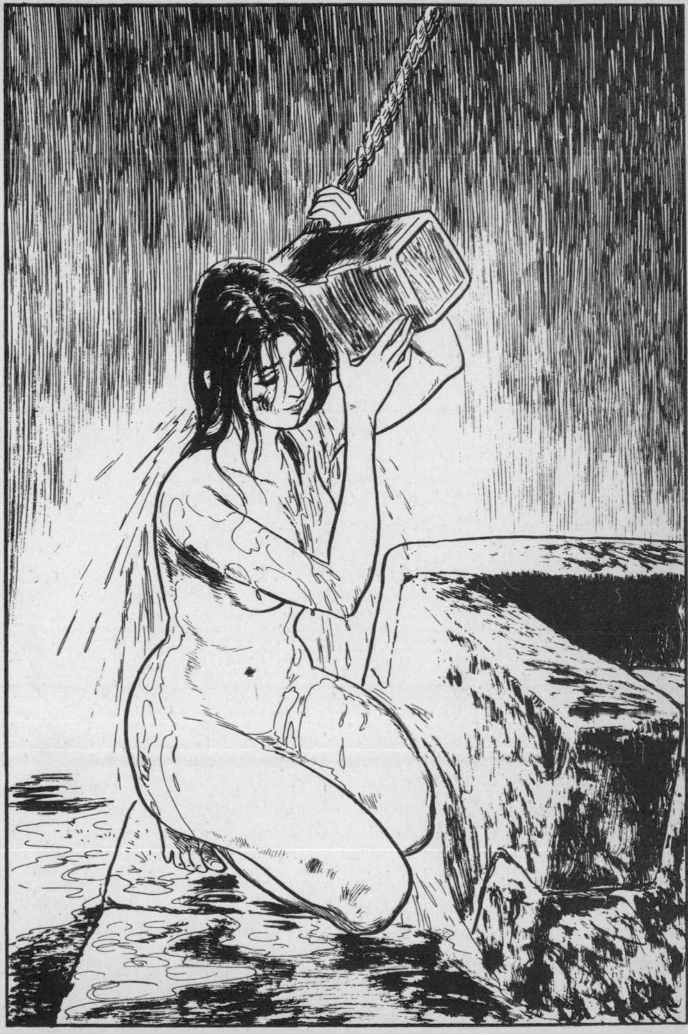

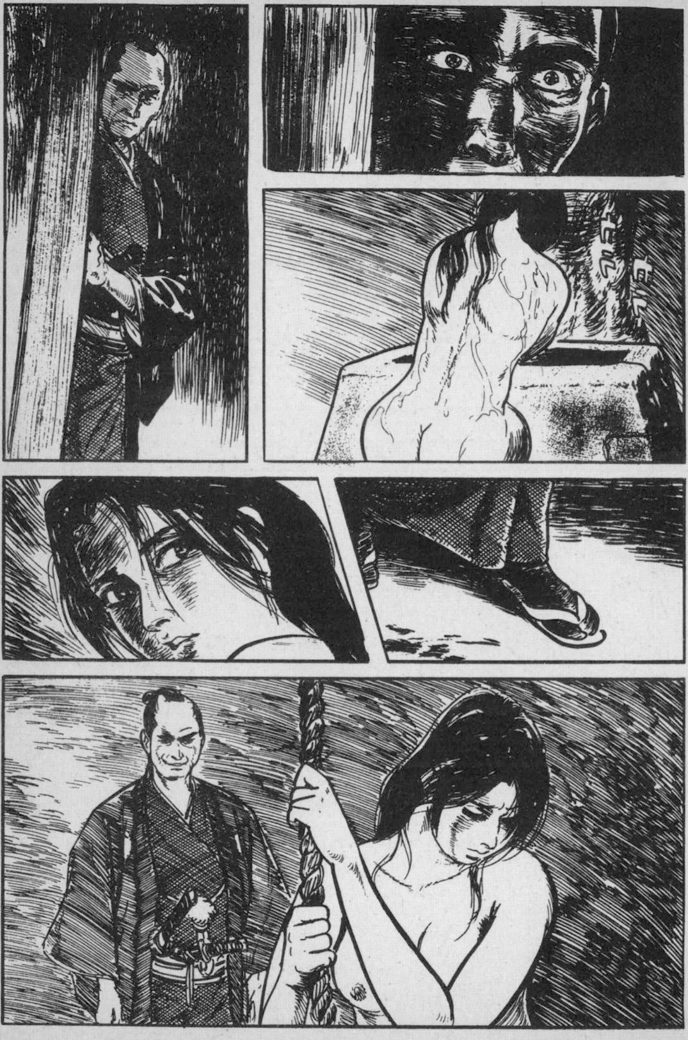

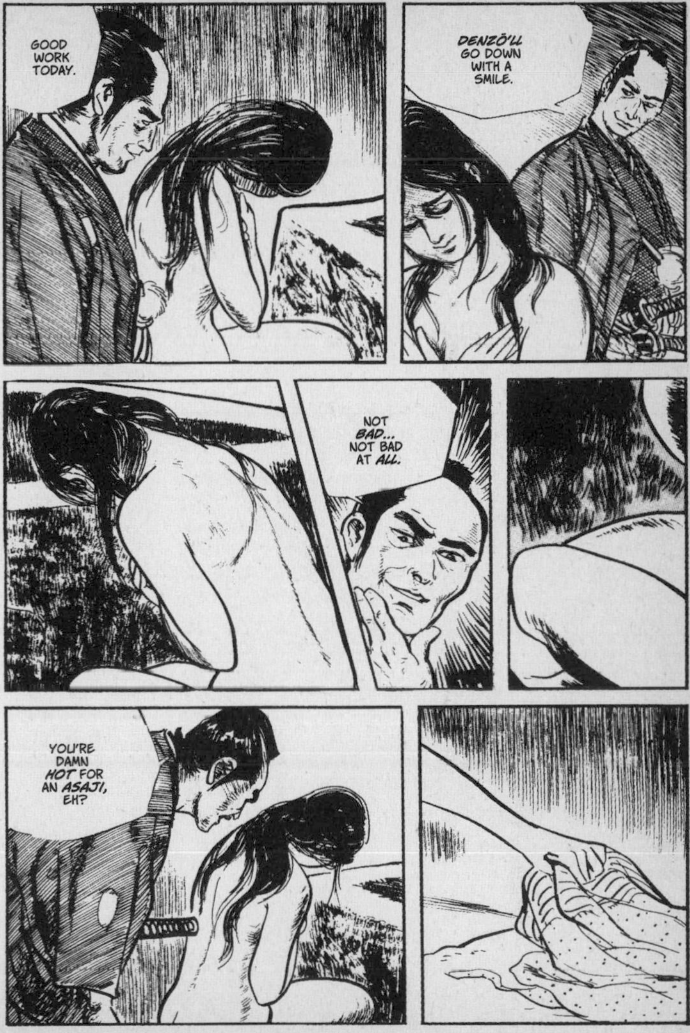
GOOD WORK TODAY.
DENZŌ'LL GO DOWN WITH A SMILE.
NOT BAD... NOT BAD AT ALL.
YOU'RE DAMN HOT FOR AN ASAJI, EH?

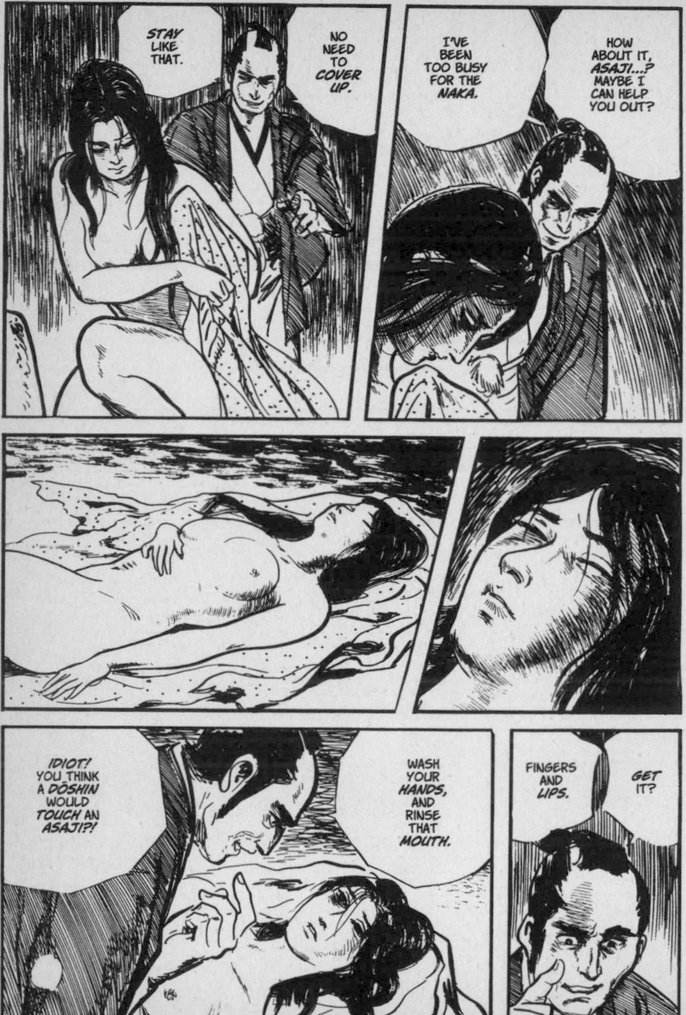
STAY LIKE THAT.
NO NEED TO COVER UP.
I'VE BEEN TOO BUSY FOR THE NAKA.
HOW ABOUT IT, ASAJI...? MAYBE I CAN HELP YOU OUT?
IDIOT! YOU THINK A DŌSHIN WOULD TOUCH AN ASAJI?!
WASH YOUR HANDS, AND RINSE THAT MOUTH.
FINGERS AND LIPS.
GET IT?

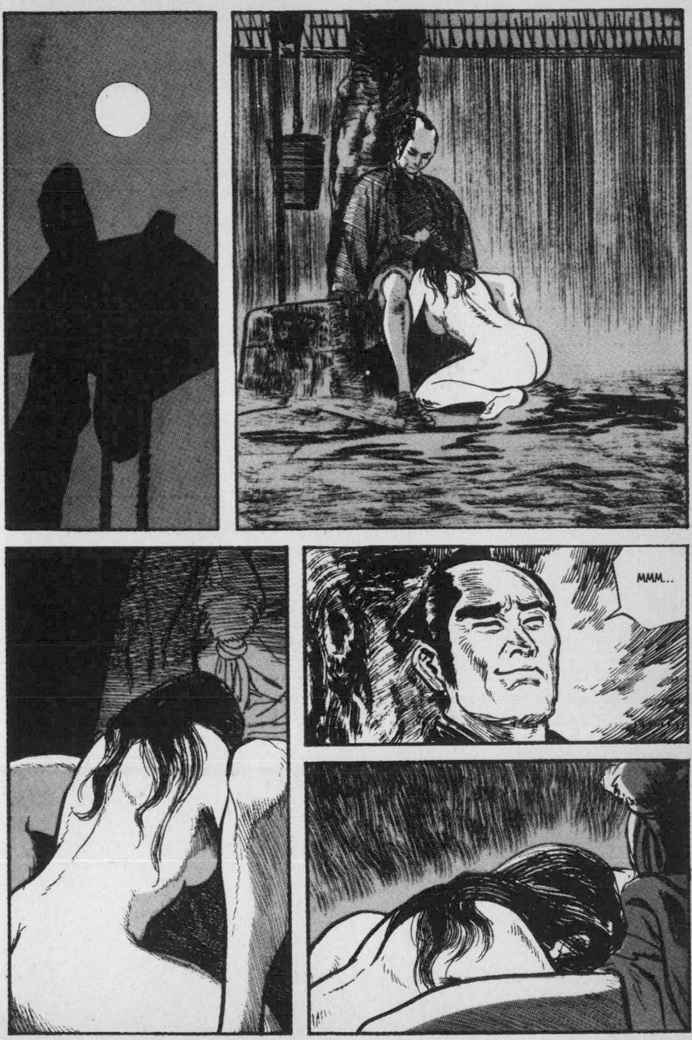
MMM...

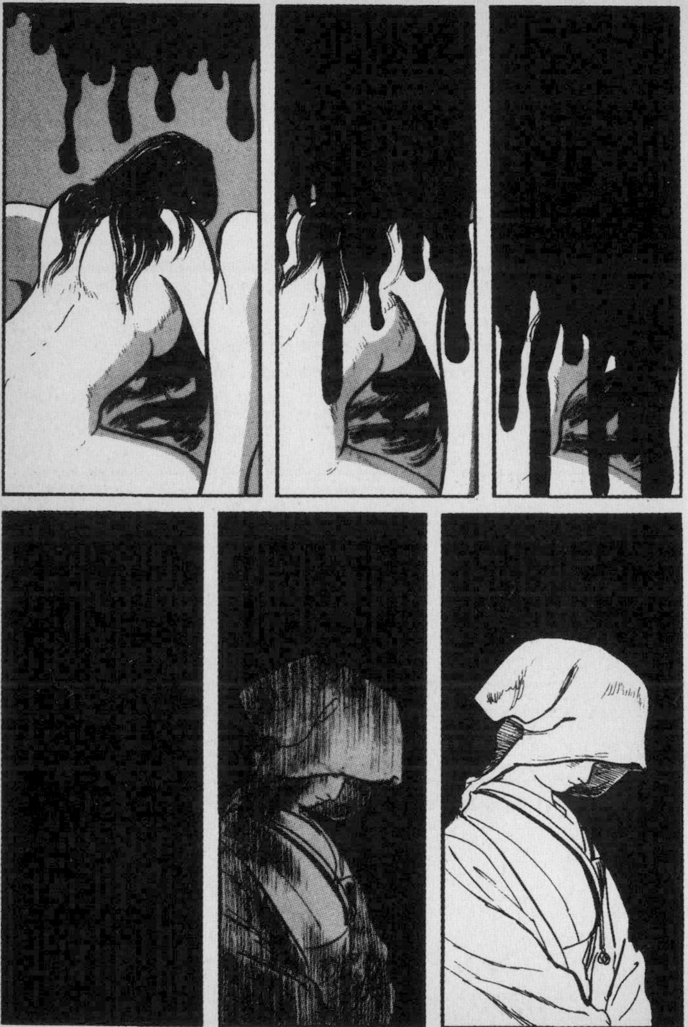

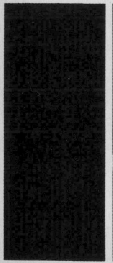

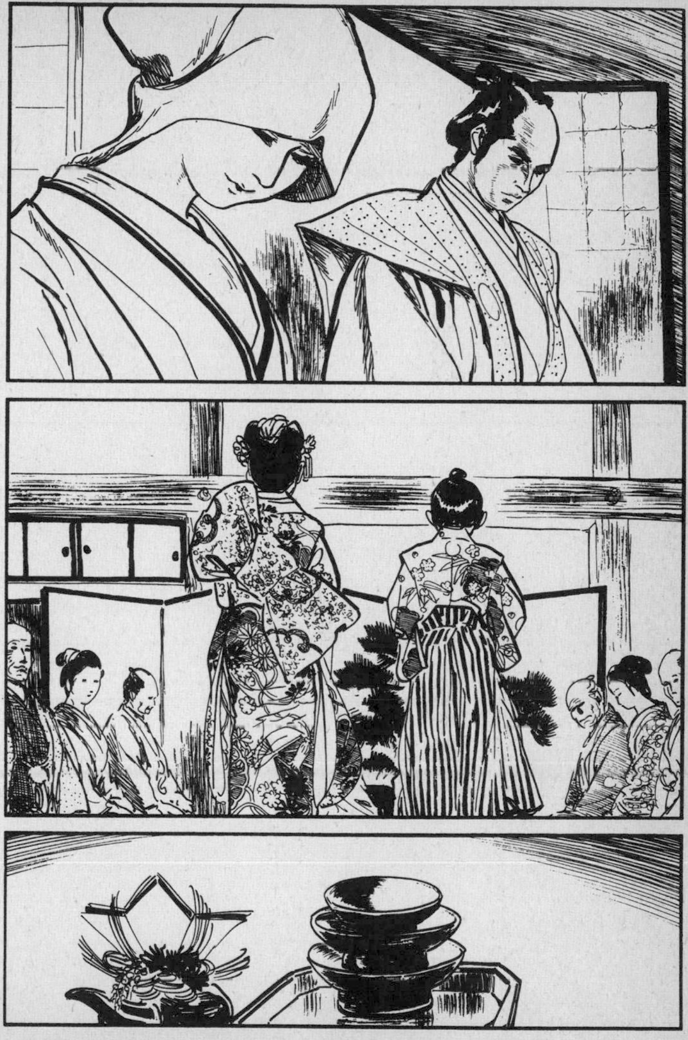

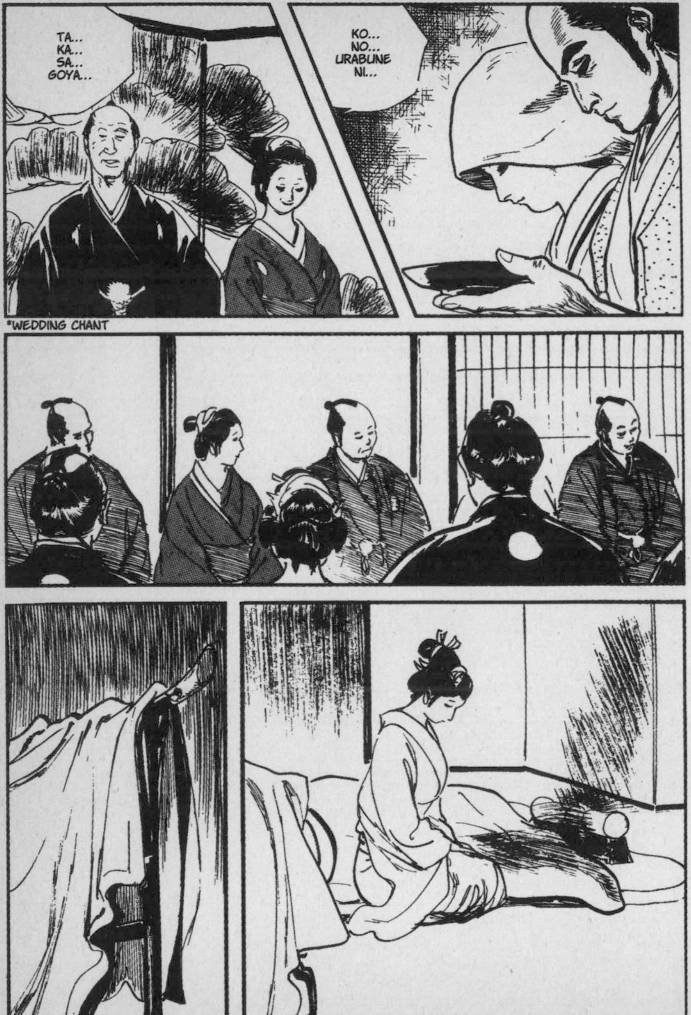
TA... KA... SA... GOYA...
KO... NO... URABUNE NI...
*WEDDING CHANT

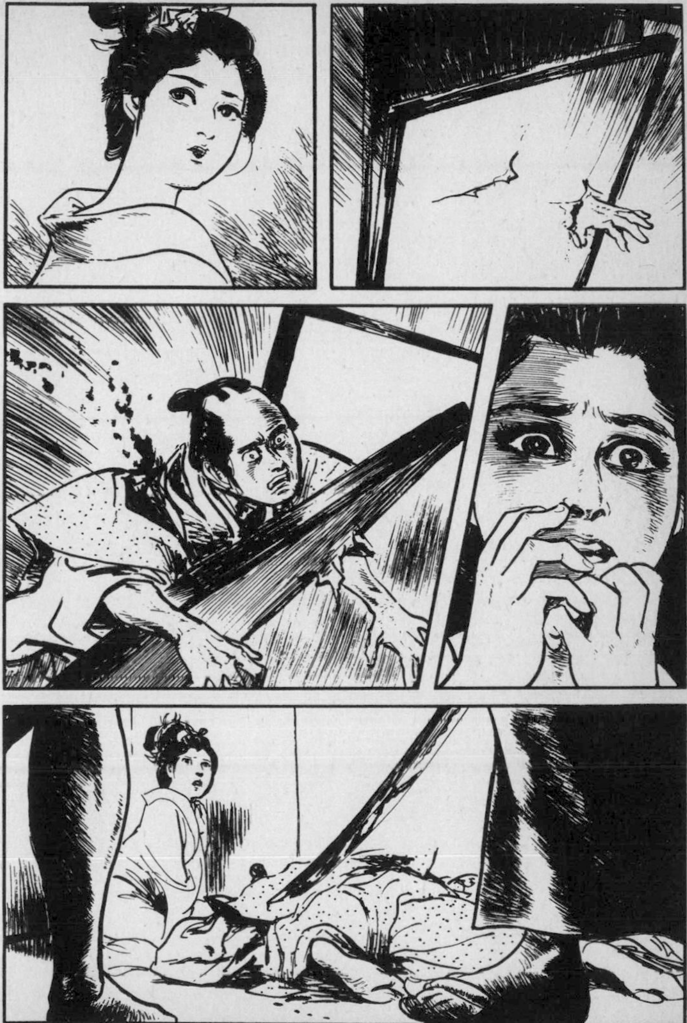

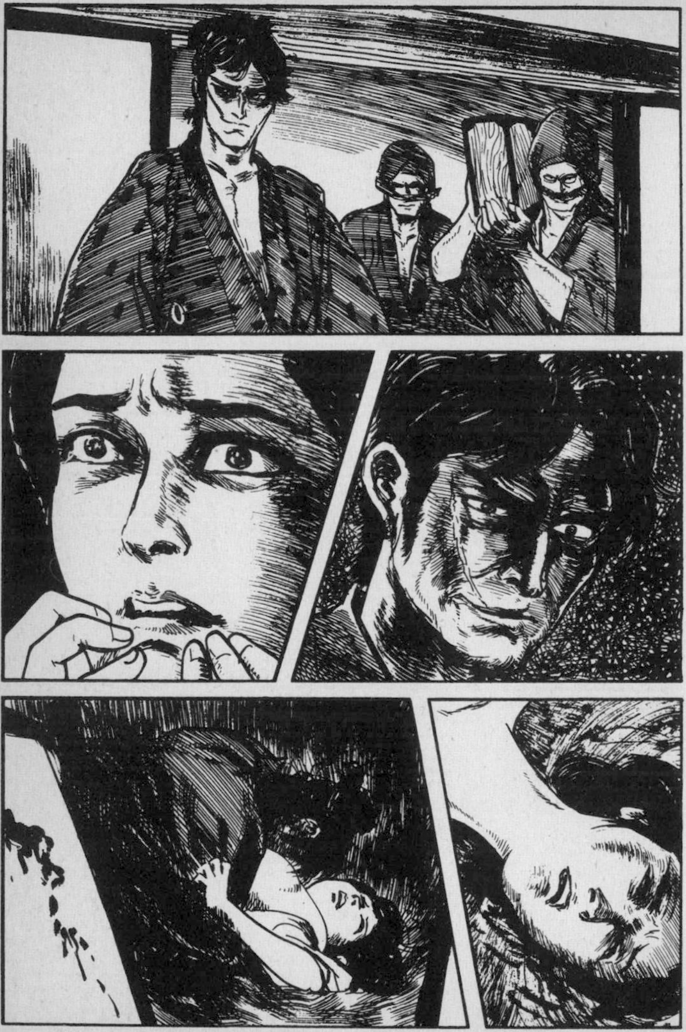

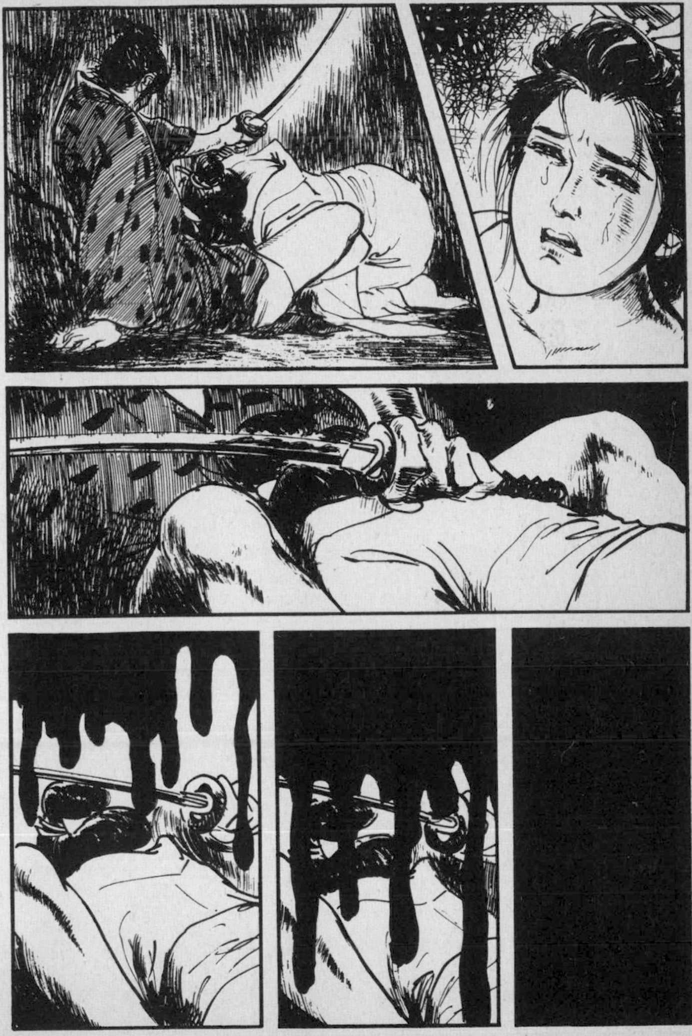

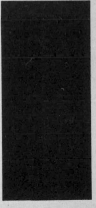

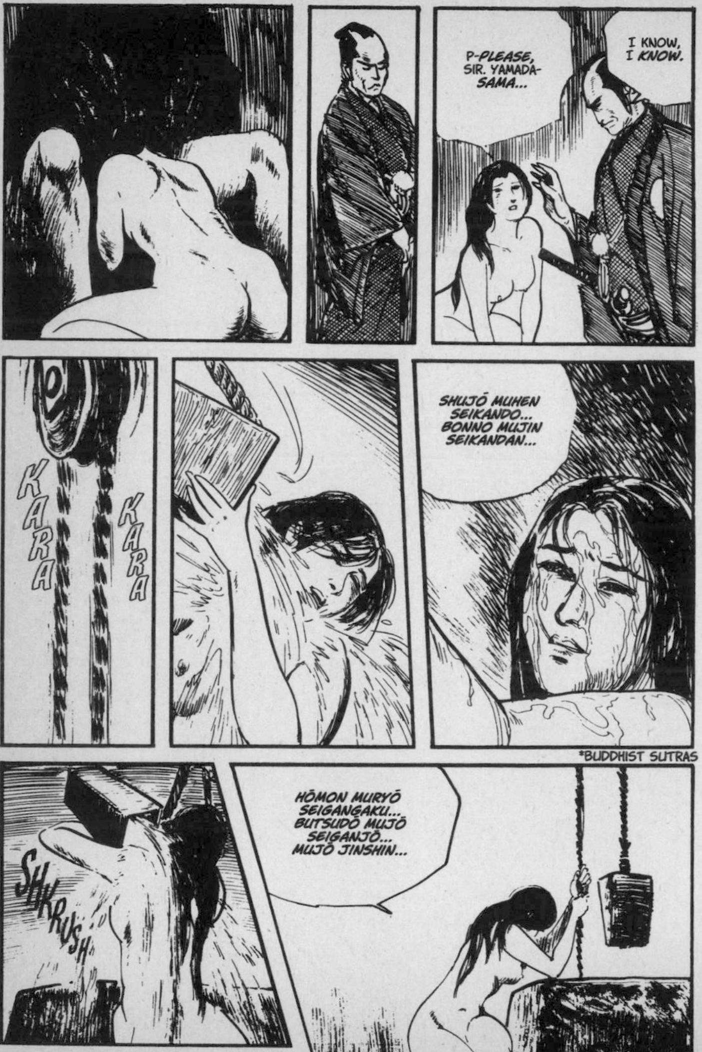
P-PLEASE, SIR. YAMADA-SAMA...
I KNOW, I KNOW.
KARA
KARA
SHUJŌ MUHEN SEIKANDO... BONNO MUJIN SEIKANDAN...
*BUDDHIST SUTRAS
SHKRUSH
HŌMON MURYŌ SEIGANGAKU... BUTSUDŌ MUJŌ SEIGANJŌ... MUJŌ JINSHIN...

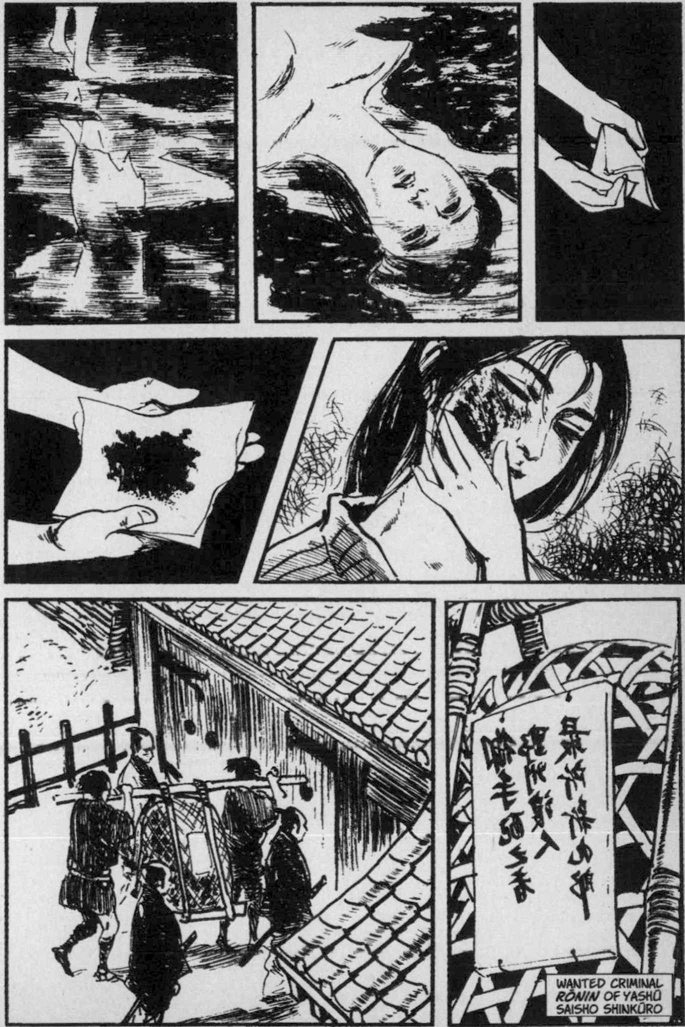
WANTED CRIMINAL
RŌNIN OF YASHŪ
SAISHO SHINKŪRO

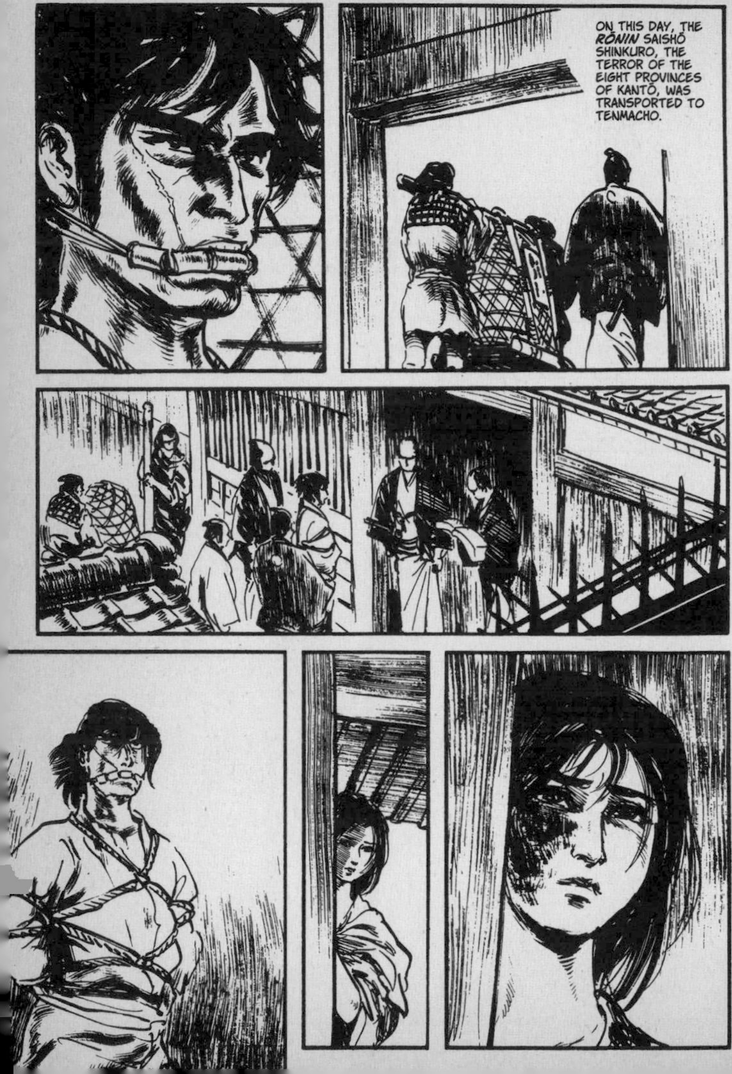
ON THIS DAY, THE *RŌNIN* SAISHŌ SHINKURO, THE TERROR OF THE EIGHT PROVINCES OF KANTŌ, WAS TRANSPORTED TO TENMACHO.

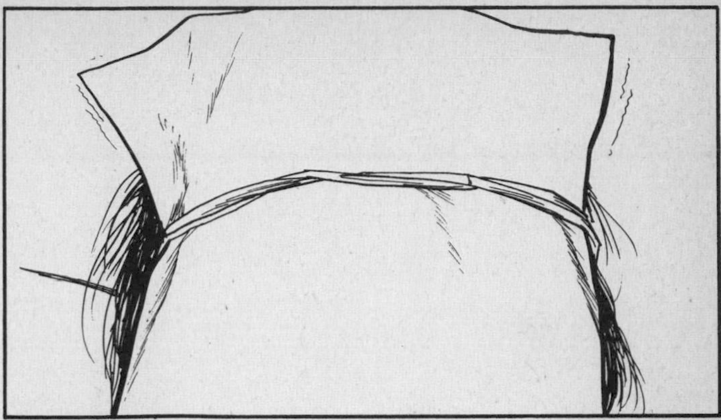
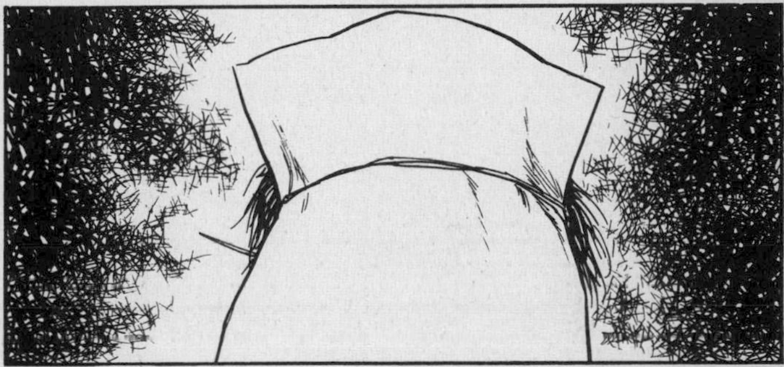
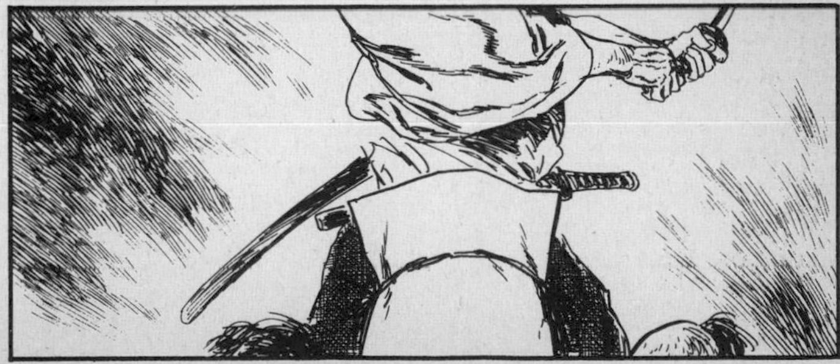

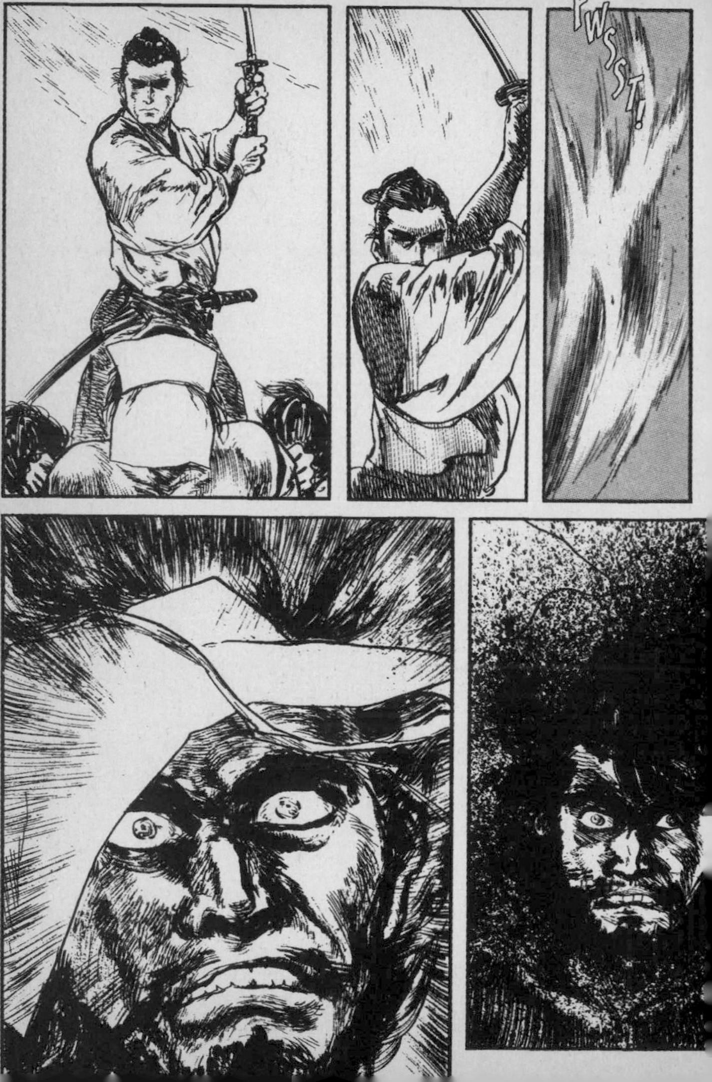
FWSST!

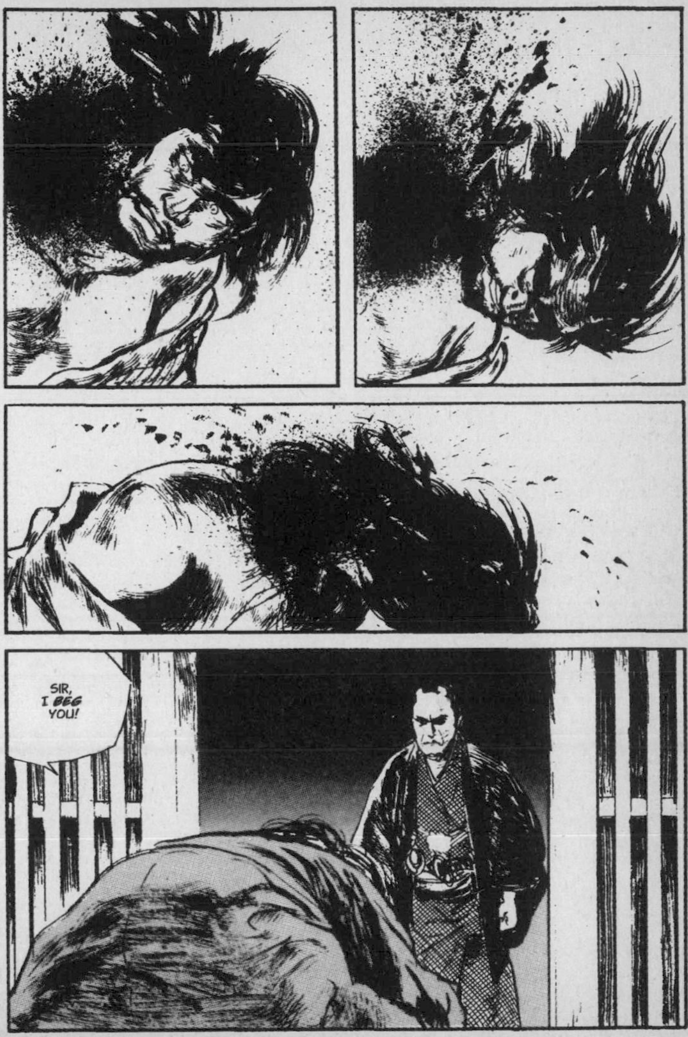
SIR, I BEG YOU!

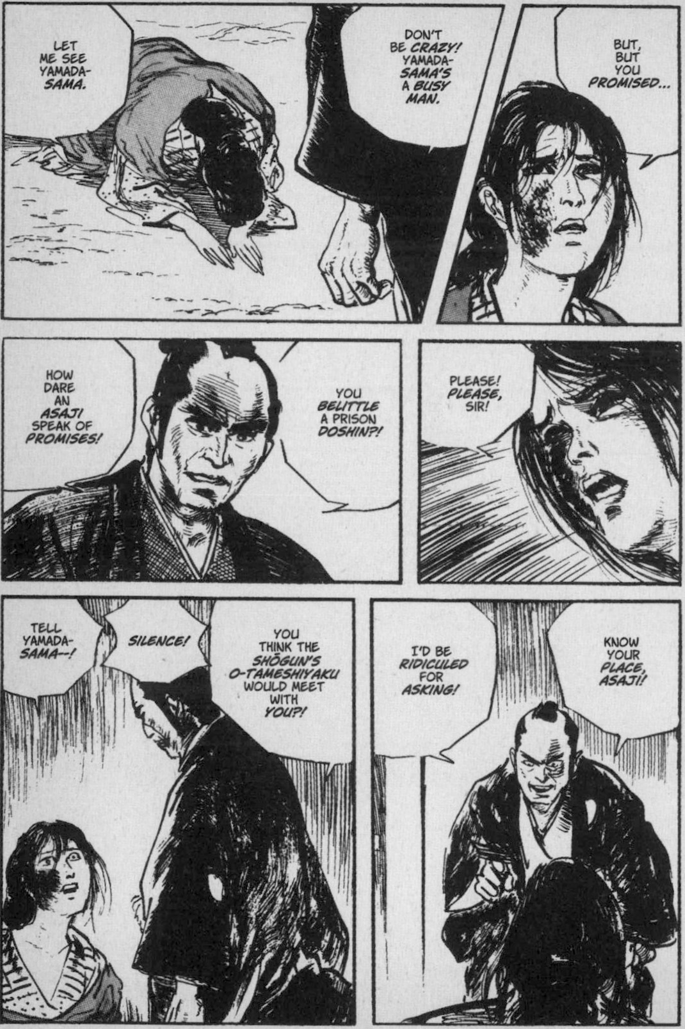
LET ME SEE YAMADA-SAMA.
DON'T BE CRAZY! YAMADA-SAMA'S A BUSY MAN.
BUT, BUT YOU PROMISED...
HOW DARE AN ASAJI SPEAK OF PROMISES!
YOU BELITTLE A PRISON DOSHIN?!
PLEASE! PLEASE, SIR!
TELL YAMADA-SAMA--!
SILENCE!
YOU THINK THE SHŌGUN'S O-TAMESHIYAKU WOULD MEET WITH YOU?!
I'D BE RIDICULED FOR ASKING!
KNOW YOUR PLACE, ASAJI!

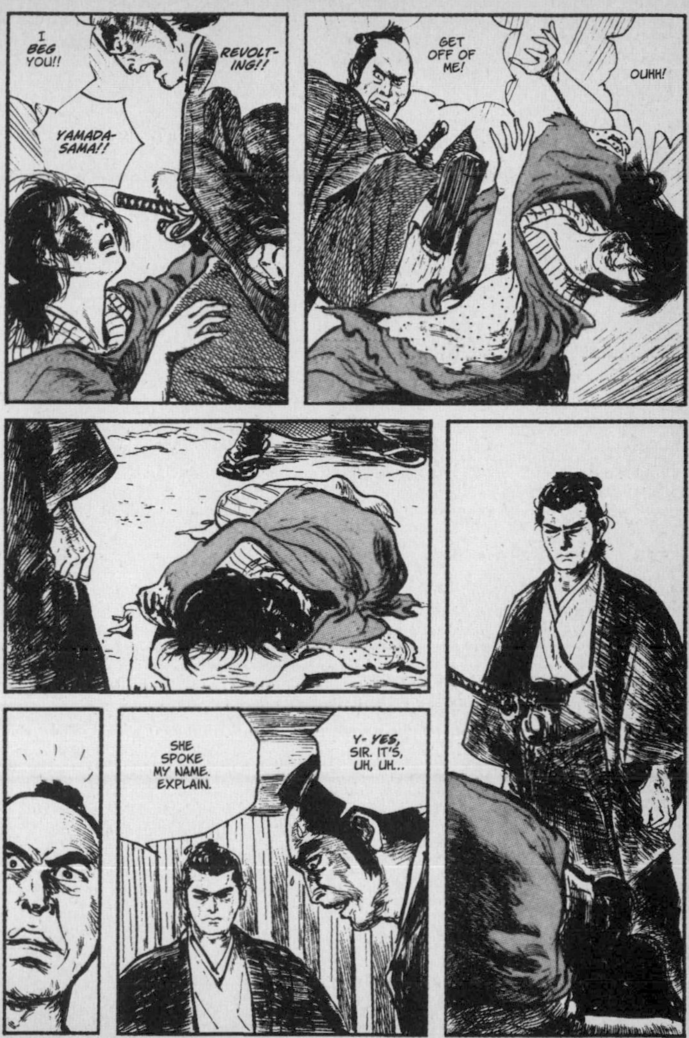
I BEG YOU!!
REVOLTING!!
YAMADA-SAMA!!
GET OFF OF ME!
OUHH!
SHE SPOKE MY NAME. EXPLAIN.
Y-YES, SIR. IT'S, UH, UH...

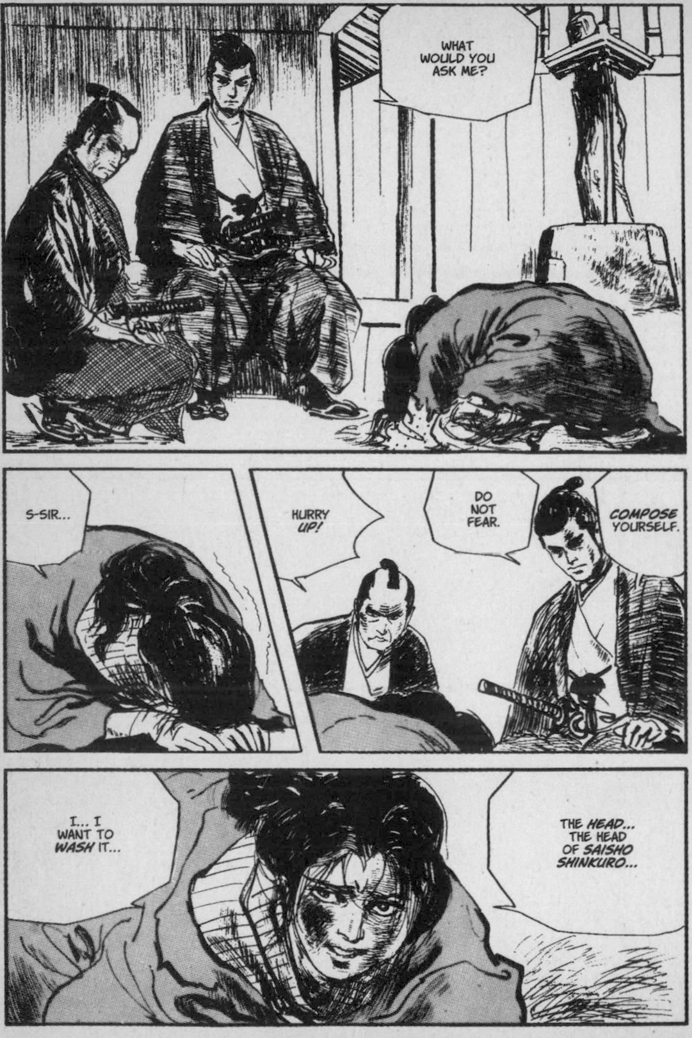
WHAT WOULD YOU ASK ME?
S-SIR...
HURRY *UP!*
DO NOT FEAR.
COMPOSE YOURSELF.
I... I WANT TO ***WASH*** IT...
THE ***HEAD...*** THE HEAD OF ***SAISHO SHINKURO...***

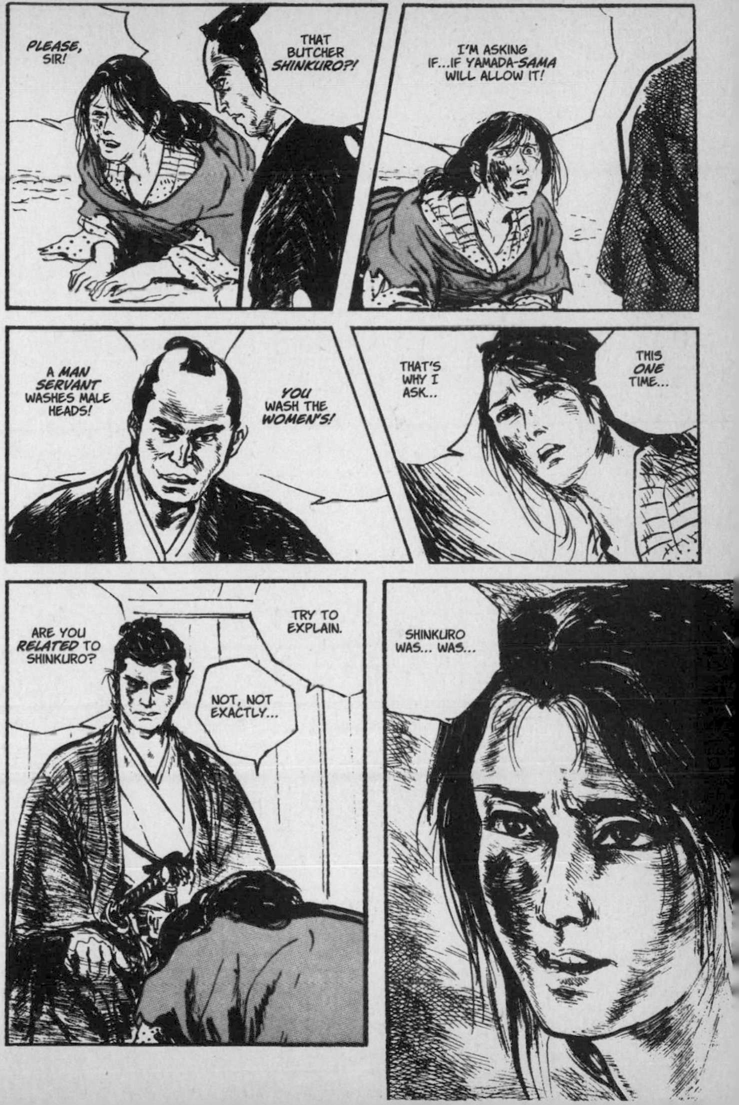
PLEASE, SIR!
THAT BUTCHER SHINKURO?!
I'M ASKING IF...IF YAMADA-SAMA WILL ALLOW IT!
A MAN SERVANT WASHES MALE HEADS!
YOU WASH THE WOMEN'S!
THAT'S WHY I ASK...
THIS ONE TIME...
ARE YOU RELATED TO SHINKURO?
TRY TO EXPLAIN.
NOT, NOT EXACTLY...
SHINKURO WAS... WAS...

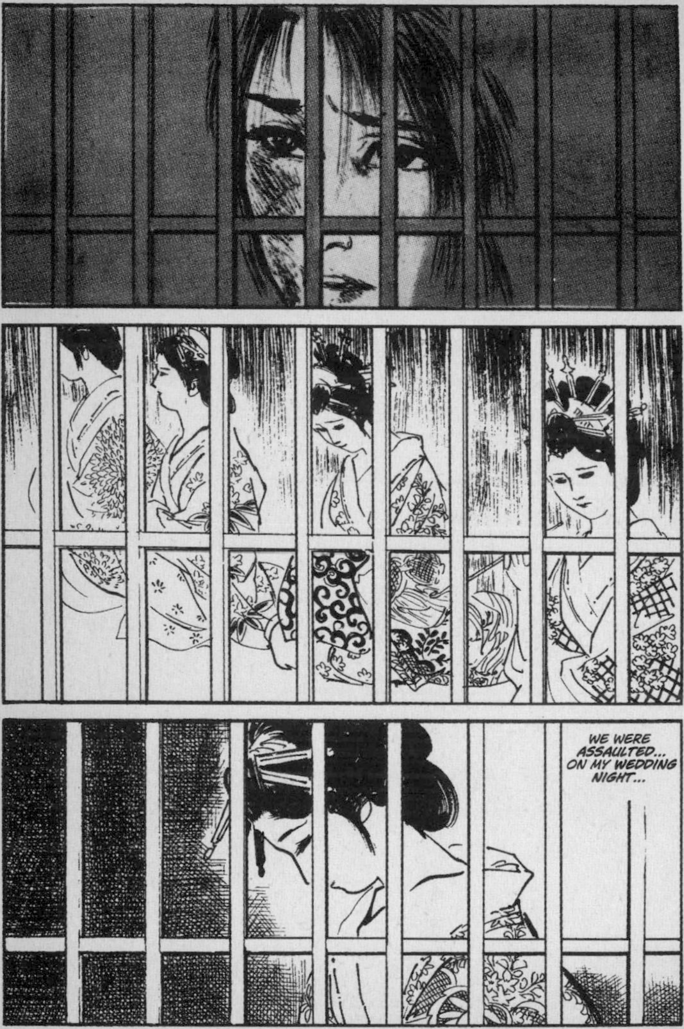
WE WERE
ASSAULTED...
ON MY WEDDING
NIGHT...

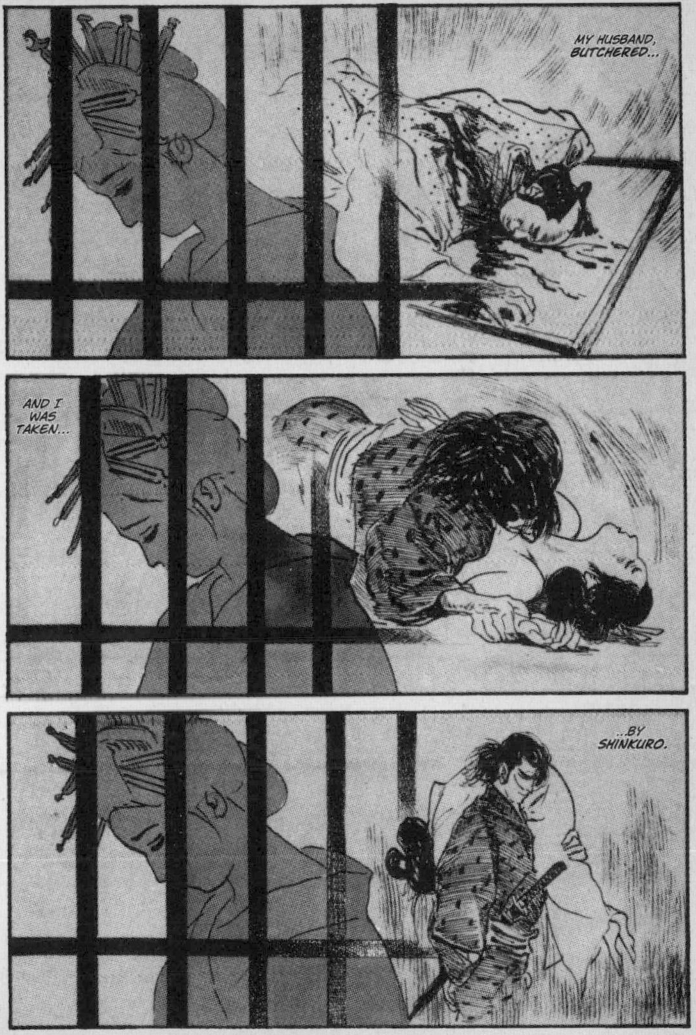
MY HUSBAND, BUTCHERED...
AND I WAS TAKEN...
...BY SHINKURO.

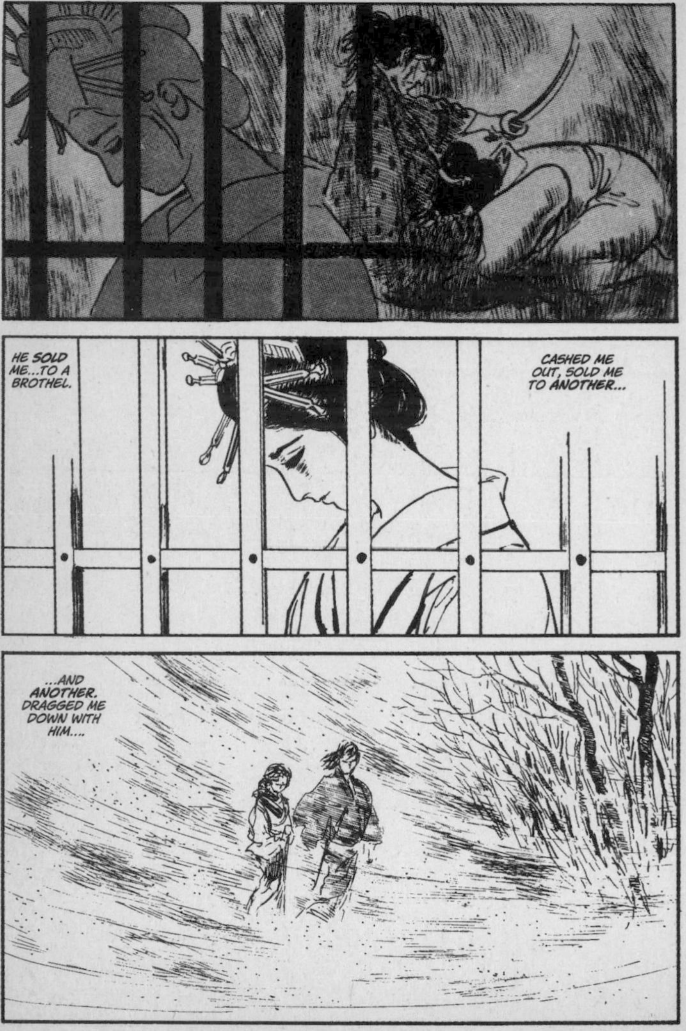
HE SOLD ME...TO A BROTHEL.
CASHED ME OUT, SOLD ME TO ANOTHER...
...AND ANOTHER. DRAGGED ME DOWN WITH HIM....

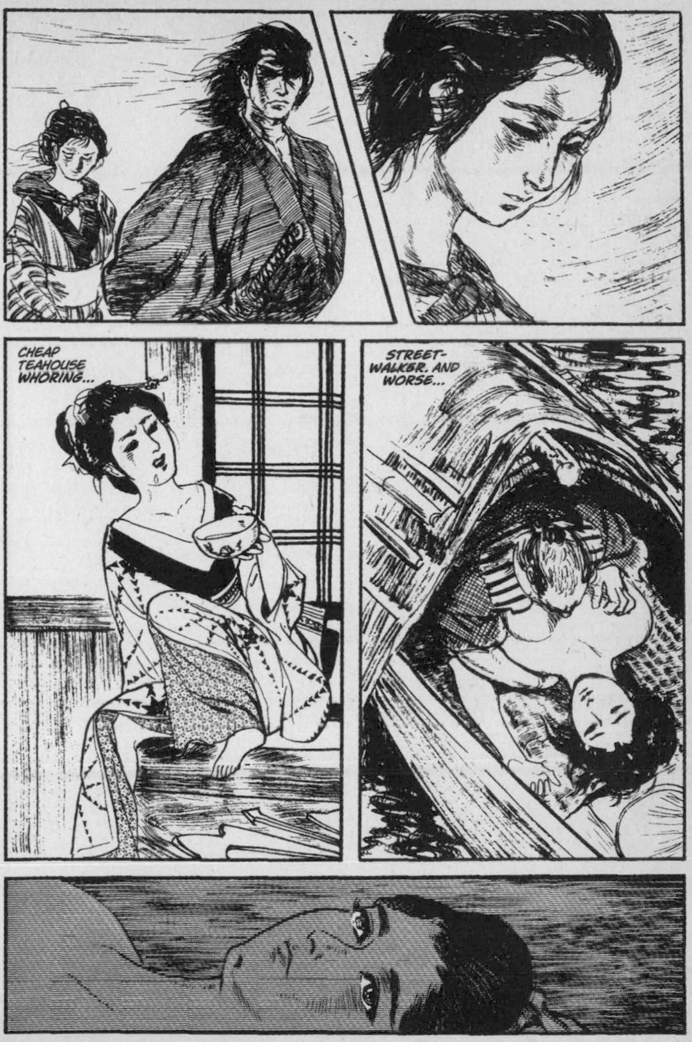
CHEAP TEAHOUSE WHORING...
STREET-WALKER. AND WORSE...

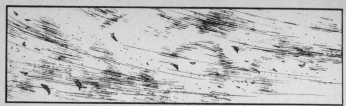

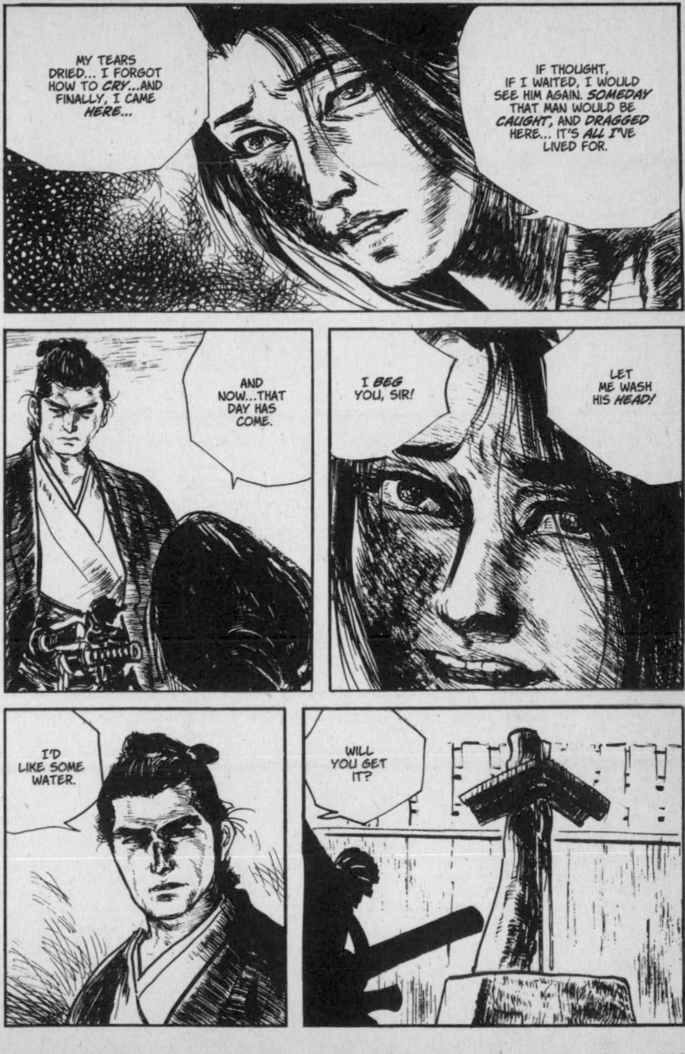
MY TEARS DRIED... I FORGOT HOW TO *CRY*...AND FINALLY, I CAME *HERE*...
IF THOUGHT, IF I WAITED, I WOULD SEE HIM AGAIN. *SOMEDAY* THAT MAN WOULD BE *CAUGHT*, AND *DRAGGED* HERE... IT'S *ALL I'VE* LIVED FOR.
AND NOW...THAT DAY HAS COME.
I *BEG* YOU, SIR!
LET ME WASH HIS *HEAD!*
I'D LIKE SOME WATER.
WILL YOU GET IT?

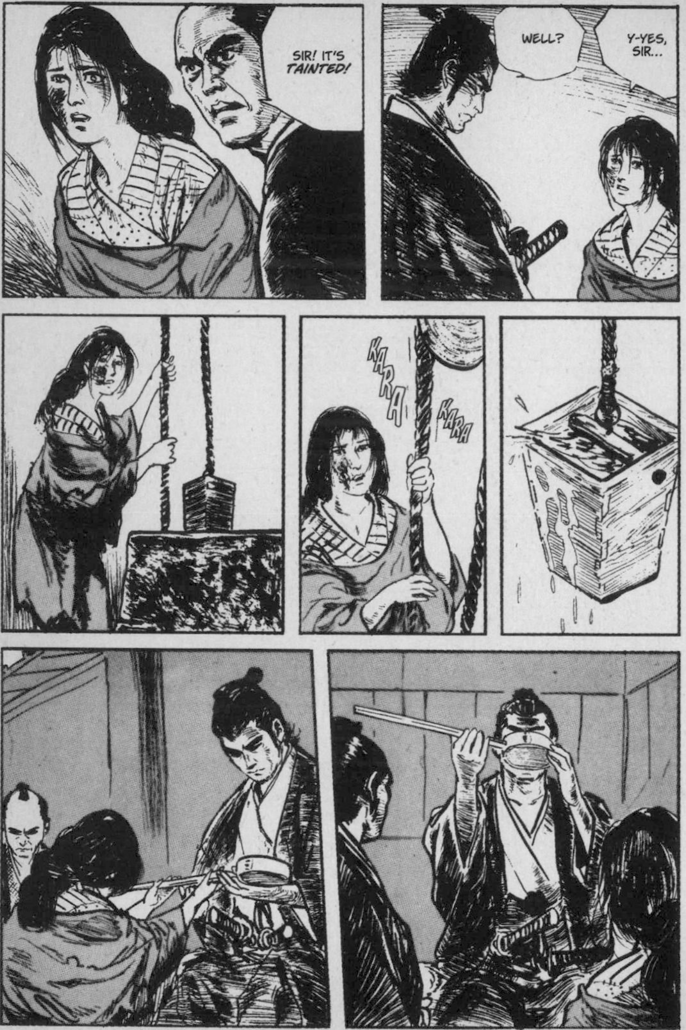
SIR! IT'S *TAINTED!*
WELL?
Y-YES, SIR...
KARA
KARA

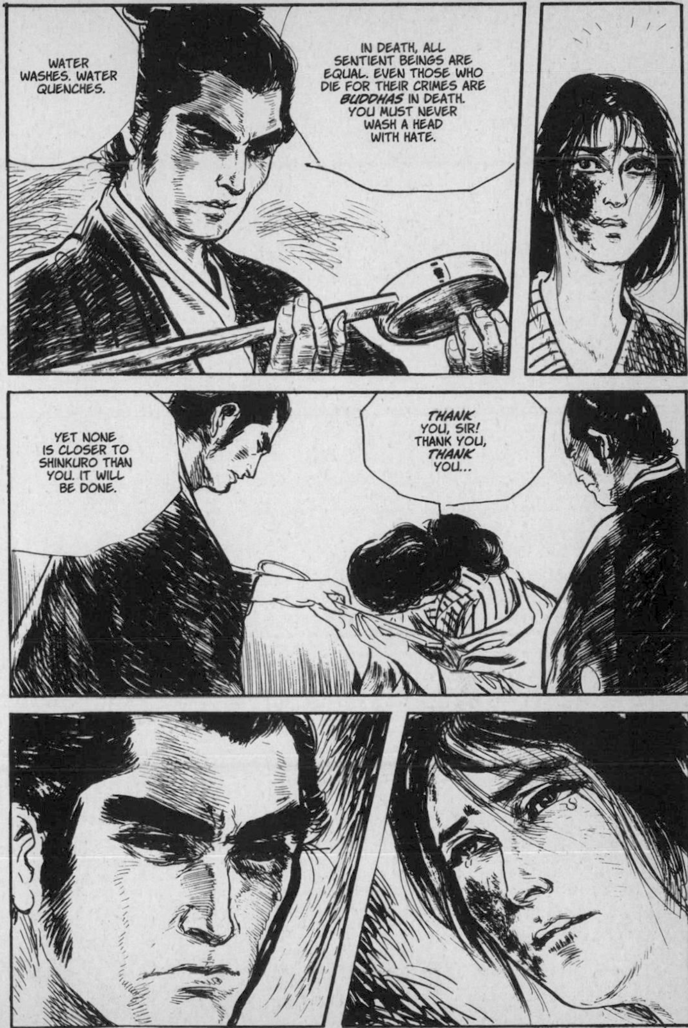
WATER WASHES. WATER QUENCHES.
IN DEATH, ALL SENTIENT BEINGS ARE EQUAL. EVEN THOSE WHO DIE FOR THEIR CRIMES ARE *BUDDHAS* IN DEATH. YOU MUST NEVER WASH A HEAD WITH HATE.
YET NONE IS CLOSER TO SHINKURO THAN YOU. IT WILL BE DONE.
THANK YOU, SIR! THANK YOU, *THANK* YOU...

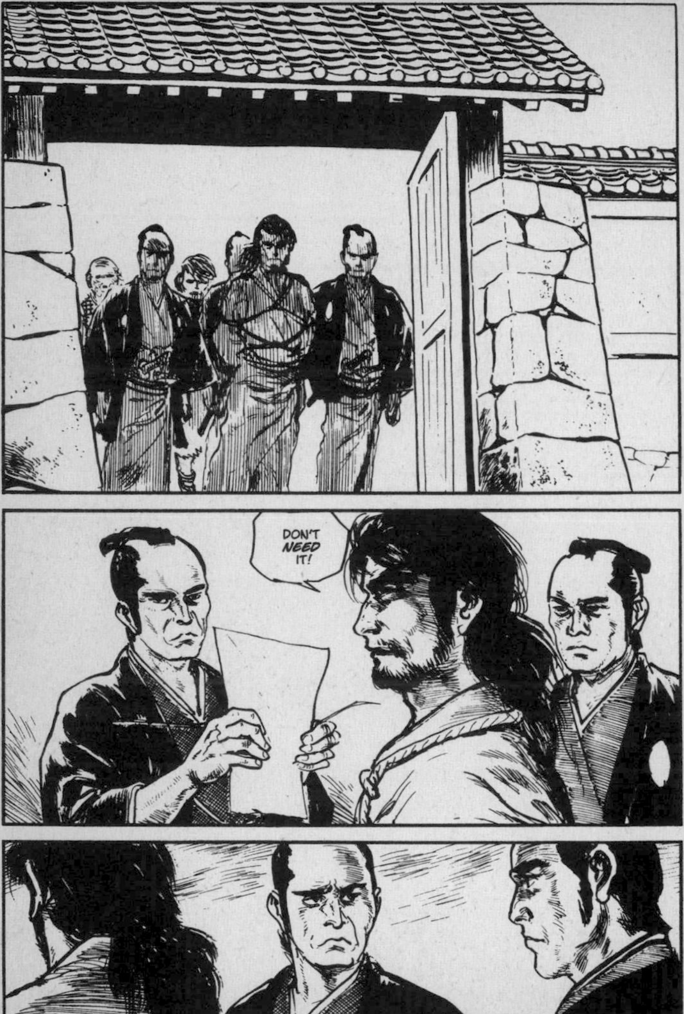
DON'T NEED IT!

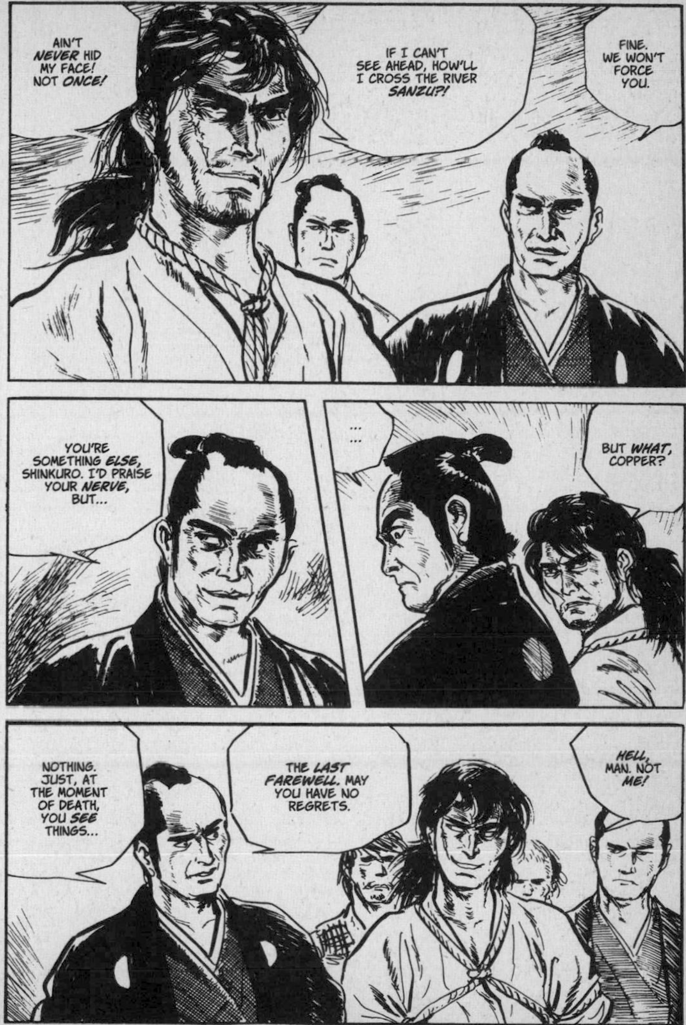
AIN'T NEVER HID MY FACE! NOT ONCE!
IF I CAN'T SEE AHEAD, HOW'LL I CROSS THE RIVER SANZU?!
FINE. WE WON'T FORCE YOU.
YOU'RE SOMETHING ELSE, SHINKURO. I'D PRAISE YOUR NERVE, BUT...
...
...
BUT WHAT, COPPER?
NOTHING. JUST, AT THE MOMENT OF DEATH, YOU SEE THINGS...
THE LAST FAREWELL. MAY YOU HAVE NO REGRETS.
HELL, MAN. NOT ME!

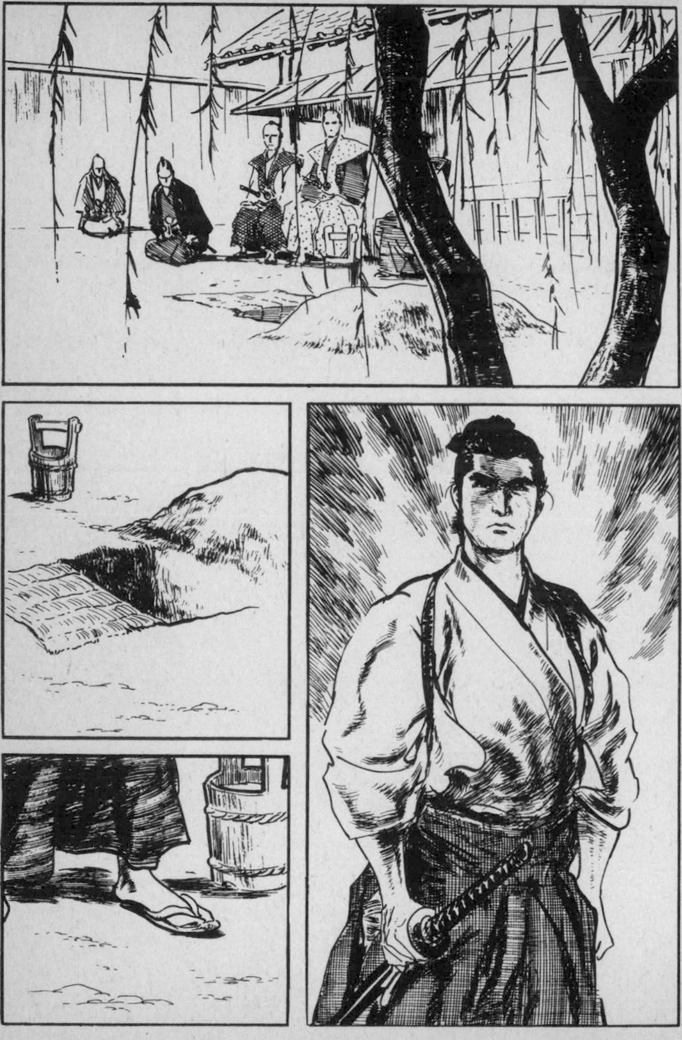

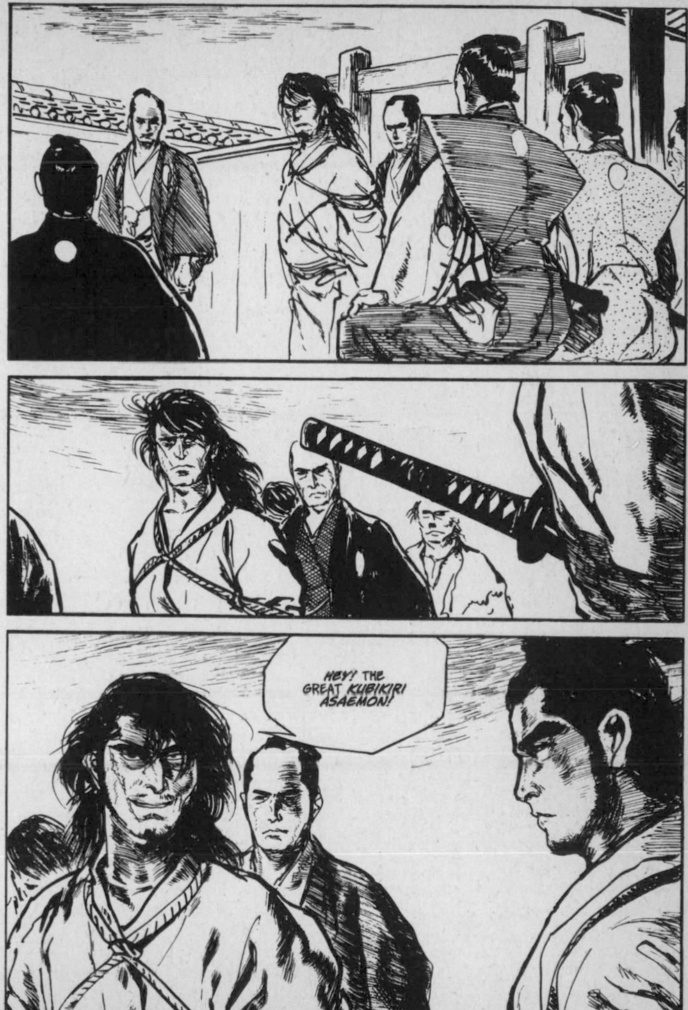
HEY! THE GREAT KUBIKIRI ASAEMON!

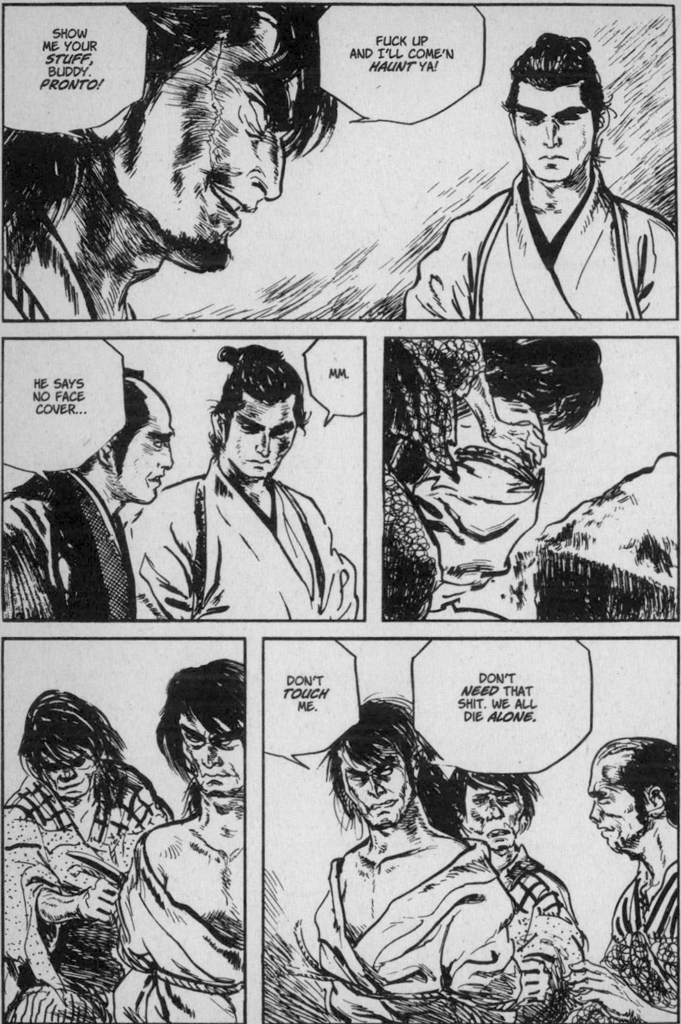
SHOW ME YOUR STUFF, BUDDY. PRONTO!
FUCK UP AND I'LL COME'N HAUNT YA!
HE SAYS NO FACE COVER...
MM.
DON'T TOUCH ME.
DON'T NEED THAT SHIT. WE ALL DIE ALONE.

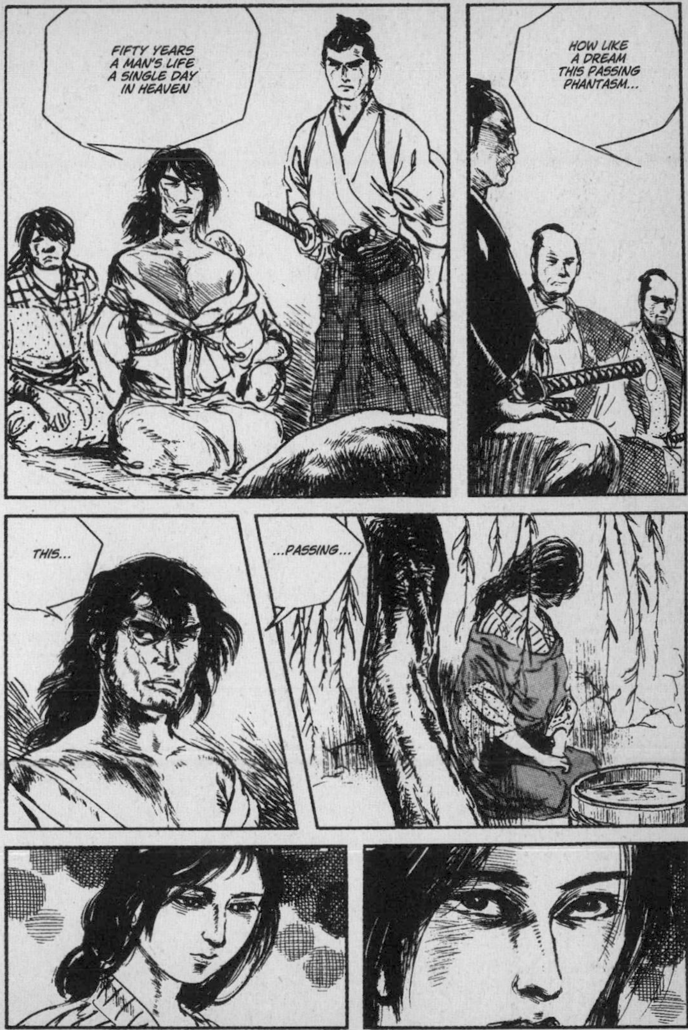
FIFTY YEARS A MAN'S LIFE A SINGLE DAY IN HEAVEN
HOW LIKE A DREAM THIS PASSING PHANTASM...
THIS...
...PASSING...

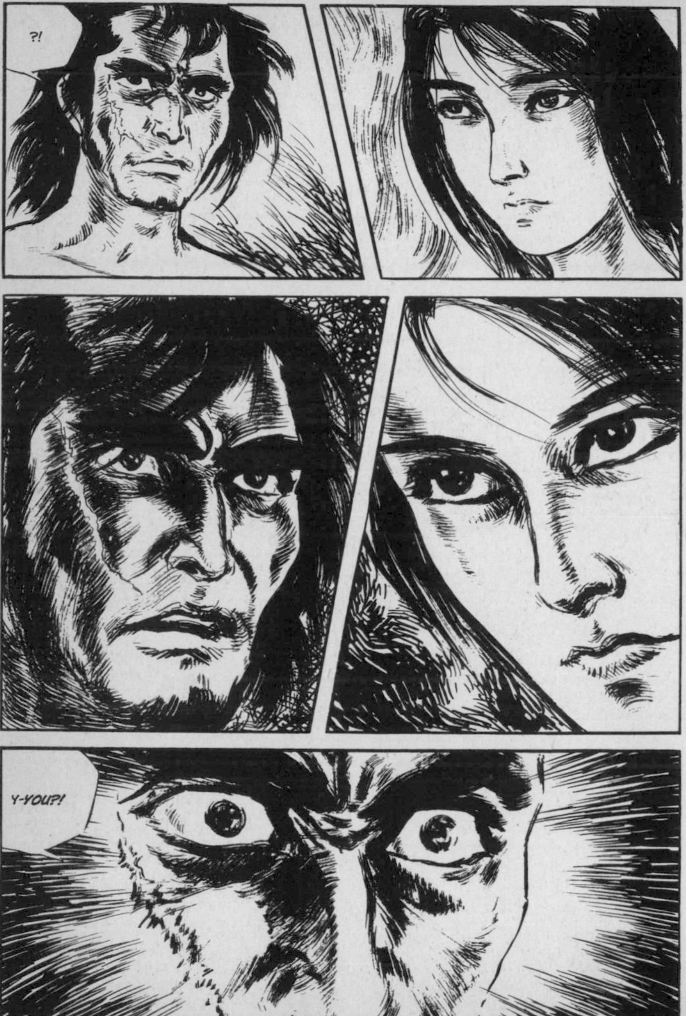
?!
Y-YOU?!

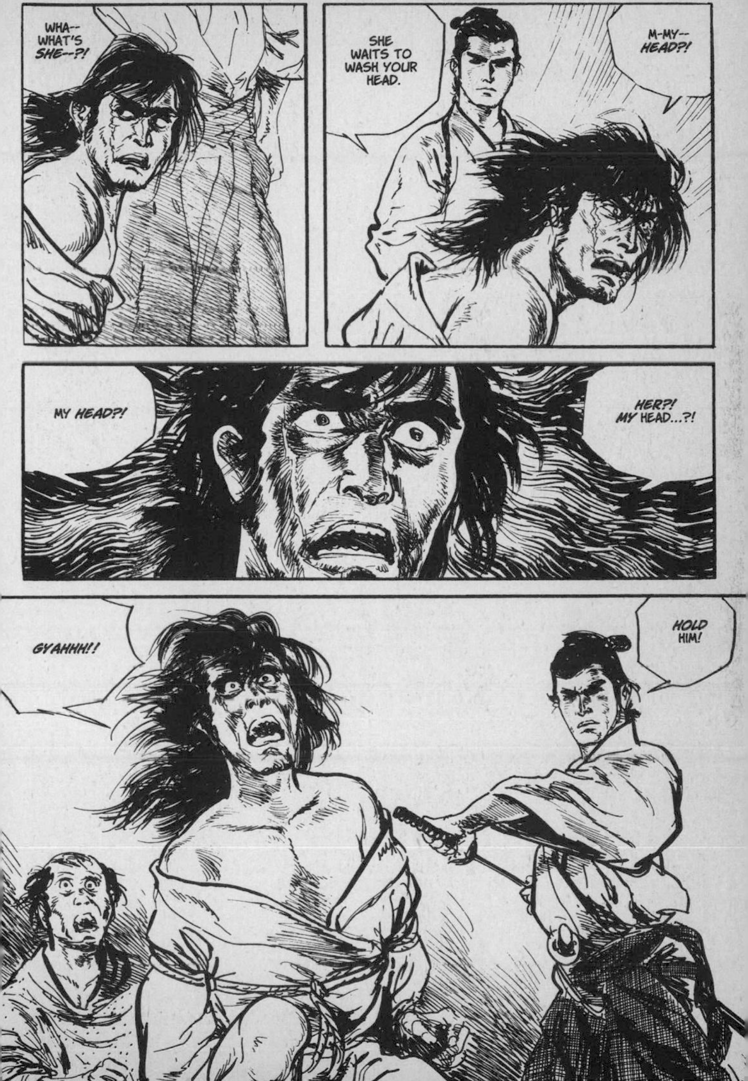
WHA--
WHAT'S
SHE--?!
SHE WAITS TO WASH YOUR HEAD.
M-MY--
HEAD?!
MY HEAD?!
HER?!
MY HEAD...?!
GYAHHH!!
HOLD HIM!

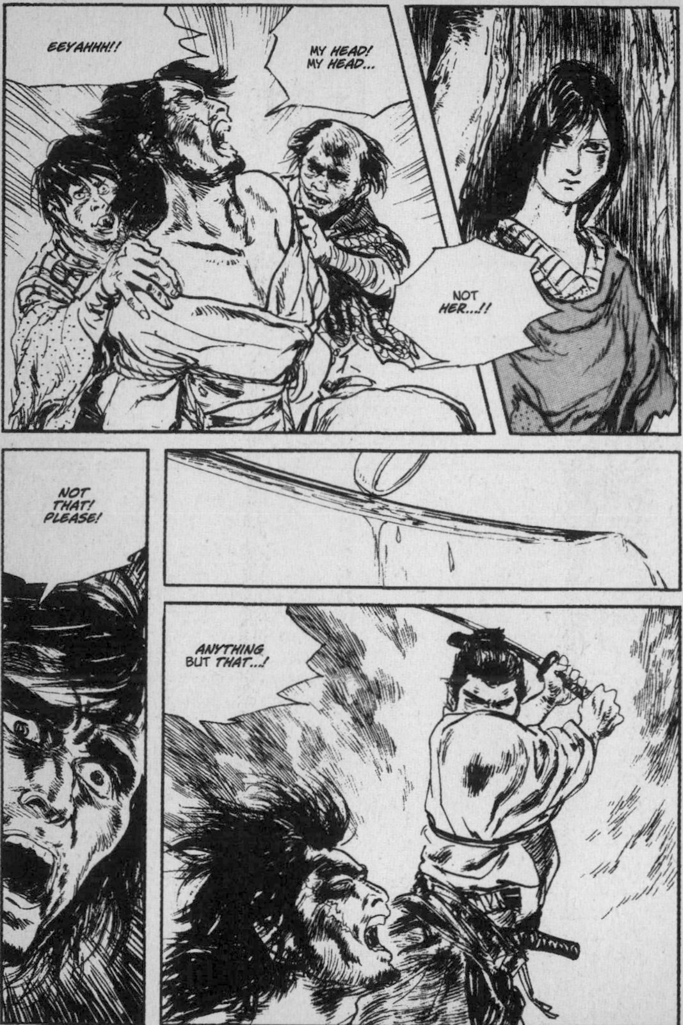
EEYAHHH!!
MY HEAD! MY HEAD...
NOT HER...!!
NOT THAT! PLEASE!
ANYTHING BUT THAT...!

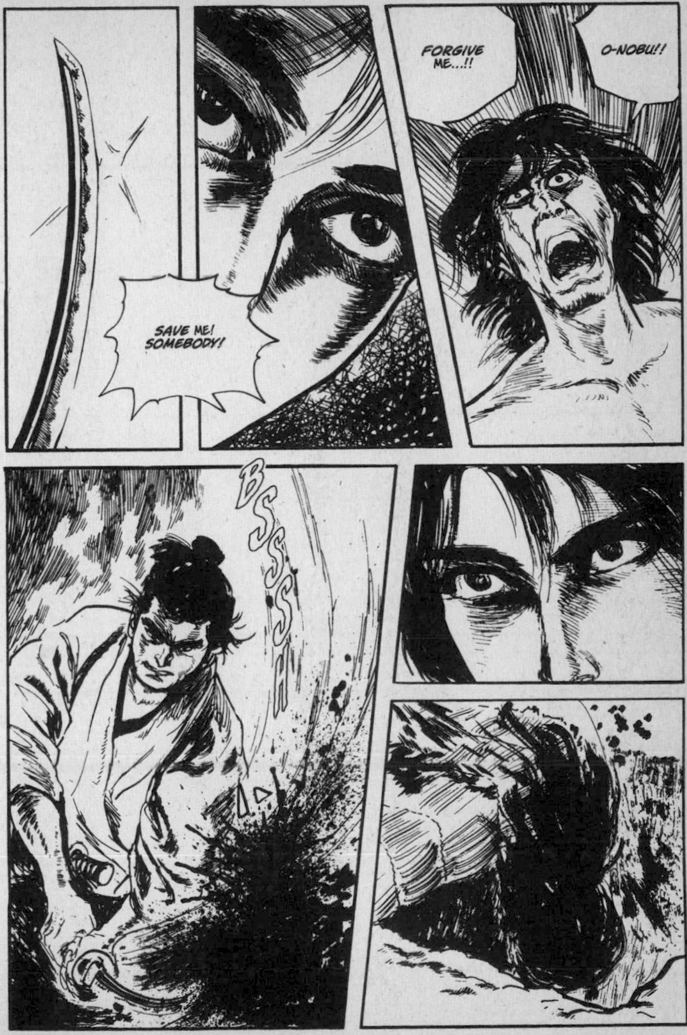
SAVE ME! SOMEBODY!
FORGIVE ME...!!
O-NOBU!!
BSSSH

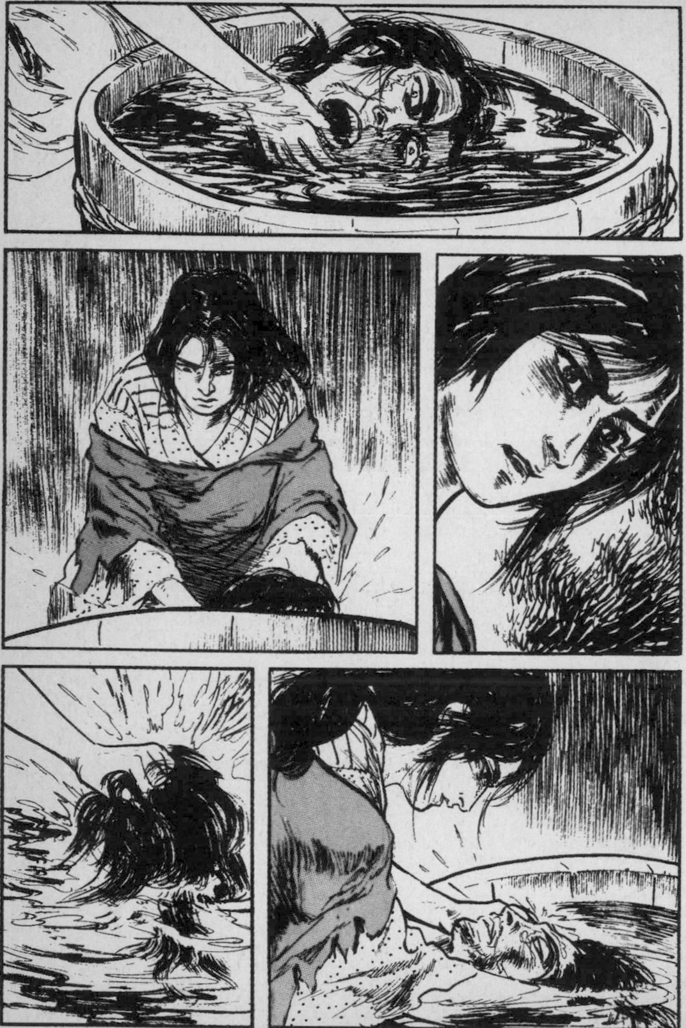

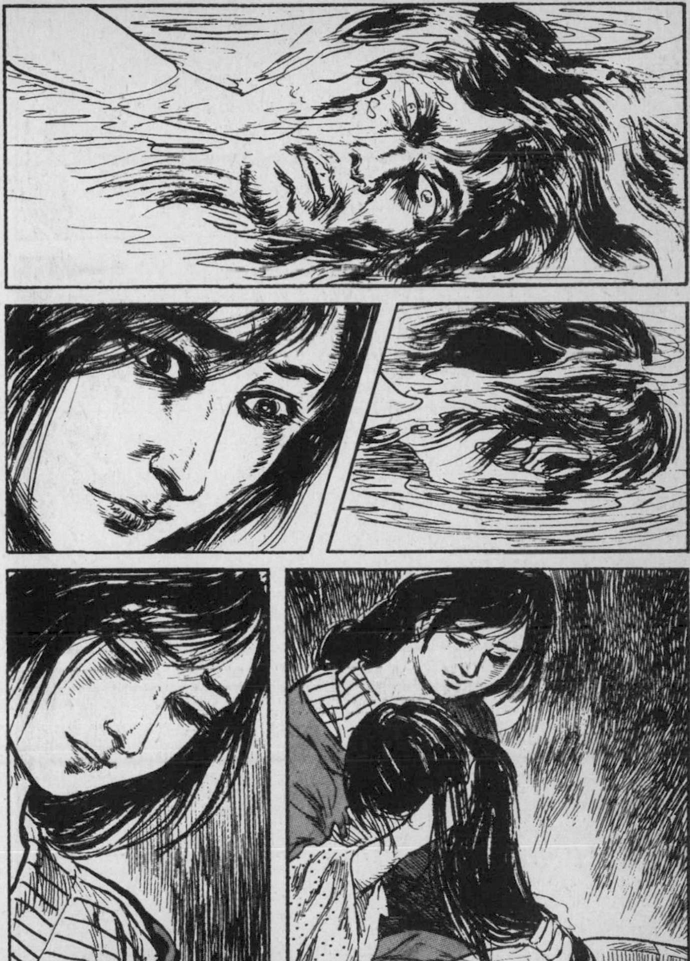

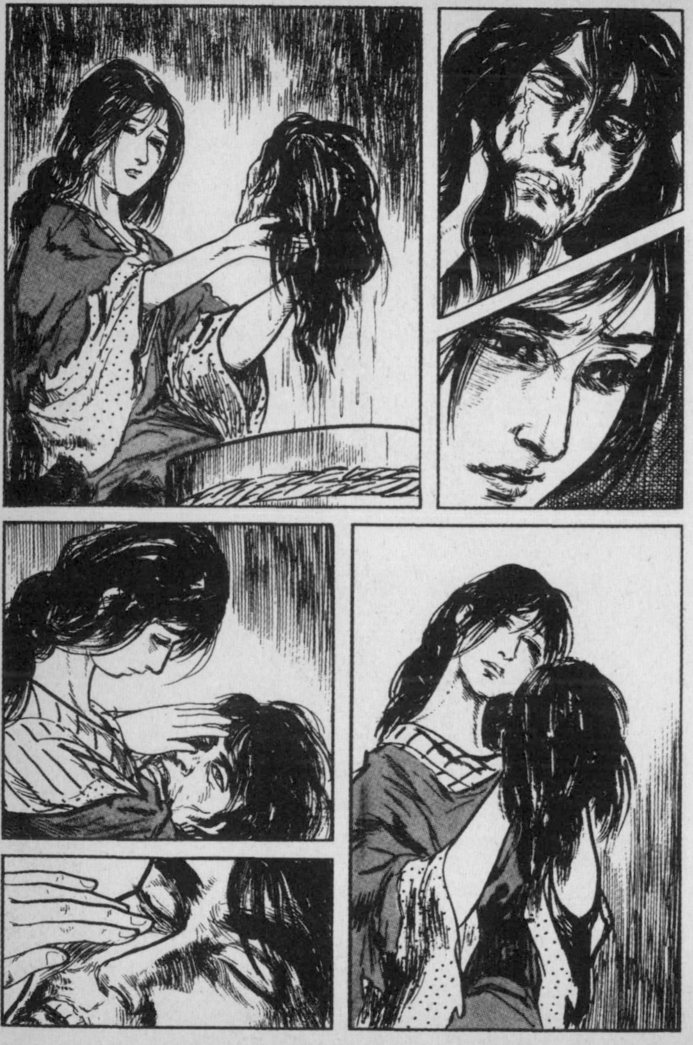

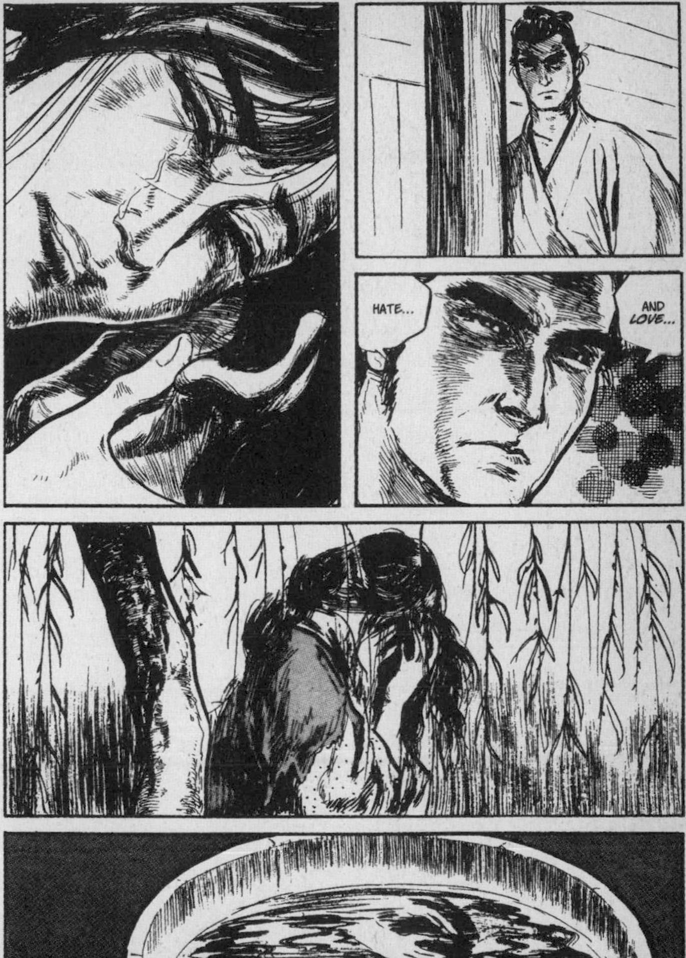
HATE...
AND LOVE...

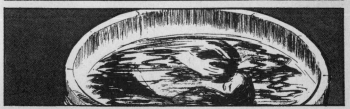

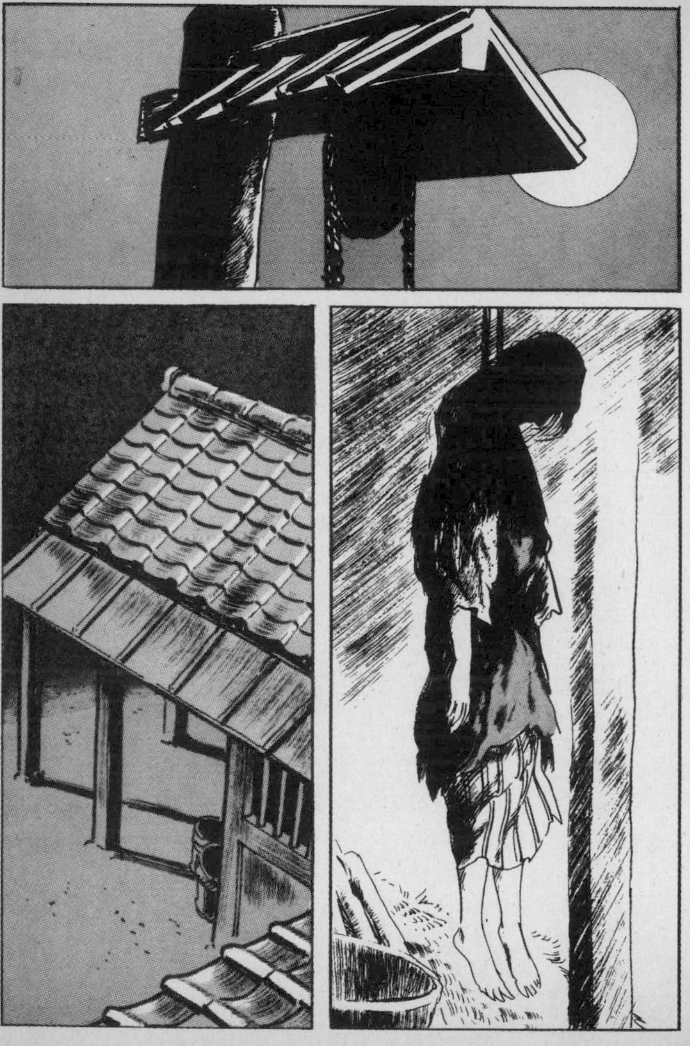

GLOSSARY

bansho
An Edo Period police box. Also *banya*.

crucifixion
One form of punishment in the Edo period was to be nailed or tied to an "X"-shaped wooden frame fixed in the ground and exposed to the elements until death.

currency
mon – A copper coin.
kan – A bundle of 1,000 mon.
monme – A silver piece.
ryō – A gold piece, worth 60 monme or 4 kan.

dairyō
Prison boss. Prison officials appointed reliable prisoners to maintain order. The *dairyō* was the cell boss.

Enma
King of the Buddhist underworld.

go-yō
Official business.

haritsuke
Crucifixion. Like the Romans on the other side of the world, Japan had discovered death by crucifixion. Particularly heinous criminals were crucified upside down.

Hayashi
Traditional festival music, with flutes, cymbals, shamisen string instruments and drums. Also, the band.

honorifics
Japan is a class and status society, and proper forms of address are critical. Common markers of respect are the prefixes o and go, and a wide range of suffixes. Some of the suffixes you will encounter in *Lone Wolf and Cub*:

chan – for children, young women, and close friends.
dono – archaic; used for higher-ranked or highly respected figures.
sama – used for superiors.
san – the most common, used among equals or near-equals.
sensei – used for teachers, masters, respected entertainers, and politicians.

katana
The Japanese sword. The honorific O- acknowledges its link to the *shōgun*.

Koshimono
A sword. "Koshi" means hip, where swords were worn.

kubiuchi
Decapitation.

machi-bugyō
The Edo city commissioner, combining the post of mayor and chief of police. A post held in monthly rotation by two senior Tokugawa vassals, in charge of administration, maintaining the peace, and enforcing the law in Edo. Their rule extended only to commoners; samurai in Edo were controlled by their own *daimyō* and his officers. The *machi-bugyō* had an administrative staff and a small force of armed policemen at his disposal.

machikata
Town policemen.

migen tatewari
A vertical cut between the eyes.

naka
Slang for the Yoshiwara, the fabled, and infamous, pleasure district of Edo.

nihontō
Japanese swords, encompassing *katana, tachi* and other sub-categories.

o-tameshiyaku
The swordmaster who performed *o-tameshi*, the testing of the *shōgun's* swords. The "o-" signifies respect for the *shōgun*.

Onibocho
Literally, "Demon Blade." The name of the second Yamada Asaemon's personal sword. Prized swords were given names.

osadamegaki
The Official Provisions.

oyakata
Boss.

rō-bugyō
The *bugyō* in charge of prisons.

rōjū
Senior councilor to the *shōgun*.

Sanzu no kawa
The river separating the land of the living and the land of the dead.

shaku
10 sun, approximately 30 centimeters.

shitōjutsu
The art of sword-testing.

sori
The curve in a Japanese sword, different from sword to sword.

sumaki
The 'concrete boots' of Edo's underworld. The victim would be tied up in a bamboo screen, and heaved overboard to drown.

sun
Approximately 3 centimeters.

tatami
A thick mat woven of rice stalks, used as flooring.

togishi
Sword polisher

KAZUO KOIKE

Though widely respected as a powerful writer of graphic fiction, Kazuo Koike has spent a lifetime reaching beyond the bounds of the comics medium. Aside from co-creating and writing such classic manga as *Lone Wolf and Cub* and *Crying Freeman*, Koike has hosted the popular *Shibi Golf Weekly* instructional television program; founded the *Albatross View* golf magazine; produced movies; written popular fiction, poetry, and screenplays; and mentored some of Japan's best manga talent.

Koike started *the Gekiga Sonjuku*, a college course aimed at helping talented writers and artsts — such as *Ranma* 1/2 creator Rumiko Takahashi — break into the comics field. His methods and teachings continue to influence new generations of manga creators, not to mention artists and writers around the world. Examples of Koike's influence range from the comics works of Frank Miller and Stan Sakai to the films of Quentin Tarantino.

The driving focus of Koike's narrative is character development, and his commitment to the character is clear: "Comics are carried by characters. If a character is well-created, the comic becomes a hit." Kazuo Koike's continued success in comics and literature has proven this philosophy true.

Kazuo Koike continues to work in the entertainment media to this very day, consistently diversifying his work and forging new paths across the rough roads of Edo-period history and the green swaths of today's golfing world.

GOSEKI KOJIMA

Goseki Kojima was born on November 3, 1928, the very same day as the godfather of Japanese comics, Osamu Tezuka. Art was a Kojima family tradition, his own father an amateur portrait artist and his great-great-grandfather a sculptor.

In 1950, Kojima moved to Tokyo, where the postwar devastation had given rise to special manga forms for audiences too poor to buy the new manga magazines just starting to reach the newsstands. Kojima created art for *kami-shibai*, or "paper-play" narrators, who would use manga story sheets to present narrated street plays, and later moved on to creating works for the *kashi-bon* market, bookstores that rented out books, magazines, and manga to mostly low-income readers.

In 1967, Kojima broke into the magazine market with his ninja adventure, *Dojinki*. As the manga magazine market grew and diversified, he turned out a steady stream of popular samurai manga series.

In 1970, in collaboration with Kazuo Koike, Kojima began the work that would seal his reputation, *Kozure Okami (Lone Wolf and Cub)*. Many additional series would follow, including this related series, *Samurai Executioner*.

In his final years, Kojima turned to creating original graphic novels based on the movies of his favorite director, the great Akira Kurosawa. Kojima passed away on January 5, 2000 at the age of 71.

NOW AVAILABLE FROM DARK HORSE COMICS AND MASTER STORYTELLER OSAMU TEZUKA!

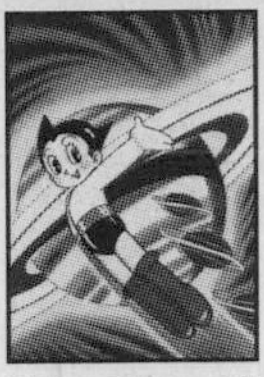

Astro Boy vol. 1
1-56971-676-5
$9.95

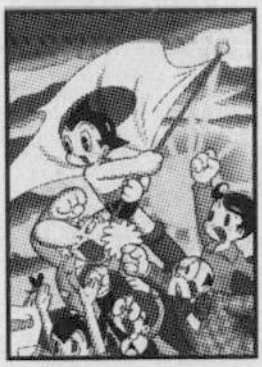

Astro Boy vol. 2
1-56971-677-3
$9.95

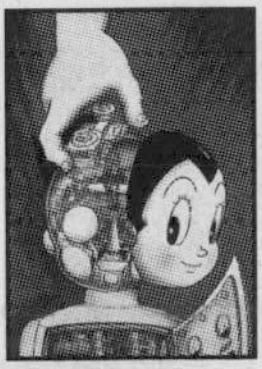

Astro Boy vol. 3
1-56971-678-1
$9.95

Astro Boy vol. 4
1-56971-679-X
$9.95

Astro Boy vol. 5
1-56971-680-3
$9.95

Astro Boy vol. 6
1-56971-681-1
$9.95

Astro Boy vol. 7
1-56971-790-7
$9.95

Astro Boy vol. 8
1-56971-79
$9.95

Astro Boy vol. 9
1-56971-792-3
$9.95

Astro Boy vol. 10
1-56971-793-1
$9.95

Astro Boy vol. 11
1-56971-812-1
$9.95

Astro Boy vol. 12
1-56971-813-X
$9.95

Astro Boy vol. 13
1-56971-894-6
$9.95

Astro Boy vol. 14
1-56971-895-4
$9.95

Astro Boy vol. 15
1-56971-896-2
$9.95

Astro Boy vol. 16
1-56971-897-0
$9.95

Astro Boy vol. 17
1-56971-898-9
$9.95

Astro Boy vol. 18
1-56971-899-7
$9.95

Astro Boy vol. 19
1-56971-900-4
$9.95

Astro Boy vol. 20
1-56971-901-2
$9.95

Astro Boy vol. 21
1-56971-902-0
$9.95

Astro Boy vol. 22
1-56971-903-9
$9.95

Lost World
1-56971-865-2
$14.95

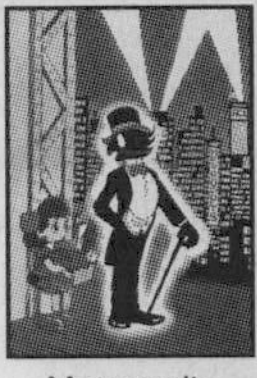

Metropolis
1-56971-864-4
$13.95

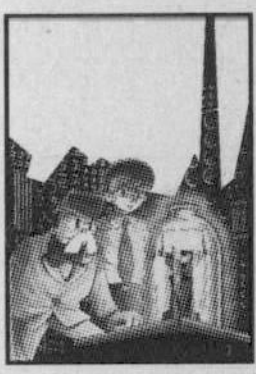

Nextworld vol. 1
1-56971-866-0
$13.95

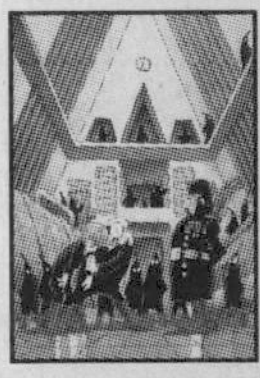

Nextworld vol. 2
1-56971-867-9
$13.95

DARK HORSE MANGA
darkhorse.com

AVAILABLE AT YOUR LOCAL COMICS SHOP OR BOOKSTORE
To find a comics shop in your area, call 1-888-266-4226 • For more information or to order direct visit darkhorse.com or call 1-800-862-0052
Mon.-Sat. 9 A.M. to 5 P.M. Pacific Time

*Prices and availability subject to change without notice

STUDIO PROTEUS
studioproteus.com

Dark Horse Comics: **Mike Richardson** *publisher* • **Neil Hankerson** *executive vice president*
Tom Weddle *vice president of finance* • **Randy Stradley** *vice president of publishing* • **Chris Warner** *senior books editor*
Anita Nelson *vice president of sales & licensing & marketing* • **David Scroggy** *vice president of product development*
Lia Ribacchi *art director* • **Dale LaFountain** *vice president of information technology*
Darlene Vogel *director of purchasing* • **Ken Lizzi** *general counsel*